Cambridge Studies in Ethnomusicology

General Editor: John Blacking

Traditions of gamelan music in Java: musical pluralism and regional identity

This book is a wide-ranging study of the varieties of gamelan music in contemporary Java seen from a regional perspective. While the focus of most studies of Javanese music has been limited to the court-derived music of Surakarta and Yogyakarta, Sutton goes beyond them to consider also gamelan music of Banyumas, Semarang, and east Java as separate regional traditions with distinctive repertoires, styles and techniques of performance, and conceptions about music. Sutton's description of these traditions, illustrated with numerous musical examples in Javanese cipher notation, is based on extensive field experience in these areas and is informed by the criteria that Javanese musicians judge to be most important in distinguishing them.

In the present day more than ever before, different regional styles of gamelan music meet and mix in a variety of contexts – formal educational institutions devoted to the performing arts, government-sponsored contests and festivals, radio and television broadcasts, and cassette recordings. In separate chapters, Sutton considers the impact of government policy, of the major media, and of the works and recordings of the highly influential and popular musician Ki Nartosabdho. Sutton demonstrates how these varied forces contribute to a heightened awareness of regional traditions, to a crystallized conception of them, and yet, at the same time, to their dilution through a process of partial homogenization with mainstream central Javanese tradition derived from Surakarta. Whatever the extent to which these traditions now blend and spread beyond their region of origin, Sutton maintains that regional differences persist in contemporary Java, not as vestigial curiosities, but rather as deep-rooted aesthetic differences that reflect varied perceptions of regional cultural identity.

Cambridge Studies in Ethnomusicology

General Editor: John Blacking

Ethnomusicological research has shown that there are many different ingredients in musical systems. The core of this series will therefore be studies of the logics of different musics, analysed in the contexts of the societies in which they were composed and performed. The books will address specific problems related to potential musical ability and practice, such as how music is integrated with dance, theatre and the visual arts, how children develop musical perception and skills in different cultures and how musical activities affect the acquisition of other skills. Musical transcriptions will be included, sometimes introducing indigenous systems of notation. Cassettes will accompany most books.

Already published:
Bonnie C. Wade, *Khyāl: creativity within North India's classical music tradition*
Regula Burckhardt Qureshi, *Sufi music of India and Pakistan: sound, context and meaning in Qawwali*
Peter Cooke, *The Fiddle Tradition of the Shetland Isles*
Anthony Seeger, *Why Suyá Sing: a musical anthropology of an Amazonian people*
James Kippen, *The Tabla of Lucknow: a cultural analysis of a musical tradition*
John Baily, *Music of Afghanistan: professional musicians in the city of Herat*
Bell Yung, *Cantonese opera: performance as creative process*
Anna Czekanowska, *Polish Folk Music: Slavonic heritage – Polish tradition – contemporary trends*
Hormoz Farhat, *The* Dastgāh *concept in Persian music*

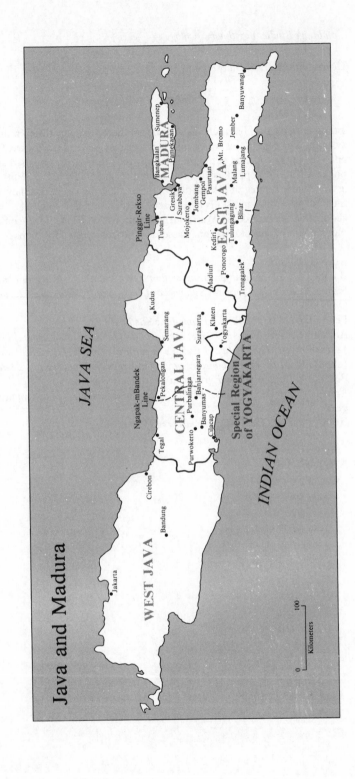

Java and Madura

Traditions of gamelan music in Java: musical pluralism and regional identity

R. Anderson Sutton

Associate Professor of Music, University of Wisconsin-Madison

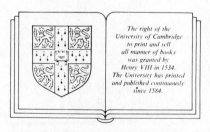

The right of the
University of Cambridge
to print and sell
all manner of books
was granted by
Henry VIII in 1534.
The University has printed
and published continuously
since 1584.

Cambridge University Press

Cambridge
New York   Port Chester
Melbourne   Sydney

Published by the Press Syndicate of the University of Cambridge
The Pitt Building, Trumpington Street, Cambridge CB2 1RP
40 West 20th Street, New York, NY 10011, USA
10 Stamford Road, Oakleigh, Melbourne 3166, Australia

© Cambridge University Press 1991

First published 1991

Printed in Great Britain at the University Press, Cambridge

British Library cataloguing in publication data
Sutton, R. Anderson
   Traditions of gamelan music in Java: musical and regional identity.
   – (Cambridge studies in ethnomusicology).
   1. Indonesian gamelan music: Javanese gamelan music
   I. Title
   784.68095982

Library of Congress cataloguing in publication data
Sutton, Richard Anderson.
Traditions of gamelan music in Java: musical pluralism and
regional identity / R. Anderson Sutton.
         p.   cm. – (Cambridge studies in ethnomusicology)
Includes bibliographical references.
Discography: p.
ISBN 0 521 36153 2
1. Gamelan music – History and criticism.   2. Music – Indonesia –
Java – History and criticism.   I. Title.   II. Series.
ML1251.I53S93   1991
784.2'2 – dc20 90–40031   CIP

ISBN 0 521 36153 2

For my parents
Eloise Chadwick-Collins Sutton and
James Anderson Sutton

And for Peggy, Maya, and Tony

Contents

ix

Plates

Figures

Preface

Ethnomusicologists and gamelan enthusiasts outside Indonesia have long recognized the major stylistic differences between Balinese, Javanese, and Sundanese gamelan music. Those who study Javanese gamelan performance are often introduced to subtler differences between the two main court-derived traditions of central Java: Yogyanese and Solonese. Yet other traditions of gamelan music continue to be cultivated today, and in the past fifteen years or so have undergone something of a revival, gaining in visibility and stature within the complex cultural fabric of contemporary Indonesia through the legitimizing forces of government support and representation in the mass media.

Early in my graduate studies, when I decided on a geographic area of specialization, I chose to study the gamelan music of the central Javanese heartland – the court-derived music mentioned above. Although for my first two major periods of field work (1973–74 and 1979–80) I was based in Yogyakarta, with frequent visits to Surakarta, the plurality of traditional gamelan music increasingly impressed me the longer I stayed. The artistic rivalry between Yogyakarta and Surakarta proved to be very much an issue, and far more complex than I had expected. Yet there were other styles as well, represented on commercial cassette recordings and to a limited extent at performing arts schools. The widely popular gamelan music composer and director Ki Nartosabdho (1925–85) championed many regional styles and repertory items.

During a trip in 1980 to Surabaya (in the province of East Java, several hundred miles from either court city), I was able to observe musical practices substantially different from those of both central Javanese court music traditions. I returned to eastern Java in 1983, 1984, and 1986 to broaden my experience and work closely with east Javanese musicians. Seeking out other areas with distinctive music traditions, I conducted research in Banyumas (in western central Java) and in Semarang (on the north coast of central Java). What I found was a diversity not only in musical style and repertory, but also in the extent to which those styles and repertories were currently known and practiced. And so substantial was the diversity that a monograph – the book that follows – seemed the best way to bring it to the attention of the scholarly world.

The story of Java's artistic diversity is only partly told in the following pages. To keep this project from turning into an encyclopedia of brief entries on the many genres of musical arts (and performing arts with musical accompaniment) I have had to establish limits. Indeed, the Indonesian Department of Education and Culture, which conducts cultural censuses and "inventories" of performing arts, lists hundreds of extant genres, many of them involving music. Rather than attempt to look at all musical activity, or even all musical activity the Javanese themselves would call traditional, I consider only those genres that involve ensembles known as "gamelan." And rather than attempt to cover the entire island of Java, I have chosen to exclude the ethnically distinct Sundanese of West Java, and the cosmopolitan community of Jakarta, Indonesia's national capital. The Madurese, though they reside within the province of East Java (on the island of Madura and in areas of the easternmost part of the island of Java), are also excluded. The people whose music is to be investigated, then, all speak some form of Javanese language and, at least at one level, identify themselves as culturally Javanese.

Orthography

The Indonesian language words in this book are spelled in accordance with the system known as "ejaan yang disempurnakan" (literally, "spelling that has been perfected"), officially adopted by the Indonesian government in 1972. The single consonant /c/ in this system, represented in earlier publications by /tj/, represents a sound close to *ch* in English. Otherwise, the sounds of the consonants in Indonesian are similar to those in English. The vowels are pronounced as follows:

> a = as in f*a*ther
> e = as in cit*e*d or as in b*a*ke
> i = as in b*ee*t
> o = as in b*oa*t
> u = as in b*oo*t

Modern Javanese orthography follows the same conventions of spelling, but distinguishes dental /t/ and /d/ (written simply *t* and *d*) from the retroflex (written *th* and *dh*, formerly indicated with subscript dots beneath the letters). A somewhat greater range of vowel sounds exists in Javanese than in Indonesian. The Javanese /a/ in final and penultimate syllables may be pronounced "aw" (as in r*aw*) if the final syllable is not closed with a consonant (e.g., p*a*r*a*). This sound is sometimes rendered with the letter /o/ (e.g., poro), but in most scholarly publications appears as /a/ without any diacritical markings. The Javanese /e/ can represent several vowel sounds, which are distinguished in many scholarly publications, including the present one, by the use of diacritical marks as shown below:

> e = as in cit*e*d
> é = as in b*ai*t
> è = as in b*e*t

For Javanese names and older bibliographic entries I have preserved whatever spelling I encountered. The diacritical markings and indication of retroflex are often omitted in these cases. Below are given the obsolete forms and their modern equivalents:

> tj = now written c and pronounced *ch* (su*ch*)
> dj = now written j and pronounced *j* (*j*et)
> j = now written y and pronounced *y* (*y*et)
> oe = now written u and pronounced *oo* (b*oo*t)

Plurals in Javanese and Indonesian may be marked by reduplication (e.g., one *saron*, several *saron-saron*), but they are only marked if plurality is unclear from context. The indigenous convention is adopted for the present study, in which I will speak, for example, of several *saron*. Where unclear from the context, an *s* is appended for plurals.

Musical notation

Despite the ongoing preference for modified Western notation in ethnomusicological publications, I have chosen to present the musical examples for this study in the Javanese *kepatihan* cipher system, now widely known throughout Java and used with great fluency by most foreigners familiar with Indonesian musics. Each pitch degree of the five-tone *sléndro* and the seven-tone *pélog* scale systems is indicated by one cipher: 1, 2, 3, 5, and 6 in *sléndro*; 1, 2, 3, 4, 5, 6, and 7 in *pélog*. Octave register, relative to the normal tessitura of an instrument or voice, can be indicated by subscript dots (for lower octave) and superscript dots (for higher octave).

The strongest beat in a grouping is normally shown furthest to the right, precisely the reverse of Western notational convention. This practice stems from the system by which Javanese musicians count beats, with the strongest being the last, rather than the first. The phrase notated 2165 has the strongest weight on the fourth and final tone (pitch 5), with secondary stress on the second beat (pitch 1). Many instrumental parts are characterized by a very steady succession of beats, each articulated. A sustained tone is indicated by a dot. With each beat equivalent to a quarter note, the phrase 2.65 would be played as a half-note on pitch 2, followed by a quarter on 6, and a quarter on 5. Articulation between beats is indicated, as in Western notation, by superscript beams: one for double subdivision (equivalent to eighth notes) and two for quadruple subdivision (equivalent to sixteenth notes). Space given between four-beat groupings does not indicate passage of time, but merely facilitates reading, like bar-lines in Western notation. For example, 3216 2165 would be played as eight continuous beats: 32162165.

Any melodic part, instrumental or vocal, can be notated with the *kepatihan* cipher system; and drum timbres and rhythms may also be notated (though no standard system of symbols for drumming has yet been adopted). The part most frequently notated by Javanese musicians, and the only one likely to be used in performance, is the instrumental melody called *balungan* (literally, "skeleton," "outline"), normally played on metallophones that are limited in range to an octave in *pélog* and slightly more than an octave (depending on the region) in *sléndro*. This part more than any other, except the vocal in some pieces, constrains or even determines the other parts and is the best identifier distinguishing one piece (*gendhing*) from another.

In addition to the ciphers for the *balungan* part, Javanese notation usually indicates the "formal structure" of a *gendhing*, which is determined by the sounding of certain gong instruments simultaneously with the *balungan* in a recurring pattern of punctuation. These are represented in this study by letter abbreviations given above or immediately following the tone with which they sound.

> G = *gong* (large hanging knobbed gong)
> N = *kenong* (large horizontally-mounted knobbed kettle-gong)
> t = *kethuk* (small horizontally-mounted knobbed kettle-gong)
> P = *kempul* (small hanging knobbed gong)
> S = *siyem* (medium-sized hanging knobbed gong)

```
                                                                        G
t P t N                    t P t                          t P t N
6 5 3 2G   is equivalent to:  6 5 3 2N/G   is equivalent to:  6 5 3 2
```

Here *kethuk* is played simultaneously with tone 6, followed by *kempul* with tone 5, followed by *kethuk* with tone 3, followed by *kenong* and *gong* simultaneously with tone 2. If the gong

```
t P t N                                    G
2 3 5 3                          t P t N  t P t N
6 5 3 2G   is equivalent to      2 3 5 3  6 5 3 2
```

punctuation is the same from one line of *balungan* to the next, the pattern of the previous line is assumed. Other punctuating gong instruments (*engkuk-kemong*, a pair of gongs in *sléndro*, and *kempyang*, a pair of gongs in *pélog*) are considered of secondary importance, reinforcing rather than determining formal structure. They are generally not notated. *Kempul* may also not be notated in cases where it plays a similar secondary role.

Acknowledgments

A list of those deserving acknowledgment includes many teachers in Indonesia and the United States, beginning with the late Prawotosaputro, who introduced me to his style of gamelan music (Surakarta) at Wesleyan University in 1970. At the University of Hawaii, Hardja Susilo provided inspiring instruction in both theoretical and practical aspects of gamelan music from both Surakarta and his native Yogyakarta. Ricardo Trimillos and Barbara Smith, together with Susilo, provided the grounding in ethnomusicology that continues to sustain me. At the University of Michigan, my teachers Judith and Alton Becker provided both stimulation in their courses and fine example in their writings. Their experience in East Java helped awaken my own interest in this area.

Friends with long experience in Java have provided valuable direction in my research: Alan Feinstein and Marc Perlman, working primarily in Surakarta; Joan Suyenaga and Roger Vetter in Yogyakarta; René Lysloff in Banyumas; and Philip Yampolsky, who has gathered enormous amounts of invaluable material on the commercial cassette industry throughout Indonesia. For language study, I am grateful to Soenjono Dardjowidjojo and Bambang Kaswanti Purwo for studies in Indonesian and Javanese, to G. DeHeer and Alton Becker for Indonesian, and to Mukidi Adisumarto and the late Subardi of Yogyakarta for Javanese.

In Yogyakarta, I owe thanks to three generous gamelan teachers: B.Y.H. Pustakamardawa (formerly Sastrapustaka), Prajasudirja, and especially Suhardi, whose encyclopedic knowledge of gamelan continues to amaze all of us lucky enough to have studied with him. I have also benefited from discussions with prominent Yogyanese dancers, R.L. Sasminta Mardawa and Benedictus Suharto. In Surakarta, I am grateful to the late R. Ng. Martopangrawit, S. Probohardjono, and Sri Djoko Raharjo for their invaluable lessons and for their patience in answering my questions about Solonese gamelan. Semarang musicians Djoko Suyono, Ponidi, and A. Salim were all generous with their time. My thanks to Ki Sugino Siswocarito, Parta, S. Bono, and especially Rasito, who helped in countless ways to introduce me to the varieties of music in Banyumas. In Surabaya, I thank Diyat Sariredjo and Munali Fatah, formerly of the national radio station (RRI), Darmono Saputro and Sutrisno at the provincial office of Education and Culture, and Soenarto R.P. and A.M. Munardi at the local conservatory (SMKI). My work in the Malang area relied on the kindness of many performers, of whom I would especially like to thank Bilal and Rasimun in Glagah Dowo, Kasdu and Karimun in Kedung Monggo, and Mohd. Soleh and Suwito in Malang city. Elsewhere in East Java, I owe thanks to Piet Asmoro in Trowulan and Mustopo in Banyuwangi.

My first period of study in Java was in summer 1973 as a member of the University of Hawaii "Music Department Abroad," coordinated by Hardja Susilo, Ricardo Trimillos, Jeanette Bennington, and then Drs. (now Dr.) R.M. Soedarsono. All subsequent study and research has been made possible by generous support from a number of sources. The East–West Center Culture Learning Institute funded my first extended stay in 1974. My doctoral research was supported by a joint fellowship from the Social Science Research Council and Fulbright-Hays Fellowship (1978–80). Subsequent research has been funded by the American Philosophical Society (1983 and 1989), the Wenner Gren Foundation for Anthropological Research and the National Endowment for the Humanities, Summer Stipend (1984), and the Social Science Research Council (1986). The University of Wisconsin-Madison Graduate School has contributed to each of these last four periods of research and is gratefully acknowledged. A Fellowship for Independent Study and Research from the National Endowment for the Humanities allowed me to take a leave-of-absence from my teaching duties at the University of Wisconsin for the academic year 1986–87 and devote full time to research and writing. And an Alumni-in-Residence Fellowship from the East–West Center allowed me to finish most of the writing in 1988.

Special thanks is due to the Indonesian Institute of Science (Lembaga Ilmu Pengetahuan Indonesia), who facilitated my field research during 1978–80 and during 1986, and to Dr. Soedarsono, who acted as my Indonesian sponsor during both these periods. Without their assistance and good faith, I could not have gathered the materials necessary for this study.

In the final stages of the preparation of the manuscript, I was fortunate to have the assistance of Mary Elizabeth Powell, whose Bolz Fellowship at the University of Wisconsin-Madison involved her in sundry tasks, from compiling the terms to be defined in the glossary to preparing the final inked versions of the staff notation for examples in chapter 2.

Many scholars who work overseas must thank their wives either for bearing up well in an unfamiliar environment (if they go along) or putting up with temporary widowhood (if they stay at home). My thanks to Peggy Choy, my wife, co-worker, and best critic, for the insights and contacts she provided me with during our several stays in Java, where she had already lived and studied from 1973–76. Only on my most recent trips (in 1986 and 1989) did she remain at home, caring for our daughter Maya during the long months of my research. For all her support both with me and away from me I am grateful.

From the initial proposal to the final editing of this book, I have benefited from the encouragement and careful attention of the editorial staff at Cambridge University Press. I would like to thank Penny Souster, who helped in the early stages of this project, and Victoria L. Cooper, who worked with the manuscript and saw it into print. And of course, I owe the deepest debt of gratitude to the editor of the Ethnomusicology Series, the late Dr. John Blacking, whose initial enthusiasm for the topic helped shape the book in fundamental ways.

Only several weeks before submitting the final revised version of this manuscript to the editorial staff at Cambridge University Press, I learned that Dr. John Blacking had just died. As we would have expected, he showed uncommon strength in his final months and continued to contribute with great energy and enthusiasm to the profession he loved. It was with a special sadness that I came to learn of his death, just as I had completed my revisions in response to his many insightful remarks on his reading of an earlier draft. I feel very lucky indeed to have enjoyed this scholarly exchange with a man who has clearly commanded the respect of so many scholars and influenced the field of ethnomusicology so profoundly. I can only hope that he would have found the revisions worthy of the hard work he managed to devote to the manuscript under very difficult circumstances.

1 Introduction: gamelan and cultural diversity in Java

With over three hundred ethnic groups living on thousands of islands stretching eastward three thousand miles from the South East Asian mainland, Indonesia is nothing if not diverse. The national motto, *Bhinneka Tunggal Ika* (usually translated "Unity in Diversity"), places that diversity at the very core of the national self-image. In the literature on Indonesia, now quite extensive, though perhaps not as extensive as one would expect for the fifth most populous nation in the world, scholars usually acknowledge the diversity, but the vast majority of their work has concerned Java and, more precisely, the Javanese. In its broadest usage, the term "Javanese" refers to the people who reside mostly in the eastern two thirds of the island of Java and who speak some form of Javanese language, and not to the Sundanese speakers of West Java, or the Madurese speakers of Madura island and much of the easternmost portion of Java. This tripartite ethno-linguistic division of the island of Java is fundamental and is widely known.

The penchant for focus on the Javanese has been particularly strong for those of us who study the performing arts. Periodically we may acknowledge our "Javacentrism," only to dive ever deeper into our study of the rich and fascinating world of Javanese dance, shadow puppetry, and gamelan music. The more we learn, the more questions arise.

Yet limiting one's attention to the Javanese need not, indeed should not, mean dismissal of the issue of cultural diversity. Within this large group of people, one finds important regional distinctions that often go unmentioned by scholars, though such distinctions are readily recognized by the Javanese. What can be observed in one locale is not necessarily to be found throughout the rest of Java. Nor does what has developed in the Javanese court centers (the "principalities" of south central Java) represent Javanese culture as a whole, nor in its purest or most essential form. What I intend in this study is to provide musical evidence of the significant regional diversity that persists within this, the largest ethno-linguistic group in Indonesia, and to see how that diversity is being represented and transformed.

It might seem untimely to be studying regional differences within a single major ethno-linguistic group when the young nation of Indonesia faces important challenges in the diversity between such groups. Yet, as will be seen in the succeeding chapters, the heterogeneity of the Javanese is an important aspect of Indonesia's diversity and one that is increasingly recognized by cultural policy at the national and provincial level. Despite the reference by some Javanese writers to different "ethnic areas" within Java, I use the term "ethnic" here as it is defined by Barth (1969), who would differentiate Madurese from Javanese, but not speakers of different dialects of Javanese from one another. The differences we encounter between the people of Banyumas, in western Central Java, and the people of Lumajang in East Java may be substantial, but we will refer to these as "cultural" or "sub-cultural," rather than ethnic.

I

Modern nations as a rule see little if any reason to foster regional differences and identities, but, as Doorn notes, one can find evidence of a revival of regionalism in many parts of the world, including Indonesia (1980:1). As recently as the 1960s, one might have forecast the demise of regionalism in Javanese culture. The trend now seems to be in the opposite direction – towards a conscious realization on the part of contemporary Javanese of their heritage of regional diversity and a taking stock to meet the challenges of the future. This type of awareness and the responses it generates constitute a dynamic that is modifying the way contemporary Javanese conceive of their indigenous arts.[1] The situation is dazzlingly complex, as numerous social and historical factors come to bear in different ways on the vitality of the arts associated with each particular region. Before considering the styles and the issues region by region, however, something must be known of the cultural geography by which the following study is organized.

Defining regions in contemporary Java

The very concept of "region" poses problems. Doorn notes the vagueness of the term, "located in the social sciences at some midpoint between the community and the nation" (1980:1). In contemporary Indonesia, the term *daerah* (literally, "region," "area") is used in a number of senses, but always in reference to an area smaller than the entire nation. One frequently encounters it as a synonym for major cultural (ethno-linguistic) grouping or for one of the twenty-seven major administrative units into which the nation is divided: twenty-four provinces (*propinsi*) and three special regions (*daerah istimewa, daerah khusus*). The island of Java is divided into the province of Jawa Barat ("West Java") and the Daerah Khusus Ibukota (Special Region of the nation's capital, metropolitan Jakarta) in the western third, the province of Jawa Tengah ("Central Java") and the Daerah Istimewa Yogyakarta (Special Region of Yogyakarta) in the central third, and the province of Jawa Timur ("East Java") in the eastern third. The island of Madura is also part of East Java. These divisions do not align accurately with cultural divisions, although national government policy often seems to assume otherwise. Javanese speakers can be found along the north coast to the north western corner of the island, well into West Java. And one finds greater similarity between the central portion of Central Java and the western portion of East Java than one does between the same portion of Central Java and the Banyumas area in western Central Java. Though Jakarta is technically a *daerah*, it is usually the less thoroughly urban areas to which most Indonesians refer when they use the term in general – opposing *daerah* both to the capital (i.e., away from the capital) and to the nation (i.e., regions within the nation).

Hatley makes the following observations about the three ethno-linguistic groups.

The ethnic homelands also are arrayed generally in sections of Java west to east, Sundanese, Javanese, and Madurese, more or less in correspondence with the three large modern administrative provinces of Java ... the most significant exception is that the province of East Java extends westward into the Javanese cultural area, making the Madurese a minority in the province, and increasing central Javanese influence there. The intrusion of Jakarta, and the extensions of Javanese along the northwest and southeast coastal plains, are recent movements, respectively post 17th, 16th and – except for the Osing people of Banyuwangi – 19th century. Of course the sectional array of ethnic regions on the island is not based on the provinces, which were organized only in this century, but on the west-to-east wet-to-dry ecologies produced by the monsoon advancing across the landscape.   (Hatley 1984:3–4)

The size and identity of a region will depend on the criteria by which it is demarcated, of course, and for Central and East Java, the provincial level can be too broad. Below the province, the next largest administrative unit currently is the *kabupaten*, an area that may be too small in many cases to constitute a cultural "region." Javanese still speak of "*ex-karesidenan*" (i.e. "former residencies"), the larger units demarcated during the colonial era and known as *residenties* in Dutch and residencies in English. Local nuances may be associated with individual *kabupaten*, more significant cultural differences with the residencies or larger *daerah*.

In assessing any attempt to define regional boundaries, it should be born in mind that most of the administrative boundaries were first imposed by the Dutch, who noted a considerable mobility in the population and wished to make the population more sedentary to facilitate economic control (Doorn 1980:8–10; Gooszen 1985:26–27).

One can say that Javanese society has long lacked clear regional demarcation; not the district boundaries but the radiating effect of the major town in a district is decisive for division of the territory.

(Doorn 1980:9)

Anderson also alludes to the Javanese conception of region in reference to sovereign territory, particularly in regard to a court center and its realm, with gradually diminishing allegiance as one moves away from the center (1972:22). Reflecting this orientation, each of the musical regions considered in this study is associated with a large city or major town.

Several views have been expressed by scholars concerning broad regional boundaries in Java. Concerned primarily with patterns of agriculture and ecology, Geertz distinguished three major regions (in addition to Sunda, west Java): *Pasisir* (= *Pesisir*; north coast), *Kejawèn* (central Java), and East Hook (the eastern tip of the island) (1963:42–43). In a critique of Geertz's study, Hüsken suggests four:

REGION	RESIDENCIES
1. Principalities and former mancanegara (outlying areas)	Yogyakarta, Surakarta, Madiun, Banyumas, Kedu
2. Pasisir (coastal residencies)	Japara, Semarang, Pekalongan, Tegal, Cirebon
3. Brantas residencies	Kediri, Surabaya, Pasuruan, Probolinggo
4. Eastern Corner	Besuki, Banyuwangi

(Hüskens 1981:10)

1.1   Major regions in Java, according to Hüskens 1981

Hatley has made regional demarcation in Java the subject of an extended essay, which serves as a basis for the musical regions to be investigated in the following chapters. Hatley pays heed to a number of ecological and cultural factors. Mapping cultural variety among the Javanese, he begins by identifying two "niches": *Tanah Jawa* (literally, "land of Java" – the south central heartland, the former realm of Mataram) and *Pesisir* (literally "coast" – the northern coastal region and "internationalized gateway through which the outside world has come to Java") (1984:4). These niches offer contrastive orientations in many aspects of culture, including religion, language, and the arts.

Two important cultural boundaries distinguish Javanese on the east–west axis. The *arèk* Javanese, who live east of the *pinggir-rekso*, the eastern edge of the lava flow from Mt. Kelud, "speak with variant vowel pronunciations and vocabularies . . . more in the style of the Madurese" (Hatley 1984:6). The Javanese of western Central Java (Banyumas) and northern West Java (Cirebon and Banten) speak distinctive dialects of Javanese and are sometimes collectively called *ngapak*. This term is simply a word for "what" or "why", pronounced in the manner characteristic of this region: with the final /k/ and the final vowel /a/ as in "father." Those Javanese residing east of Tegal and Banyumas would pronounce the same word "ngawpaw" (written "*ngapa*"): without final /k/ and with the /a/s pronounced *aw* (as in "law"). The latter practice, characteristic of the great majority of Javanese speakers, is called *mbandhèk*. What is *aw* (as in "law") east of this line, is pronounced *a* (as in "father") west of the line.

Both the *ngapak–mbandhèk* line and the *pinggir–rekso* line represent ancient boundaries, which Hatley states are "of an ethnic character and fairly precisely definable" (Hatley 1984:7). Distinction between the *Pesisir* and the *Tanah Jawa* heartland is less clear, and is less manifest in language than in other aspects of culture, such as religious practice and the arts.

The major regional traditions of Javanese gamelan music to be considered in the following chapters demonstrate the significance of these various boundaries. The investigation begins in Java's heartland, with the gamelan music associated with the two major court cities of south central Java: Surakarta and Yogyakarta. Standing in contrast to these within the province of Central Java are the traditions of Banyumas, west of the *ngapak–mbandhèk* line, and of Semarang, on Java's north coast (*Pesisir*). Even further removed from the influences of the central Javanese courts are the traditions east of the *pinggir–rekso* line: the main *arèk* tradition of Surabaya, Mojokerto, and Malang and – most distinctive – the tradition of the Osing people of Banyuwangi. Their local music often resembles Balinese music more than it does any other type of gamelan music from the rest of Java, and is not covered in the present study. Though speaking a dialect of Javanese (Osing) and not a separate language, the Osing are considered exotic by most other Javanese.

Exchange between these regional musics has not been even. The Surakarta tradition has spread throughout all of Java and can clearly be called Java's "mainstream" or "standard" tradition. While this spread has affected other regional musics, it has usually not replaced them. Musicians who operate primarily in the mainstream are exposed to the music of other regions and, to a limited extent, may incorporate stylistic influences and items of repertory into their own performance. Mass media, government institutions, and key individual artists all play important roles in both the definition and the dispersion of these traditions and are discussed in the final chapters of this study.

Gamelan and *karawitan*

One approach to regionalism in music would be to consider the great variety of songs, solo instruments, and small ensembles found in villages throughout Java. I have opted for a different approach: to consider the music performed on larger ensembles whose styles and repertories contrast but whose instrumentation varies only to a small degree from one region to another. Smaller ensembles will be mentioned when they are particularly prominent in a given region (*calung* in Banyumas, *sronèn* in East Java), but to attend to each ensemble would require many volumes. It is not the intention of this work to be all-inclusive in the form of an encyclopedia or dictionary, but instead to present significant examples of regional differences and interpret their meaning in terms of musical aesthetics and regional cultural identity today. And one is afforded more meaningful comparison when, to the extent that it is possible, some element is held constant – avoiding the charge of comparing apples to oranges. For example, to compare Yogyanese court gamelan, with its forty or more instruments and chorus of singers, to a group of four women pounding out interlocking patterns on a riceblock in rural Banyumas speaks less of regional differences than of urban–rural or court–village differences. Only three kilometers from the Yogyanese palace, in rural Bantul, one can find women playing riceblock music that differs only subtly from that of Banyumas.

The topic of this study, then, is intentionally limited to the music played on ensembles that are usually referred to simply as "gamelan," and not the more specialized ensembles, such as the gamelan *monggang* (the three-tone ensemble associated with antiquity) or gamelan *bumbung* (the bamboo ensemble found in parts of East Java). Regardless of region, the gamelan will consist predominantly of metal idiophones (bronze or iron gongs, gong-chimes, and metallophones) and one or more double-headed drums. The instrumentation for pieces with vocalists will involve at least some of the "soft"-sounding instruments: metallophones struck with two padded beaters (*gendèr barung* and *gendèr panerus*), xylophone (*gambang*), two-string fiddle (*rebab*), flute (*suling*), and zither (*siter* or *celempung*).

My focus on large ensembles is not an arbitrary one. Residents of all the areas under investigation speak of their local gamelan tradition in reference to these large ensembles. At least as far back as older living musicians can remember, the large ensembles were present locally and used to perform local repertory. As the Javanese become increasingly aware of each other's regional music, it is the music of the large ensembles that is best known. And for the most part, this is the traditional music chosen to be broadcast on radio and television, recorded and disseminated on commercial cassettes, and taught at schools of performing arts.

For some, this music would be categorized as *karawitan*, a word coined only earlier this century (Supanggah 1984:2–3, as quoted in Sri Suyamti 1985:17) and deriving from the root *rawit*, best translated as "intricate." This term applied originally to a variety of refined arts and later came to refer exclusively to traditional gamelan music associated with the courts, in distinction to the music made by villagers on ensembles that struck the upper classes as crude (whether or not the music performed on those ensembles imitated the court style and repertory). But the gloss of this term has widened considerably in recent years. Officially, it has become a general word for any indigenous music in any part of Indonesia, and for some its meaning has widened to incorporate all the performing arts.[2] However, in its everyday usage the word suggests the refinement and respectability of the particular art to which it refers and, outside of government schools and publications, is preeminently a Javanese term for Javanese arts, usually gamelan music. If a particular event is said to include *karawitan* performance, most Javanese would expect to hear a full gamelan and not riceblock stamping or Jew's harp playing. And most of the works by Javanese on *karawitan* deal with the music of a large gamelan ensemble, whether it be *karawitan* Banyumas, *karawitan* Jawa timur (east Javanese), or *karawitan* Solo.

Traditions, styles, and repertories

Several of the terms I have used up to this point in relation to music require elucidation. One could argue that all the regional musics I propose to cover are actually part of one Javanese tradition and merely represent local variant styles. Indeed, the Javanese themselves speak consistently about Banyumas "style," Yogyakarta "style," and so forth, using the Javanese *gagrag* or the Indonesian *gaya* (both translated as "style"). But the way in which they use these words in reference to music and other performing arts corresponds more precisely with our notion of tradition than with our notion of style. Musicians tend not only to speak of the *gaya* of a musical process, but also to assign particular items of repertory to one or another *gaya*. Recent symposiums devoted to the defining of regional *gaya* have gone far beyond what we would think of as "style" to subsume not only the describable aspects of musical structure (rhythmic and melodic character, instrumentation, and so forth), but also repertory, terminology, transmission, even function and social meaning. It is for this reason that I choose to speak of Banyumas tradition, Yogyakarta tradition, and so forth. The reader accustomed to the terms *gaya*, and the Javanese *gagrag*, can simply substitute them as he encounters my "tradition" throughout this study.

The distinction between style and repertory is an important one. Each of the areas under investigation has associated with it a body of *gendhing* (gamelan pieces) that may be said to constitute a regional repertory. These pieces will usually be performed in the style of the area from which they come, though not always. Like pieces in many repertories around the world (though not the compositions of Western art music), Javanese *gendhing* are not fully fixed either in notation or memory. Rather, they are identified by aspects of melodic and rhythmic structure that remain constant from one rendition to another. More than any other element, it is the melodic line known as *balungan* (literally, "skeleton," "outline") and usually sounded in single-octave form on *saron* and *slenthem* (single-octave metallophones) that identifies a particular *gendhing*, although in some cases the vocal part may be the primary identifier.

The nature of the other parts can be described in several ways. The sparser gong parts may be said to punctuate the *balungan*, sounding in a cyclical "colotomic" pattern. Other parts, sounding at higher densities, weave around the *balungan*, decorating or elaborating it in a stratified heterophonic relationship (see further Sutton 1982:33–82; Vetter 1981). A drummer directs the ensemble, determining tempo, dynamics, and number of repetitions in accordance with the needs of a particular performance context. For some of the instruments one finds little difference from one regional tradition to another, but for others the differences are sharply defined. Thus, it is possible for styles to mix within an item of repertory associated with a single region.

It is also important to realize that, despite efforts by some factions to the contrary, all these styles, repertories, and traditions, are undergoing some degree of change – some would say gradual evolution, others radical or deep change. It is perhaps a shortcoming of the present study, whose approach is primarily synchronic rather than diachronic, that more attention is not paid to the development of these traditions. For the court-derived traditions, a moderate amount of data is available and some scholars (notably Lindsay, Yampolsky, Feinstein) are piecing together musical history. For others, such as Banyumas and eastern Java, what little historical data is known suggests numerous conflicting interpretations. And for Semarang, too little survives to posit any line of historical development. What concerns me in this study is the state of these traditions in the late twentieth century and the responses of their carriers to contemporary conditions.

Javanese musical diversity and the scholarly literature

It is well known to Javanists, though less apparent to other scholars, that most of the recent work on Javanese music has focused on the gamelan music associated with the two major court centers: Yogyakarta and Surakarta. And since most Javanese musicians today have at least some familiarity with one of these traditions (usually Surakarta), such a focus is not without justification. Awareness of traditions centered in regions away from the courts has been less evident. What I intend here is a brief review of writings on Javanese music as they have contributed to a conception of regional musical diversity and a patterning of that diversity into recognized traditions.

Prior to 1900

Javanese music is mentioned in numerous early accounts by Dutch and English writers (see discussion in Kunst 1973 1:5–10), but usually with no indication of regional identity or diversity. The most significant exception is an account by Cornets de Groot, a *resident* (chief Dutch official) in Gresik, East Java during the early nineteenth century, whose writings on Javanese "manners and customs" distinguish gamelan *surabayan* (i.e., of the Surabaya area) and gamelan *mentaraman* (a term referring to the central Javanese kingdom of Mataram/Mentaram and used well into the twentieth century by east Javanese to identify gamelan thought to derive from central Java) (Cornets de Groot 1852; see also Kunst 1973 1:12–13). Nevertheless, the extensive passages devoted to music do not otherwise suggest diversity along regional lines; the author claims to be writing of "Javanese" music in general, rather than any particular local variant.

The same might be said for early Javanese treatises containing information on gamelan.[3] Most widely cited is the *Serat Centhini*, which, like many works of Javanese literature, exists in a number of manuscript versions. Though it chronicles the wanderings through rural Java of several young men from east Java, the best known version is a lengthy one written by court scribes in Surakarta during the early nineteenth century.[4] Its lists of musical pieces and accounts of performance and aesthetics do not directly indicate a regional association with either east Java or Surakarta; but because the scribes would have been likely to incorporate their own locally-based knowledge of gamelan practice, this version of the work is generally understood by musical scholars to represent practice in the region of Solo.

Towards the end of the nineteenth century, two important works were written pertaining specifically to gamelan musical practice in Yogyakarta. Groneman's *De Gamelan te Jogjakarta* was published in 1890. Even in the title ("Jogjakarta" is one of several older spellings of Yogyakarta), Groneman demonstrates an understanding that what he describes concerning gamelan music in the main court (*kraton* Yogyakarta) and in the lesser court (*pura* Pakualaman), both within the city of Yogyakarta, would not necessarily apply to Javanese music elsewhere. The most comprehensive early Javanese work on music (begun in 1889) still exists only in manuscript form and is generally known as the *Pakem Wirama*, attributed to K.R.T. Kertanegara and his aristocratic assistants.[5] This is quite clearly and self-consciously a

Yogyanese document, one intended to perpetuate the musical repertory, playing styles, terminology, and concepts – indeed, the tradition – associated with the Yogyakarta court. I know of no comparable work for any other tradition.

The early twentieth century

In the early twentieth century, several important works were published on gamelan music of Surakarta. Djakoeb and Wignjaroemeksa published lengthy commentary in Javanese script on gamelan music, including its performance contexts (1913), and cipher notation for 128 pieces (1919). The tradition they cover is Solonese, though they seem less overtly concerned with distinguishing it from other traditions than were the authors and compilers of the *Pakem Wirama*. Richer in detail on musical techniques, such as interlocking (*imbal*) and dance drumming (*ciblonan*), are the two volumes in Javanese script compiled by the Komisi Pasinaon Nabuh Gamelan (literally, "committee for the study of gamelan playing") of the Radya Pustaka in Surakarta (1924 and 1925).

Dutch scholars writing about Javanese music during the 1920s and 1930s, unlike the Javanese with whom they often worked closely, were concerned not with providing manuals or study guides for performers, but instead with descriptive documentation and, sometimes, with broad theoretical issues in the new field of comparative musicology. Their writings almost always identify by locale the music they describe and bear witness to a staggering regional diversity, often based on first-hand field research. J.S. Brandts Buys and A. Brandts Buys-van Zijp knew and wrote of the court gamelan music, but also explored many types of music outside of the courtly sphere: riceblock pounding music (1925), diverse aerophones (1925–26; 1926–27), slit gong ensembles (1928a), and two landmark studies on the music of distinct groups residing in what is now the province of East Java: the Osing of Banyuwangi (1926) and the Madurese (1928b).[6] These latter two works demonstrate well the existence of what can properly be called distinct traditions (and not merely isolated instruments or performance styles) away from the courts and, in the case of Banyuwangi, carried by an identifiable regional group of Javanese.

Jaap Kunst, the most prolific Dutch scholar of Javanese music, was always careful to identify as precisely as possible the geographic locus of the instruments and practices he reported. In his *De Toonkunst van Java* (1934; rev. 1949, 1973), he lists and describes numerous "gamelan" ensembles, many of them in areas far from the courts (and some of which would no longer generally be referred to as gamelan – see further below). Yet when he writes of gamelan performance (styles and repertories), his data is almost exclusively from Yogyakarta and Surakarta – the principalities of south central Java. He provides extensive evidence for separate Yogyanese and Solonese traditions.

While one finds in this work some information pertaining to all the regions to be covered in the present study, Kunst gives the reader no sense of any viable traditions away from the court areas. Only assorted "village" ensembles and genres seem to dot the countryside, many of them employing instruments judged crude in comparison to the gamelans of the court areas. Indeed, his interest in these other areas is limited to individual instruments and to ensembles that clearly contrast with the larger gamelans associated with the court regions, even though these larger gamelans have long been used widely throughout Java. He does not describe performance practice for large gamelans outside the court areas, and thereby he obscures any stylistic traits that might have been characteristic of other regions.

Aside from providing valuable tables and maps showing distribution of gamelans and the predominance of *sléndro* or *pélog* scales in vocal music and gamelan tunings (Appendices 57 and 58), Kunst refrains from mapping musical characteristics in any explicit fashion and does not tend to generalize from the various data obtained outside the court regions. He documents the use of some technical terms and practices in given locales, but does not go beyond this to speak, for example, of a Banyumas tradition or even a Banyumas style of gamelan performance.

It is likely that regional differences in gamelan music were more numerous and more pronounced during Kunst's time than they are presently. And it is also possible that the myriad local variants have since coalesced into more readily identifiable styles and traditions. At any rate, the present study is indebted to Kunst for his careful reporting, but focuses from a different angle on far more recent data.

Concerned primarily with drama and dance, and only marginally with music, Pigeaud's encyclopedic *Javaanse Volksvertoningen* (1938) organizes its wealth of data by region as well as by genre. For instance, masked plays (usually accompanied by gamelan or some derivative ensemble) are described first as performed in the court areas (*vorstenlanden*, literally, "principalities") and then as performed outside these areas: in central Java to the west, west Java, central Java to the east, north east coast, east Java, Madura, and the extreme eastern corner (*oosthoek*) of Java. Pigeaud reports local variation within all these regions, but, perhaps more importantly, he provides evidence in arts other than music for the regional distinctions drawn today and reflected in the present study.

First three decades of Indonesian independence (1950s–1970s)

From 1949 – a year marked both by the final defeat of the Dutch in Indonesia and the publication of a revision of Kunst's 1934 work in English – through the 1970s, the substantial body of writings on music in Java scarcely mentions music in regions other than Solo and Yogya. It is during this period that Westerners from countries other than the Netherlands developed scholarly interest in Indonesia, including Javanese music, and that Javanese themselves began to write extensively, producing not only practical manuals and books of notation, but descriptive studies and theoretical works that have profoundly influenced all scholarship in this field. My commentary here on the literature of this period will be limited to the question of regional concerns.

Hood's 1954 study of *pathet* (Javanese modal classification) is based entirely on music from the two courtly traditions, despite the existence of significant regional differences in the *pathet* concept. And though he is careful throughout to mention which manuscript sources derive from Yogya and which from Solo, his argument and conclusions propose a single concept of *pathet*, obscuring differences even between these two court areas (see chapter 2). His subsequent work usually acknowledges the courtly rivalry, but makes no mention of other regions.

Javanese musician–scholars writing during this period have mostly been faculty members at the several conservatories in Surakarta, and they have concentrated heavily on the mainstream, Solonese tradition, often explicitly identifying the music they notate or discuss as

Solonese. The offices of the Department of Education and Culture have sponsored a great variety of publications on traditional culture throughout much of the nation, including many – some non-Javanese Indonesians would say disproportionately many – works on performing arts in Java. Whether directly through the Education and Culture offices or through the schools and conservatories, it is the government that funds the publication of almost all of this research on traditional arts, with the lion's share of resources allocated to institutions in Surakarta (and, to a lesser extent, Yogyakarta). I use the term "traditional" here and throughout this study in the same sense as the Javanese, who speak of traditional arts as indigenous, regional arts, rooted in the cultural past of a people. This in distinction to the complex of acculturated "modern" and "national" arts, such as the popular *dangdut* genre (Frederick 1982). In most cases, *kesenian tradisional* (literally, "traditional arts") and *kesenian daerah* (literally, "regional arts") are considered to be synonymous and are used interchangably.

The works of Sindusawarno (1955) and Martopangrawit (1969, 1972a) on gamelan music theory offer much valuable material on the techniques and conceptions within the Surakarta tradition. Affiliated with the first music conservatory, Konservatori Karawitan Indonesia (later known as Sekolah Menengah Karawitan Indonesia – "SMKI Solo"), and with the college-level Akademi Seni Karawitan Indonesia (recently renamed Sekolah Tinggi Seni Indonesia – "STSI"), both these men explain their Solonese tradition rigorously. Notation of the *balungan* melodies for much of the Surakarta *gendhing* repertory is contained in Mloyowi-dodo's three volumes (1976). Martopangrawit and others at STSI/ASKI and SMKI Solo have notated vocal and other instrumental parts in a flourishing of limited-edition stencil copies, many of which were produced in the 1960s and 1970s and are now difficult to obtain.

Despite a significant outpouring of works on Yogyanese dance tradition, very little is published on Yogyanese gamelan music. What is available is mostly notation, with little if any theoretical or scholarly commentary. The three volumes compiled by Sukardi, Sukidjo, and Dibyomardowo of *balungan* notation of Yogyanese pieces (Sukardi and Sukidjo 1976a and 1976b; Sukidjo and Dibyomardowo 1976) is nowhere near as extensive for Yogya as Mloyowidodo's for Solo. Nor is their notation of Yogyanese drumming (Sukardi and Sukidjo 1976c) as extensive as Martopangrawit's for Solo (1972b). Siswanto's recent book on Yogya-nese music (1983), intended as a handbook for high school students, identifies some aspects of Yogyanese style, but betrays, rather ironically, the considerable influence of the Solonese on conception and practice in contemporary Yogya.

In her 1972 dissertation (published in revised form in 1980), Judith Becker also draws heavily on the writings of the Solonese theorists for her explanation of gamelan music. Although she resided in east Java for much of her stay in Java from 1969 to 1971 and was aware of gamelan styles outside the mainstream, she chose not to focus on regional issues, except to report that regional diversity in instrumentation was fast disappearing in east Java as musicians attempted to conform to central Javanese standards (1972:15–16; 1980:9). Never-theless, her account of the role of contemporary gamelan composers, Ki Nartosabdho and Ki Wasitodiningrat (formerly Wasitodipuro and, before that, Tjokrowasito), demonstrates that the vitality of Javanese gamelan music has depended on a wider base than the courts (Becker 1972, 1980). And recently she has spoken of the resurgence of regional traditions in an interview published in *Balungan* (Devereaux 1986:21–22).

One can point to only a few exceptions to the focus on the court areas and the mainstream tradition by scholars prior to the late 1970s. In 1971 the east Javanese musician and puppeteer Ki Piet Asmoro published a collection of *gendhing* in *kepatihan* notation that he identifies explicitly as "east Javanese." Although presented as a "manual" (*tuntunan*), it consists almost entirely of notation, with only minimal commentary on performance, context, or theory. Margaret Kartomi's descriptive studies of village trance music in the Central Javanese areas of Banyumas and Semarang (1973) and of village processional music and dance (*reyog*) of Ponorogo, near the western edge of the province of East Java (1976), are detailed and carefully documented, with transcriptions and photographs that enable us to imagine more clearly the events she describes than is possible from the briefer accounts of these genres in Pigeaud (1938) and Kunst (1973). But like Pigeaud and Kunst, she does not choose to scrutinize gamelan performance in these areas and does not speak of a Semarang, Banyumas, Ponorogo, or east Javanese "tradition" (or "style").

Unpublished work has also been heavily concentrated on the court traditions. The large number of theses (*skripsi*, Ind.) on gamelan music have been written mostly at institutions in Indonesia and abroad which offer training in gamelan performance.[7] Javanese and foreigners alike tend to study Solonese gamelan performance primarily, with some interest (mostly by foreigners) in Yogyanese gamelan; and this interest and experience is usually reflected directly in the topics chosen for theses.

Recent focus on gamelan outside the court regions (late 1970s and 1980s)

Works that either convey an awareness of regional plurality in gamelan playing or focus specifically on practices outside the mainstream have only begun to appear since the mid-1970s. Civil servants at various regional offices of the Department of Education and Culture in Java have for some time been documenting certain local genres, but their reports rarely circulate. In the latter 1970s, however, the Department of Education and Culture in East Java published several substantial studies devoted to traditional arts in East Java (Proyek Penelitian 1976 and Kartamihardja 1978). And around the same time faculty members at the SMKI (formerly KOKARI) conservatory and Sekolah Tinggi Kesenian Wilwatikta ("STKW" – a private college for the arts) in Surabaya began to publish technical studies of music, dance, and *wayang kulit* (shadow puppetry) in East Java (e.g., Munardi 1975, Proyek Rehabilitasi 1979).

The literature on music and other arts appearing from these institutions and from the provincial office of the Department of Education and Culture reflects methodological influence from the earlier work of Javanese musician–scholars in Surakarta. In fact, the major collection of east Javanese *balungan* melodies and *rebab* (fiddle) parts appears in two volumes compiled under the direction of Tasman Ronoatmodjo (Ronoatmodjo *et al.* 1981a and 1981b), who lives in Surakarta, teaches at STSI/ASKI, and travels to Surabaya only as a guest instructor and advisor. Soenarto R. P.'s brief but informative work (1980) represents the only theoretical discussion of east Javanese gamelan playing (the Surabaya–Mojokerto–Malang tradition), with examples of instrumental techniques and extensive notation of drum patterns for major repertory items. But his approach also reflects Solonese conceptions and categories. Though born in East Java (Nganjuk), he was trained in Surakarta before assuming his current reaching post at SMKI Surabaya.

A more recent student handbook written by teachers at SMKI Surabaya (Munardi *et al.*

1983) presents a general overview of indigenous music in East Java, including notation of vocal pieces and several instrumental rhythmic patterns. It is significant that this work, intended for high school students at SMKI (in Surabaya and elsewhere), describes a number of genres associated with small village ensembles throughout the various regions of the province of East Java and not just the more complex genres taught at SMKI. More scholarly studies of East Javanese performing arts have been carried out by Soenarto Timoer: on *reyog* (1978–79), on *topèng* (masked dance-drama) (1979–80), and on *wayang kulit* (1988). The extensive musical notation in the last work is an important and reliable supplement to the collections cited above by Ronoatmodjo and others. Though not published and uneven in quality, an important body of literature on East Javanese traditions is taking shape at STKW as students there complete their undergraduate and graduate theses (e.g., Saputro 1984, 1987, and Sri Suyamti 1985).

Writing on music in Banyumas has only recently begun and, like most of the writing on East Javanese music, bears a clear Solonese imprint. The first work to appear, as far as I have been able to determine, was the ASKI thesis on *calung* (bamboo ensemble) by Soebiyatno (1979), a musician born and raised in Purwokerto in the heart of the Banyumas region. Though concerned primarily with the construction of *calung* instruments, Soebiyatno provides *balungan* notation for sixty-two pieces commonly performed on *calung*. The following year a committee from the local office of the Department of Education and Culture completed a brief report on Banyumas gamelan music, including notation of drum patterns and *balungan* notation for fifty traditional *gendhing* (Departmen PDK 1980). Complementing these contributions is the recent and much lengthier book on Banyumas shadow puppetry published by the prestigious Balai Pustaka press in Jakarta (Sekretariat Nasional 1983), which provides notation of the puppeteer's songs (*sulukan*) and lists of pieces appropriate for various scenes. Despite some serious quibbles among Banyumas performers on the information the book contains, it clearly enhances the prestige of Banyumas as a cultural region in modern Indonesia (see further Sutton 1986a). Aside from these works, writing on Banyumas music is limited mostly to the senior papers prepared by students at SMKI Banyumas.

I have searched in vain for any Indonesian sources of information, published or not, on gamelan music in Semarang, but have found no evidence that any exists. Bearing on some recent developments in Semarang is the brief study of traditional Semarang *macapat* singing (Hardjo 1982). And, aside from a few photocopied sheets of musical notation from the local office of the Department of Education and Culture, the only materials available on gamelan music in the Malang area are given in the several studies on masked dance drama, by Munardi (1975) and by Murgiyanto and Munardi (1979–80).

As the new body of literature on different regional traditions began to appear in Indonesia, *The New Grove Dictionary* was published: without coverage of Banyumas or Semarang, but with Michael Crawford's article on East Java (Crawford 1980:201–07). Though limited by the constraints of encyclopedia entries, this article brings before the world of musical scholarship clear descriptions of several musical traditions within the province of East Java as Crawford encountered them during his field work there in the early 1970s. In his overview of major musical genres throughout the province, he provides examples of east Javanese gamelan techniques, and discusses the *pathet* system there as it relates to east Javanese *wayang* performance and as it contrasts with *pathet* in central Java.

Several lengthy studies of the gong-chime *bonang barung* and its repertory appeared as master's theses, both identifying pieces and playing styles by regional tradition: McNamara's study of Solonese *gendhing bonang* (1980) and Lysloff's study comparing Yogyanese and Solonese *bonang* playing. Lysloff's is of special significance in the context of the current study as a study specifically addressing differences between Yogyanese and Solonese practice. Moreover, he notes the existence of other styles (Semarang and east Java) besides those associated with the courts (1982:292–94).

My own work has only recently begun to reflect a concern with regional diversity. My master's thesis and dissertation (1975, 1982) and articles published between them (1978, 1979) are based primarily on the standard associated with Surakarta, though most of my closest study took place in Yogyakarta with musicians familiar with both traditions. Since my dissertation, I have written on a range of issues pertaining to regional traditions (1984, 1985a, 1985b, 1986a, 1986b), in preparation for tackling the more formidable task I have set myself in the present study. The article on musical pluralism (1985a), in particular, provides an overview of a number of issues and three of the traditions explored in greater detail in this study.

An important recent perspective on regional consciousness in performing arts is provided by Yampolsky in his study of the national recording company Lokananta (1987). His analysis of the exhaustive data he provides concerning discs and cassettes released by this company and his "dictionary of genres" bring regional identity to the fore. We are given a precise view of the classification systems (including regional classifications) used by this company – probably the most respected of the many cassette companies in operation and, thus, arguably, most likely to influence people's conceptions about the music and theater they record. Yampolsky notes a marked decline over the years in the recording by Lokananta of genres from outside Central and East Java, but at the same time a greater output of gamelan music from Banyumas, Surabaya, and Banyuwangi – Javanese regions outside the court areas (Yampolsky 1987:11, 14–19). This company, then, is finding a profitability and, as Yampolsky suggests, an aesthetic respectability, in the diverse regional traditions of music in Java.

The literature that bears on regional diversity in Javanese music, then, has been uneven, though in some cases substantial. While the sources mentioned above provided valuable data and perspectives for the present study, it has been primarily my direct encounter with musical practice in the field over the last fifteen years that has formed the basis of my understanding of the regional configurations within the traditional arts of present-day Java. During my two long periods of musical research in Yogyakarta (1973–74 and 1979–80), the Yogyakarta–Surakarta rivalry proved to be a persistent and burning issue among musicians and local bureaucrats. As of early 1989, debate was still raging in the local newspaper (*Kedaulatan Rakyat*) over aspects of a distinctive Yogyakarta tradition and the merits of delimiting and preserving it. If debate and disagreement are signs of vitality, as I believe they are, we are surely witnessing signs of a continued or even renewed vitality in the plurality of Java's gamelan music.

Notes on the approach taken in this study

During the 1980s my field research was mostly in areas far from the courts: Banyumas, Semarang, Surabaya, and Malang, with visits to various smaller towns and villages. The basis of understanding I had built during my study in Yogyakarta and Surakarta has been gradually put into regional perspective as I have come to know musicians elsewhere in Java and the range of sensibilities they bring to their love and performance of gamelan music. Though I devoted a greater portion of my time in these other regions to observation and interviews than to lessons in performance – certainly more so than during my long stays in Yogyakarta, where I took lessons almost daily for several years – I found myself always reacting emotionally to the music I heard, with a performer's interest in what to me were fascinating alternatives to the traditions I had studied before. I confess here a sense of awe at both the variety of gamelan performance styles and the persistence of so many of these styles in the context of contemporary Indonesian life, in which one could so easily envision the demise or homogenization of traditional arts. In the gamelan performance courses I teach, I have introduced some of the repertory and techniques I encountered during my research, in hopes of providing my students with a pluralistic view of gamelan music. It is this same pluralism, and the social context that shapes it, that this book is intended to address.

The book divides into two main parts, the first on the major regional traditions as I have come to know them and the second on the ways these traditions have been represented in Java in recent years. My discussion in the first part (chapters 2–5) is devoted in large measure to particulars of musical structure and context. I do not wish by taking this approach to imply that we attain an "understanding" of particular performances representative of these traditions merely by being able to recognize something as Yogyanese and something else as east Javanese. I would argue, however, that without this ability, our understanding is very likely to be deficient. Clifford Geertz writes disparagingly of the structuralist belief that

technical talk about art, however developed, is sufficient to a complete understanding of it; that the whole secret of aesthetic power is located in the formal relations among sounds, images, volumes, themes, or gestures.   (Geertz 1983:96)

Nor do I wish my description of various technical constraints or "rules" operating in a given region to be taken as the goal of my investigation – cf. Geertz's now famous call for the study of culture not as "an experimental science in search of law but an interpretive one in search of meaning" (Geertz 1973:5). Rather, it is my intention to alert the reader to the more readily identifiable traits that Javanese themselves recognize as characteristic of a particular region as a necessary step in the search for meaning. A full interpretation, were one possible, of the way any particular instance of gamelan music is meaningful to those who apprehend it would clearly involve exploration of many other dimensions. But I see this study as a contribution to such an interpretation precisely because the regional identity of a particular piece or its performance is an important component in its meaning.

Decoding such regional identity, which many Javanese seem to do routinely, with relative ease and consistency, is part of what we can call "informed listening." To know that a piece, or its performance style, comes from Banyumas is more than just to be able to point in a self-satisfied manner to that region on the map with the assurance that one knows from whence it came. Rather its very identification with that region allows it to conjure certain emotions, or more accurately a certain *rasa* (a Javanese word that Geertz, in an earlier work, translates as "feeling meaning" – 1960:310). At the same time that a performance of a certain piece calls to mind a given region, it also calls to mind, for the informed listener, characteristic feelings, or *rasa*, that the listener associates with that region. These may differ substantially from local residents – insiders to the region – to Javanese from other regions. And they may differ as well, though to a lesser extent, between members of different social classes in the same area or even between neighbors with very similar backgrounds.

The final three chapters, constituting the second part of the book, discuss the ways in which regional traditions are represented and transformed – crystallized and redefined – through the formal educational system, the complex of contests and festivals, the major public media, and the practices of major musicians (with focus on the most famous, Ki Nartosabdho). While some of the information conveyed in this second part of the book might have been incorporated into the previous chapters, region by region, the many instances of juxtaposition and blending across regional boundaries led me to choose to discuss the impact of these modern institutions and media, and of Ki Nartosabdho in particular, in a context that allows us to see patterns and issues attendant to the nature of these institutions, rather than to their impact on any one particular regional tradition.

PART I

2 Rival traditions in the courtly centers: gamelan music of Surakarta and Yogyakarta

The traditions of Surakarta and Yogyakarta are the most widely known in Java and the most frequently discussed in the scholarly literature. They are also the most problematic with respect to regionalism. In the broad schemes of cultural boundaries mentioned in the previous chapter, both Surakarta and Yogyakarta fall within the same south central Javanese heartland, the "Tanah Jawa" of the former Mataram kingdom. The artistic differences that developed between them reflected what was at first a political division, growing out of rivalry within a single royal family. In what sense are Surakarta and Yogyakarta "regions"? Yogyakarta is the name of a special administrative region (Daerah Istimewa Yogyakarta) and Surakarta the name of a former administrative region (ex-*karesidenan* Surakarta). Yet today these words refer most often to the two major urban centers in south central Java, located only sixty kilometers apart. Moreover, they are also the names of the two *kraton* (major courts) which have coexisted in Java for over two hundred years and which share the same heritage from the time before their division.

It was around the courts that the urban centers and administrative regions arose, and for most Javanese it is the courts which are seen as the locus of the artistic traditions called Solonese and Yogyanese. But this perception is problematic, particularly in an era which no longer recognizes the courts as legitimate centers of government and is generally apprehensive about the feudal nature of the court culture. Complicating matters further are the two lesser courts: the Mangkunegaran in the city of Surakarta and the Pakualaman in the city of Yogyakarta. Both of these lesser rivals borrowed artistic practices from the more distant major court (Mangkunegaran from Yogyakarta, Pakualaman from Surakarta), thereby setting themselves off from their more powerful immediate neighbors. While the often subtle differences between the arts of these four courts makes for fascinating study, it is my intention here to focus on the major distinctions, those between what is called "*gaya* Solo" and "*gaya* Yogya." The borrowings of the lesser courts are to be seen as something of a mediating between the two. I must begin with the courts, as the limited historical data on the arts pertains primarily to them. My major concern, which will be dealt with subsequently, is the present state of these two traditions – their repertory and style and their regional significance.

The court of Surakarta was established by the ruler Paku Buwana II, who decided in 1743 to abandon his ravaged court in Kartasura and rebuild twelve kilometers east on the Solo river.[1] Paku Buwana II's court was in disarray. The combination of his capitulation to Dutch demands for territory and his refusal to pay his brother Mangkubumi a promised reward for quelling rebellion, led Mangkubumi himself to rebel against Paku Buwana in 1746 in a war of succession that was not entirely settled for more than ten years.

Just before his death in 1749, Paku Buwana II ceded his kingdom to the VOC (Dutch East

India Company). The Dutch insured the succession of the Crown Prince to the throne, despite substantial popular support for Mangkubumi. In 1755, unable to defeat the allied forces of his nephew (Paku Buwana III) and the Dutch, Mangkubumi agreed to sign the Treaty of Giyanti, a compromise engineered by the Dutch, guaranteeing him half of the former kingdom of Mataram. Paku Buwana III would remain in the Surakarta court. Mangkubumi would found a new court, which he named Yogyakarta, sixty kilometers to the south west of Surakarta and just west of the old Mataram capital (Kota Gedhé). The VOC then assisted Mangkubumi in defeating Mas Said, who attacked and nearly burned Mangkubumi's court shortly after it was built. In 1757, Mas Said was made vassal ruler over a small realm (the Mangkunegaran) carved out of Paku Buwana III's territory.

Mangkubumi was to remain antagonistic to the Dutch, and passed on this legacy to his successors, whereas rulers in the *kraton* Surakarta have been somewhat more accepting of Dutch rule and European culture. This is not to say that the Solonese liked Dutch rule any more than the Yogyanese, but merely that they seemed less inclined to display their dislike. In contrast to Sunan Paku Buwana XII of Surakarta (r. 1944–present), for example, Sultan Hamengku Buwana IX of Yogyakarta (r. 1939–88) played an active role in resisting the Dutch during the revolution (1945–49).

By all accounts, important differences of all sorts soon arose between the two major courts with the intention of setting off one from the other.[2] Oral tradition has it that the process began when Mangkubumi met with Paku Buwana III to divide the royal regalia, only days after the signing of the treaty of Giyanti. Yogyanese say that Paku Buwana III, younger and weaker, conceded that Mangkubumi and the Yogyakarta court should inherit the Mataram tradition, while he and his Surakarta courtiers would develop a new tradition. Solonese say that Paku Buwana III, in a position of greater authority, graciously offered Mangkubumi a choice between "tradition" and "modernity" and that Mangkubumi's choice of the former paved the way for the progressive advances in Surakarta.[3]

Neither of these versions should be seen as entirely accurate, particularly since neither leader was inclined to view the partition of the kingdom as a permanent one, but both versions are consistent with an interpretation of more recent developments in the two courts: the fulfilment of a need for distinction and what appears to be a more conservative orientation in Yogyakarta. Carey provides evidence for the much earlier adoption of Dutch clothing and manners in Surakarta than in Yogyakarta, and for the general impression by European observers in the nineteenth century of a more "old fashioned" style in Yogyakarta (1986:20–21). Ricklefs writes of Yogyakarta that "in its cultural life it consciously conserved traditional forms, considering its arts more 'authentic' than those of Surakarta, while the latter regarded them as more 'antiquated'" (1974:425). He also notes Yogyakarta's special need for legitimization as "the new court, the second court" (1974:184). And Carey remarks that "the onus of developing a new style (or, as in the case of Yogyakarta after 1755, reasserting a more 'traditional' one) was on Mangkubumi's upstart kingdom rather than on the rival court of Surakarta which could, after all, continue to pass itself off as the legitimate successor of Mataram" (1986:19).

In addition to its more traditional orientation, the Yogyakarta court also developed – or one could say maintained – a reputation for militancy and bravery, in keeping with the character of its first ruler. By contrast, early Dutch observers sometimes noted a more decadent quality in Surakarta, calling the Solonese "wasteful, voluptuous, and effeminate to the highest degree," in contrast to the Yogyanese, who were "courageous, heroic, and more attached to the old traditions."[4] This militant character figures prominently and proudly in the self-image today of those who consider themselves Yogyanese. Together with this are the associated qualities of boldness, strength, steadfastness, and straightforwardness – all of which are seen today as quintessentially Yogyanese and as much manifest in the arts as in any sphere of social action.

The Solonese, of course, do not see themselves as decadent or weak, but rather as *alus*. Though this term is often translated as "refined," it is more complex, as Anderson elucidates:

The meaning of this term [*alus*], which eludes precise definition in English . . ., is to a certain extent covered by the idea of smoothness, the quality of not being disturbed, spotted, uneven or discolored. Smoothness of spirit means self-control, smoothness of appearance means beauty and elegance, smoothness of behavior means politeness and sensitivity. Conversely, the antithetical quality of being *kasar* means lack of control, irregularity, imbalance, disharmony, ugliness, coarseness, and impurity. Since being *kasar* is the natural state of man, in which his energies, thoughts, and behavior lack all control and concentration, no effort is required to achieve it. Being *alus*, on the other hand, requires constant effort and control to reach a reduction of the spectrum of human feeling and thought to a single smooth "white" radiance of concentrated energy.   (Anderson 1972:38)

Alus also implies intricacy, subtlety, even ambiguity. The Javanese spoken by the Solonese, their manners, their *batik*, and their arts, have generally been seen as the most *alus* in Java and, partially because of this, have assumed the status of Javanese standards. However, the quality of *alus* is not necessarily or always positively valued. In language use, for example, someone of clearly superior rank is expected to speak *kasar* language (*ngoko*) to those of inferior rank, and the latter is expected to speak *alus* language (*krama*) in response. What is sought by all parties is the appropriateness or fit (*cocog*) in the use of language levels. Furthermore, the *alus*ness in which Solonese pride themselves is sometimes interpreted negatively – as slickness or even slyness – by Yogyanese. Solonese, on the other hand, may interpret Yogyanese straightforwardness as unsophisticated and even clumsy and uncultured (thus, in a certain sense, *kasar*).

Alus and *kasar* are not merely two poles on a single continuum. In the categories of Javanese male dance, the refined style (*alusan*) contrasts not with *kasar* style but with "strong male" style (*gagahan*). In gamelan music *alus* sections of a piece contrast not with *kasar* sections, but with *lincah* (light, happy) or *ndhugal* (joking, mischievous) sections.

It would be a vast oversimplification to say that Solonese music is *alus* and Yogyanese is not. But it is true that Yogyanese music is generally more robust and less florid in its melodic elaborations than is Solonese. Though both traditions include purely instrumental performance and a more refined combination of vocal and instrumental performance, the emphasis in Yogyakarta has been on the former and in Surakarta on the latter. Moreover, at least with regard to the court ensembles, the percussion instruments are normally larger and more numerous in Yogyanese gamelan than in Solonese.

It is my intention below to become considerably more specific in identifying features which distinguish the gamelan music of these two traditions, but a word of caution is needed. Those expecting an exhaustive catalogue of differences will be disappointed, for such an endeavor would be impossible. Over the course of the past two centuries, neither of these traditions has remained static. I would suspect that the differences between Solonese and Yogyanese gamelan today are less profound than the differences between Yogyanese practice today and

Yogyanese practice two hundred years ago, although such a claim would be difficult to substantiate. With an eye on the past, then, my main focus is on present perceptions of present practice.

One of the important problems in any effort to describe or define a musical tradition is the choice of data. An empirical approach might include as Yogyanese any music made within the region of Yogyakarta, or within the city, or within the court. But none of these would reflect the perceptions of the Javanese, who recognize that much of the gamelan music played today in the city and region of Yogyakarta, and even some of what is played in the court, represent Solonese tradition. Individual perceptions differ in this regard, however; what one person thinks of as Solonese another might think of as Yogyanese. Such confusion has periodically prompted discussions and seminars aimed at delineating Yogyanese style, usually yielding little in the way of concrete results. My inquiry here should not be mistaken as a claim to solve the problems addressed in those discussions, nor as a prescription for performance. My findings are based to a considerable extent on the shared perceptions of my gamelan teachers and other Javanese I came to know in Yogyakarta and Surakarta, together with written sources. I wish to identify the types of contrasts that have evolved, but would emphasize at the same time the flexibility within both traditions.

The focus here is not on the court traditions, *per se*, though what has come to be known as Solonese and Yogyanese owes much to court practices. My inquiry is directed towards the gamelan music made in numerous settings, comprising what I call the "court-derived" traditions of Yogyakarta and Surakarta. This is perhaps a bit misleading, since some of what came to be known as court tradition undoubtedly derived from the surrounding rural areas.[5] Both of these traditions are seen by the Javanese to have close ties with the courts – though perhaps more so for Yogyakarta, which does not have nearly as wide a popular base of support as the Solonese tradition, nor an alternative locus of musical standards (STSI/ASKI). Yet even in Solo, the standards set by STSI/ASKI derive directly from the older teachers there, most of whom received their training in the court. In the ensuing discussion, characteristics peculiar to the gamelan music practiced inside the courts will be identified as such explicitly.

Instrumentation

Descriptions of "the Javanese gamelan" abound in the literature. In some cases these descriptions may indicate that the gamelan being described is standard central Javanese. Only rarely is it identified as either Solonese or Yogyanese. One can talk with a fair degree of accuracy about a standard ensemble used both in Solonese and Yogyanese tradition, as long as it is understood that certain features will distinguish Solonese from Yogyanese gamelan (see plates 1–3). I am talking here of "full gamelan" (gamelan *lengkap*, gamelan *gedhé*), rather than any of the smaller ensembles that omit some of the full gamelan instruments (gamelan *gadhon*, *siteran*, and so on) or the ceremonial court gamelans (*sekati*, *monggang*, and so on). Figure 2.1 lists the instruments common to most Surakarta and Yogyakarta gamelan presently.

One of the ways the two traditions distinguish themselves today is in the pitch vocabulary within some of these categories. Yogyanese *kempul* and *kenong* sets normally consist of a gong for each pitch in each tuning system, except pitch 4 in *pélog*, as follows: 3, 5, 6, i, and 2 in *sléndro* and 3, 5, 6, 7, i, and 2 in *pélog*. In addition, one often finds a lower-pitched *kenong*

1 Solonese gamelan at Taman Budaya Surakarta, *bonang* in foreground, *kenong* and *saron* in center, *gendèr* on right.

2 Yogyanese gamelan *Kangjeng Kyahi Medarsih* (*sléndro*) and *Kangjeng Kyahi Mikatsih* (*pélog*) in the dining pavilion at the Yogyakarta palace (*kraton*), *bonang* player in foreground, *saron* on left, *kempul* in background. Musicians are rehearsing for an upcoming *uyon-uyon hadiluhung* (July, 1989).

3   Yogyanese gamelan *Kangjeng Kyahi Medarsih* (*sléndro*) and *Kangjeng Kyahi Mikatsih* (*pélog*) in the Pagelaran pavilion at the north entrance to the Yogyanese palace. Musicians are accompanying a *wayang golèk* performance during Yogyakarta's Arts Festival (July, 1989).

```
gong ageng (largest gong)
gong suwukan or siyem (medium hanging gong)
kempul (small hanging gong)
kenong (large kettle gong-chime)
kethuk (small kettle gong)
kempyang (small kettle gongs for pélog)
saron family (single-octave metallophones with trough resonators):
    saron demung, saron barung (ricik), and saron panerus (peking)
bonang family (double-octave gong-chimes):
    bonang barung, bonang panerus
gendèr family (metallophones with keys floating over tube resonators):
    slenthem (gendèr panembung), gendèr barung, gendèr panerus
gambang (multi-octave xylophone)
suling (bamboo flute)
celempung or siter (zither)
rebab (spike fiddle)
kendhang family (double-headed laced drums):
    kendhang gendhing, kendhang ciblon or batangan, kendhang ketipung
```

2.1   Instruments used in Yogyanese and Solonese gamelan

known as *kenong japan*, tuned to pitch 5 in the octave below the other *kenong*. Solonese *kempul* sets usually omit the high 2̇ and sometimes the 3, and Solonese *kenong* sets begin from pitch 2 and proceed up to pitch 1̇, again with no 4 in *pélog*. While in Yogyanese gamelan the *kethuk* is tuned to 2 in both tuning systems, in Solonese ensembles the *pélog kethuk* is tuned to pitch 6 in the octave below the *sléndro kethuk*. Yogyanese *kempyang* consist of two kettle gongs tuned to pitch 6 and 7, struck simultaneously, whereas most Solonese *kempyang* are tuned only to pitch 6. Yogyanese *suling* sound pitch 1̩ with all holes open, the Solonese *suling* pitch 2̩. One often finds two *pélog suling* in Solonese gamelan, one in *barang* (with pitch 7) and the other in *bem* (with pitch 1), but only one *pélog suling* in Yogyanese gamelan. Finally, the *sléndro saron* and *bonang* have a slightly larger ambitus in Solonese gamelan than in Yogyanese. These differences are summarized in the figure below.

Instrument	Solonese Pitch Vocabulary	Yogyanese Pitch Vocabulary
kempul (sléndro)	3 5 6 i̇	3 5 6 i̇ 2̇
(pélog)	3 5 6 7 i̇	3 5 6 7 i̇ 2̇
kenong (sléndro)	2 3 5 6 i̇	3 5 6 i̇ 2̇
(pélog)	2 3 5 6 7 i̇	3 5 6 7 i̇ 2̇
kethuk (pélog)	6	2
kempyang (pélog)	6	6 7
suling (sléndro)*	2̣ 3̣ 5̣ 6̣ 1 2 3 5 6 etc.	1̣ 2̣ 3̣ 5̣ 6̣ 1 2 3 5 etc.
suling (pélog)	2̣ 3̣(4̣)5̣ 6̣ 7̣ 2 etc.	1̣ 2̣ 3̣ 4̣ 5̣ 6̣ 7̣ 1 2 etc.
	2̣ 3̣(4̣)5̣ 6̣ 1 2 etc.	
saron demung (sléndro)	6̣ 1 2 3 5 6 i̇	1 2 3 5 6 i̇
saron barung (sléndro)	6̣ 1 2 3 5 6 i̇	1 2 3 5 6 i̇
saron peking (sléndro)	6̣ 1 2 3 5 6 i̇	1 2 3 5 6 i̇
bonang barung (sléndro)	1̣ 2̣ 3̣ 5̣ 6̣ 1 2 3 5 6 i̇ 2̇	2̣ 3̣ 5̣ 6̣ 1 2 3 5 6 i̇
bonang panerus (sléndro)	1̣ 2̣ 3̣ 5̣ 6̣ 1 2 3 5 6 i̇ 2̇	2̣ 3̣ 5̣ 6̣ 1 2 3 5 6 i̇

```
* The range of the suling spans several octaves, not shown fully here.
  Half-holing and special fingering can yield other tones besides those of
                         the fixed scale.
```

2.2 Pitch vocabulary on Solonese and Yogyanese instruments

Though instrumentation in the two traditions is nearly identical, Yogya has demonstrated some conservative tendencies over the course of its history, substantiating the claim that Yogyanese are more "traditional". One of these is simply the maintenance of a smaller pitch vocabulary on the *sléndro bonang* (ten kettles *vs.* Solo's twelve) and *saron* (six keys *vs.* Solo's seven). Comparing lists of instruments in the court gamelans of Surakarta and Yogyakarta from the late nineteenth and early twentieth centuries indicates that Yogyanese ensembles maintained some instruments, such as the knobless gong (*bendhé*) and cymbals (*kecèr* and *rojèh*), that were no longer used in Surakarta, except in ceremonial ensembles.[6]

The past several centuries have seen an increase in the number of *kempul* and *kenong* from one or two per tuning system to the present standard of a *kempul* and a *kenong* for almost every tone in each tuning system. Formerly these instruments marked points in the gong cycles both by their distinctive timbre and their constant pitch. Nowadays the pitch played usually matches that of the other instruments at these points, making the *kempul* and *kenong* strokes themselves less clearly audible than they were. Though both traditions contributed to this development, the proliferation seems to have begun in Surakarta. In the late nineteenth and early twentieth centuries, some Solonese gamelan already included two or three *kempul* and three *kenong* – all tuned in the same octave register that they are today. Yogyanese gamelan, however, usually had only one *kempul*, two *kenong* in the register of modern-day *kenong*, and a more archaic-sounding one in the lower octave (the *kenong japan*).[7]

In addition to these differences in range and pitch vocabulary, further contrast between Yogyanese and Solonese instrumentation is afforded in the use of instruments associated only with one or the other tradition. In some Yogyanese gamelan, one finds a third member of the *bonang* family, tuned an octave lower than the *bonang barung* and called *bonang panembung* (one in each tuning system) (see plate 4). Some Solonese gamelan, particularly those used to

4   Yogyanese gamelan in the Daerah Istimewa Yogyakarta (Special Region of Yogyakarta) pavilion at Taman Mini, 1986. *Saron* on left, *bonang panembung* in foreground.

accompany shadow puppetry and other related dramatic forms, include one or two nine-keyed *saron* (*saron sanga* or *saron wayang*). Also frequently used in Solonese tradition for dramatic accompaniment is the *kendhang wayang*, larger than the *kendhang ciblon*, though not as large as the *kendhang gendhing*. The large tacked drum *bedhug* is found in some Solonese ensembles, but is more common in Yogyanese. On the other hand, the pair of *sléndro* kettle-gongs known as *engkuk-kemong* is almost always included in Solonese gamelan and only rarely in Yogyanese.

Because of the stress on loud-playing style in Yogyanese tradition, one is likely to find a greater number of *saron* instruments in Yogyanese gamelan than in Solonese. The norm in Solo is one *saron demung*, one or two *saron barung*, and one *saron peking* in each tuning system. Solonese court ensembles, especially those favored for loud-playing style, may have a larger number.[8] Some older ensembles in Solo have two *saron peking* for each tuning system, played in interlocking alternation with one another.[9] In Yogyanese gamelan it is preferable to have two *saron demung* and three or four *saron barung* in each tuning, though this number may be compromised to cut expense. Some Yogyanese court ensembles include as many as four *saron demung* and eight *saron barung*, which can produce a thunderously loud sound.[10]

Contributing to the louder Yogyanese sound is the tendency to use thicker *saron* keys and larger *bonang* kettles than one finds in Solo. The Solonese preference is for smaller instruments, even for the playing of their instrumental pieces, *gendhing bonang* (see below).

Another difference that strikes most observers immediately is the design of the wooden resonators and cases that hold the sonorous keys and gongs. In general, these are thicker and heavier in Yogyanese gamelan. The ends of Solonese *bonang* racks and *gambang* resonators are often intricately carved in open filigree. The Yogyanese may be decoratively carved, but are less ornate and rarely filigree. Solonese *saron* resonators are flat on top, curling downward at both ends. In Yogyanese tradition, these resonators arch upwards at both ends before curling downwards (see plates 1 and 2). Overall, Yogyanese gamelan appear sturdier and Solonese gamelan more delicate. The physical appearance of the ensembles, then, reflects the same aesthetic differences that are manifest in the musical sound.

Tuning system and pathet

Throughout Java, regions may contrast in their relative emphasis on one or the other of the two tuning systems: *sléndro* (five nearly equidistant intervals per octave) or *pélog* (seven uneven intervals per octave, usually only five or six tones used in a single piece). However, neither Solonesse nor Yogyanese gamelan music today demonstrates a marked preference for one tuning system (*laras*) over the other. Based on a census of gamelan ensembles conducted during the 1920s, Kunst noted a slight preference in the Surakarta region (residency) and a stronger preference in the Yogyakarta region for gamelan ensembles tuned in *sléndro*, and a clear preference in both areas for *sléndro* in vocal music. In the courts, though gamelan names usually refer just to a *sléndro* or a *pélog* ensemble, two are usually paired to enable performers to use both tuning systems during the course of a performance. For the large ensembles, the number of *pélog* and *sléndro* ensembles is the same in both the Yogyakarta and Surakarta courts. While economic constraints may enable individuals to purchase instruments in only one tuning system, it is considered desirable to have both *sléndro* and *pélog* available for public performances in both traditions. While I do not have access to present-day data of the kind Kunst presents, I believe there may still be a slight preference in both regions for *sléndro*. But, as will be seen below, there is substantial repertory in both tunings.

Scholars have spent much time in the study of tunings in Java, but many questions remain unanswered. Javanese musicians I worked with were highly conscious of subtle differences from one ensemble to another in tuning, and generally viewed tuning as an individual matter, rather than a regional one. But several points emerged. One is the preference in old Yogyanese ensembles, particularly ones in the court (such as *Kyahi Guntur Sari*), for instruments to be slightly "out of tune" with one another (*umyung*). The shimmering effect of the beats produced by sounding the instruments together, more widespread in Bali than in Java today, is considered desirable in Yogya for the loud, instrumental pieces and not the pieces with voice and softer instruments.

A set of *sléndro* and *pélog* instruments that are set out and played as one large ensemble will almost always have one or more tones in common (*tumbuk*) between the two systems. Preference has been given to pitch 5 in Yogya, sometimes with *sléndro* 6 equal to *pélog* 7 and *sléndro* 1 equal to *pélog* 1. The result is felt by many Solonese to be "awkward," forcing intervals to be stretched or compressed a bit more than they find tolerable (especially the squeezing of the two *pélog* intervals 5–6 and 6–7 into one *sléndro* interval 5–6, and stretching *pélog* 7–i to the size of the *sléndro* interval 6–i). In Solo, and now increasingly in Yogya, the preferred *tumbuk* is pitch 6, usually with *sléndro* 5 equal to *pélog* 4. I have not heard this criticized by Yogyanese as awkward or otherwise undesirable, but the *tumbuk* 5 is still preferred by older Yogyanese musicians. A hypothetical case is given below. The dotted line is for reference and should not be misconstrued as a Javanese theoretical construct for the derivision of scales comparable to Indian *sruti* division of the octave.

```
pélog:      1  2  3     4  5  6  7     i
            ................................  Tumbuk 5, Yogyanese
sléndro:    1  2     3     5     6     i


pélog:         1     2  3     4  5  6  7     i
               ................................  Tumbuk 6, Solonese
sléndro:    1     2     3        5     6     i
```

2.3   Common tumbuk in Yogya and Solo

Pathet, the Javanese system of modal and tonal classification, is understood in a variety of ways by musicians and scholars and remains a subject of debate today. Both Solonese and Yogyanese traditions recognize three main *pathet* in each tuning system and, with very few exceptions, assign each piece to one *pathet* or another. The standard categories are given here; their associations with time of day and mood are discussed elsewhere, along with several theories concerning their musical determinants (see Hood 1954, Sutton 1975:32–45, Becker 1980:78–99, and Powers 1980:436–41).

Sléndro pathet:	Pélog pathet:
nem (stresses 2, avoids 1)	lima (stresses 1 & 5, avoids 7)
sanga (stresses 5, avoids 3)	nem (stresses 5 or 6, avoids 7)
manyura (stresses 6, avoids 5)	barang (stresses 5, 6, or 7, avoids 1)

2.4   Standard central Javanese *pathet* categories

In *pélog*, both *lima* and *nem* partake of the *bem* scale, consisting of pitches 1, 2, 3, 5, and 6 (with 4 as an alternate for 3). *Pathet barang* uses the *barang* scale, consisting of 2, 3, 5, 6, and 7 (with 4 as an alternate for 5). The distinction between the two *pathet* of the *bem* scale (*lima* and *nem*) is the weakest. Sometimes pieces may be classified by Yogyanese simply as *pathet bem*, although the court maintains the *lima–nem* distinction. One also hears of pieces classified as *pélog pathet manyura* or *pélog pathet nyamat* – pieces whose tones, if played in *sléndro*, would clearly be *pathet manyura*. These are often pieces that were more commonly played in *sléndro*, but have been "transposed" to the *pélog bem* scale.

Another addendum to the basic *pathet* categories in Yogya is the designation of a few pieces heard at the end of all-night shadow puppet performances as *sléndro pathet galong*. Some view this as a subcategory of *manyura*, as these pieces are heard at the very end of the *manyura* section of the *wayang*. They stress pitch 3, which is prominent in *manyura*, though usually less so than 6 (or 2).

For certain pieces or passages played in *sléndro*, the vocal part employs intervals approximating *pélog*, a practice known variously as *minir* (from Dutch *mineur* – "minor"), *miring* (literally, "slanted," "deviating") or *barang miring* (see further Martopangrawit 1972a, in Becker and Feintstein 1984:231–41).

Pathet distinctions are generally not given for the few pieces played on the small ceremonial gamelan (gamelan *monggang* and *kodhok ngorèk*). In the case of *kodhok ngorèk*, a *sléndro* melody is played simultaneously with a melody whose two tones suggest *pélog*.

Repertory

One of the ways in which Yogyakarta and Surakarta have distinguished themselves over the years is in their repertory of *gendhing*. The earliest sources pertaining to musical practice are manuscripts with lists of gamelan pieces. Thus, it is repertory and some terminology that can be traced furthest back. It should be noted from the outset, however, that the repertories of these traditions still overlap to a great degree down to the present day. In cases where the same piece is played in both traditions, the style of performance and often the basic instrumental melody will differ.

Categories of gamelan pieces

Before beginning to consider the various sources pertaining to repertory in historical perspective, we need to examine the important categories of gamelan pieces practiced currently in Surakarta and Yogyakarta. For the most part, categories pertain to types of punctuating gong structures and to the relative emphasis on instrumental and vocal melody.

Almost all the gamelan repertory can be grouped under the heading *gendhing*. Whether or not *gendhing* emphasize vocal parts, they all involve a *balungan* part, usually played by more than one player simultaneously on the single-octave metallophones *saron* and *slenthem*, with a recurring pattern of interlocking and coinciding gong punctuation. *Gendhing* are often grouped according to the relation of the gong punctuation to the *balungan*, from "short *gongan*" with eight or sixteen beats between each stroke of the large *gong*, up to "long *gongan*" with 256 beats per large *gong* stroke.[11] Both Yogyanese and Solonese make a distinction between "large *gendhing*" (of sixteen or more beats per *kenong*) and "small *gendhing*" (eight, four or two beats per *kenong* stroke). The latter employ the set of small hanging gongs (*kempul*); the former do not. The latter are considered to be somewhat lighter in mood and easier to learn than the former.

The large and small *gendhing* share the characteristic of regular *gong* phrase lengths, in contrast to the pieces, sometimes called *gendhing lampah* (literally, "walking") in which phrases marked by the large *gong* (or *gong suwukan*) vary in length and the *kempul* sounds simultaneously with every second *kenong* stroke, rather than between *kenong* strokes as in the "small *gendhing*." The term *gendhing lampah* is more prevalent in Yogyanese tradition. Nevertheless, in Solo these pieces are also thought of as comprising a single category, often simply referred to with two or all three of the Solonese terms (e.g., *Srepegan-Sampak*).

Structure	Solonese Term	Yogyanese Term

I. Small Gendhing (8 or fewer beats per kenong stroke, use of kempul)

A. 2 kenong per gong

1. 16 bb/G	Ketawang	Ketawang

B. 4 kenong per gong

1. 8 bb/G	Lancaran	Lancaran/Bubaran
2. 16 bb/G	Lancaran mlaku	Bubaran
3. 32 bb/G	Ladrang	Ladrang

II. Large Gendhing (16 or more balungan beats per kenong stroke)

A. 2 kenong per gong:

1. 32 bb/G	Ketawang Gendhing kt. 2 kerep	[Ketawang Alit?] (lit. "small")
2. 64 bb/G	Ketawang Gendhing kt. 4 kerep	[Ketawang Tengahan?] (lit. "middle-sized")

B. 4 kenong per gong:

1. 64 bb/G	Gendhing kt. 2 kerep Minggah kt. 4	Gendhing Alit (lit. "small")
2. 128 bb/G	Gendhing kt. 2 arang Gendhing kt. 4 kerep Minggah kt. 8	Gendhing Tengahan (lit. "middle-sized")
3. 256 bb/G	Gendhing kt. 4 arang Gendhing kt. 8 kerep Minggah kt. 16	Gendhing Ageng (lit. "large, great")

Key: bb = balungan beats   kt = kethuk
     G = gong (large gong)   kerep = "frequent" (bb 4, 12, 20 etc.)
     N = kenong   arang = "sparse" (bb 8, 24, 40 etc.)

2.5   Solonese and Yogyanese terms for "regular" formal structures

Structure	Solonese Term	Yogyanese Term
8 bb/P	--none--	Ayak-ayakan
4 bb/P	Ayak-ayakan	Srepegan/Slepegan
2 bb/P	Srepegan/Slepegan	Playon/Sampak
1 bb/P	Sampak	Sampak Gara-gara

2.6   Solonese and Yogyanese terms for "irregular" formal structures

Becker has shown how these pieces are "regular," only with *kempul* serving as a substitute gong. The resulting structure consists of many short *gongan*, occurring every second *kenong* stroke (like a compressed *ketawang*). Longer phrases, consisting of a concatenation of these short *kempul gongan*, are marked by the use of a large *gong* rather than a *kempul* (see Becker 1980:105–47). But despite their structural regularity, these pieces are felt by Javanese to stand apart from the others. The difference is reflected in their function as the standard dramatic accompaniment for scene changes, arrivals and departures, and fights.[12]

Though most of the *gendhing* in the categories mentioned thus far can have vocal parts and soft-sounding instruments, the pieces in which a vocal melody is in some senses primary may be designated with other terms, which may not delimit the formal structure. *Jineman* are short pieces featuring a vocal melody whose gamelan accompaniment excludes *rebab*. The gong punctuation may be based on that of "small *gendhing*" (*ladrang, lancaran*) or "walking *gendhing*" (*srepegan*). The most widely heard *jineman*, *Uler Kambang*, resembles a piece in *ladrang* form, but neither begins nor ends with the large *gong*.

In Yogyakarta, the pieces associated with the singer–dancer (*talèdhèk*) tradition and featuring solo singing and the lively *gembyakan* drumming style of the *kendhang batangan* were formerly classified separately as *gendhing talèdhèkan*. Especially in court circles, this category implied a lower status in relation to the instrumental pieces (*soran*) and the other pieces (*lirihan*) with vocal parts that were accompanied by the more subdued drumming of the *kendhang gendhing* and *ketipung*. Some of the *talèdhèkan* pieces were large *gendhing*, but most were small (*ladrang*, primarily), with some special forms. For most Yogyanese the *talèdhèkan* pieces – at least the ones still performed – are no longer differentiated from the larger, standard repertory.

In both Yogyakarta and Surakarta, beginning in the latter part of the nineteenth century, a corpus of small *gendhing* were composed based on solo vocal melodies (*tembang* in low Javanese, *sekar* in high Javanese). These pieces, mostly *ketawang* and *ladrang*, were used in the genres of dance drama in which characters sang all their lines (*langen driyan* and *langen mandrawanara*) and were called *sekar gendhing*. Now, like the *gendhing talèdhèkan* mentioned above, these have become standard pieces in concerts and other dramatic forms and are no longer seen as a separate body of repertory. Also deriving from the *langendriyan* and *langen mandrawanara* genres are the freer vocal pieces accompanied by the gamelan, but with *balungan* instruments and *bonang* silent – pieces that do not fall under the category of *gendhing*, but rather *palaran* (the Solonese term) or *rambangam* (the Yogyanese term). Though the punctuating gong pattern is identical to that of the walking *gendhing*, with large *gong* sounding only on signal from the drum, there is no *balungan* to punctuate, but instead a rather free-floating melody, sung by a soloist (male or female).

Consisting mostly of new compositions, the category of *lagu* (literally, "song," "melody") or *lagu dolanan* (literally, "play/game song") is becoming an increasingly significant part of the gamelan repertory in Yogya and Solo, although few of these are identified specifically as "Yogyanese" or "Solonese."[13] These pieces place strong emphasis on a vocal melody, often sung by a chorus in unison (occasionally in counterpoint!) with a *lancaran* or *srepegan* formal structure. Some of the traditional *lagu dolanan* are associated with children's games. The many new compositions are not, but their rhythmic simplicity (in most cases, at any rate) is reminiscent of the older *lagu dolanan*. Along with these one finds gamelan imitations of the Javanese *kroncong* pieces known as *langgam*. These may also be labelled *lagu*, although the style of singing resembles that of *kroncong* and even the instrumental accompaniment may imitate that of the *kroncong* ensemble.

All of the categories of repertory mentioned thus far are usually played on a standard gamelan, rather than any specialized ensemble. Some pieces are performed with no singing or soft-sounding instruments. These are called *gendhing soran* (literally, "loud pieces") in Yogyanese tradition and *gendhing bonang* (or *gendhing bonangan* – literally, "*bonang* pieces") in Solonese, and include pieces in most of the regular forms, though in Solo the term usually refers to a small repertory of large *gendhing*. The vast majority of the repertory heard today consists of pieces with some singing and soft instrumentation. It is not uncommon, especially in Solonese tradition, to omit the *saron* and *bonang* instruments in performance of some pieces, thereby enabling the listener to hear the softer instruments and vocalists more clearly. In this case, *balungan* is sounded only on the *slenthem*.

In the courts of Yogya and Solo one finds other, small repertories for the ceremonial gamelan ensembles. The gamelan *sekati*, a loud ensemble with large *pélog bonang* and *saron*, and no soft instruments, has associated with it some pieces that are exclusively *gendhing sekati*. In both Solo and Yogya, however, many of the pieces performed on gamelan *sekati* are also part of the standard gamelan repertories. The smaller ensembles, gamelan *kodhok ngorèk* (literally, "croaking frog") and gamelan *monggang*, consist only of gongs, drums and archaic cymbals or bell-trees and, at least now, only sound one piece each (Gendhing *Kodhok Ngorèk* and Gendhing *Monggang*, respectively). The gamelan *kodhok ngorèk* is usually supplemented by a few other instruments, which perform the melody *Ayamsepenang* simultaneously. In keeping with their emphasis on loud playing, the Yogyanese add three *saron* (one *demung* and two *saron barung*), while the Solonese add a soft-sounding *gendèr* along with a multi-octave metallophone known as *gambang gangsa* (literally, "bronze *gambang*"). Another ceremonial gamelan, now found in Surakarta and elsewhere, but not (no longer?) in Yogyakarta, is gamelan *carabalèn*, which some believe to be an imitation of Balinese gamelan. The contemporary repertory for this ensemble in Surakarta is quite limited (about ten pieces), although the ensemble may have enjoyed wider use and a larger repertory in the past (see below).

I have mentioned these special ceremonial ensembles because they will be occasionally referred to below. My concern, however, is with the repertory for the standard gamelan ensemble.

Yogyanese and Solonese repertories, past and present

The earliest extensive list of gamelan pieces appears in the opening section of the encyclopedic poem *Serat Centhini*, the version written down by court scribes in Surakarta during the first decades of the nineteenth century. Among the several passages devoted to the performing arts, one lists 153 pieces.[14] Most of these, at least the *gendhing* to which these titles refer today, are now performed in soft-playing style and are part of the *klenèngan* repertory – pieces played for listening enjoyment, rather than for accompaniment of dance, drama, or special ceremonies. A few of the pieces listed are strictly instrumental (*gendhing bonang*), one (*Jalaga Bonang*) listed explicitly as such.

An untitled Yogyanese manuscript that I was shown by Lindsay's and my mutual teacher, Pustakamardawa, gives a list of 351 pieces dating from 1847.[15] Both sources classify the *gendhing* according to tuning system (*sléndro* or *pélog*) and modal category (*pathet*). This

Yogyakarta manuscript, from the court of Sultan Hamengku Buwana V and hereafter referred to as HBV, also classifies the *gendhing* according to prominent instrument or playing style (e.g., *gendhing gendèr*) – a practice no longer found in Yogyakarta, but still frequent in Surakarta.

Since neither of these lists includes any musical notation, one cannot be sure when comparing lists that the same title appearing in both lists actually refers to the same piece in both court traditions. Correspondence in tuning (whether *sléndro* or *pélog*) and in *pathet* may be taken as further evidence of a match, but a lack of correspondence here may not mean that two pieces are different. Transposition between tuning systems and between *pathet* within one tuning system has long been common (see further Vetter 1986:564–603 on "*gendhing* traits"). But given the common heritage shared by these two courts and the fact that many of the pieces known by the same name in both courts today are musically quite similar, it seems that a comparison of titles can offer some indication of the extent of repertory shared between the two.

Bearing in mind that the HBV list is more comprehensive (including more than just *klenèngan* pieces), it would be a mistake to suggest that the Yogyanese repertory in the early nineteenth century was larger. But what is fairly certain is that most of the Solonese *klenèngan* repertory was also known in Yogya. Of the 153 pieces listed in the *Serat Centhini*, about three-quarters appear in the Yogyanese HBV.[16]

Thus, both the names of the pieces and the method by which they are classified in the Yogyanese manuscript suggest that Yogyanese and Solonese gamelan traditions in the first half of the nineteenth century were more closely related than one might have expected given the professed rivalry between the two courts. In the *Pakem Wirama*, a Yogyanese manuscript existing in a number of variant forms and whose title page indicates that the first version was begun in 1889, a much larger number of *gendhing* appear, complete with *titilaras andha* ("ladder notation") of the *balungan*, drum, and punctuating gong parts. In the versions I examined I found a total of 703 pieces, some of which were clearly added during the twentieth century. Though listing twice the number of *gendhing* as the HBV manuscript, the *Pakem Wirama* contains no more pieces (only 119) from the *Serat Centhini* list than the HBV manuscript (see Lindsay 1985:314–40). One no longer finds *gendhing* classified by Solonese categories, but instead by drum pattern – a practice maintained today in the Yogyakarta court and seen as an important distinction between the two traditions. Where Solonese tradition usually lists pieces today according to their formal structure (e.g. *gendhing kethuk 2 kerep*, *minggah 4*), Yogyanese tradition lists pieces by drum pattern (e.g., *kendhangan candra*). The formal structures imply specific drumming patterns for Solonese, and the drumming patterns imply specific formal structures for the Yogyanese.

Apparently no comprehensive manuscript was produced by the Solonese as a counterpart to the *Pakem Wirama*. The most extensive source on Solonese gamelan music dating from before 1950 is the *Wedha Pradangga* (Warsadiningrat 1979), in which *gendhing* titles are given and pieces discussed in their historical context, though they are not notated. The *Wedha Pradangga* mentions most of the *Serat Centhini gendhing* (137 of 153, see Lindsay 1985:314–40). The most authoritative Solonese source today, however, is the three volume set of *gendhing* notation compiled by Mloyowidodo and published by ASKI Surakarta in 1976. This work contains 902 *gendhing*, including nearly all of the *Serat Centhini* pieces (147 of 152) and just less than two-thirds of the *gendhing* listed in the HBV manuscript (depending on one's caution in matching titles, from 213 to 235 of the 351 in HBV). A similar work dealing with Yogyakarta repertory was compiled in three volumes by Sukardi, Sukidjo and Dibyomardowo and published by ASKI Surakarta in the same year, but it is smaller in scope (445 entries) and generally not taken as a near-comprehensive collection of Yogyanese repertory. The *Pakem Wirama* remains the most authoritative source on Yogyanese pieces, despite the fact that it has not been published and thus remains relatively inaccessible.

Another approach to repertory is to identify the pieces that are actually performed and not merely listed or notated. While it would not be possible to take this approach in historical perspective, since program listings are extremely rare, it is possible either through observation or through an examination of the discs and cassettes recorded to do so for the present. In his dissertation on gamelan music, in the Yogyakarta *kraton*, Vetter kept track of all the repertory used for a period of one year and made cipher notation of the *balungan* for most of it (Vetter 1986:327–562). Of the 245 pieces in regular forms collected by Vetter, only about one quarter (61–65) appear in the HBV manuscript and only an eighth (32) in the *Serat Centhini*. Three-fifths (146–151) appear in the more recent Yogyanese source, the *Pakem Wirama*, and nearly one half (112–16) in the still more recent Solonese source Mloyowidodo. This suggests a substantial repertory change over the last 150 years, but also points to a continued overlap between Yogyanese and Solonese repertories.

In my own compilation of pieces recorded either commercially or by researchers (including myself), I find 656 *gendhing* and 46 *palaran* that can be said to belong to the contemporary "mainstream" repertory – associated with Solo, though played throughout much of Java. But my list of active repertory differs markedly from that notated by Mloyowidodo, sharing only 250 pieces (38 percent of the *gendhing* in my compilation and 28 percent of the *gendhing* in Mloyowidodo). Many of the large *gendhing* Mloyowidodo included are rarely, if ever, performed and are not available as recordings. Much of what is often heard and recorded consists of new pieces (*lagu* or *lagu dolanan*) and *gendhing lampah*, neither of which are included in Mloyowidodo's work.

Before going on to scrutinize the distribution of the repertory in these sources with respect to formal structure, tuning, and *pathet*, we can gain some measure of the distinction between Yogyanese and Solonese repertory by comparing the pieces listed in either the *Pakem Wirama* or Vetter 1986 with those listed in either Mloyowidodo 1976 or in my compilation. Though neither combination represents a definitive listing of repertory, either Yogyanese (in the first two) or Solonese (in the second two), the results should provide a reasonable picture of the extent to which the two overlap. Of the total 815 *gendhing* in the Yogyanese sources, approximately one third occur in at least one of the Solonese sources. Limiting the comparison to categories that are included in all four sources (large *gendhing*, *ladrang*, *ketawang*, and *lancaran/bubaran*), we find an even more significant overlap. Of the total 785 Yogyanese pieces, more than one half are found in the Solonese repertory.

It would be somewhat misleading to present data based on comparison of these various sources without pointing out that their intentions and the types of repertory they incorporate are not uniform. The least comprehensive is the *Serat Centhini*, which, as stated above, is the *klenèngan* repertory and consists mostly of pieces known today as large *gendhing*, with only a few *ladrang* and no *gendhing lampah*. Small *gendhing*, especially *ladrang*, are now a prominent fixture in contemporary *klenèngan*, as are the *gendhing* lampah. The extent to which they were played 150 years ago, but simply not deemed worthy of listing, cannot be accurately determined. The emphasis on large *gendhing* also characterizes the HBV list. Only a few pieces are listed explicitly as small *gendhing* (five as *ladrang*, one as *ketawang*, two as *bubaran*). Of the 343 remaining pieces on the HBV list, only fifty-five appear elsewhere as *ladrang*, five as *ketawang*, and seven as *bubaran* or *lancaran*. Thus, the large *gendhing* outnumber the small by nearly four to one (276 large *gendhing*, 75 small *gendhing*). Nor does the HBV list include any *gendhing* lampah.[17]

In contrast to the *Serat Centhini*, however, the HBV list includes pieces identified as *gendhing* Sekati (i.e., pieces for the large *pélog* ensembles known as gamelan *sekati* found only in the Yogya and Solo courts and sounded only for special occasions). Only twenty-five of the 351 pieces in HBV are listed as "*sekati*", and four of these appear as non-*sekati* pieces as well.[18] In current practice, most pieces played on the *sekati* gamelan are also heard in other contexts as part of a more "standard" repertory. Also included in HBV are *gendhing cara wangsul* (= *cara bali*) – presumably for, or in the style of, the now archaic gamelan *carabalèn* which, notably, is no longer represented in Yogyakarta, though it is in Surakarta and elsewhere. Another category appearing in the HBV list is *gendhing Madunten* (= Madura), which suggests some borrowing from Madurese culture, though no one has substantiated this. Still, most of the *gendhing* titles classified in HBV as *cara wangsul* or as Madunten have been known as part of standard Central Javanese repertory, played on full gamelan ensembles in both Yogyakarta and Surakarta.

The *Pakem Wirama* contrasts with these earlier sources both in the systems of classification and in the balance between the different formal structures. To begin with, fifteen *gendhing lampah* are included, with drum patterns indicated as *patut* (literally, "fit," "appropriate"; i.e., what is appropriate for the particular context). Though the *sekati* repertory for the Yogyakarta palace is notated in the same format as that used in the *Pakem Wirama*, it is bound separately and generally thought of as a separate manuscript (see Toth 1970). Pieces in the *Pakem Wirama* are classified by drum pattern and *pathet*, with a special category for *talèdhèkan* pieces (whose drum patterns are listed as *gembyakan* and not notated) and for *sekar gendhing* (the vocally oriented pieces). It is neither difficult nor a misrepresentation of the data to list formal structures, rather than drum patterns. For the sake of consistency with the other data in this study, I have chosen to do so with the *Pakem Wirama* pieces in Figure 2.7 below, which maintains the separation of *gendhing talèdhèkan* and sekar *gendhing* from the other, basic repertory (unmarked). The distribution by tuning system and *pathet* will be discussed later.

Though the number of large *gendhing* is high (296), the most significant contrast with the earlier sources is the great number (382) of small *gendhing* – *ladrang*, *ketawang*, *lancaran*, and the smaller *talèdhèkan* pieces. It is unlikely that these were all newly composed, though some of them were (particularly the *sekar gendhing*). Rather, it seems to reflect increased stature for the little pieces as distinct repertory items.

As a measure of the continuity of this trend, we can compare the *Pakem Wirama* data with that gathered by Vetter (1986) for the Yogyakarta court music activity during 1982–83 (Figure 2.8). Again we see a preference for smaller forms, particularly *ladrang*. The *gendhing sekati* pieces transcribed – twenty-nine of the thirty listed – all resemble *ladrang* form most closely. If we include these in the figures for *ladrang*, we have an even more pronounced emphasis on this one small *gendhing* form: 143, more than half of the entire active repertory for 1982–83.

	BASIC	REPERTORY				GENDHING SEKAR			TALEDHEKAN	OTHER	
	Gen-dhing	Lad-rang	Keta-wang	Lcn/Bbr.	Gd. Lamp.	Gen-dhing	Lad-rang	Keta-wang	Gen-dhing	Small Gd.	TOTALS
Pélog											
lima	25	13	–	–	1						39
nem	38	31	3	6	2		(Gendhing Sekar and Gendhing Talèdhèkan only listed in Sléndro)				80
barang	33	70	7	2	2						114
Pélog Totals:	96	114	10	8	5	–	–	–	–	–	–	233
Sléndro											
nem	40	20	–	–	4	–	3	–	–	–	–	67
sanga	49	37	13	7	4	–	10	2	4	13	–	139
manyura	92	72	3	2	2	4	20	5	11	50	–	261
Sléndro Totals:	181	129	16	9	10	4	33	7	15	63	–	467
Other (ceremonial): Monggang (quasi pélog) and Kodhok Ngorék (mixed)										3	3
TOTALS:	277	243	26	17	15	4	33	7	15	63	3	703

2.7 Distribution of *gendhing* in the *Pakem Wirama* (Yogya)

In Mloyowidodo's notation of Solonese *gendhing*, although *gendhing lampah* are not included, we find a balance comparable to that listed in the *Pakem Wirama* for Yogya between the large and small *gendhing* (in Mloyowidodo, 415 and 487 respectively). The total number of *gendhing* in Mloyowidodo 1976 and their distribution across the formal structural categories and *pathet* are given in Figure 2.9. Although Mloyowidodo notates more *gendhing* than he does *ladrang* (415 vs. 368), it is *ladrang* that represents the most prominent single formal structure, for under the heading *gendhing* are included six or seven large *gendhing* structures. It is also the category of *ladrang* that accounts for the greatest distribution through the *pathet* of both tuning systems (428, vs. 424 for all *gendhing*).

For comparison, I include data on active repertory associated with Surakarta in Figure 2.10. The categories used are based on those listed on the recordings (cassette covers and record jackets) and reflect the importance of vocal music (*lagu dolanan, langgam, jineman,* and *palaran*). Again, the small *gendhing* outnumber the large *gendhing*. Even excluding the vocally-oriented pieces, we find 301 small *gendhing* (*ladrang, ketawang* and *lancaran/bubaran*) and only 136 large *gendhing*. The number of *ladrang* alone (190) is 40 percent greater than the number of all large *gendhing*. And clearly there is a great emphasis on the vocally-oriented pieces, particularly the *lagu dolanan*, which often employ *lancaran* or *ladrang* form.

Given that these sources of repertory inventory differ in comprehensiveness and in intent, what can be said about the differences between Yogya and Solo with regard to the formal structures? Most important is to note the similarities between the distributions of the

Total no. of gendhing listed (exlusive of multiple pathet and laras listing):

Gd. 51	Ldr. 114	Ktw. 28	Bbr. 17	Lcn. 3	Gd. Lamp. 21	Gd. Skt. . 30	Other 2	TOTAL 266

	Gen- dhing	Lad- rang	Keta- wang	Lcn/ Bbr.	Gd. Lamp.	Gd. Sekati	Other	Totals
Pélog								
lima	4	4	–	1	–	6	–	15
nem	8	26	8	5	4	15	–	66
barang	11	30	11	8	7	23	–	90
Pélog Totals:	23	60	19	14	11	44	–	171
Sléndro								
nem	9	10	–	1	2	–	–	22
sanga	15	23	9	5	4	–	–	56
manyura	7	37	9	4	7	–	–	64
Sléndro Totals:	31	70	18	10	13	–	–	142
Other: (gamelan monggang and kodhok ngorèk)							2	2
TOTALS:	54	130	37	24	24	44	2	315

Excluding gendhing sekati, pélog = 127 (9 pl lima, 51 pl nem, 67 pl barang)
cf. sléndro = 142 (22 sl nem, 56 sl sanga, 64 sl mnyr)

2.8   Distribution of *gendhing* in Vetter 1986 (Yogya)

gendhing through the various formal structures. Taking only the categories represented both in Vetter's and my data on active repertory, *ladrang* are most numerous, followed by (in order) large *gendhing*, *ketawang*, *gendhing lampah*, and *lancaran/bubaran*.

The other categories deserve some explanation. It is not that *lagu dolanan* or *langgam* are unknown in Yogya, but most are recent additions and generally understood to be part of a more generalized central Javanese repertory, based on Solonese tradition, but combined with new additions. Though some *lagu dolanan* have been composed by a renowned musician from Yogyakarta, Ki Wasitodiningrat, he has long been a champion of Solonese style and his pieces are not generally felt to be "Yogyanese." Yogyakarta has a strong tradition of *palaran* performance (the Yogyanese term is *rambangan*), though this is rarely heard in the palace. Yet the repertory is mostly shared by Solo and Yogya, with stylistic differences in the singers' contours being the primary distinguishing feature. The *rambangan* and *gendhing lampah* of Yogyakarta are probably the best known Yogyanese pieces outside the region and are often incorporated as purposefully "Yogyanese" offerings in a concert that might otherwise be devoted to Solonese repertory.

There is also a corpus of pieces that are still widely known in Yogyakarta, and to some

Total number of <u>titles</u> (some of which are used x2 or x3 for different pieces):

Gendhing	Minggah	Ladrang	Ketawang	Lancaran	TOTAL
388	8	349	76	34	847

Total number of <u>pieces</u> (two diff. pieces may have same title):

Gendhing	Minggah	Ladrang	Ketawang	Lancaran	TOTAL
407	8	368	80	39	902

Distribution by form and pathet (incl. multiple listings; a single piece may appear in more than one category, e.g., sl 9 & pl 6):

	Gendhing	Minggah	Ladrang	Ketawang	Lancaran (& Bubaran)	Totals
Pélog						
lima	62	3	41	5	4	115
nem	77	–	104	25	1	207
barang	69	–	95	18	15 (4 untitled)	197
Pélog Totals:	208	3	240	48	20	519
Sléndro						
nem	61	1	29	1	–	92
sanga	80	1	66	17	9	173
manyura	67	3	63	22	10 (1 untitled)	165
Sléndro Totals:	208	5	173	40	19	430
TOTALS:	416	8	428	88	39	949

2.9   Distribution of *gendhing* in Mloyowidodo 1976 (Solo)

extent elsewhere, as a kind of canon of Yogyanese tradition. The same cannot be said for Solo, probably because so much of what is heard is Solonese. These Yogyanese pieces symbolize a Yogyanese presence – or what I have called elsewhere an "idea of Yogya" as a distinctive cultural entity, be it court or, nowadays, region (see Sutton 1984). I list below only the pieces that I found to be widely known and recognized as Yogyanese. Solonese pieces exist for most of these titles.

Gendhing *Bondhèt*
Gendhing *Jangkung Kuning – Arum-arum*
Gendhing *Lambangsari*
Gendhing *Méga Mendung*
Gendhing *Pandhélori*
Ladrang *Asmaradana Kenya Tinembé*
Ladrang *Clunthang*
Ladrang *Liwung*

Ladrang *Lung Gadhung*
Ladrang *Pamularsih*
Ladrang *Srikaton*
Ladrang *Surèngrana*
Ketawang *Gajah Éndra*
Gangsaran – Ladrang *Bima Kurda*
Gangsaran – Ladrang *Roning Tawang*

Total No. of

Gen-dhing	Lad-rang	Keta-wang	Lcn/Bbr.	Gd. Lamp.	Lagu Dol.	Lang-gam	Jine-man	Pala-ran	Other	TOTAL
136	190	76	35	37	144	14	9	46	5	702

Distribution by form and pathet (including multiple listings):

	Gen-dhing	Lad-rang	Keta-wang	Lcn/Bbr.	Gd. Lamp.	Lagu Dol.	Lang-gam	Jine-man	Pala-ran	Other	Totals
Pélog											
lima	10	6	6	4	2	1	-	2	-	1	32
nem	27	46	23	12	6	45	5	5	10	2	181
barang	32	48	20	8	9	24	6	4	16	2	169
lima/nem*	3	4	4	-	1	2	-	-	9	-	23
other**	1	-	-	-	-	3	-	-	-	-	4
Pélog Totals:	73	104	53	24	18	75	11	11	35	5	409
Sléndro											
nem	16	8	-	1	6	1	-	-	6	-	38
sanga	26	48	18	8	7	38	2	4	20	1	172
manyura	40	45	14	7	12	11	-	1	24	0	154
barang miring+	-	-	-	-	-	1	1	-	-	-	2
not listed	-	-	-	1	-	21	-	-	-	-	22
Sléndro Totals:	82	101	32	17	25	72	3	5	50	1	388
TOTALS:	155	205	85	41	43	147	14	16	85	6	797

* same piece, with different pathet listing in different sources
** employ all seven tones and not classified by pathet
+ use of vocal scale that deviates from sléndro and sounds like pélog.
++ for some sléndro pieces no pathet listing was given.

2.10 Distribution of *gendhing* and *palaran* in active Solonese repertory, compiled by the author from recordings

Javanese often distinguish these pieces from the Solonese versions by appending the word "Mataram" when referring to the Yogyanese versions, for example, Gendhing *Bondhèt Mataram* (or *Mataraman*). This term is somewhat ambiguous, however. Mataram is the name not only for the region in which the Yogyakarta court was founded, but also for the undivided kingdom of south central Java that preceded the division into Yogyakarta and Surakarta. The term invokes the memory of a powerful, united central Java and suggests continuity with that tradition; but it may also be interpreted as "old fashioned". Less well known than the pieces listed above, but identified as Yogyanese, are pieces whose titles refer to the region: Ladrang *Prabu Mataram* (literally, "Ruler of Mataram") and Gendhing *Ngèksi Ganda* (*ngèksi* = "to see"; *ganda* = "fragrance"; suggesting *mata* ["eye"] + *arum* ["fragrant"] → Mataram).

Finally, the *ladrang* pieces known as *gati* or *mares* (from the Dutch for "march") are unique to Yogya and number at least forty. (I count forty titles in the *Pakem Wirama* and Vetter 1986.) These are *kraton* pieces used for dance entrances and exits and are often performed with gamelan augmented by Western brass, woodwinds, and snare drum. The drum pattern for all these pieces is a special *ladrang* pattern known as *sabrangan* (literally, "from across the sea," "foreign"). In this case, the Yogyanese appear to have moved further away from whatever they may have inherited from the old Mataram kingdom than have the Solonese, whose repertory shows Western influence only in the recent *lagu dolanan*.

In summary I offer some figures based on analysis of the Solonese *gendhing* (in Mloyowidodo 1976 and on recordings) and the Yogyanese *gendhing* (in the *Pakem Wirama* and reported by Vetter 1986). Based on these sources, I find 1,310 gamelan pieces in the Solonese repertory (1,257 *gendhing* and forty-five *palaran*) and 852 in the Yogyanese repertory, to which one can add fifteen *rambangan*. There is considerable overlap between these two groups. I find 305 pieces that are shared, with an additional thirty-six that are probably related (notation or recording unavailable). The potential for considerable distinction by repertory alone should be clear. Even if a lengthy performance in one area presents many pieces shared between repertories, a few pieces belonging exclusively to one tradition or the other can make a strong regional statement – which can be greatly enhanced by aspects of playing style.

Tuning system and *pathet*

No strong preference is shown for one tuning system over the other in the repertories of either tradition. A summary of the data from Figures 2.7, 2.8, 2.9, and 2.10 is given below. The only source that suggests a clear preference is the *Pakem Wirama*, in which one third of pieces are *pélog* and two-thirds *sléndro*. But given that the *sekati* pieces (all *pélog*) are not included and that many of the pieces notated only in *sléndro* have often been played in both tuning systems, the *sléndro* preference is not as pronounced as the data might make it seem. Vetter's data, which includes *sekati* pieces, shows a slight preference for *pélog*, but discounting these thirty pieces, we obtain an almost exact balance in the repertory between *pélog* (141) and *sléndro* (142). Though both the data from Mloyowidodo and my own compilation suggest a slight preference for *pélog* in Solonese tradition, this is not marked enough for musicians to identify *pélog* with Surakarta tradition or *sléndro* with the Yogyanese.

Amplifying this data on repertory is the aesthetic articulated within both traditions for the alternation between tuning systems in gamelan music concerts. The *Pakem Wirama* gives

| | YOGYAKARTA | | SURAKARTA | |
	Pakem Wirama	Vetter 1986	Mloyowidodo 1976	Recordings
Pélog				
lima	39	15	115	32
nem	80	66	207	181
barang	114	90	197	169
lima/nem	–	–	–	23
other				4
Pélog Totals:	233	171	519	409
Sléndro				
nem	67	22	92	38
sanga	139	56	173	172
manyura	261	64	165	154
other	–	–	–	24
Sléndro Totals:	467	142	430	388

2.11   Summary of data on distribution by tuning system and *pathet* in four sources (2 Yogya, 2 Solo)

explicit directions for the mounting of a three-day (!) *uyon-uyon* (gamelan concert, not in accompaniment of dance or drama), in which each piece or piece medley is followed by one in the other tuning system. In both Solo and Yogya, this same type of balanced alternation is the norm – observable, for example, in radio broadcasts (including those from the palaces).

If the two traditions appear not to distinguish themselves from each other in the choice of tuning system, neither do they on the basis of *pathet*. The number of pieces in *sléndro pathet nem* and *pélog pathet lima* is markedly lower than for the other *pathet*. Most of the pieces in these two *pathet* are felt to be subdued, even austere. As such, the contexts for their performance are more restricted. A few points of subtle contrast emerge from the data. The Yogyanese sources contain a greater number of entries in *sléndro* for *pathet manyura* than for *pathet sanga*; in the Solonese sources it is the reverse. In *pélog*, the Yogyanese sources contain a greater number of entries for *pathet barang* than for *pathet nem*, while the Solonese sources contain a greater number for *pathet nem* than for *barang*. Again these are not significant enough to be mentioned by most musicians when discussing differences between Yogya and Solo. Rather, the differences most musicians mention in contrasting the *pathet* systems of the two traditions are in the Yogyanese use of *pathet galong* in the *manyura* section of the *wayang* and the use, outside the palace, of the category *pathet bem* as a catch-all for pieces that would otherwise be classified either as *pathet lima* or *pathet nem*.

Prescribed uses of *gendhing*

In addition to the sheer enumeration of pieces that comprise a repertory, an important aspect of musical tradition is the association that develops between certain pieces or practices and the contexts in which they are heard. Concerts and new dance dramas have a relatively low level of prescription in this regard. But in *wayang kulit* and wedding ceremonies, the choice of pieces for certain events may be determined entirely by tradition. To offer a complete account of these associations for both Yogyakarta and Surakarta would be a lengthy and complex task. A few examples are chosen here to demonstrate the differences that persist between Yogya and Solo.

Wedding music can vary for some stages of the ceremony, but for the appearance of the bride and groom in front of the guests, Yogyanese tradition calls for Lancaran *Kebo Giro*, whereas Solonese tradition calls for the archaic piece *Kodhok Ngorèk*. Rarely would any Solonese other than royalty have a gamelan *kodhok ngorèk* present. The piece is played, instead, on a standard gamelan, using *pélog* for the basic ostinato and *sléndro gendèr* for the contrasting melody.

In former times, if we can judge from manuscript sources from both regions, the use of pieces in *wayang kulit* was highly constrained from beginning to end. The appearance of a certain character, or the locus of action at a certain place, required the use of a specific piece. Books still appear with these associations listed (see Probohardjono 1957; Mudjanattistomo *et al.* 1977), but in practice only a few persist. One association that is very clearly maintained is the choice of *gendhing* for the first scene in the entire performance (*jejer sepisan*). Yogyanese use their version of Gendhing *Krawitan* regardless of the place in which this scene is to take place.[19] Solonese use Gendhing *Kawit* for the first scenes either in the court of the Pendhawa brothers' or in the realm of the gods and Gendhing *Kabor* for the first scenes in the court of the Korawa brothers. These account for many of the *wayang* plays. Only for first scenes in other kingdoms do they use their version of Gendhing *Krawitan*. In the first scene of the *wayang*, then, Yogyanese and Solonese tradition already prescribe different treatment. Nowadays, as the night progresses, the choice of *gendhing* is less determined by scene or character than it was formerly. Depending on the disposition of the puppeteer, one may find anything from partial adherence to the standard prescription to near total disregard for it.

The musical hallmark of shadow puppet performances are the *sulukan* of the puppeteer and the *gendhing lampah*. In both categories, clear contrasts abound between Yogya and Solo: in the melodic contours and the instrumental accompaniment of the *sulukan*, and in the structures, melodies, and treatment of the *gendhing lampah*. One can drop into a performance at any time and learn very quickly which of the two traditions is being represented, or at least being used as a basis, even though the former differences in prescription for certain *gendhing* may no longer be evident. In addition, Yogyanese recognize some disparity in *wayang kulit* between palace or "inside" style (*cara njero*) and "outside" style (*cara njaba*), just as Solonese distinguish sulukan padésan ("village" *sulukan*) from those of the main court (*kasunanan*) and their variants at the Mangkunengaran. These make for fascinating study, but are on a less significant level of contrast than those between the two main traditions.

Solonese and Yogyanese musical styles

Balungan

Though the repertories of Yogyakarta and Surakarta overlap to a considerable extent, *balungan* for pieces shared by both often contrast. In fact, even within one tradition a number of slight variants may exist for the *balungan* of a single piece, but the differences between

Yogyanese and Solonese *balungan* are usually more pronounced. One could argue that Yogyanese and Solonese versions of a piece actually represent two pieces – related, but distinct. Outside of Yogyakarta, the Yogyanese version of Ladrang *Bima Kurda*, for example, is usually referred to as Ladrang *Bima Kurda* "*gaya* Yogya" (also as Ladrang *Bima Kurda Yogya* or Ladrang *Bima Kurda Mataram*) and the Solonese version simply as Ladrang *Bima Kurda*. In Yogyakarta it is the reverse. *Balungan* notation, with gong punctuation, for two versions is given in Figure 2.12 in cipher notation as well as Western staff notation.[20] Some important features are shared by these two versions: the emphasis on pitch 5 in the first *gongan* and on the gong stroke in all *gongan*, the use of the characteristic passage .25. 6765 (and its rhythm, .xx. xxxx), and sequence of six *gongan* (AABBCC or AABB'CC). Yet the two melodies contrast clearly in every *gongan*, beginning with the first *kenongan* (first line, as written). Contrast is even more pronounced in performance. The Solonese version is played softly with vocal and soft instruments sounding, whereas the Yogyanese version is normally played in loud (*soran*) style.

It would be a vast undertaking to conduct a comprehensive survey of *balungan* in the large Solonese and Yogyanese repertories. Nevertheless, by examining several versions of some *gendhing*, representing different formal structures, it will be possible to identify some general traits more prevalent in one repertory than in the other. From the start, it should be pointed out that there is some degree of stylistic overlap. Often, it is not that a *balungan* is in Yogyanese or Solonese "style" but that it is the version which happens to have come to be associated with one or the other court or region.

```
        Solonese                          Yogyanese

     t    t N                          t    t N
    ...5 .235                         .5.5 .2.5
    ...5 .235      A (x 2)            .5.5 .2.5      A (x 2)
    ...5 .235                         .5.5 .2.5
    .25. 6765G                        .25. 6765G

     t    t N                          t    t N
    .77. 7656                         ..57 5676
    567. 7656      B (x 2)            7576 7576      B
    567. 7656                         756. 6725
    .53. 2365G                        .25. 6765G

     t    t N                          t    t N
    .22. 2327                         ..57 5676
    672. 2327      C (x 2)            7232 .765      B'
    6732 .756                         ..57 5676
    .53. 2365G                        7232 .765G

                                       t    t N
                                      6352 3565
                                      7656 3532      C (x 2)
                                      6567 6532
                                      1216 5365G
 KEY:
   t = kethuk (beats 2 and 6 of every line)
   N = kenong (8th beat of every line)
   G = gong (with every 4th kenong)
  [P = kempul (4th beat of 2nd, 3rd and 4th line in each gongan), not shown]
```

2.12 Ladrang *Bima Kurda*, *pélog pathet barang*, Solonese and Yogyanese versions

2.12   Continued.

One characteristic that musicians often mention is the tendency for Yogyanese *balungan* to be "denser" or more filled in than the Solonese. The part is frequently twice as dense in the Yogyanese version and sometimes four times, depending on the *irama* – the level of subdivision of the *balungan* beat in performance. For example, the popular Ladrang *Clunthang* is known in two densities for *irama* level I: *nibani* (Solonese) and *mlaku* (Yogyanese).

```
Solonese--nibani              Yogyanese--mlaku

  t   t N                       t    t N
.5.6 .2.1                     5616 5321
.5.6 .5.6      A              5616 5356     A
.5.6 .3.5                     5612 1635
.2.1 .6.5G                    2321 3265G

  t   t N                       t    t N
.1.6 .3.5                     1216 3235
.1.6 .3.5      B              1216 3235     B
.1.6 .3.5                     1216 3235
.2.3 .2.1G                    2353 2121G

(Mloyowidodo 1976I:94)       (Sukardi & Sukidjo 1976:68)
```

2.13   Ladrang *Clunthang*, *sléndro pathet sanga*, two versions

As the piece slows in performance to *irama* level II (half the speed of *irama* I) and *irama* level III (half the speed of *irama* II), the Solonese *balungan* remains the same, only with greater time intervals between successive tones. The Yogyanese, already twice the density of the Solonese in *irama* I, may double again to become four times the density of the Solonese for the A *gongan* and the final *kenongan* of the B gongan, a *balungan* style called *ngracik*.

```
A:   t        t  N        B:    t         t  N
 55.61656 51525321             1 2 1 6   3 2 3 5
 55.61216 ..635616             1 2 1 6   3 2 3 5
 ..6.6612 53216535             1 2 1 6   3 2 3 5
 23532121 35321635G           22.35653 65212321
```

2.14   *Ngracik* version of Ladrang *Clunthang*, *sléndro pathet sanga* (Yogyanese)

A more subtle distinction may be found in pieces for which both *balungan* versions have the same density. The first section of Ladrang *Sri Karongron* differs only by the manner in which the fifth *gatra* (group of four *balungan* beats) emphasizes tone 5. While in a Yogyanese version one tone may receive emphasis by its appearance in the initial and final positions of a *mlaku* style *gatra*, in a Solonese version it may be sustained or repeated with no other melodic motion in the *gatra*, a device known as *gantungan* (literally, "hanging," "suspended"). The *gatra* 5235 and 55.. are in paradigmatic relationship, appearing in the same context. Yet, while

```
Solonese                      Yogyanese

  t   t N                       t    t N
2126 2165                     2126 2165
6165 2321                     6165 2321
55.. 6165                     5235 6165
3216 2165G                    3216 2165G
```

2.15   Ladrang *Sri Karongron*, *sléndro pathet sanga*, two versions of first *gongan*

both emphasize 5, their meaning is not identical, for it is by their contrasting structure that one is able to distinguish one as Yogyanese and the other as Solonese.

This is not to say that gantungan is unique to the Solonese repertory. Many Yogyanese *gendhing* contain passages of *gantungan*. In notation these passages may appear to be identical in both Yogyanese and Solonese versions, as in the following excerpt from Gendhing *Capang* (in Yogya, sometimes called *Caplang*): 5653 2123 ..35 2353N. In Yogyanese style performance the *saron barung* and *demung* players often execute a technique known variously as *cecegan* or *ngencot*. The player damps the key as he strikes it, yielding a staccato sound. This technique is used on even-numbered beats (i.e., the strong beats) in passages of *gantungan*. Whether one conceives of the result as two slightly different *balungan* or as the same *balungan* realized in variant styles, the difference is quite apparent in performance.

```
Yogyanese style:    5 6 5 3   2 1 2 3   . 3̄3̄3 5   2 3 5 3N

Solonese style:     5 6 5 3   2 1 2 3   . . 3 5   2 3 5 3N

                                          / = cecegan (ngencot)
```

2.16   Passage from Gendhing *Capang*, *sléndro pathet manyura*, two versions

The use of *cecegan* (*ngencot*) is yet another means of filling in, and is identified with Yogyanese style.

One important exception to this penchant for density – and also a hallmark of Yogyanese style, though one that is now fading from popularity – has been the playing of a less filled in *balungan* (*lamba*) in the first *gongan* of many pieces. Below is the opening *gongan* of Gendhing *Montro*, *sléndro pathet manyura*, in both styles. By the gong tone, the Yogyanese *balungan* has doubled, but in the first portion it is the Solonese which is twice the density of the Yogyanese.

```
        Solonese                    Yogyanese (lamba)

   t        t   N                 t        t   N
.132 .132 5653 2126           .1.2 .3.2 .5.3 .1.6
.132 .132 5653 2126           .1.2 .3.2 .5.3 .1.6
33.. 3356 3561 6523           .5.3 .1.6 .2.1 .5.3
..61 2321 3216 .523G          6521 2321 3216 1523G
```

2.17   Gendhing *Montro*, *sléndro pathet manyura*, first *gongan*, two versions

The contrast is immediately apparent. Within the first few beats one can tell whether the *gendhing* is being played in Yogyanese or Solonese style from the density of the *balungan* alone. The association of *lamba* with Yogyakarta suggests that the need to be distinctive is a more basic constraint than the aesthetic preference for greater *balungan* density. One could also argue that the Yogyanese preference is for changing the *balungan* density in response to changes in tempo (*irama* level), much as the *bonang* and other higher density parts do in both Solonese and Yogyanese tradition.

Another criterion by which different versions of *gendhing* are distinguished is length: greater number of *gongan*, more expanded *gongan*, or both. A remarkable contrast is found in the *gendhing lampah*: *Ayak-ayakan*, *Srepegan*, and *Sampak*. A Solonese version of *Ayak-ayakan*, *sléndro pathet sanga*, is given in Figure 2.18 on the left, with a Yogyanese version on the right. It is possible to see that these pieces cover the same overall contour, by nature of the proposed alignment of large units ending on the same tones. The number of *gongan* units, here marked most often by *kempul*, is greater in the Yogyanese version (thirty in all, nineteen in the repeated portion) than in the Solonese (twenty-five in all, seventeen in the repeated portion). More important is that the melodic contours within the Yogyanese are more filled in.[21]

```
           Solonese                                    Yogyanese
       P     P     P                             P            P
     N N   N N   N N   N N                   N        N        N        N        N        N
     .2.1  .2.1  .3.2  .6.5G   }——I——{     .2.1   .2.1    .2.1    .2.1    ..1.    1121G
                                            22.3   1232    35.2    3565G
     1656  5356  5356  3565G   }——II——{     66.1   5616    161.    1656    5323    1232G
   [:3235  3235  1656  5321G              35.2   3565    61..    1561    5652    5321G
                                        {[:2635  2321    2635    2321    22..    22.3P
     2321  2321  3532  5356G   }——III——{    55.2   3565    61..    1561    5652    3216G
           5356  5356  2321G   }——IV——{    2153   2356    2153    2356    2353    2121G
                 2321  3565G   }—— V——{    2635   2321    2635    2321    6532    3565G
                                            1612   1615    1612    1615    2253    2253P
   3235  3235  3212  3565G:]}——VI——{                                      2523    5615G
                              II'——{     1623   5615    1623    5615    6152    5321G:]
```

2.18   *Ayak-ayakan, sléndro pathet sanga*, two versions

Clearly the Yogyanese would be the harder to memorize because of the sheer number of notes. Advocates of Yogyanese style stress the discipline required to learn and perform such pieces, and they make similar comments about Yogyanese dance. They imply that Solonese performing arts are easier and less spiritually uplifting. Lengthiness is associated with grandeur. Those who prefer Solonese style remark that the Yogyanese is too cumbersome and that Solonese versions represent essence without clutter. Both may claim theirs to be more original (*asli*), but the arguments usually have to do with aesthetic criteria such as grandeur, elegance, smoothness, and liveliness.

Musicians who prefer Solonese style speak of its smoothness, an important measure of which is the degree of conjunct versus disjunct motion. The degree of disjunction can be quantified as a ratio of the number of disjunct intervals to the total number of instances of tonal motion. *Gantungan*, whether by immediate repetition or sustaining, is not counted. Thus, in the *gatra* 2253, for example, there are two instances of tonal motion: 2 to 5 and 5 to 3 – the first disjunct, the second conjunct. (In *pélog*, tone 4 is only used as an alternate for either 3 or 5 and not as a step between them; *sléndro* contains no tone 4.) Clearly the Solonese version of *Ayak-ayakan, sléndro pathet sanga* (shown in Figure 2.18), is more conjunct than the Yogyanese version. In ninety-one instances of tonal motion only nine (about 10 percent) are disjunct. In the 201 instances of tonal motion in the Yogyanese version, forty-seven (about 23 percent) are disjunct.

Less spectacular but still significant is the contrast between *gongan* of equal length, such as the repeatable *gongan* in the *mérong* section of Gendhing *Montro* (see Figure 2.19). In the Solonese version, fourteen of the fifty-two instances of tonal motion are disjunct (27 percent). In the Yogyanese version, twenty of the sixty-three instances of tonal motion are disjunct (32 percent). Again, the Yogyanese is the more disjunct both in number of occurrences and in percentage relative to all tonal motion. Yet it is important to realize that the comparison is valid only for different versions of the same *gendhing*. One need only look back at *Ayak-ayakan* to see that the Solonese version of one piece (Gendhing *Montro*) can be more disjunct

```
        Solonese (mérong)              Yogyanese (dados)

     t        t    N                  t        t    N
    .132 .132 5653 2126              1312 3132 5653 2126
    .132 .132 5653 2126              2132 3132 5653 2126
    33.. 3356 3561 6523              3523 .516 3561 6523
    ..61 2321 3216 .523G             6521 2321 3216 1523G

    (Mloyowidodo 1976I:127)          (Larassumbogo et al. 1953:75)
```

2.19   Gendhing *Montro, sléndro pathet manyura*, repeatable *mérong gongan*, two versions

than the Yogyanese version of another (*Ayak-ayakan*): 27 percent and 23 percent respectively.

Even when we limit the comparison on two versions of a particular *gendhing*, we may not be able to predict the regional identity based on degree of disjunction alone. The examples above have been confined to *mlaku balungan*. In cases of *nibani balungan*, such as the second section of large *gendhing*, known as *inggah* (Solo) or *dhawah* (Yogya), greater disjunction is just as likely to occur in Solonese versions as in Yogyanese. In a sample of twenty–one *gendhing* that occur in both repertories, I found the Solonese to be more disjunct in nine cases and the Yogyanese in eight. In the remaining four, though the *balungan* differed in all but one, the amount of disjunction was equal in both versions (see Sutton 1982:120, note 11.)

Much is shared in the *balungan* styles of these two traditions. Many of the basic syntactical constraints, which I have discussed in detail elsewhere (Sutton 1982:127–29), are the same. That is, for the most part, Yogyanese *balungan* are "grammatically acceptable" in Solonese tradition, as are Solonese *balungan* in Yogyanese tradition. Yet within the larger system, some tendencies have evolved representing aesthetic preferences that mark off the two styles from one another. In a similar fashion, as we shall see below, contrasts abound in the playing techniques and patterns for many of the instruments.

Instrumental playing techniques

Punctuating gongs

Very little flexibility is given to the players of the punctuating gongs that mark the formal structure of a piece. But even here we find some traits that distinguish Yogyanese and Solonese styles. While the large *gong*, the most revered of all the gamelan instruments, sounds its deep penetrating tones together with the last tone of the *gongan* phrase in both traditions, the Yogyanese seem to like to use this large *gong* in some contexts where the Solonese would use the *gong suwukan*: for example, for some *gongan* in *gendhing lampah* and *lancaran*. Furthermore, in *ladrang* and large *gendhing*, the Yogyanese make more abundant use of the *gong suwukan* than the Solonese to enrich the sound of certain tones that appear at points other than the end of a *gongan*. Yogyanese say this practice adds life to pieces. In some cases, Solonese may find it excessive and complain that it indicates a lack of restraint on the part of the Yogyanese, a sort of unsophisticated exuberance. Younger Solonese musicians seem to find it appealing.

The contrasting pitch vocabulary of the *kenong, kempul,* and *kethuk* provide a clear opportunity for contrast. Low 2 on the *kenong* is simply "Solonese." And high *kenong* or *kempul* tone 2, regardless of context, is simply "Yogyanese" to most people, though some performing ensembles now use these tones in playing Solonese *gendhing lampah* (e.g., Ki Nartosabdho's famous group, Condhong Raos).

Seemingly the most routine of timekeepers, with no pitch variation throughout the entire repertory, the *kethuk* may in fact be a stylistic indicator. In both traditions, the *kethuk* is played on certain prescribed beats. In Solonese style, however, when the *gongan* has expanded to *irama* level II or greater (III or IV), the *kethuk* is normally struck four or five times in very rapid succession, a ricochet technique that enables it to be better heard than when it is only struck once. One now hears this in some Yogyanese performances, but the older musicians comment that it is Solonese influence.

Single-octave metallophones and *bonang panembung*

The *saron barung*, *demung*, and *slenthem* usually sound the *balungan* in unison and thus are known collectively as "the *balungan* instruments". Little can be said about contrast in the playing of the *balungan* in these two traditions, other than the rather important fact that the balungan is more often played loudly in Yogya than in Solo. For expanded sections of pieces with vocal parts and soft instruments, it is not uncommon in Solonese style for the *saron barung* and *demung* to drop out entirely, leaving the *slenthem* alone to play the slow-moving *balungan*.

In some contexts the *balungan* instruments do something other than sound the *balungan*. Solo and Yogya have developed contrasting processes of variation on these instruments for the elaboration or abstraction of the *balungan*. When the *balungan* is in *nibani* format, as in the second section (*inggah/dhawah*) of many large *gendhing*, the *saron barung* in Yogyanese style is expected to add a single *pancer* tone between all the *balungan* tones – usually pitch 1 (in *pélog barang* pitch 7), but other pitches (particularly 5 and 3) also serve as *pancer* in some contexts. For example, the passage .6.5 .2.3 could be rendered on the *saron barung* as follows: 1615 1213. Solonese *saron* do not normally insert *pancer*, and in fact may be silent during the playing of *nibani balungan* in soft-playing pieces, allowing the *slenthem* to sound the *balungan* alone. The *engkuk-kemong* or the *kempyang* can be seen to serve a *pancer* function in Solo and it is clearly a pan-Javanese musical trait, but in Yogya the *pancer* becomes prominent, sounded by as many as eight *saron barung* simultaneously.

One of the hallmarks of Yogyanese style, especially suited to the performance of loud-playing pieces, is the interlocking alternation of two *demung* parts, known as *imbal demung*. This practice gives prominence to the *demung* and is now generally considered inappropriate for soft-playing, since it obscures the vocal and soft instrumental parts. While *imbal* is a widely practiced technique, popular in some Solonese genres and throughout Java, the use of the *demung* for this interlocking is rare outside Yogya – probably in part because most gamelan outside Yogya have only one *demung* per tuning system (and only one player).

One does occasionally hear *imbal demung* in the instrumental pieces (*gendhing bonang*) of Surakarta, but the basic paradigm is the opposite of that found in Yogya. In Yogyanese style, the part coinciding with the *balungan* beat (*demung* I) most often plays the tone one step above the tone of the *balungan*, while the second part (*demung* II) plays the *balungan* tone, but between the beats of *demung* I. The use of the *balungan* tone rather than its upper neighbor in the *demung* I part provides variation, a transposition down one key of the original paradigm.

```
balungan:        .   3   .   2

demung I:        .5.5.5...3.3.3..

demung II:       3.3.3.3.2.2.2.2.
```

2.20   Yogyanese *imbal demung*

The strokes coinciding with the *balungan* tones may be deleted (*pejah*, literally, "dead") or played (*gesang*, literally "alive"), as shown in Figure 2.21.

```
balungan:        .   3   .   2        A = transposition down,
                                            played gesang.
demung I:        .3.3.3.3.3.3.3..
                                      B = normal position,
demung II:       2.2.2.2.2.2.2.2.           played pejah.
                 A       B
```

2.21   Yogyanese *imbal demung*, *gesang* and *pejah* variation

In Solonese style, the *demung* part coinciding with the *balungan* beats (here *demung* I) would normally sound the *balungan* tone, with the second *demung* playing the upper neighbor tone. Thus, the Yogyanese and Solonese practices are literally mirror images of one another.

In Yogyanese style, pieces or sections in which the *balungan* is in *nibani* format call for a *slenthem* technique known as *gemakan* (literally, "like [the sound of] a quail").[22] Instead of sounding the *balungan* tone together with the *saron*, the *slenthem* anticipates each *balungan* tone, as shown in Figure 2.22.

```
balungan:    .  3  .  2         .  3   .  2

slenthem:    3.3.2.2.           3 3 3 . 2 2 2 .
             (irama I)          (irama II and III)
```

2.22   Yogyanese *gemakan* technique for *slenthem*

Often the *gemakan* technique is used together with *imbal demung* and *saron pancer*, creating a richly textured sound in which the *balungan* is sounded (between the *pancer* tones) on the *saron*, but elaborated as well.

As something of a counterpart to Yogya's quail analogy (*gemakan*), the Solonese tradition employs all three *balungan* instrument types in a technique known as *banyakan* (literally, "like [the sound of] a goose"). In this style, the *balungan* itself is implied but not stated explicitly. The *saron* usually plays the second *balungan* tone of each *gatra* on the first and second beats, and the fourth tone on the third and fourth beats (e.g., for *balungan* 6532, *saron* plays 5522). The *demung* sounds the *saron* tones but adds an upper or lower neighbor tone between the beats, and the *slenthem* plays the *demung* part delayed by a quarter of a *balungan* beat, in rhythmic interlocking with the *demung*, as shown in Figure 2.23.

```
[ balungan:           .   1   1   1   2   3   2   1 ]

  saron barung:     ...1...1...1...1...3...3...1...1

  demung:           .2.1.2.1.2.1.2.1.2.3.2.3.2.1.2.1        banyakan

  slenthem:         ..2.1.2.1.2.1.2.1.2.3.2.3.2.1.2.1
```
2.23   Solonese *banyakan* technique for *sarons* and *slenthem*

The result is a rather different sound than that of the Yogyanese practices discussed above. The *saron* part is characterized by repetition, involving none of the jumps to a *pancer* tone every other beat characteristic of Yogyanese style. The *demung* part emphasizes the *balungan* tones on the strong beats, rather than only on the weak beats as in the normal Yogyanese style of *imbal demung*. And the *slenthem* echoes the *demung*, rather than sounding a contrastive drone tone leading to each *balungan* as it does in Yogyanese style.

While the term *balungan* is used by carriers of both Yogyanese and Solonese traditions today to refer to the "*saron* part", the only melody played by more than one player in contemporary performance, the Yogyanese used the term until fairly recently to refer to an abstraction of the *saron* part, played on the *slenthem* and (if the ensemble included one) the *bonang panembung*. Regardless of the *saron* density, this *balungan* was a very regular two tones per *gatra*, the first usually an upper or lower neighbor to the second, as in this excerpt from Ladrang *Oyag-oyag*:

```
bonang panembung (& slenthem):   2 1  5 6    5 3   6 5

      saron barung & demung:  2121 2156   5523 5635
```
2.24   *Saron* part and abstract *balungan* in Yogyanese tradition

This more abstract *balungan* is unchanging in density and resembles the *lamba* in its rhythm. The presence of this layer of melodic activity, though increasingly rare even in Yogya, is an unmistakable mark, imbuing a performance with a Yogyanese feel.

Most closely related to the *balungan* instruments, though usually seen as an elaborator and subdivider of the *balungan*, the *peking* has become an important indicator of regional style in gamelan music. In very fast passages, the *saron peking* will sound the *balungan*. Otherwise, it usually provides a simple elaboration of the *balungan*, sounding at a greater density. In *irama* I the *peking* states each tone twice, once simultaneously with the *balungan* beat and the other a half beat before or after the *balungan* beat, a technique known in Solo as *nacah lamba* ("single chopping"), as shown in Figure 2.25.

```
                  YOGYANESE                        SOLONESE

balungan:          5 6 5 3         balungan:        5 6 5 3

peking:            55665533        peking:          55665533
                  (anticipating)                   (following)
```
2.25   Yogyanese and Solonese *peking* playing, *irama* I

Peking playing is fairly well standardized in Solonese style, and may reflect the former preference there for two *peking* in each gamelan. In *irama* II (and other contexts in which the *balungan* tones are played at slower tempi), a pattern of alternating anticipation groups the *balungan* in units of two, a technique known as *nacah rangkep* (literally, "double chopping"), as shown in Figure 2.26. In Yogyarkarta, where the *peking* figured less prominently than in Solo during the past, debate in recent discussions on musical style has focused on a properly Yogyanese method for playing the *peking* in the slower tempi (*iramas* II and III). The Yogyanese treatise *Pakem Wirama* states explicitly that the *peking* should anticipate (*ngru-miyini* – literally, "go before," "go first") and decorate (*miraga* – literally, "act alluring," "move attractively"). One could interpret the Solonese *nacah rangkep* pattern shown below as doing just that, but devotees of Yogyanese style offer several other techniques, contrasting with the widely practiced Solonese one.

	YOGYANESE					SOLONESE			
balungan:	5	6	5	3		5	6	5	3
peking:	5566556655335533					5566556655335533			
or	5 5 6 6 5 5 3 3								
						("nacah rangkep")			

2.26   *Peking* playing in *irama* II

Palace musicians tend to choose the sparser playing, in which the *peking* part maintains a constant ratio with the *balungan* part, slowing down as the *balungan* slows down. The denser playing in Yogyanese style is simply the Solonese *nacah rangkep* moved ahead one *peking* beat, representing a greater anticipation than the Solonese, analogous to the difference between the two styles in *irama* I.

The choices in Yogyanese style become more complex in cases where the *saron barung* is playing *pancer*. Some players choose to include the *pancer* as part of the melody from which they derive their *peking* part, others do not. Although Yogyanese *peking* playing has not been standardized, a player can play "in Yogyanese style" by taking any of the choices other than the Solonese. This sort of negative definition of style serves in cases where only two traditions are to be distinguished from one another. Later we shall see that other regional traditions also use one or another of the techniques attributed here to either Solo or Yogya.

Bonang

When asked which instrument other than the *balungan* instruments most clearly sets off Yogyanese and Solonese styles, Javanese musicians will almost always cite the *bonang*. Most of what is said in discussions of *bonang* playing concerns the *bonang barung* and this focus is reflected in my own coverage below. The *bonang panerus* is a less important instrument and plays the same kind of patterns as the *bonang barung*, only at a greater density (usually twice that of the *bonang barung*).

Javanese often say of two related things that they are "basically the same" (*dhasaré padha, pokoknya sama*). This is an important point in understanding Yogyanese and Solonese *bonang* techniques. *Bonang barung* is said by the Javanese to be the melodic leader, anticipating *balungan* tones in various ways. The technique known in Yogya as *mlaku* (= *mlampah*;

literally, "to walk," "to proceed") and in Solo as *mipil* (literally, "to pick off one by one") can be the most explicit as a leader. Each group of two *balungan* beats can be played in an alternating anticipation whereby each *balungan* tone is sounded by the *bonang* before it occurs in the *balungan*. Beginners in both traditions are taught to play as follows in *irama* I and II, for example.

balungan: 5 6 5 3 (irama I)   5   6   5   3 (irama II)

bonang barung: 56565353   565.5656535.5353

2.27 *Mipil/mlaku bonang* playing

But Yogyanese *bonang* players usually vary the durational values of the tones, especially in the slower *irama* (II and III), whereas the Solonese vary by omitting some of the tones. One possibility for each is given in Figure 2.28 (the dotted line is included to facilitate reading the precise rhythmic values).

balungan: 5   6   5   3   (irama II)
                    ....

bonang (Yogya)   5 6 .5. 5 6 5 65. 3 .5. 5 3 5 3

bonang (Solo)   5 6 5 . . 6 5 . . 3 5 . 5 3 5 .

2.28 Rhythmic variation in *mipil/mlaku bonang* playing

The principle of alternating anticipation (recalling the Solonese style of *peking* playing, *nacah rangkep*) is operating in both styles, but the rhythm can set one style off from the other. Further variations can occur in the choice of tones, as shown in Figure 2.29.

balungan: 5   6   5   3   (irama II)
                    ....

bonang (Yogya)   5 6 .1. 6 6 1 65. 3 .2. 2 3 5 3

bonang (Solo)   5 6 5 . . 6 5 . . 2 5 . 3 3 5 .

2.29 Variation with alternate tones in *mipil/mlaku bonang* playing

Yogyanese *bonang* playing tends to obscure the regular binary pulse of the music, seeming to hurry some beats and delay others. This is contrary to the Solonese aesthetic for smoothness, but delights lovers of Yogyanese style as animated and strong.

In addition to the Yogyanese preference for syncopated rhythms and the Solonese preference for understatement by omission, both *bonang* styles involve some flexible melodic formulas that act as stylistic signatures. The following is used widely in Yogyanese pieces, corresponding with one of several *balungan* configurations. (In performance, players would

```
        balungan:           .       2       .       1

          (or:          2       3       2       1   )

          (or:      2   3   5   3   2   1   2   1   )

   bonang Yogya:      2 5 2 3 5 3 2 1 6 5 6 1 2 1
                    2 2 2
```

2.30   A standard formula in Yogyanese *mlaku bonang* playing

normally add rhythmic syncopation, such as that described previously.) This whole pattern can be transposed up one key (to fit with *gatra* .3.2, 3532, and so on). Solonese patterns would be different for each of the *gatra* shown, none of them duplicating the Yogyanese pattern. The following is a widely used pattern in Solonese style, serving in a similar capacity as a "signature." (For other characteristic Solonese *bonang mipil* patterns, see Lysloff 1982:280.)

```
        balungan:           .       1       .       6

          (or:          2       1       2       6   )

          (or:          .       2       .       6   )

   bonang Solo:    2 1 5 5 5 1 . . 5 1 5 . 6 6 1 .
```

2.31   A standard formula in Solonese *mipil bonang* playing

In keeping with the Solonese emphasis on refinement, realized in music partially through understatement, it is usual practice for the *bonang* to play at half the normal density (*lamba*) in the calmer sections of some pieces. Yogyanese and Solonese versions of a passage from Gendhing *Mudhatama* are given in Figure 2.32:

```
        balungan:       2       6       2       1       2       3       1       2

 bonang Yogya:  2 6 .2. 2 6 2 6 2 1 2 . 1 1 2 1 2 3 .2. 3 3 2 3 1 2 .1. 1 2 1 2

 bonang Solo:       2   6   2   .   2   1   2   .   2   3   2   .   1   2   1   .
```

2.32   Yogyanese *mlaku* and Solonese *mipil lamba bonang* playing

Somewhat less obvious to the casual listener, but no less important in the minds of musicians, is the difference in conception of octave register in the two traditions. As much as is possible, given the limitation of the instrument, Solonese *bonang* parts reflect the multi-octave implications of the *balungan*: what Sumarsam (1984) has called "inner melody" (*lagu batin*), and my teacher Suhardi calls "*lagu*" (Sutton 1979). In the writing of Solonese *balungan*, it is customary to include subscript and superscript dots to indicate register – not only for the single-octave *balungan* instruments themselves, but as an indication for players of other parts (and for singers) of which register they should choose. Though the checkered notation of the *Pakem Wirama* gives indications of register for the soft instruments and vocals, more recent Yogyanese collections do not (e.g., Larassumbogo *et al.* 1953; Sukardi and Sukidjo 1976a and 1976b; and Sukidjo and Dibyomardowo 1976).

Representing register is somewhat problematic because the two-octave range of the *bonang* (slightly greater in Solonese *sléndro bonang*) does not fully cover the larger range possible in the conceptual melody. The latter is based on vocal range and its limits are essentially those of the singing parts in gamelan music. Solonese *bonang* playing may indicate register in several

		Octave I		Octave II		Octave III	
RANGES:	Conceptual melodies:	1̣	-->	1	-->	1̇	--> 5̇
	Bonang pélog:	1̣	-->	1	-->	7	
	Bonang sléndro (Solo):	1̣	-->	1	-->	1̇ 2̇	
	Bonang sléndro (Yogya):	2̣ -->		1	-->	1̇	

2.33   Range and register in *bonang* and conceptual melody

ways. In *mipil*, it may sound tones in the lower register of the *bonang* only in passages whose conceptual melody is also low register. Use of the middle register (octave II) is ambiguous, since it may indicate either middle or upper register in the conceptual melody. Though a passage such as 5 6 1̇ 2̇ could be realized on a Solonese *sléndro bonang* utilizing the high 1̇ and 2̇, the many passages reaching higher in register, such as 3̇ 2̇ 1̇ 2̇, require a shift down to the middle register (octave II) to enable the *bonang* part not to have to leap from high 2̇ down to middle 3 and back up. Thus, one hears 32321212, rather than 3̇2̇3̇2̇1̇2̇1̇2̇ in the *bonang*.[23]

Another means of indicating register is the reiteration of a single prominent tone (*nduduk*), either duplicated at the octave (*nduduk gembyang*) or not (*nduduk tunggal*). *Nduduk* is almost always used for *balungan* passages that also sustain a single tone (*gantungan*), but may also be played to suggest that a moving passage is cadencing in the middle or upper register. The Yogyanese technique known as *gembyangan* is essentially the same as Solonese *nduduk gembyang*, but carries with it no connotations of register, as shown in Figure 2.34. Most Yogyanese *bonang* players vary the rhythm of the *gembyangan*, as they do in the "walking" style.

Aside from the *bonang* techniques described above, both Yogyanese and Solonese styles involve an interlocking technique between *bonang barung* and *bonang panerus* (called *imbal* or *pinjalan*) and a technique of octave playing (*gembyangan nyegat*) in which the *bonang barung* played on the off beats or weak beats, anticipating only the fourth (or second and fourth)

```
balungan:          .      3̣   3̣    .//         .      3     3     .

Solonese                                      3     3     3     3     3
bonang:     3̣ 3̣ 3̣ .(3̣)3̣ .(3̣)3̣ .(3̣)3̣ .(3̣)3̣ .//   3̣ 3̣ 3̣ .(3̣)3̣ .(3̣)3̣ .(3̣)3̣ .(3̣)3̣ .
                   nduduk tunggal                          nduduk gembyang


Yogyanese      3     3          3     3              3     3          3     3
bonang:     3̣ 3̣ 3̣ . 3̣ 3̣ . . 3̣ 3̣ 3̣ . 3̣ 3̣ . .//   3̣ 3̣ 3̣ . 3̣ 3̣ . . 3̣ 3̣ 3̣ . 3̣ 3̣ . .
                  gembyangan                               gembyangan
```
2.34 *Nduduk* and *gembyangan bonang* patterns

tones of a *gatra*. Individual nuances have developed for *bonang imbal*, but the patterns are remarkably similar in both traditions, at least today. A slight difference is found in the *bonang panerus* playing for *gembyangan nyegat*, however. Solonese play three tones for every two in the *barung* part: either in groupings of two and three fast beats, or in a triplet three-against-two with the *balungan*. Yogyanese simply play between the beats of the *balungan* and the off-beats of the *bonang barung*.

```
balungan:              6        5        3        2

                    5  .  5  .  2  .  2  .
bonang barung:      5̣     5̣     2̣     2̣


bonang panerus (Solo):  . . 5 . 5 . . 5 . . 2 . 2 . . 2
                            5̣   5̣     5̣     2̣   2̣     2̣

bonang panerus (Yogya): 5 . 5 . 5 . 5 . 2 . 2 . 2 . 2 .
                        5̣   5̣   5̣   5̣   2̣   2̣   2̣   2̣
```
2.35 *Gembyangan nyegat bonang* patterns

At a discussion session in Yogyakarta I attended in 1979 devoted to defining Yogyanese *bonang* style, no consensus could be reached on ruling certain patterns to be correct Yogyanese style or not. Many of the musicians argued that one aspect of Yogyanese tradition was its lack of stylistic standardization, allowing for more individual input than in Solonese *bonang* playing. It would take us too far afield here to go into the kinds of individual variants that came under consideration at that meeting, but it was clear that none of the musicians present was willing to alter his own playing to conform with some newly established standard. All the musicians, however, played in ways that clearly stood out from Solonese style, and agreed that it is possible to speak of Solonese style and Yogyanese style in *bonang* playing, so long as one is not forced to limit the possibilities too narrowly.

Indeed, some important aesthetic differences persist, despite the heavy encroachment of Solonese tastes in Yogyakarta over the last fifty years. Javanese partial to Solonese style complain that Yogyanese *bonang* playing upsets the smooth rhythmic flow of the piece with its syncopations and ignores register in its melodic style. In contrast, they say, Solonese *bonang* playing is subtle, smooth, and more logical in relation to the multi-octave conception of the *gendhing*. Essentially, then, they see Solonese style as both more *alus* and more *maju* (advanced). The defenders of Yogyanese style see their *bonang* style – in all its individual variants – as spirited, and more interesting than the regular and predictable Solonese style. Though viewed differently, these contrasts in *bonang* playing are apparent to all gamelan musicians and constitute one of the most consistent identifying characteristics of the two styles.

Soft instruments

An investigation into the performance styles of the soft instruments could fill many volumes. Nowadays people do not normally speak of differences between Yogyanese and Solonese styles in most of these instruments, though only a generation ago such differences were recognized. It is generally thought that the heavy influx of Solonese styles in the Yogya area all but eradicated any distinctive Yogyanese style for these instruments.

Older musicians in Yogyakarta, however, mention some general characteristics that set the styles apart, at least for *gendèr barung* (hereafter, simply *gendèr*) and *gambang* playing. Yogyanese *gendèr* playing was less florid than Solonese, and followed the melody of the *balungan* (i.e., the *saron* part) more closely than it does in Solonese style. The two hands were less independent of one another and, in calm musical contexts, created a texture consisting mostly of parallel octaves and parallel *kempyung* (close to a fifth, but defined as an interval "separated by two keys" *let loro*). Solonese *gendèr* patterns (*céngkok*) always begin and end on either octave or *kempyung*, but otherwise are characterized by greater variety both in rhythm and in intervallic relationship between the two hands. For the lively sections of pieces with *batangan/ciblon* drumming, the *gendèr* part is correspondingly more animated in both traditions. In this context, some Yogyanese patterns contained brief reiterations of a single tone in the right hand part, in which the key was damped as it was struck – just as in the *cecegan/ ngencot saron* technique described above.

These traits are only rarely heard today. Where one finds a contrast now between the *gendèr* playing of Yogyanese and Solonese traditions is in the accompaniment of the puppeteer's songs (*sulukan*) in *wayang kulit* and related genres. For the calmer pieces, known as *lagon* in Yogyanese terminology and *pathetan* in Solonese, Yogyanese *gendèr* playing consists primarily of regular duration and a fairly steady underlying pulse. The rhythm of Solonese *gendèr* in this context is in parlando style, more prone to accelerandi and ritardandi. The *sulukan* known as *ada-ada*, for dramatic situations that are tense and emotionally charged, are accompanied by more agitated *gendèr* playing in both Yogyanese and Solonese styles, but again the two styles contrast. The Solonese *ada-ada* accompaniment is steadier in rhythm than the Solonese *pathetan* accompaniment, but goes through dazzling accelerandi that require technical virtuosity. Yogyanese *ada-ada* accompaniment is not as virtuosic as the Solonese. It is even more regular in rhythm than the *lagon* accompaniment – almost indistinguishable from the *gendèr* playing in *gendhing*.

Yogyanese *gambang* style, at least as musicians remember it from a generation or two ago, incorporated several contrasting techniques. What is now prevalent in both Solo and Yogya is the continuous motion in both the left and right hand parts, playing on every beat of the fastest regular pulse – a technique known as *banyumili* (literally, "flowing water"). Yogyanese *gambang* style involved passages in *banyumili* style, but partook of others. The technique my teachers identified as most characteristic of Yogyanese style is known as *glebeg*, in which the left hand damps the key it is striking, or the key which it has just struck (both occurred). Thus, the simultaneous damping and striking of a key is not only a Yogyanese characteristic in *saron* and *gendèr* playing, but in *gambang* playing as well. Another technique, characteristic of both Yogyanese and Solonese styles but more prevalent in the former, is *geter*, a quick reiteration or ricochet, used only in the right hand. The frequent use of *geter* was referred to by Yogyanese as *grontolan* (literally, "like kernals of corn") and was still prevalent in the playing of the Yogyanese musician Bapak Durmo, who performed with the studio musicians of the national radio station (RRI) in Yogyakarta in the 1950s and 1960s (see Sutton 1975:85–87 for notation and further commentary on these techniques).

Little is said about *gendèr panerus* and *celempung* playing. Most Javanese, at least, would not look to these instruments for stylistic differences between Yogya and Solo. Nor does the *rebab* figure prominently in the contrast today, since many Yogyanese imitate Solonese *rebab* style. Formerly, the *rebab* melody stayed very close to the *saron* part in Yogya, exhibiting less of the independence that characterizes Solonese playing. Today, the Yogyanese cite the main difference to be that Solonese *rebab* playing is more standardized than Yogyanese, with only minor differences in nuance between players in Solonese style. Older Yogyanese *rebab* players, such as Pak Lokasari and Pak Gonjang Anom (both active in the palace and in outside groups), state that they underwent no formal training on the *rebab* when they were young, but merely listened to others and worked out their own fingering and bowing techniques. Solonese *rebab* playing requires certain patterns of bowing and standardized finger positions for melodic passages in certain registers. But even for players who still use unorthodox bowing and finger positions, the Yogyanese today tend towards Solonese style in the melodic patterns they play on the *rebab*.

The *suling*, on the other hand, can be a clear indicator of style, even though it is in some senses a marginal instrument and one particularly conducive to individual expression.[24] *Suling* rhythm in both traditions is quite free. One cannot even predict when it will begin to play or when it will finish its phrase. Usually it will play in proximity to the end of a melodic phrase (at the *kenong*); elsewhere it depends on the whims of the player. The main feature that my teachers suggested set off Yogyanese from Solonese *suling* playing was the more frequent departure from the fixed scale of the percussion instruments in Solonese playing. Through special fingering and half-holing, a far greater pitch vocabulary is available to *suling* players than to players of *gambang*, *gendèr*, and other instruments of fixed pitch. In some cases, the voices and *rebab* may systematically employ pitches from outside the instrumental scale (*miring* or *minir*), usually to set a mood of sadness of pathos. The *suling*, however may vary from the fixed scale in many pieces, often with humorous intent, and does so more often in Solonese performance than in Yogyanese.

The coverage of the soft instruments, important as they are to gamelan aesthetics, reveals relatively little contrast between the two traditions. The differences were more pronounced even twenty or thirty years ago, but the younger generation of gamelan musicians has been applying Solonese practice on these instruments even to the playing of Yogyanese pieces in which the *bonang* and other loud instruments adhere to Yogyanese style. The very nature of the soft instruments – that they sound softly and do not stand out – makes them appropriate for individual expression which, though more varied among the Yogyanese, is nevertheless important in Solonese tradition as well.

Drumming

The drums used in Yogyanese and Solonese styles are the same. Only for *wayang* accompaniment does Solonese style require the special *kendhang wayang* and the lively but subdued style known as *kosèkan* (or *kosèk*). The playing of *batangan/ciblon* is subject to a fair amount of individual interpretation, making distinction between Solonese and Yogyanese patterns somewhat problematic. This drum was formerly excluded from the court ensembles, making its way into the Solonese court before the Yogyanese (where it only occurred around the turn of the present century). Solonese musicians claim that much of what the Yogyanese perform on this drum represents a derivative of Solonese practice. It would be difficult to substantiate this claim, however, since this type of drumming is rarely notated and thus cannot be compared diachronically across traditions.[25]

Clear differences are to be heard primarily in the use of this drum to accompany dance. In Solonese style, the drum is played much louder in dance accompaniment than in concert settings (*klenèngan*). Yogyanese style tends not to make such a sharp distinction, playing a medium level in both (dance and *uyon-uyon*).

The patterns played on the kendhang *gendhing* ("one drum" style) and on that drum in combination with the *ketipung* ("two drum" style) represent well-established, standardized models in both traditions. One scarcely needs to hear more than the first few beats of a *gendhing* performed with these drums to know whether the drumming is Yogyanese or Solonese. Contrasting but related patterns exist for almost all of the "regular" formal structures. If one knows each pattern, one can easily recognize whether a drummer is using Yogyanese or Solonese – or some combination of the two. What drummers normally play is a slight variation of the so-called "basic" patterns that have been notated for both styles. What the notaters have felt to be basic are (1) the "dhung," the high-pitched resonant stroke on the large drum or *ketipung*, (2) the "dhang" (or "bem" or "bah"), the deep stroke on the large drum, and (3) the "tak," the short crisp sound on the small head of either drum. Figure 2.36 gives notated versions of the drum pattern for the first repeated section of most *sléndro gendhing* with four *kenongan*, sixteen beats per *kenong*. In Yogya this is known as "*kendhangan Candra*," in Solo as "*kethuk 2 kerep, sléndro.*"

```
        CANDRA (YOGYANESE)                    KETHUK 2 KEREP, SLENDRO (SOLONESE)

     t           t         N               t            t          N

 D d . D . . . d  . . d . . d . .       . . . D . . . T . d . D . . . D

 d . d .  . d d D . . . d . d . T̄d      d . d .  . d . d D . d . . d . T

 .d.D̄d D . . . d  d D d . D̄d.d. d       . d . D . . . d d D d . . d . D

 D T̄dd d  D d . d  d . d T  D d . .      d . d .  . d . D . d . . D d . .

     (from Prajasudirja, ms.)               (from Martopangrawit 1972a)

 D = "dhang" ("bem"); d = "dhung"; T = "tak"; . . . . = one gatra
```

2.36 *Candra* and *kethuk 2 kerep, sléndro* drum patterns

Though related, the two patterns are different enough to make for easy distinction. In this case only the fifth, eighth, tenth, eleventh, and sixteenth (last) *gatra* are identical – less than one third. Javanese listeners would also feel a similarity between passages where the drum stroke is the same at points of structural weight (ends of *gatra* and especially ends of *kenongan*), but here that would only add the first *gatra*. As we might expect, it is the Yogyanese pattern that exhibits the greater density, with forty strokes as compared to Solo's twenty-eight, and with three *gatra* containing strokes on the off-beat (ninth, twelfth, and thirteenth *gatra*).

The *ketipung* in large *gendhing*, if it is played at all, will sound an ostinato varied only at the approach of a gong stroke (see Sutton, 1982:322–23). In Yogyanese tradition the ostinato for the first section is double what it is in Solonese, sounding four times per *gatra*, instead of two:

```
        balungan:     5   6   5   3     2   1   2   6   etc.

ketipung (Yogya):    d̄d̄  .   d̄d̄  .     d̄d̄  .   d̄d̄  .

ketipung (Solo):      .   d   d   .     .   d   d   .
```

2.37   *Ketipung* ostinati in large *gendhing*

This contrast is consistent with those we have identified previously, Yogyanese versions representing greater density, and more activity.

In the realm of smaller forms, one finds patterns unique to one or the other tradition – most notably the *bubaran* drumming of Yogyakarta for pieces with sixteen beats per gong, four per *kenong*. In Solo, this form is called *lancaran mlaku*, with *lancaran* drumming. *Ladrang*, the most popular form in both traditions, also has substantially different drumming in Solo than in Yogyanese tradition, for "one drum style" (*kendhang gendhing*) and for "two drum style." In the latter, for example, Solonese style requires a special pattern to be used for the playing of the first *gongan* of a passage in higher register, known as *ngelik* (literally, "get smaller" – i.e., go up in pitch) (notated in Martopangrawit 1972b:29–33). While one can generalize that the Solonese drumming tends to be less filled in, the first *kenongan* of this special *ngelik* drumming is far more active than the usual *ladrang* drumming in either Solonese or Yogyanese styles.

The *bedhug* is considered an optional instrument in standard gamelan. It is more common in Yogyanese ensembles. Solonese only use it in accompanying the dances of *gagah* (strong male) and *raksasa* (ogre) characters. Yogyanese use this loud drum for similar kinds of dances and, in addition, some *gendhing* in *ketawang* form. Even though *ketawang* are normally played in soft style, with vocal parts, Yogyanese tradition calls for a loud stroke on the *bedhug* to coincide with each of the "dhang" strokes in the pattern of the *kendhang gendhing*. While this does not alter the drum pattern, which is fairly similar in both styles, it very sharply distinguishes the two styles aurally.

Drumming is a stylistic indicator throughout Java. Solonese and Yogyanese styles are relatively closer to one another than to any other drumming styles. I have suggested that Yogyanese style demonstrates a tendency for greater density. Most important, however, is the fact that contrastive patterns developed for all the major forms. As with *balungan*, listeners familiar with both styles may not consciously distinguish between the two on stylistic criteria, but simply recognize the particular patterns as Solonese, Yogyanese, or something resembling one or the other.

Vocal style

Vocal style is, as a rule, less prescribed than instrumental playing. Solo singers, usually female (*pesindhèn*), develop individual styles that may only subtly reflect Yogyanese or Solonese orientation. In 1980, the local government in Yogyakarta sponsored discussions aimed at identifying certain traits of Yogyanese *pesindhèn* style, but most musicians present protested that solo singing was too personal a form of expression to be defined along regional lines. Little was concluded, other than the very general observation that Yogyanese style is more *lugu* (ordinary, unadorned) than Solonese (Anon. 1980).

Over the years there has been some difference in the alignment of *pesindhèn* phrases with the *balungan* and other instruments. In the earlier part of the century, Yogyanese *pesindhèn* tended to arrive at the final tone of their phrases at the same time as the *balungan*. With some exceptions, Solonese delayed their phrases so that the *pesindhèn* phrase carried over the end of the corresponding *balungan* phrase, finishing after the next *balungan* phrase had begun. This preference for delayed cadence was then adopted and exaggerated by some Yogyanese so that now the greater displacement may be found among Yogyanese *pesindhèn*. But today the contrast is slight, and almost all Yogyanese *pesindhèn* show continuing influence from the famous *pesindhèn* of Surakarta. Nyi Tjondrolukito, a *pesindhèn* raised and trained in Yogyakarta and the one most popular with champions of Yogyanese gamelan style, now incorporates many Solonese elements in her unique singing style. Yet the fact that she does stand apart from those in the Solonese mainstream makes her a "Yogyanese" *pesindhèn* in many people's minds.

Gérongan

Male choral singing (*gérongan*) is, of necessity, more standardized than solo singing, since all voices are expected to execute the same melody simultaneously. It is generally true of both styles that the *gérongan* is in heterophonic relationship with the *balungan*, coinciding with it at the end of most *gatra* and often more frequently. In Yogyanese style, the *gérongan* is likely to be less independent of the *balungan* than in Solonese style and less ornate. The following two versions of the *gérongan* for the widely known Ladrang *Wilujeng* demonstrate the difference. From the first *gatra*, the Solonese version is more independent, veering away from the sustained 6 at the end of the *gatra*, where the Yogyanese does not. The beginning of the second and fourth *kenongan* (here second and fourth systems) best demonstrates the Solonese preference for florid *gérongan*, as contrasted with the simpler Yogyanese version. Yogyanese say that their *gérongan* is more *prasaja* (plain, straightforward, simple). The Solonese agree, but do not value this quality highly aesthetically. Yogyanese, on the other hand, suggest that it is a good quality – both in everyday human interaction and in aesthetic expression.

Rambangan and palaran

Singing in the context of *gendhing* performance, whether *gérongan* or solo *pesindhèn*, is constrained by the *balungan* and its implied register. Singers of the freer genre of pieces known as *rambangan* in Yogya and *palaran* in Solo (and referred to without regional

```
balungan:         .        .      6      .      1      5      1      6N
        (Yogya):         6   6   6 i 6              i   2      i 2 i   6
gérongan
        (Solo):          6   6   6 i 5      6      i   2    3 i 2 i   6
text:                    Pa- ra- bé Sang         Ma- ra      Ba-  ngun


balungan:     3      5      6      1      6      5      3      2N
        (Yogya):         i   i   i 2 i              6   5      6 3 5 3   2
gérongan
        (Solo):          3   3   352 i      2      6   5      6 3 5 3   2
text:                    Se- pat dom-ba           ka- li      O-   ya

balungan:     6      6      .      .      1      5      1      6N
        (Yogya):         6   6   6 i 6              i   2      i 2 i   6
gérongan
        (Solo):          6   6   6 i 5      6      i   2    3 i 2 i   6
text:                    A-  ja  do- lan          lan wong   pri-  ya


balungan:     1      1      3      2      .      1      2      6G
        (Yogya):         3   3   3 5 2           3 5 3      1 2 1   6
                         Nggera- mèh no-         ra pra-    sa-    ja.
gérongan
        (Solo):    i   2   i 6 3 5 3   2         3 5 3      1 2 1   6
                   Ngge-ra-   mèh   no-          ra pra-    sa-    ja.
```

2.38 Yogyanese and Solonese style *gérongan* for Ladrang *Wilujeng*, *sléndro pathet manyura*

connotation as *uran-uran*) have evolved some marked differences in melodic contour for pieces that have the same poetic meter and the same basic tonal outline. Examples of *Pangkur* melodies in the two traditions demonstrate this trait as well as any, as shown in Figure 2.39. In the Yogyanese version (*rambangan*) every new phrase begins high and descends, sometimes an octave or more. The contours of the Solonese phrases are more varied, often beginning in the middle register and rising before cadence. Contour is the characteristic most often mentioned by Javanese in regard to differences between the two styles, not only in *Pangkur*, but in other *rambangan* and *palaran*. Here, the most obvious contrasts occur in the first, second, and sixth phrases. Though the phrase finals are the same in all cases (not so in all *rambangan* and *palaran* variants), the intermediate contours are never identical and are fairly close to one another only in the fourth and seventh phrases.

Musicians ascribe the differences in the style of *palaran* and *rambangan* not only to the musical tastes of the Solonese and Yogyanese, but also to the fact that it is males who normally sing *rambangan* and females who normally sing *palaran*. Both developed, it is generally believed, as vehicles for poetic text in dance-dramas in the late nineteenth century. *Langen mandrawanara*, a dance-drama enacting stories from the Ramayana, is attributed to K. P. H. Yudanegara III, who became Yogyarkarta's prime minister in 1915. All of the roles were taken by men. *Langen driyan*, enacting stories of the indigenous hero Damar Wulan, is attributed to the Solonese dance master R. M. Tandakusuma, servant in the lesser court of Surakarta (the Mangkunegaran). All roles were taken by women. Both genres are accompa-

(Yogya): 　6　i　2̇　2̇　　2̇i̇　i̇ 2̇ 3̇　　i̇2̇ i̇ 6　　3̇ 212 1
I　　　Mingkar mingkur　ing　u-　　　ka-　　　ra

(Solo): 　1 323　3　3　3　　3 23 2 2 35 356　　3 53　3　5 32 12 1
　　　　Ming-　kar mingkur　ing　u-　　　ka-　ra

(Yogya): 　6　i　i　i　i　i　i　　i̇2̇3̇　2̇i̇2̇ i̇6　　5 353 2　　1 6 1　6
II　　　A- ka-ra-na ka-re-nan　mar-　di　　si-　　wi

(Solo): 　3　3　5　6 535 3　3　3　3　　3 2　2 3 5　　2 3 5　　32 161　6
　　　　A- ka-ra-na　　　ka-re-nan mar- di　　si-　　wi

(Yogya): 　3̇　3̇　3̇　3̇　2̇　　2̇ 3̇　　2̇ i̇2̇　i̇　2̇
III　　　Si- na- wung res- mi- ning　　ki-　dung

(Solo): 　6 i̇ 6i̇2̇　2̇　2̇　　2̇ 6 2̇ i6i　6　2̇ 3̇ i̇2̇i6 i̇　2̇
　　　　Sina-　wung res-　mi-ning　　ki-dung

(Yogya): 　2̇　2̇　2̇　　2̇ i̇ 2̇ 3̇　　2̇ i̇　6　　3 532 12　1
IV　　　Si- nu- ba　si- nu-　　kar-　ta

(Solo): 　i̇　2̇　3̇　　3̇ i̇ 2̇i̇2̇ i6　　3 5　3　5 3 212　　1
　　　　Si- nu- ba　si- nu　kar- ta

(Yogya): 　3̇　3̇ 3̇ 3̇　3̇ 3̇ 3̇ 3̇　　3̇5̇3̇ 3̇　　i̇ 2̇ i̇　6　3 5 323 2
V　　　Mrih kretarta　pa-karti-ning ngèl- mu　lu-　　hung

(Solo): 　3̇　3̇ 3̇ 3̇　2̇ 2̇ i̇2̇ 3̇ i̇ 2̇　6 65 32 35 6　6 i̇2̇ i̇ 6　6i65 3　2
　　　　Mrih kretarta　pa-kar- tining ngèlmu　　lu-　hung

(Yogya): 　6　i　2̇　2̇　　2̇i̇　i̇ 2̇　3̇　　i̇2̇ i̇ 6　　3 532　1
VI　　　Kang tum-rap ing ta-　nah　　Ja-　　wa

(Solo): 　3　3　3　3　3　2 35 3235 6　　3 53　3 2　32 12 1
　　　　Kang tum-rap ing ta- nah　　Ja-　wa

(Yogya): 　6　6　6　6　6 i 2̇　i　6　　5 35 3 2　161　6
VII　　　A- ga- ma a- ge-　ming　a-　　ji

(Solo): 　6 2̇ i6i 6　6　6　6　6 i 2̇　6 535　2353 2　161　6
　　　　A-　ga-ma a- ge-　ming　a-　ji

2.39　Two versions of *Pangkur*, *sléndro pathet manyura*: *rambangan* (Yogya) and *palaran* (Solo)

nied by full gamelan, with *saron* and *bonang* dropping out for the *rambangan/palaran*. Dancers sing all their lines in both genres. Some say the Yogyanese phrases begin high in order to enable audiences before the era of microphones to hear the words clearly. The female voice, it is felt, can be heard more clearly than the male in the middle and lower registers. Whatever the reasoning, this difference in style remains, even though microphones and recordings today enable singers to be heard through their entire range. *Rambangan/palaran* have become important elements in other genres of performance today: *kethoprak* (popular drama, stories from Javanese history and legend, associated with Yogya), *wayang wong panggung* (commercial dance-drama, stories from Indic epics, associated with Solo), and gamelan concerts (Yogyanese *uyon-uyon* and Solonese *klenèngan*).

Tempo and treatment

Melodic phrases expand and contract in both traditions through the same process of subdivision (*irama* level). Solonese and Yogyanese use different terms, but both identify five levels, defined by ratio between the *balungan* beat and the faster parts that subdivide that beat. Subdividing parts, such as the *gambang*, maintain a more or less constant tempo

Yogyanese Term	Solonese Term	Balungan Beat	Gambang Beats
Irama 1/2	Irama lancar ("swift")	ratio 1 :	2
Irama I	Irama tanggung ("in between")	ratio 1 :	4
Irama II	Irama dadi ("become," "settled")	ratio 1 :	8
Irama III	Irama wilet ("intricate," "curly")	ratio 1 :	16
Irama IV	Irama rangkep ("double density")	ratio 1 :	32

2.40   Yogyanese and Solonese terms for *irama* levels

throughout, adjusting their relationship with the *balungan* in order to do so.

Though *irama* levels do not distinguish the two styles, one does find a preference for slightly slower tempos within a given *irama* level in Yogya rather than in Solo. This trait is sometimes subtle, but it is tenacious, persisting even when Yogyanese play Solonese pieces today. The difference is most striking in dance accompaniment. Yogyanese preference, particularly in the accompaniment of female and refined male dances, is for tempi noticeably slower than are normal for concert music (*uyon-uyon*). Solonese, on the other hand, often choose tempi for dance accompaniment that are even faster than those chosen for their concert music (*klenèngan*). The following shows tempi of the fastest pulse (what Hood has called the "density referent"), manifest on the *gambang* and *celempung* in sections of steady tempo in *irama* levels II/*dadi* and III/*wilet*.

The result is that musicians and listeners who prefer Solonese style may find Yogyanese tempi unbearably slow, and those who prefer Yogyanese style find Solonese too rushed. Both Yogyanese and Solonese agree that the slower tempi are probably more "traditional." Solonese musicians claim that their tempi represent an advancement, an improvement more appropriate for the modern age, and that they lend to the dancers' movements a quality of grace, fluidity, and motion. R. L. Sasminta Mardawa, a famous Yogyanese court dancer and choreographer, who often directs tempo on the *keprak* (small wooden slit gong), feels that dance should be contemplative. Slow tempi are crucial to this aspect of Yogyanese dance, he says.

Related to the Yogyanese preference for slower tempi in style is the practice, mentioned above, of beginning pieces with a passage of *lamba* (literally, "single," i.e., not yet doubled). All large *gendhing*, and most *ladrang* and *ketawang*, in both traditions begin with a solo introduction (*buka*) followed by the entrance of the full ensemble with a fast *balungan* beat (*irama* ½ or *lancar*), slowing to *irama* I/*tanggung* and then usually to *irama* II/*dadi*. With few exceptions, the Solonese pieces require the *saron* players simply to play the *balungan* fast at the beginning. But the Yogyanese *lamba* represents a reduction (every other beat) of the

Gendhing Title	Style	Dance or Concert?	Tempo of Gambang	Performers	Source
Lambangsari	Yogya	dance	208–216	Mardawa Budaya dir. by R. L. Sasminta Mardawa	Golek Lambangsari (Borobudur, com- mercial cassette)
"	Yogya	concert	236–240	Yogyakarta court musicians (dir. not listed)	Javanese Court Gamelan, Vol. III (Nonesuch H-72138)
"	Solo	concert	296–304	RRI Solo Studio Musicians, dir. by P. Atmosoenarto	Lambangsari (ACD-106, Lokananta com. cassette)
Clunthang	Yogya	dance	232–240	Mardawa Budaya, dir. by R. L. Sasminta Mardawa	field recording (RAS-061179)
"	Yogya	concert	252	RRI Yogya studio musicians, dir. by Mudjiono	field recording (RAS-092374)
"	Solo	concert	252–264	RRI Solo studio musicians, dir. by P. Atmosoenarto	Klenengan Gobyog (ACD-001, Lokananta com. cassette)
"	Solo	concert	276	RRI Solo studio musicians, dir. by P. Atmosoenarto	Larawudhu (ACD-070, Lokananta com. cassette)
"	Solo	dance	340–352	Sanggar Budaya Dwi Tunggal, dir. by Soegito	Gendhing Beksan (PS2C commercial cassette)

2.41   Tempo in Yogyanese and Solonese performance

balungan that is to be played once the tempo has slowed and settled (see Figures 2.17 and 2.19). The result is that the *saron* players do not have to play the *balungan* fast, but instead maintain a more or less constant level of activity, as opposed to the Solonese initial burst of energy and gradual dissipation as the piece slows down.

For large *gendhing* in both traditions, performance requires at least two major (repeatable) sections, the first calmer in mood than the second. Solonese refer to the first as the *mérong* and to the second as the *inggah* or *minggah* (literally, "rise"). Yogyanese have no single term for the first section other than *dadi/dados* (literally, "become," "settle"), which is the settled passage that comes after the *lamba*. The second section they refer to as *dhawah* (literally, "fall"). Despite much speculation, there is no agreement on how or why the same section is called "rise" in Solo and "fall" in Yogya. Some lengthy and unusual pieces in Yogya (e.g., *Pramugari*) contain a *minggah* section followed by a *dhawah* section, but more often the term *minggah* is used to refer to the continuation from a large *gendhing* to a smaller form (usually *ladrang* or *ketawang*): "Gendhing *Gambir Sawit minggah* Ketawang *Rajaswala*," for example.

Stylistic differences – summary

The points of difference in musical style between Yogyakarta and Surakarta seem to confront one at every turn. Above I have surveyed a number of the characteristics most often mentioned by Javanese musicians today. It becomes problematic to group all points under a few general headings. In many ways, Yogyanese style involves greater density and activity than Solonese – in the more filled-in and disjunct *balungan*, the busier and denser drumming patterns, the more rhythmically varied *bonang* playing, and, in former times, more varied *gambang* playing. Yet in *gendèr* playing, in vocal style, and in tempo, it is Solonese style that exhibits greater density and activity. Underlying the Yogyanese preferences is the conception of an assertive, strong, bold Yogyanese character in contrast to the Solonese obsession with refinement. The Yogyanese musical "activity" – the focus of aesthetic attention by musicians and audience – is in the extroverted instruments (the loud playing ensemble), whereas in Solo it is in the vocal and the soft instruments, such as *gendèr* and *rebab*. Yet Solonese style can present loud and strong playing, as in their dance accompaniment and in the fast and loud *Sampak* pieces that accompany *wayang kulit* and other dramatic forms. The range of expression in Solonese style seems presently to be greater than in Yogyanese style. And this leads to the ironic conclusion that the contrasts within Yogyanese style may actually be subtler than the contrasts in Solonese style, even though the most subtle and refined playing is that associated with Solo.

Regionalism in the traditions of Yogyakarta and Surakarta

After this lengthy overview of ways in which Yogyakarta and Surakarta gamelan music contrast, I return to the issue of regionalism itself, which, as I stated at the outset, is problematic with regard to these two traditions. The question presents itself, however, for the very reasons that Javanese conception of these traditions is regional, despite the undeniably important role of individual creativity in their history. Even the activities of individual musicians today and in the recent past, in my experience, are most often spoken of in relation to what are seen as regional norms. Moreover, the differences between Yogyanese and Solonese music are not generally attributed to individual musicians, but are seen to be emblematic of an idealized Yogyanese- and Solonese-ness, and to represent aesthetically the traits and values shared by one regionally-based Javanese social group, and not another.

We cannot know the extent to which the present contrasts between the two traditions might be traceable to differences already extant more than two centuries ago between Solo and the area in which Mangkubumi founded his court. It is generally thought that no clear regional differences existed here in the mid-eighteenth century. Carey suggests that

Certainly, in the artistic sphere (especially in music and dance), the evolution of a unique "Yogyakarta style" appears to have been a self-conscious process with much of the impetus being given by the rulers themselves.   (Carey 1986:21)

The differences between Yogyanese and Solonese styles of performance and repertories have resulted most directly from the creative decisions and sensibilities of talented individual musicians, to be sure. But various forces, most notably those associated with the courts and their need to define themselves dialectically in relation to one another, have contributed greatly to the institutionalization of these differences, and very likely to the favoring of certain developments and rejection of others. Evidence supports the idea that the more robust Yogyanese style was encouraged from the very early days of the division of Mataram. And certainly for some time now the conception of each region's quintessential character – no matter how artificial such a notion might strike us – is, to a considerable extent, both constituted and reaffirmed in the kind of gamelan music associated with each. Even a Yogyanese who prefers to perform or listen to Solonese music, or does not limit his musical tastes to Yogyanese gamelan music, is still very likely to point to a loud Ladrang *Liwung* as something deeply Yogyanese, just as a Solonese will point to a soft and subtle Gendhing *Onang-onang* as deeply Solonese.

Given that the issue of regionalism is pertinent, however, we must ask to what extent these two traditions are actually supported by the population of an identifiable region in the late twentieth century. In another paper, I have argued that most of what is seen as Yogyakarta tradition – while widely understood in popular conception to represent the region (the Daerah Istimewa Yogyakarta) – is in fact primarily limited in actual practice and appeal to the *kraton* and the nobility associated with it (Sutton 1984). In other words, while most Javanese – Yogyanese and others – might identify a particular musical piece or playing style with the Yogya region, close scrutiny of musical practice finds relatively few musicians within this region adhering primarily to this style or repertory. Yet, in order to maintain the image of Yogyakarta as a meaningful cultural entity, local government officials together with the nobility have attempted to define Yogyakarta gamelan music as the appropriate tradition for all the residents of the province, though the sources to which they look for authority are mostly court manuscripts and court musicians.

Formerly, direct imitation of courtly arts was proscribed. During this century the proscription has been relaxed and is now, ironically, turned around completely, with the nobility all but begging the masses to support the shrinking tradition of the court through their own participation. But a gap remains between the practices developed in the court and the tastes of the people. Solonese tradition has made ever increasing inroads in Yogya since the 1920s, through certain influential *karawitan* groups (especially, early on, Daya Pradangga), through radio broadcasts, recordings, and the strong presence of Solonese in the local Department of Education and Culture. The few who wish to resist this trend have felt that the entire region should be urged to make Yogyakarta gamelan music "master in its own house" (*tuan rumah di rumahnya sendiri*).

The association of this tradition primarily with the court, though attractive for tourists, is a liability for most Indonesians (Javanese and non-Javanese) in the current era of democratic government. By stipulating that performing arts contests and radio broadcasts in Yogyakarta feature "Yogya style," it is believed that the tradition stands a better chance of survival than if it is left only to the court itself.[26] As people are asked not only to recognize a responsibility for maintenance of Yogyakarta tradition, but are judged on their adherence to a Yogyakarta style, many are asking what defines the style. My discussion throughout much of this chapter points to a number of salient features of Yogyanese tradition, but is far from the kind of comprehensive list of rules that is currently being sought and which, I argue, is unlikely ever to be produced (see Sutton 1984 and Lindsay 1985:72–74).

Solonese tradition has known a rather different set of circumstances. Though the association with the Solonese court is not to be denied, it has played a less crucial role than the Yogyanese court for Yogyanese tradition. Some aspects of Solonese court tradition were forbidden to outsiders – the sacred *bedhaya ketawang* dance, to take only the most obvious example. But musical influences, it is generally agreed, were allowed to pass in and out of the court more easily there than in Yogyakarta. And more importantly, while Yogyanese tradition does not enjoy popularity even within the region, Solonese tradition has spread beyond the palace, beyond the ex-*karesidenan* Surakarta, even beyond the boundaries of the province of Central Java, to become the standard tradition of ethnic Java.

Its wide popularity in comparison to other regional styles, and especially in comparison to Yogyanese style, makes it in some ways a "supraregional" tradition, at least in Javanese conception. Yet even as far away as East Java, this style is more often referred to as "Solonese" than "Central Javanese" and rarely, if ever, as simply "Javanese." The regional association is still very much in evidence, and it lends prestige to the music because of Solo's image as the center and standard-bearer of Javanese culture. The court is clearly part of this image, but the music has managed to take on characteristics that make it less a statement of courtly grandeur than Yogyanese gamelan music seems to be.

The Yogyanese emphasis on loud playing means that a large number of *saron* instruments is preferred and, if possible, a *bonang panembung*. As it is these instruments that are to be featured, it is desirable that they be made out of the most sonorous and expensive material: bronze (Ind. *prunggu*, Jav. *gangsa*), rather than the cheaper brass (*kuningan*) or iron (Ind. *besi*, Jav. *wesi*). The Solonese emphasis, on the other hand, is on soft instruments, which are cheaper to manufacture than the loud, and on that most widely distributed of all instruments, the human voice. I have pointed out a few Yogyanese characteristics for vocal and soft instrument parts, but the essence of the tradition as it is currently conceived is the loud playing style, with its *imbal demung* and varied *bonang* playing. Solonese tradition is typified by the intricacies of the soft playing and is more appropriate for the much cheaper ensembles that may have only a few *saron*, no *bonang panembung*, and whose metal keys and gongs may be made of iron. As such, a minimal ensemble for Solonese playing costs only a fraction of what is needed for Yogyanese. Several Solonese musicians stated to me that Solonese style is more accessible to the masses (*lebih merakyat*) than Yogyanese, and that in this era it was inevitable that Solonese style would be more widely practiced than Yogyanese. As will be seen in the chapters below, while there is undoubtedly a great deal to their argument, the situation is more complex. Some *rakyat* traditions thrive, others may not fare so well. The means by which the music is transmitted, its availability through the mass media, and its evaluation by prominent people in the local and national government also combine to create an environment favorable to some traditions and not to others.

3 A flourishing tradition in west central Java: gamelan music of Banyumas

Located at the western periphery of the province of Central Java, on the Sundanese side of the *ngapak–mbandhèk* line, the region of Banyumas stands apart from the rest of Java in its dialect, its local legendary history, and its performing arts. The region was formerly an administrative unit (*residentie*) under the Dutch and currently comprises four *kabupaten*: Cilacap, Banyumas, Purbalingga, and Banjarnegara.[1] The largest city within the region is Cilacap on the south coast. More centrally located and representing more of a cultural center is Purwokerto, lying some seventy kilometers to the north east. Purwokerto is the home of some of the leading musicians and puppeteers, the Banyumas studio of the national radio station (RRI Purwokerto), the small cassette companies Hidup Baru and Nusah Indah, and the original site of the high school conservatory of traditional performing arts (SMKI Banyumas, now moved sixteen kilometers south to the town of Banyumas). Yet musicians and puppeteers versed in Banyumas performing styles are spread throughout the ex-residency. Indeed, one finds here a stronger sense of a shared regional tradition than in Yogyakarta, whose distinctive performing arts are primarily court-based, or in Surakarta, whose gamelan and *wayang* styles have spread far beyond the Surakarta region.

Banyumas culture is often described by local residents and by others as a mix of Sundanese and Central Javanese. If we consider its location, midway between the main Sundanese city of Bandung to the west and the court cities of Yogyakarta and Surakarta to the east, such a blend should not be surprising. Yet the blend is not an even one, either in music or in any other aspect of culture. Though some Sundanese words are used in Banyumas dialect, and the final /a/ is pronounced "a" (as it is in Sunda) rather than "aw" (as it is in the rest of Java), the vocabulary is mostly Javanese (Esser 1927, Hardjowigati 1957, Mardjana 1933). The most popular legend in the Banyumas region is the story of Raden Kamandaka, a Sundanese prince who lived in the Banyumas area and met his bride there (Oemarmadi and Poerbosenojo 1964). Yet the forms of traditional theater most popular in Banyumas are those most widespread in the rest of central and east Java: *wayang kulit* and *kethoprak*. The wooden puppet genre (*wayang golèk*), so popular in Sunda, is very rare in Banyumas, as are most other forms of Sundanese performing arts.

The Banyumas area has been under central Javanese jurisdiction for over two hundred years. At the partition of Java with the Treaty of Giyanti in 1755, Banyumas remained part of the Surakarta realm, despite its greater proximity to the rival Yogyakarta.[2] Since the revolution (1945–49) it has been administered as part of the province of Central Java. This is an area which looks to Surakarta as a cultural center, and it is not surprising that one finds many influences at many levels from this revered city, particularly since the end of the revolution.

The long-standing ties with Surakarta have not precluded influence from Yogyakarta, however. Although Banyumas was officially under Solonese administration, the *bupati* (regional ruler) in charge at the time of the partition of Java, Radèn Tumenggung Yudanegara, came to Yogyakarta as *patih* (prime minister) under the first Yogyanese sultan, Mangkubumi. Yudanegara's son remained as *bupati* of Banyumas, thereby establishing a line of high-level family contact between the two areas (Ricklefs 1974:68–70). Whether this contact was the impetus for cultural exchange or not would be difficult to ascertain, but one does find some specific connections between Banyumas and Yogyakarta in music and *wayang kulit*. Legend tells of influential puppeteers coming from Yogyakarta during the late nineteenth and early twentieth centuries. The major gamelan pieces used during the first major portion of contemporary Banyumas *wayang* – *Ayak-ayakan*, *Srepegan*, and *Sampak* (or *Playon*) *Lasem*, *sléndro pathet nem* – are very similar to those of the Yogyakarta repertory.[3] In addition, the medley of pieces played before a *wayang* performance (the *talu* sequence) is often very similar to the sequence used in Yogyakarta, at least during the early twentieth century: Gendhing *Gambir Sawit*, Ladrang *Gonjang Ganjing*, Ketawang *Rajaswala*, *Ayak-ayakan*, *Srepegan*, and *Sampak*, *sléndro pathet sanga*.[4] The rhythmic knocking by the Banyumas puppeteer against the puppet chest (*dhodhogan*) bears some resemblance to that typical of Yogyanese puppeteers, though here the Javanese with whom I have discussed this find more of a middle ground between Yogya and Solo. Otherwise, Banyumas *wayang* music shows greater similarity to Solonese than to Yogyanese practice.

While Solonese tradition is admired in Banyumas, and is seen by some as a threat to distinctive Banyumas culture, there is an overriding sense of optimism among many musicians and others about the state of indigenous Banyumas tradition and its prospects for the future. As I have discussed elsewhere, the champions of Banyumas music and related arts have made a number of strides towards winning an unprecedented legitimacy for their tradition in the modern era (Sutton 1986a:115–32 and Sutton 1986b:79–101). The use of Solonese methods of formal transmission in Banyumas and the opening of a formal course of study in Banyumas gamelan music at the prestigious STSI/ASKI (university-level academy of performing arts) in Surakarta have contributed substantially to this new legitimacy. But the fact remains that Banyumas residents view themselves and their arts as distinctive.

Where the Solonese have a reputation for refinement and the Yogyanese pride themselves on their boldness and straightforwardness, the overriding element in Banyumas self-image is humor. Almost no social interchange occurs without a great deal of joking and laughing, open but not boisterous. Beyond the specific element of humor, the local people see themselves as more direct and even blunt (*blag-blagan*), more egalitarian, more "relaxed" (*santai*, *rilak*) than either the Solonese or Yogyanese. The deference that characterizes social interaction between all but the most intimate friends and family in Surakarta and Yogyakarta, especially in urban circles, is noticeably absent in Banyumas. A visitor might take an hour or more to bring up an important issue with his or her host in the court areas, but in Banyumas it is considered no breach to etiquette to state one's intentions immediately after a brief salutory greeting. Being direct is not only accepted, it is expected and positively valued. Those readers familiar only with the areas of the court centers may have noted a similar contrast between city dwellers and villagers, but I encountered a much greater directness and relaxed manner in urban and rural Banyumas than I usually encountered in either the cities of Yogyakarta and Surakarta or the villages around them.

Banyumas local residents see their music and other performing arts as an important embodiment of these regional traits. Humor is evident in instrumental style, dance move-ments, and dramatic plots. Song texts are often humorous, more *risqué* and direct than in Yogyanese or Solonese tradition. The Banyumas arts are seen as egalitarian, with wide appeal, as summarized in this statement by a committee of Banyumas authors:

Banyumas *karawitan* has a fresh quality, full of humor, and has a folk/democratic nature. Because of this it is easily absorbed by the village people and easily becomes popular.

[karawitan Banyumas bersifat segar, penuh humor, dan bersifat kerakyatan. Karenanya mudah dicerna oleh rakyat pedesaan dan mudah menjadi populer.]   (Departemen PDK 1980:12)

While these qualities would have made it difficult for Banyumas music and other arts to gain prestige during the centuries of court supremacy, the modern democratic era has at least provided an atmosphere more conducive to the wide acceptance of arts seen by some as "folk" (*kesenian rakyat*). At the same time, recognition at educational institutions and dissemination through the mass media has given Banyumas music a more equal footing with the court and court-derived arts of Yogya and Solo, raising it from the "folk" category, or at least making that classification more ambiguous. More will be said about the role of modern institutions and about the spread of Banyumas tradition in later chapters, but it is important to note here that Banyumas tradition is seen by many to be flourishing in the 1980s.

Though I have alluded to Solonese and Yogyanese influences in the region, there is much that sets off Banyumas tradition from either of these. An examination of instrumentation, tuning and *pathet*, repertory and performance style will enable us to identify elements that are distinctive to the *karawitan* of Banyumas.

Instrumentation

Gamelan

Many of the gamelan used in Banyumas are identical to those used elsewhere in Java to play Solonese or Yogyanese music.[5] Indeed, performances often involve a combination of Banyu-mas pieces played in Banyumas style with pieces from other traditions, primarily Surakarta. Two publications listing Banyumas gamelan instruments give the following.

gong	slenthem
kempul	gendèr barung
kenong	gendèr panerus
kethuk	gambang
kempyang	rebab
saron demung	siter
saron barung	seruling (suling)
saron peking	kendhang ciblon (= gambyakan)
bonang barung	ketipung
bonang panerus	(kendhang gendhing)*

*not included in Departemen PDK 1980

3.1   Instrumentation of Banyumas gamelan, from Departemen PDK 1980:8 and Sekretariat Nasional 1983:95

The instrumentation of the gamelan ensembles I observed during periods of research in Banyumas was nearly identical to this. *Rebab* plays a far less crucial role than in Yogyanese and Solonese traditions and is often absent, despite its prominence in Sundanese music. I usually found three drums, as in Yogya and Solo, though each of them tended to be smaller than their equivalents to the east. In some cases, a fourth drum is added for playing Sundanese-inspired rhythms. The pitch ranges of the *kempul* and *kenong* are not standardized, but in my experience more often resemble Solonese than Yogyanese ranges, without high 2. *Saron* and *bonang* ranges, however, tend to duplicate those of Yogya, with only six keys on *sléndro saron* (1,2,3,5,6, high 1) and ten kettles on the *sléndro bonang* (low 2 to high 1). Some of the gamelan used for *wayang* accompaniment contain one or two nine-keyed *saron* (*saron wayang*).

Calung

The large gamelan described above can be used for dance accompaniment and for music concerts, but today it is most often heard in the accompaniment of dramatic forms: *kethoprak* and especially *wayang kulit*. The much smaller and more affordable ensemble popular throughout Banyumas is *calung*, consisting of only a few bamboo instruments, but capable of playing most of the Banyumas repertory. Though never used to accompany *wayang kulit* or other dramatic forms, I was told, it is now the preferred ensemble for accompanying the singer–dancers known as *lènggèr* (see plate 5).

5   Three young *lènggèr* facing *calung* musicians in performance in Papringan, west of the town of Banyumas, 1986. Two *gambang calung* in center.

Musicians betray an ambivalent attitude about the *calung*. Its bamboo construction and its use with singer–dancers, who have often been associated with prostitution, have given *calung* a lowly image in contrast to the large bronze ensembles, which not only resemble the gamelans of the court traditions but accompany the more revered *wayang kulit*. Some feel reluctant to include *calung* music under the category *karawitan*. And yet it is the most common vehicle for the Banyumas pieces that are also played on the large bronze gamelan. Given that the term *karawitan* itself derives from the court areas, where it referred first to court arts, and that it only recently has been applied more broadly, it is small wonder that musicians from areas such as Banyumas encounter difficulty in reaching consensus on its usage. The ambivalence on the status of *calung* is demonstrated in the following excerpts from the publication on Banyumas *karawitan* by the local office of the Department of Education and Culture. After *calung* is listed as something other than *karawitan*, it is said to be one of the main vehicles of Banyumas *karawitan*, if not the single most important vehicle.

Aside from *karawitan*, some of the other traditional musical arts that thrive in this area are: 1 Banyumas *siteran* [zither ensemble], 2 *calung* [bamboo xylophone ensemble], 3 *jani-janèn* [songs in Arabic accompanied by tambourines and frame drums], 4 *genjring* [Banyumas and other Javanese songs accompanied by tambourines and frame drums] and 5 *slawatan* [like *jani-janèn*, but less overt Islamic content].

[Disamping Karawitan, seni musik tradisional yang juga hidup subur didaerah ini antara lain: 1 Siteran Khas Banyumasan, 2 calung, 3 Jani-Janen, 4 Genjring, 5 Slawatan.]   (Departemen PDK 1980:7)

calung is a/the basic vehicle for Banyumas *karawitan*.

[Calung adalah pendukung pokok bagi karawitan Banyumas.]   (Departemen PDK 1980:8)

In a short typescript by Rasito, one of the most talented and well respected young Banyumas musicians, the ambiguity again appears as he contrasts *calung* with *karawitan* (1986:2) but later indicates that *calung* is taught as part of the curriculum in Banyumas *karawitan* at SMKI Banyumas and ASKI Surakarta (1986:8).

In a similar way, one finds no consensus on whether the *calung* ensemble is a kind of gamelan or not. Soebiyatno, a young musician from Purwokerto who wrote a thesis at ASKI Surakarta, used the term "gamelan *calung*" (1979). Yet the team of musicians who wrote *Sumbangan Pikiran Tentang Karawitan Banyumas* (Departemen PDK 1980) consistently oppose the terms: gamelan (larger ensembles with metal keys and gongs) and *calung* (smaller ensemble with bamboo keys). Kunst used the term gamelan widely to refer to almost any ensemble, including *calung*, but it is not clear to what extent this reflects popular usage at the time of his research.

Because of the ambiguity and because *calung* ensembles are used for the same Banyumas repertory heard on the larger ensembles, it is appropriate in the context of this study of regional traditions of gamelan to describe the instrumentation. Most see this ensemble as an imitation of the larger gamelan. Though the technology of building a *calung* is related by local lore back to bamboo sounding devices such as *bongkel*, *gumbeng*, and *angklung* (Departemen PDK 1980:8; Rasito 1986:1), the *calung* ensemble is said to have developed only in the early twentieth century – *c.* 1918, according to one source (Departemen PDK 1980:8).

Kunst describes the ensemble as follows:

This combination consists in the first place, of three *chalungs* ... mounted upon a sledge-shaped resilient underframe of bent bamboo-laths, played like a *gambang*, similar as regards tuning and pitch, but having a different function and distinguished by the names of *demung*, *pembabar*, and *penitir* ... Other instruments forming part of the *chalung* orchestra are a number of tubular bamboo keys, collected together on a single underframe and also consisting of segments cut on the slant into a point, distinguished respectively by the names of *kempul*, *kethuk*, and *kenong* (of the latter there are three). Further there is a blown *gong*, a *kendhang*, asymmetrical and pot-bellied (with two skins), and a *ketipung*.   (Kunst 1973:292–93)

The standard ensemble today is similar, though terminology has changed, reflecting Solonese influence in the region.

Now it is normal to find only two *gambang*-like instruments, one of which is called *gambang panerus*. The other is referred to as *gambang penggedhé* (literally, "the large one"; although it is no larger than the other), *gambang pengarep* (literally, "the one in front"), *gambang penodhos* (literally, "the one that drills"), or *gambang barung*. The last term is common only among musicians at the local conservatory and seems to represent an accommodation to Solonese norms, as I have suggested elsewhere (Sutton 1986b:84). Though Solonese do not speak of *gambang barung*, they do use the term *barung* in opposition to *panerus* (for *saron*, *bonang*, and *gendèr*). None of the other three terms are used in reference to either Solonese or Yogyanese instruments. These two *gambang* consist of fifteen or sixteen keys, ranging from a low 3 or 5 up to 5 three octaves higher. They play fast elaborations, often interlocking.

The single-octave instrument known as *slenthem* (a Solonese and Yogyanese term) and more rarely as *jengglong* (a Sundanese term for a gong-chime) plays a *balungan* part and may correspond in function to what Kunst reports as *demung*. The range is normally from pitch low 1 or 2 to pitch 1 (five or six bamboo tubular keys). The instrument Kunst says served three functions (*kempul*, *kenong*, *kethuk*) is now generally referred to as *kethuk-kenong*, and consists of the same number of keys as the *slenthem*, but tuned one octave higher. Occasionally the *kethuk-kenong* may have a seventh key (1, 2, 3, 5, 6, high 1, high 2).

The blown *gong* and the two drums are the same as those described by Kunst. The larger is now more often referred to with the Solonese term *ciblon*, but the older term *gambyakan* is still in use. This latter term is used by Yogyanese not for an instrument, but as the general word for the lively drumming that is associated with the *batangan* (= *ciblon*). A similar term (*gambyak*) is found also in east Java, where it refers to the uniquely east Javanese drum which accompanies dance and lively, light-hearted pieces. As in some of the larger gamelan, it is not unusual today to find an extra one or two *kendhang* in *calung* ensembles for Sundanese-derived drumming.

Other ensembles

Though relatively rare in comparison to *calung* and (metal) gamelan, several other ensembles distinctive to the Banyumas region should be mentioned. The *angklung* ensemble is similar to the *calung* ensemble and is seen by some as a precursor to it. The drums, *gong*, and *kethuk-kenong* are the same as those of the *calung*. But instead of a separate *slenthem* and two *gambang*, the *angklung* ensemble has a single *angklung* chime, consisting of fifteen *angklung*. The lowest octave serves as a *slenthem*, while the middle and upper octaves serve as melodic elaborators, usually played in interlocking alternation. The one *angklung* chime, then, is played by three players. The few extant *angklung* ensembles are found mostly in the north eastern portion of the Banyumas region, in the *kabupaten* of Banjarnegara. Like *calung*, the *angklung* normally accompany a singer–dancer, known either as *lènggèr* or *ronggèng*.

The well-known Banyumas musician Rasito mentions a reduced ensemble comparable to the gamelan *klenèngan* of Surakarta and known in Banyumas as gamelan *kemagan* or gamelan *climènan*. It consists of *kendhang, siter, gambang, gendèr barung, gendèr panerus, slenthem, gong kemodhong* (also called *gong anggang-anggang* – two metal slabs, resonating over a large pot encased in a box), but with no *kempul, kenong*, or *kethuk*. Despite the two Banyumas terms for the ensemble, it is thought to have originated from the court areas to the east and has been used more for the Yogya and Solo repertoires than for what is now seen to be Banyumas *gendhing*.

Now rarely heard, the gamelan *ringgeng* and gamelan *mondrèng* were at one time popular ensembles for itinerant street musicians. Though serving the same functions as their counterparts in the large gamelan, the *bonang* and punctuating gongs consisted of suspended keys, usually made of iron. Even at the time of Kunst's research, the terms *ringgeng* and *mondrèng* were used interchangeably, though he points out that the *ringgeng* keys formerly had no raised boss, whereas the *mondrèng* did. In the one gamelan *ringgeng* located by René Lysloff during his research in the Banyumas region in 1986–87, the keys of the two *bonang* and the *kethuk-kenong* (only four keys, on one frame) are bossed. This ensemble also has a single-keyed gong *kemodhong* and a small hanging gong (*kempul*), as well as a small *kendhang* and two *saron*. This is slightly smaller than the *ringgeng* instrumentation given by Rasito: *kendhang*, several *saron, bonang barung, bonang panerus, kethuk*, three *kenong*, three *kempul*, one or two *gong* (1984, personal communication).

Similar iron ensembles may be used to accompany the Banyumas hobby-horse trance dance *èbèg*, sometimes complemented by a double-reed (*selomprèt*) or, in the last few years, by *pesindhèn* (see Kartomi 1973: 167–79, Sutton 1986a:123–24 and Sutton 1985b:37). The basic *èbèg* ensemble, according to Rasito, consists of two *kendhang*, one *saron*, one or two metal-slab *kenong, kethuk*, hanging *kempul*, and hanging *gong*. He lists neither the *selomprèt*, observed by Kartomi, nor the two *bonang*, which Lysloff observed in 1986.

Finally, mention should be made of the characteristic musical ensemble known as *jemblung*. Though Kunst shows a bamboo ensemble of this name in Banyumas, it is a term now used for a performance in which all gamelan instrument sounds are imitated by the human voice. The ensemble consists of four or five individuals, usually seated around a table. The leader (*dhalang*) tells a story, with the other members commenting and taking the roles of some of the characters. As the *dhalang* sings an opening phrase, the others join in, imitating the sounds of gamelan instruments (*kendhang*, gong punctuation, *balungan* and its elaboration). Usually a *pesindhèn* provides a vocal line. The effect is often hilarious, and intentionally so, fitting well with the reputation of the region for humor. (On *jemblung* see further Lysloff 1990.) The music performed will usually include Banyumas pieces, although in the one performance I witnessed in its entirety, most of the pieces were from Solonese or Yogyanese tradition. The *dhalang*, Ki Parman, explained that the use of Banyumas pieces for such a long performance (8:30 p.m. to 4:00 a.m.) would have been too taxing on the performers, exhausting them much earlier in the evening.

Instrument tuning systems

Ensembles with both *pélog* and *sléndro* instruments are now preferred in Banyumas by those who can afford them, but *sléndro* is the dominant scale system in the region. Even the entirely vocal *jemblung* employs *sléndro* music throughout. In the survey published by Kunst the preference for *sléndro* is dramatic. For the districts of Cilacap, Purwokerto, Banyumas, Purbalingga, and Banjarnegara, Kunst shows more than ten bronze gamelan in *sléndro* to every one bronze gamelan in *pélog* (566 to 47) (Kunst 1973 II:552). And in addition to the bronze ensembles, he lists smaller ensembles with either bamboo or iron keys (*calung*, *ringgeng*, *angklung*), with 286 tuned to *sléndro* and only thirty-six tuned to *pélog*. That the entire traditional Banyumas repertory is normally played in *sléndro* is usually cited as the reason for such a strong preference for *sléndro* in the region, though one could argue that the repertory has been shaped by the wide availability of *sléndro* instruments.

The precise tuning of these *sléndro* instruments is standardized neither in Banyumas nor in the court areas to the east. But musicians note a significant difference between "Banyumas *sléndro*" and "Solonese *sléndro*" (Rasito 1986:5). The *calung* constructed by A. L. Suwardi, a teacher at STSI/ASKI Surakarta, and intentionally tuned to Solonese sensibilities was felt to be noticeably unsettling by musicians from Banyumas.

Repertory

The repertory of Banyumas gamelan music contrasts with those of Yogyakarta and Surakarta in a number of ways. First, it is much smaller, consisting of between two and three hundred pieces. (My count, based on available data as of 1986 is 224; see further below.) Second, it is weighted heavily on short form pieces, mostly *lancaran*. And third, it emphasizes one tuning system (*sléndro*) and two *pathet* (*sanga* and *manyura*). In this section I will discuss at some length the nature of the Banyumas repertory, beginning with an assessment of what is considered to be the standard, traditional repertory.

One source gives *balungan* notation for fifty pieces and mentions an additional three, which it claims to be the entire standard repertory (Departemen PDK 1980). This source groups *gendhing* by formal structure, employing the same terms as found in contemporary Solonese tradition. The adoption of Solonese terms apparently does not supplant an indigenous Banyumas system, as musicians told me they knew of no other terms. With such a small repertory, it has not been necessary to specify formal structure when naming a piece, since each is fully identified by title alone. Yet the widespread familiarity with Solonese tradition makes the application of these terms to indigenous repertory unproblematic. The fifty pieces notated in the PDK source consist mostly of *lancaran*, with three *ketawang*, two *ladrang*, and four "special" forms (*pamijèn*), three of which are essentially *lancaran* with some unusual treatment.

Ladrang	Ketawang	Lancaran Mlaku	Lancaran	Pamijen	TOTAL
2	3	18	33	4	50

3.2   Distribution of traditional Banyumas repertory as given in Departemen PDK 1980

This collection excludes the fast growing body of recent *lagu dolanan* (mostly *lancaran*) and the distinctive *gendhing lampah* used in Banyumas *wayang*, *kethoprak*, and *dhagelan* (comedy).

Soebiyatno's earlier study of *calung* (1979) provides notation for sixty-two pieces, consisting of a few recent pieces and a *gendhing lampah* in addition to what is essentially the same corpus of *lancaran*, *ketawang*, and *ladrang* found in Departemen PDK 1980. The pieces classified by Soebiyatno as *lancaran* include all *lancaran mlaku* and three of the pieces listed as *pamijèn* in the PDK source. He also indicates *pathet*, whereas the PDK source does not.

Pathet	Ladrang	Ketawang	Lancaran	Gendhing Lampah	TOTAL
Nem:	--	--	12	1	13
Sanga:	1	1	16	--	18
Manyura:	1	1	29	--	31
TOTALS:	2	2*	57	1	62

*Crebonan, listed as ketawang in Departemen PDK 1980, but notated as a lancaran in Soebiyatno 1979.

3.3   Distribution of Banyumas *gendhing* in Soebiyatno 1979

Both these sources are limited to those Banyumas pieces one is likely to hear in concert or in a *lènggèr-calung* performance. Usually one also hears at least a few pieces from the "east" (i.e., Yogya and Solo), particularly during the early part of the evening. The choices are usually limited to a few of the best-known pieces shared by both Yogya and Solo, such as Ladrang *Pangkur*, Ladrang *Asmarandana*, Ladrang *Kutut Manggung*, Ladrang *Rujak Jeruk*, Jineman *Uler Kambang*, and Gendhing *Gambir Sawit*.[6] However, most of the repertory in a lengthy *lènggèr-calung* performance, lasting from about 7:00 or 8:00 p.m. until 4:30 or 5:00 a.m., consists of a mixture of traditional Banyumas pieces with recent Banyumas *lagu dolanan* and popular songs from other genres, such as the acculturated *dangdut*.[7] The vocal melodies of the popular songs employ the Western tempered (*diatonis*) scale, which is maintained in *calung* performances even though the instrumental accompaniment is *sléndro*.

New pieces for gamelan in Banyumas style are being composed by a few prominent musicians in the region. Rasito (see plate 6), who teaches at the local conservatory (SMKI Banyumas) and is musical director of the group that accompanies the most popular Banyumas *dhalang* Ki Sugino Siswocarito, says he believes he has composed over sixty pieces, although when asked to provide a list, could only remember forty-two. Like many composers who work in what remains primarily an oral tradition, he does not publish his works, nor bother to keep an archive of manuscripts, though he normally writes some of the parts (*balungan* and vocal) when he composes. Most of his pieces use a *lancaran* formal structure. Some he classifies simply as *lancaran*, others as *langgam*, *jaipongan*, or *dangdut*, depending on vocal and drumming styles. The *jaipongan* pieces are a Banyumas response to a popular genre of music originating in West Java but which spread over all of Java (see Baier and Manuel 1986). The *dangdut* pieces display the characteristic rhythm of the popular pan-Indonesian genre, but the melodies use the gamelan scales (usually *pélog*, rather than *sléndro*) and not the Western tempered (*diatonis*) scale. Rasito's earliest work was *Banyumas Kowèk*, a *lancaran* written in 1973. Most of his composing occurred during the late 1970s (1978–79), corresponding to the opening of the local SMKI conservatory. He remained active throughout the 1980s.

S. Bono, another composer, is a member of Rasito's group, a renowned singer, and active producer of *calung*, *angklung*, and gamelan groups from Banyumas. Like Rasito, he could only provide a partial list of his works. He tends to classify his output simply as *lagu*, but says

6   Pak Rasito playing drum with his group Mudha Budhaya (= Purba Kencana), accompanying *wayang kulit* in the town of Banyumas, 1984.

Tuning & Pathet	Ketawang	Lancaran	Langgam	Jaipongan	Dang-dut	TOTAL
Pélog						
Nem:	1	7	3	2	--	13
Barang:	--	6	2	--	1	9
Sléndro						
Sanga:	--	7	1	1	--	9
Manyura:	--	11	--	--	--	11
TOTALS:	1	31	6	3	1	42

3.4   Distribution of new compositions by Rasito, a partial listing as of October 1986, compiled by Rasito and Lysloff

that most employ a *lancaran* formal structure. In addition to thirty pieces he composed, he lists five that use *balungan* of traditional pieces to which he has added new vocal parts, or texts, and one that he simply transposed to *pélog*. Bono has been composing since the 1970s, but does not date his pieces. Suyoto, former *kroncong* violinist, former director of several gamelan groups, and currently the *rebab* player in Rasito's group, lists seven compositions. His most famous piece is also his earliest, *Mendhoan* (the name of a favorite Banyumas soybean patty), written in 1972. Several of his pieces derive from his days as a violinist, borrowing *kroncong* tunes and recasting them, with new texts, for gamelan. A few other pieces well-known locally are attributed to Suharti, who performs at RRI Purwokerto, and Tuslah, a musician from Purbalingga. The earliest "modern" Banyumas piece with a known composer dates from the 1960s: *Gethuk Goreng* (a sweet snack food) by S. Kartomintarga, from Sokaraja, a small town famous for its *gethuk goreng*.

In addition to the many *lancaran* and the few other pieces in small, regular forms, the Banyumas repertory includes pieces used for *wayang* accompaniment. The musical repertory heard currently in performances of Banyumas (*wayang kulit* represents a mixture of pieces considered to be indigenous to the region with a substantial body of pieces borrowed from Solo and Yogya. The recent publication on Banyumas style *wayang kulit*, though it gives notation for thirty-nine Banyumas *sulukan*, lists only a few Banyumas *gendhing*, scattered among pieces from Solonese repertory (Sekretariat Nasional 1983: 161–64). The Banyumas *gendhing* one hears, in addition to pieces from the concert and *calung* repertory, are a special Banyumas version of Gendhing *Bondhèt* and a group of *gendhing lampah* that are unique to the Banyumas region. The former is heard in every *wayang*, regardless of the characters or location of the first scene, just as Gendhing *Krawitan* is in Yogyanese tradition.

In performance, *Bondhèt* is preceded by two *gendhing lampah*, usually referred to as *Ayak-ayakan Lasem* and *Srepegan Lasem*, *sléndro pathet nem*. Though closely resembling the Yogyanese pieces of the same name (see below), these are considered to be Banyumas versions. This *srepegan* is sometimes identified as *Srepegan Lasem Arang* ("sparse"), since the relationship between *kenong*, *kempul*, and *balungan* is like the Yogyanese *srepegan* form (four beats per *kempul*), rather than the Solonese (and other Banyumas) *srepegan* form (two beats per *kempul*). The usual *Srepegan Lasem* has two beats per *kempul* and is nearly identical to Yogyanese *Playon Lasem*.

Sometimes the Banyumas *gendhing lampah* are identified explicitly as "Banyumasan" or as "Pesisiran," but these terms are not applied consistently, nor is their meaning clear. Though the term *pesisirian* usually refers to Java's north coast, in Banyumas it refers to the southern coast, the area south of the Kendeng mountain range, which cuts the Banyumas region into a northern half (*lor gunung* – "north of the mountains") and a southern half (*pesisiran*). One does find some subtle intraregional variation in the *wayang* tradition, including differences in the *gendhing lampah* in the early portion of the *wayang*. But on recordings that identify a piece as *Ayak-ayakan Pesisiran*, or *Srepegan Pesisiran*, it is not clear whether it is meant in distinction to a more normal Banyumas version, or in distinction to Yogyanese and Solonese versions. Proliferation of labels notwithstanding, there appear to be several closely related versions of both *Ayak-ayakan* and *Srepegan* in *pathet nem*. One of the important differences is the initial gong tone (6 or 5).

For the remainder of the *pathet nem* section, the Banyumas pieces *Srepegan Lasem* and

Srepegan Mandras are played, sometimes in alternation with Solonese *Srepegan* and *Sampak*. For *pathet sanga* and *pathet manyura* sections, the *gendhing lampah* again bear some resemblance to those from Yogya and Solo. And one often hears Solonese *gendhing lampah* used during these sections as well. The Banyumas *Srepegan* in *sanga* normally proceeds to a repeated section known as *Jalak-jalak Pita* (literally, "small yellow birds"), characterized by a unique *balungan* melody and an emphasis on vocal parts. The Banyumas *Ayak-ayakan* in *manyura* is sometimes called *Ayak-ayakan Arum Dalu* (literally, "night fragrance"), and bears some obvious similarities to Solonese *Ayak-ayakan pathet manyura*.

Ki Soegito Purbocarito, a purist by his own estimation, distinguishes sharply between his performances in Solonese style, for which he uses Solonese repertory with Banyumas pieces only during clown scenes, and in Banyumas style, for which he uses Banyumas *Ayak-ayakan*, *Srepegan*, and *Sampak* consistently throughout all three *pathet*. In the latter, he employs a variety of Banyumas *Srepegan* and *Sampak* in *sléndro manyura*, which, he told me, mark the four divisions of the *manyura* section in Banyumas *wayang*: *Srepegan "Manyura, suwuk 6"*; *Srepegan "Manyuri"*; *Sampak "Pancer 5"*; and *Sampak "Tayungan"* (= *Sampak "Bima Perang"*)(Notated in Sutton 1986b). According to Soegito, such a progression is less common today than it was a generation ago, due to the strong Solonese influence. No comparable division of the *manyura* section is found in Solonese *wayang*. Some aspects resemble those of Yogyanese *wayang* music, however, as discussed below. In the recent publication on Banyumas *wayang*, the various *gendhing lampah* pieces in *manyura* discussed above are not listed, nor is the *manyura* section divided into four phases (Sekretariat Nasional 1983:161–64).

Other *gendhing lampah* that can be seen as part of the Banyumas repertory are the *Srepegan* pieces used as staples in *kethoprak* and *dhagelan*, played in *sléndro* and *pélog*. Some of the Banyumas *wayang* pieces are now also played in *pélog*, both in the context of *wayang* performance and in concerts, broadcasts, and cassette recordings. Banyumas *gendhing lampah* are listed below, in Figure 3.5.

The repertory of Banyumas *gendhing*, then, consists mostly of pieces in *lancaran* form, with a few *ketawang*, *ladrang*, and *gendhing lampah*, and only one large *gendhing* (*Bondhèt*). Recent recordings have featured what is labelled as "Palaran Banyumasan," but the melodies are essentially Solonese, with Banyumas nuance in ornamentation. Other larger *gendhing* are also frequently heard in the region, borrowed from Solo. Yet the populace appears to be aware of the identity of these pieces as something other than "*asli* Banyumas" ("original," "authentic" Banyumas). The heavy borrowing of Solonese *gendhing*, especially in *wayang*, is seen by some as a potential threat, but the more usual attitude is one of openness in which borrowing is seen as enrichment. The Banyumas repertory is still very much alive in performance; it is not replaced by borrowings but supplemented by them.

Below is a summary of the repertory, based on the sources mentioned above, as well as my own extensive inventorying of cassette recordings during my research. The data excludes pieces that are generally seen to be borrowed from other repertories (Solonese, Yogyanese, Sundanese, and Indonesian popular musics), but includes locally-composed pieces that may reflect influences from other genres.

Classifying pieces by form is somewhat more problematic here than it is for Yogyanese or Solonese pieces, simply because formal structure is often not given. While most undesignated pieces are normally played as *lancaran*, I have listed them together with *lagu* in order to reflect

I. Wayang Kulit Tradition:

```
Ayak-ayakan Lasem (begins on 5)      sléndro pt. nem
Ayak-ayakan Lasem (begins on 6)      sléndro pt. nem
Srepegan Lasem (begins on 5)         sléndro pt. nem
Srepegan Lasem Arang                 sléndro pt. nem
Srepegan Lasem (begins on 6)         sléndro pt. nem; pélog pt. nem
Srepegan Mandras                     sléndro pt. nem
Ayak-ayakan                          sléndro pt. sanga
Srepegan (--> Jalak-jalak Pita)      sléndro pt. sanga; pélog pt. lima
Srepegan Tangisa                     sléndro pt. sanga
Sampak                               sléndro pt. sanga
Ayak-ayakan (Arum Dalu)              sléndro pt. manyura; pélog pt. barang
Srepegan (suwuk 6)                   sléndro pt. manyura; pélog pt. barang
Srepegan "Manyuri" (suwuk 3)         sléndro pt. manyura
Sampak "Pancer 5"                    sléndro pt. manyura
Sampak Tayungan ("Bima Perang")      sléndro pt. manyura
```

II. Other:

```
Srepegan Kethoprakan                 sléndro [pt. sanga]; pélog [pt. nem]
Srepegan Dhagelan                    sléndro [pt. sanga?]; pélog [pt. nem?]
```

3.5   Banyumas repertory of *gendhing lampah*

the potential for alternative structures. The four pieces listed as *pamijèn* in Departemen PDK 1980 are listed below as *lancaran*, since that is their designation in Soebiyatno and elsewhere. The categories *langgam*, *dangdut*, and *jaipongan* refer more to influences from other genres than to single formal structures; most are played with *lancaran* formal structure and with drumming characteristic of the particular genre indicated. In the table below these are combined under the heading "derivative" (see Figure 3.6). Some pieces are played in both tuning systems, others may appear with more than one *pathet* designation. And in many cases, only a title is given, with indication neither of *pathet* nor of tuning. Therefore, the total number of pieces (224) is somewhat less than the total obtained by adding the figures in all the columns showing distribution by *pathet* and tuning (257). *Lancaran* is clearly the most popular formal structure in the region. If we bear in mind that most pieces classified as *lagu dolanan* (= *lagu* = *lelagon*) or as one of the derivative types are normally played with *lancaran* formal structure, the predominance of this one form becomes all the more striking: nearly 90 percent (198) of the total 224 pieces in the repertory.

Tuning system and *pathet*

Based on the data presented in Figure 3.6, one can see a strong preference for *sléndro* in the region. All of the traditional Banyumas pieces, whether those for concerts and dance or for *wayang*, are normally performed in *sléndro* and are said by Banyumas musicians to be *sléndro* pieces, even if they are occasionally played in *pélog*. Some Javanese, both in the region and elsewhere, point to the limited nature of the Banyumas repertory: its emphasis on small forms, and its limitation to one tuning system (*sléndro*) and only two *pathet* (*sanga* and *manyura*). The transposition of pieces to *pélog* and the composition of new pieces in *pélog* by local musicians represents, I believe, an attempt to give Banyumas tradition wider appeal and greater stature, in answer to this charge.

The *pathet* question is another matter. In fact, *pathet* has not played a very prominent role

I. Distrubtion of Banyumas Repertory by Formal Structure:

Gen-dhing	Lad-rang	Ket-awang	Lanc-aran	Gd. lampah	Lagu dolanan	Deri-vative	TOTAL
1	4	5	95	16	77	26	224

II. Distribution of Banyumas Repertory by Tuning and Pathet:

Tuning & Pathet	Gen-dhing	Lad-rang	Ket-awang	Lanc-aran	Gd. lampah	Lagu dolanan	Deri-vative	TOTALS
Sléndro								
nem	1	--	--	13	5	--	--	19
sanga	--	2	1	25	4	12	2	44
manyura	--	1	3	55	5	13	1	78
Pélog								
lima	--	--	1	1	1	5	--	8
nem	--	1	2	10	2	5	6	26
barang	--	--	1	8	2	7	4	22
Pathet/Tuning Not Given	--	--	--	2	2	35	13	52

3.6   Distribution of Banyumas repertory

in the classification of pieces in Banyumas, at least outside of *wayang kulit*. According to Soegito, the *wayang* in Banyumas formerly consisted of only two *pathet*: *sanga* and *manyura*. Indeed, these two categories are by far the largest in the data presented in Figure 3.6. Incorporation of *pathet nem*, Soegito suggests, was due to influence from the court traditions to the east during the late nineteenth century. But in what I have argued is an attempt to fill out the three *sléndro pathet* categories, musicians in conservatory circles are now classifying some of the traditional Banyumas repertory as *sléndro pathet nem* – pieces that are otherwise listed as *manyura*.

The choices appear to have been made entirely on the basis of melodic structure, especially gong tone, and not on associations with mood. The Solonese and Yogyanese associate *sléndro pathet nem* with a calm, introspective mood, but the Banyumas pieces now sometimes classified as *sléndro pathet nem* are just as lively as the rest of the repertory (for example, Lancaran *Éling-éling*). At any rate, a repertory that was confined until recently to *sléndro pathet sanga* and *sléndro pathet manyura*, exclusive of *wayang* pieces, can now be seen to encompass all three *pathet* in both tuning systems.[8]

Banyumas *gendhing* and the Solonese and Yogyanese repertories

Many of the titles of Banyumas pieces turn up in Yogyanese and Solonese repertories, but usually in reference to very different pieces. The following table lists the titles (other than *gendhing lampah*) shared by Banyumas with one or both of these court-derived traditions and gives their most common designation in Banyumas, followed by those found in the other repertories.

Title	BANYUMAS	YOGYAKARTA	SURAKARTA
Angleng	lcn sl 9	gd tld [sl 9]	ktw sl 9
Blèndèran	lcn sl mnyr	--	[lcn] pl 6
Cèlèng Mogok	[lcn]	ldr sl mnyr	--
*Éling-éling	lcn sl mnyr	ldr sl 6, sl mnyr	ldr pl 5/6, br, sl 9, sl mnyr
*Gandaria	lcn sl mnyr	gd tld sl mnyr	ldr sl m, pl 6
**Grompol Kethèk	lcn sl mnyr	--	ldr sl 6, mnyr
Gula Kelapa	[lg]	--	lcn pl 5
Gunungsari	ktw sl mnyr	ktw & gd tld sl mnyr	ktw pl br
**Ijo-ijo	lcn sl mnyr	ldr sl 9; gd tld sl mnyr	ldr & gd sl mnyr
Ilir-ilir	[lg]	--	lg pl 6, sl mnyr
Kembang Peté	[lg] pl 5	gd sl mnyr	ldr sl mnyr
*Lung Gadhung	ldr sl mnyr	ldr pl 6	ldr pl br
*Ondhé-ondhé	lcn sl mnyr	--	lg pl br
*Pacul Gowang	lcn sl mnyr	gd sl mnyr	ldr pl br
Pengantèn Anyar	[lg] pl br	--	ldr pl 6, br
*Pisang Bali	ktw sl 9	ldr sl 6	ktw sl 9
Randha Nunut	lcn sl mnyr	--	gd sl mnyr
Ricik-ricik	lcn sl mnyr	ldr sl mnyr	lcn pl br, sl mnyr
**Samiran	lcn sl mnyr	gd tld sl mnyr	ldr pl 6
*Sekar Gadhung	lcn sl mnyr	ldr sl mnyr	ldr sl mnyr
Sontoloyo	lcn sl 9	gd sl mnyr	ldr sl 9, pl 6
Surung Dhayung	lcn sl mnyr	ldr sl 9	ldr pl 6
Waru Dhoyong	lcn sl mnyr	gd tld sl [9?]	--

KEY:
```
 br = barang        gd = gendhing       ktw = ketawang    lcn = lancaran
ldr = ladrang       lg = lagu (lelagon) mnyr = manyura    pl = pélog
 sl = sléndro      tld = talèdhèk(an)
  5 = lima          6 = nem                9 = sanga
[ ] = not listed as such in written source(s)
```

** = Banyumas gendhing similar to Yogyanese and/or Solonese gendhing of same
     title

* = Banyumas gendhing related to Yogyanese and/or Solonese gendhing of same
    title

3.7   Banyumas *gendhing* titles found in Yogyanese and Solonese repertories

A few other Banyumas *gendhing* bear titles similar to those of Yogyanese or Solonese *gendhing*, listed in Figure 3.8. In my analysis of these pieces, too lengthy to include here, I find that most Banyumas *gendhing* bear little if any resemblance to Yogyanese or Solonese pieces of the same or similar name, and in only one case (*Samiran*) could one justifiably call them "the same piece." Though the *balungan* for this piece is identical in Solonese and Banyumas versions, the formal structure is not (nor, of course, is the treatment by drums and elaborating instruments). Two other pieces are quite close to the Yogyanese and Solonese pieces with the same names: *Grompol Kethèk* (= *Grombol Kethèk*) and *Ijo-ijo*.

   Some degree of resemblance can be seen for eleven others: *Angleng, Béndrong Jawa, Bribil Buntung, Éling-éling, Gandaria, Gunungsari, Lung Gadhung, Ondhé-ondhé, Pacul Gowang,*

BANYUMAS	YOGYAKARTA	SURAKARTA
*Béndrong Jawa (lcn sl mnyr)	Béndrong (lcn sl mnyr, pl br, 6)	Béndrong (lcn sl mnyr, pl br, 6)
Béndrong Kulon (lcn sl 9, mnyr)		
*Bribil Buntung (lcn sl mnyr)	Bribil (various) (gd tld sl mnyr)	Bribil, Bribil Gonjol (lcn sl mnyr, ldr sl 9, ktw sl 9, mnyr)
Ilogondhang (lcn sl mnyr)	--	Logondhang (gd pl 5, ktw pl br)
Lambangsari Kenyol (lcn sl mnyr)	Lambangsari (gd sl mnyr, pl br gd tld sl mnyr)	Lambangsari (gd sl mnyr, pl br)
Lobong Ilang (lcn sl mnyr)	Lobong (gd sl mnyr)	Lobong (gd sl mnyr, pl br)

(abbreviations as in Figure 3.7)

* = Banyumas gendhing related to Yogyanese and/or Solonese gendhing of same
title

3.8   Banyumas *gendhing* titles similar to Yogyakarta and Surakarta titles

Pisang Bali, and *Sekar Gadhung*. Yet these resemblances may not be immediately apparent. Consider, for example, the *balungan* of the popular Lancaran *Éling-éling* from Banyumas, and the *balungan* of the most closely related *ladrang* of the same name from Surakarta:

```
    BANYUMAS (Lancaran):                    SURAKARTA (Ladrang):

    N P N  P N P N/G            t         t   N         t         t   N
    1 6 1 5  1 5 1 6     A:  1 6 5 3  2 3 5 6    B:  5 3 5 6  5 3 5 2
    1 6 1 5  1 5 1 6         1 6 5 3  2 3 5 6        5 3 5 6  5 3 5 2
    3 2 3 2  3 5 6 5         2 2 . .  2 3 5 2        1 6 . 1  6 . 5 6
    6 5 3 2  5 6 1 6         5 3 5 6  5 3 5 2G       1 6 5 3  2 3 5 6G
```

3.9   *Éling-éling*, Banyumas and Surakarta versions

There are several ways of analyzing these two versions in relation to one another. The similarity pointed to by those Javanese to whom I have spoken about this is limited mostly to the first *gongan* of the *ladrang*. Both begin with a repeated eight-beat phrase that moves away from pitch 6 and back to it. This is followed by emphasis on pitch 2, in the third *gongan* of the *lancaran* and in the third *kenongan* of the *ladrang* (the third line as written here), but the *lancaran* moves up to pitch 5 and in the fourth *gongan* moves back to pitch 6, while the *ladrang* never features pitch 5 and arrives back at pitch 6 only five *kenongan* (forty beats) later. For three of the remaining titles listed above I have insufficient notation or recordings for comparison; for the other twelve, I find no resemblance.

Musicians themselves suggest that a close relationship exists between the *wayang* repertories of Banyumas and the court-derived traditions. Though resembling the Yogyanese and Solonese versions of Gendhing *Bondhèt* in overall contour, the *mérong* of the Banyumas version is expanded to 128 beats per *gong* (*kethuk* 4 *kerep*), rather than the sixty-four in the other two (Yogya: *candra*, *gendhing alit*; Solo: *kethuk 2 kerep*). Below is given one version from each tradition (all in *sléndro*).

```
                    BANYUMAS VERSION (pathet nem)

                      (from Srepegan ...5N/G)
merong:    t            t            t            t
        22.3 6532 1216 2165 1216 3563 6516 2165N
        22.3 6532 1216 2165 1216 3563 6536 2165N
        3321 3216 1621 3216 ..66 2321 3265 1653N
        5653 5653 1216 3563 1231 3216 2253 5635N/G


umpak minggah (transitional gongan, leading to inggah section):

           t            t            t            t
    232.2353 6532  2 3 6 5  1 6 5 3  2 1 6 5N
          2 3  5 2  . 3 6 5  2 3 5 2  . 3 5 6N
          2 1  2 6  2 1 2 6  3 5 6 1  6 5 2 3N
          1 5  1 6  1 5 2 3  .2355 .  6 5 3 2  . 6 . 5N/G


inggah:    t            t            t            t
        . 6 . 5  . 3 . 2  . 3 . 2  . 6 . 5N
        . 6 . 5  . 3 . 2  . 3 . 2  . 6 . 5N
        . 1 . 6  . 1 . 6  . 2 . 1  . 5 . 3N
        . 5 . 6  . 5 . 3  . 2 . 3  . 6 . 5N/G
(transcribed from performance by Purba Kencana, group led by Rasito,
   accompanying wayang kulit dhalang Ki Sugino Siswocarito)

- - - - - - - - - - - - - - - - - - - - - - - - - - - - - - - - -

YOGYAKARTA VERSION (pathet nem):        SURAKARTA VERSION (pathet sanga):

Buka:  5353 1653 2132 55.5N/G             Buka: .55. 6656 2612 .165N/G

merong (dados)                          merong:
       t    t    N                              t    t    N
[: 2312 .365 1653 2165                      ..53 6535 22.3 5635
   3565 3235 2523 5616                  [: ..53 6535 22.3 5616
   2126 2132 5321 6523*                     .... 6656 3561 6523**
   5353 1653 2132 1635G :]                  .333 5653 2353 2165G
                                            22.. 22.3 5653 2165 :]


pangkat ndhawah: (from *)               umpak minggah: (from **)

   .1.6 .5.3 .2.3 .6.5G                    .5.6 .5.3 .2.3 .6.5G

dhawah:                                 inggah:
    t    t    t    t N                       t    t    t    t N
[: .6.5 .3.2 .3.2 .6.5                  [: .6.5 .3.2 .3.2 .6.5
   .6.5 .3.2 .3.2 .1.6                     .6.5 .3.2 .3.2 .6.5
   .1.6 .1.6 .2.1 .5.3                     .1.6 .1.6 .2.1 .6.5
   .1.6 .5.3 .2.3 .6.5G :]                 .5.6 .5.3 .2.3 .6.5G :]
(from notation by Pustakamardawa)       (from Mloyowidodo 1976 I:87-88)
```

3.10   Gendhing *Bondhèt*, Banyumas, Yogyanese, and Solonese versions (all in *sléndro*)

The *umpak minggah* in the Banyumas version resembles the Yogyanese *mérong* for most of the first three *kenongan*, and undergoes an unusual transformation in which the fourth *kenongan* has four more beats than the others. The *inggah*, though close to the Yogyanese version, is identical to the Solonese.

The *wayang* in Banyumas begins with *Ayak-ayakan*, *sléndro pathet nem*, a piece resembling Yogyanese *Ayak-ayakan* in melodic contour. A feature unique to the Banyumas version is the change in gong structure to something resembling *ladrang* in the middle section. The *kenong* sounds every eight beats, *kethuk* on the second and sixth beat of each *kenongan*, and *kempul* on the fourth beat of each *kenongan*, rather than every second *kenong* as is normal in *gendhing lampah*. The *gong*, however, occurs irregularly, not every thirty-two beats as in a normal *ladrang*.

```
         BANYUMASAN                                  YOGYANESE

    Ayak-ayakan Lasem                           Ayak-ayakan Lasem
    Buka kendhang ... 2 3 5N/G                  Buka kendhang 5 .5.5N/G

          P    P    P    G                             P         P
        NN   NN   NN   NN                           N    N    N    N
        [:    6565 6565 2356                       .6.5 .6.5 .6.5 .6.5
           1616 1616 3253 2121                     .6.1 .5.6 .1.6 .5.6
              2121 2121 3565 :]                    .2.3 .5.3 .2.1 .2.1
                                                   .2.3 .2.1 .6.5 .3.5
irama II:  P        P        G                     .1.6 .5.6 .1.6 .5.6
        N     N     N     N     N     N                      5323 1232G
        5 3   1 2   3 2   5 3   6 5   3 2      #   [: 5323 5653 6523 5653
        5 6   5 3   5 6   5 3 2132 5635            6523 5653 1123 1635G
                                                        P              P
        t  P     t    N     t    P    t    N       N      N      N      P
      3 6 3 2  3 6 3 5  3 6 3 2  3 6 3 5       1 6 1 2  1 6 1 5  1 6 1 2  1 6 1 5
      3 6 2 1  3 5 2 3G 2 5 2 3  2 5 2 3       3 3 . 5  2 3 5 3  5 6 5 3  5 6 5 3
      5 5 3 2  3 6 3 5G 3 6 3 5  3 6 3 5       5 5 . 2  3 5 6 5  3 2 3 5  3 2 3 5
      2 2 5 3  6 5 3 2G 1 3 1 6  1 3 1 2       2 2 . 3  6 5 3 2  3 1 2 6  3 5 3 2
      1 3 1 6  1 3 1 2  5 5 3 2  3 6 3 5G      3 1 2 6  3 5 3 2  5 5 . 2  3 5 6 5
      3 6 3 5  3 6 3 5  6 6 2 1  3 2 1 2G      3 2 3 5  3 2 3 5  6 6 . 1  5 6 1 6
      3 2 5 3  6 5 3 2G 5 6 5 3  5 6 5 3       1 6 5 3  6 5 3 2G 5 3 2 3  5 6 5 3
      6 5 2 3  5 6 5 3  2 1 3 2 36213216G      6 5 2 3  5 6 5 3  6 5 2 3  5 6 5 3
                                               1 1 2 3  1 62356G

    Srepegan ("Arang"):                        [Srepegan]:
         P    P    P    G                            P         P         P         P
        NN   NN   NN   NN                          N    N    N    N    N    N    N    N
           1616 1616 3561                       2 6 2 6  2 6 2 6  1 1 2 1  2 3 2 1
           2121 2121 3565                       6 5 3 5  6 1 5 6  1 6 5 6
           6565 6565 2356                       (if tempo slows, play:  53231232G
           1616 1616 5312                           then return to #)
              3653 6532
                                               (if tempo does not slow, then
     [: 5653 5653 6526 2365                        play rest of Srepegan:)
          6535 6235 3123                                          5 3 2 3  1 2 3 2G
       5353 5235 1653 6532                                                 5 3 2 3
              6612 3565                         5 6 5 3  5 6 5 3  6 5 2 6  2 1 6 5
          6121 2132 5616                        3 2 3 5  3 2 3 5
              5323 6532 :]                          suwuk:      62.262. 6165.1.6G

         (from Rasito)                      (from Sukardi & Sukidjo 1976a:110-111)
```

3.11   Opening music for *wayang kulit*: *Ayak-ayakan* and *Srepegan*, Banyumas and Yogyakarta versions

The Banyumas *Srepegan Lasem* is identical to the Yogyanese version (more correctly called *Playon* in Yogyanese terminology), except for the first phrase, which is shorter in the

Banyumas version by two *saron* beats. The second Banyumas *srepegan*, known as *Srepegan Mandras*, follows closely the melody of Solonese *Srepegan*, *sléndro pathet nem*.

```
        BANYUMASAN                              SOLONESE

Srepegan Mandras, sléndro pt. nem:      Srepegan, sléndro pt. nem:

   Buka kendhang:   ...5N/G               Buka kendhang: ...5N/G

     P   P   P  G  P   P              P   P    P   P    P   P    P  G
   N N N N  N N N N  N N N N        N N N N  N N N N  N N N N  N N N N
         [: 6 5 6 5  6 3 6 3                [: 6 5 6 5  2 3 5 3
   6 3 6 3  6 5 6 5  6 2 6 2        5 3 5 3  5 2 3 5  1 6 5 3  6 5 3 2
            6 2 6 2  6 5 6 5                 3 2 3 2  3 5 6 5 :]

                                    (optional ngelik, only played once)
                                             2 1 2 1  3 2 3 2  5 6 1 6
                                    1 6 5 3  2 3 2 1  3 2 6 5  3 2 3 5 :]
```

3.12   Two *srepegan* in *sléndro pathet nem* (Banyumas and Surakarta)

The basic contour of the non-*ngelik* portion of the Solonese piece is the same as that of *Srepegan Mandras*, the latter characterized by a *pancer* 6 in every *gatra*. In the *sanga* and *manyura* sections of the *wayang*, one normally hears Banyumas and Solonese *gendhing lampah*, and not Yogyanese. Though one can detect a relationship in overall melodic contour between the Banyumas *gendhing lampah* in these two *pathet* and those of Yogyanese and Solonese tradition, they are considered to be distinctive pieces, without the ambiguous identity associated with the *sléndro nem* pieces.

Also significant in articulating a *wayang* repertory unique to Banyumas are the four pieces for *pathet manyura* used by Ki Soegito (notated in Sutton 1986b:90). Though clearly identifiable as Banyumasan, three share some important traits with Yogyanese *gendhing lampah* used in the *manyura* section and the other with corresponding Solonese pieces. First, *Srepegan "Manyura, suwuk 6"* ends on pitch 6, just as Yogyanese *Playon Manyura* does, despite a contrast in melodic contour between the Banyumas piece and either Solonese *Srepegan* (which ends on pitch 2) or Yogyanese *Playon*. Second, the *srepegan* reserved for later in the *manyura* section in Banyumas, called *Manyuri* by Soegito, ends on pitch 3, just as the *sampak* classified in Yogya as *pathet galong*. *Sampak "Pancer 5"* is, as the name suggests, characterized by the use of pitch 5 on the weak beats. The *balungan* of Yogyanese *Sampak Galong* also consists entirely of *gatra* with *pancer* 5. The final *Sampak Tayungan* follows the general pitch progression of Solonese *Srepegan* and *Sampak* (beginning on pitch 2, followed by gong tones 1, 6, 2), but the *gatra* shapes are distinctively Banyumas.

Summarizing the findings on Banyumas repertory, then, we find that the main body of pieces, despite some shared titles and a few shared musical traits, are clearly set off from the repertories of the court-derived traditions of Yogya and Solo. The Banyumas *wayang* repertory, too, is set apart from those of Yogya and Solo, but with a number of instances of close resemblance, particularly with Yogya. One would assume the direction of influence to have been from the courts (in this case, primarily Yogya) to the rural area (Banyumas), rather than the other way round. While this is likely, we still lack written documentation supporting this view. But by accepting the idea of Banyumas receiving music from outside (as it does today with a variety of other genres), we find evidence of a strong impetus to localize pieces – changing melodic contours, formal structures, and styles of performance.

Musical style

Banyumas gamelan style is distinguished by its consistently lively instrumental playing, and light and often humorous singing. Musicians in Banyumas list *bonang*, drumming, and vocal parts as the main indicators of this style. More generally, they state that Banyumas pieces are all fundamentally vocal in conception (Departemen PDK 1980:9; Rasito 1986:2). One hears instrumental renditions of the Banyumas *lancaran* in *èbèg* (trance dance), but recently a vocalist has been added to the *èbèg* ensemble, first on commercial cassettes and now in live performance as well.[9] There exists no Banyumas repertory of *gendhing bonang* or *soran*, such as we find not only in Surakarta and Yogyakarta but also elsewhere (Semarang and east Java). The primacy of the vocal line rather than any particular instrument makes the repertory, exclusive of the *wayang* pieces, equally well suited to the large gamelan and the smaller ensembles (*èbèg* and especially *calung*). Below I will consider instruments of the large gamelan, along with some techniques employed in *calung* playing and *èbèg* accompaniment, and then consider the vocal music of the region.

Gong punctuation

In the large gamelan, the *gong*, *kethuk*, and *kenong* are usually not played any differently from the way they are in Yogyanese or Solonese styles. Yet in both the new pieces and the older repertory of Banyumas *lancaran* the *kempul* part may take one of two orientations: *wétan* ("eastern") or *kulon* ("western"). The "eastern" style is an exact duplication of the rhythmic pattern used in Solonese and Yogyanese *lancaran* (subdividing each *kenongan* but the first). The "western" style is said to be Sundanese, with *kempul* subdividing each *kenongan*, including the first, and sounding together with the third *kenong* beat, as follows:

```
"eastern" (Javanese) kempul:   .   .   P   .   P   .   P   .

"western" (Sundanese) kempul:   P   .   P   .   P   P   P   .

  kethuk, kenong, and gong:  t . t N t . t N t . t N t . t N/G
```
3.13   *Kempul* patterns in Banyumas *lancaran*

There is some freedom in the choice of these patterns. Some of the traditional repertory (e.g., *Béndrong Kulon*, *Malang Dhoi*) are said to be Sundanese-derived and most appropriately played with the Sundanese *kempul*. And a new piece with *jaipongan* rhythm would normally employ this pattern as well, since *jaipongan* is a Sundanese genre. Other pieces may incorporate the Sundanese pattern, at least at the slower, settled tempo.

Gong punctuation in the smaller ensembles, *calung* and *èbèg*, can vary from the standard heard in the large gamelan. Due to the fast sound decay of bamboo, the *calung* instrument said to function as *kethuk-kenong-kempul* may sound a dense part that, while still serving the function of punctuation, may actually omit the very beats that would normally constitute the *kenong* and *kempul* tones. I have often heard the following repeated pattern sounded between the beats where one would expect *kenong* or *kempul*: i̇ 6 i̇ 2 i̇ 6 i̇. Tone 2 represents the normal *kethuk* beat (and the normal *kethuk* tone, although in other cases tone 1 serves as the *kethuk* tone in *calung*). The alternation between i̇ and 6 is comparable to *engkuk-kemong* or the rarely heard *kemanak* (banana-shaped idiophones) of Solonese and Yogyanese traditions – while it provides a regular pattern of punctuation, the listener must, as it were, fill in the *kempul* and *kenong* tones himself. Other patterns I have heard include a straight two-tone ostinato (i̇.i̇6 i̇.i̇6 and so on) or a combination of *pancer* with *balungan* (e.g., i̇.i̇3 i̇.i̇2 i̇.i̇1 i̇.i̇6, for *balungan* 3 2 1 6). Preferences vary from group to group.

In the accompaniment of the hobby-horse trance dance (*èbèg*), pieces played with normal *lancaran* gong punctuation in other contexts are usually played with a special *èbèg* pattern.

```
kempul & gong:            P       P       P       G
                                                 ‾ ‾
   kenong:        6 3 6 . 6 3 6 . 6 3 6 .6.63 6 .

  balungan:       . 1 . 6 . 1 . 5 . 1 . 5 . 1 . 6
```
3.14   *Kenong* and *kempul* for *èbèg*

The *kempul* sounds on the *kenong* beats and the *kenong* plays between these beats a denser pattern, alternating between two tones, resembling the *calung* punctuation described above. The two-tone alternation and the syncopation leading towards the *gong* make this *kenong* part precisely the same as the *kemanak* playing in stately Yogyanese and Solonese court dance accompaniment (*srimpi* and *bedhaya*), but here it is found in the most rustic of genres. Occasionally one hears *lancaran* played on the larger gamelan in which the *kempul* and *kenong* imitate the *èbèg* treatment (*garapan èbèg*) – not in accompaniment of trance dancers, but merely recalling the excitement of an *èbèg* performance.

Bonang

One of the most characteristic sounds of the Banyumas style is the interlocking between the two *bonang* (*barung* and *panerus*). In the very fast introductory and concluding passages, without vocal parts, the two *bonang* play octaves in the same style as Yogyanese *gembyangan*. Both parts sound the same tone, (anticipating the prominent tones of the *balungan* melody), with *barung* sounding between the beats of the *balungan* and the *panerus* sounding between the beats of the *barung*. For the main section of most *lancaran* pieces, in which the tempo of the *balungan* has slowed and voices are heard, it is the *bonang barung* that takes the highest level of subdivision, still anticipating the prominent tones of the *balungan* melody – usually every second tone. The *panerus* takes the upper neighbor of the *barung* tone, sounding it three times, before descending to reiterate the *barung* tone together with the *saron*, as shown in Figure 3.15. This technique distributes the difficulties between the two *bonang*. The *barung* must play off-beat at what are sometimes rather fast tempi, but it simply reiterates the prominent *balungan* tone it anticipates. The *panerus* is on beat, but must play the neighbor tones for three beats before it joins the *saron* on the note the *barung* has been sounding. One encounters a variety of terms for this interlocking, even at the local SMKI conservatory. In senior recital papers the *bonang barung* part shown in Figure 3.15 can be called *gembyangan*, *imbal*, or *mipil*; the *panerus* part may, in addition to these three terms, also be labelled

```
              t     t  N  t     t  N
balungan:   .  1  .  6  .  1  .  5


bonang      6 . 6 . 6 . 6 . 5 . 5 . 5 . 5 .
 barung:    6̣  6̣  6̣  6̣  5̣  5̣  5̣  5̣


bonang      i̇  i̇  i̇  6  6  6  6  5
panerus:    1  1  1  6̣  6̣  6̣  6̣  5̣

   (or      i̇  5  i̇  6  6  3  6  5 )
            1  5̣  1  6̣  6̣  3̣  6̣  5̣
```

3.15 *Bonang* interlocking for Banyumas *lancaran*

ngentrungi or *ngentul*. The terms shared with, and presumably borrowed from, Surakarta (*gembyangan, imbal, mipil*) do not carry the same meaning in Banyumas as they do in Solo. Most telling is the labelling of lively interlocking playing in Banyumas as *mipil*, a term which in Solo refers to the most refined and subdued kind of *bonang* playing (see Sutton 1986b:91–96).

For *lancaran* that slow to a different *irama* level, the same technique is used, only with the *barung* sounding the same tone eight times instead of four and with the *panerus* playing neighbor tones for seven of its beats, joining the *balungan* when it reaches the prominent tone:

```
              t          t     N
balungan:   .        1  .     6

bonang      6 . 6 . 6 . 6 . 6 . 6 . 6 . 6 .
 barung:    6̣  6̣  6̣  6̣  6̣  6̣  6̣  6̣


bonang      i̇  i̇  i̇  i̇  i̇  i̇  i̇  6
panerus:    1  1  1  1  1  1  1  6̣
```

3.16 *Bonang* interlocking for Banyumas *lancaran* (expanded)

The style of *bonang* interlocking found in Banyumas *lancaran* is quite unlike that found in the *bonang* playing of Yogya and Solo. Nevertheless, it resembles the *imbal demung* technique used in Yogyanese *gendhing soran* with the instrument at the highest level of subdivision (off-beat) sounding the *balungan* tone, while the other member of the pair sounds a neighbor tone, usually upper neighbor, on the beats. I do not wish to suggest a direct link in this case, however, because we find a similar interlocking style in east Java as well. Rather, it seems to be a structure widely known in Java, but realized on different instruments in different regions.

For the few pieces in *ketawang* and *ladrang* form, a similar kind of interlocking is heard, but realized differently. In this case it is the *bonang panerus* which sounds the prominent tone on the off-beat, with the *barung* sounding neighbor tones and concluding by joining the *balungan* tone. Figure 3.17 shows an excerpt from the most popular Banyumas *ketawang*, *Gunung Sari* (often called *Gunungsari Kalibagoran*). This is the only Banyumas *bonang* technique that does not have both *bonang* playing in octaves; the *barung* plays tones one at a time, reminiscent of Solonese *pipilan* (literally, "pick off one at a time") and Yogyanese *mlaku* ("walking"), but its derivation in relation to the *balungan* is different.

```
                  t                P                t              N/G
balungan:     .   2        .       3        .      1        .      6

bonang
barung:    1  3  1  2    2  5  2  3    6̣  2  6̣  1    5̣  1  5̣  6̣

bonang     2 . 2 . 2 . 2 . 3 . 3 . 3 . 3 . i̇ . i̇ . i̇ . i̇ . 6 . 6 . 6 . 6 .
panerus:   2̣ 2̣ 2̣ 2̣ 3̣ 3̣ 3̣ 3̣ 1 1 1 1 6̣ 6̣ 6̣ 6̣
```

3.17   *Bonang* interlocking for Banyumas *ketawang* and *ladrang*

These distinctive *bonang* techniques are heard in Banyumas only in the basic repertory of pieces in regular forms. For the *wayang* pieces (Gendhing *Bondhèt* and all of the *gendhing lampah*) the *bonang* techniques associated with Yogya and Solo are used. An experienced listener might note that the nuances are different – in other words, that the playing is neither especially Solonese nor especially Yogyanese. Yet the application of these techniques with such strong associations and probable derivation from outside the region suggests that, though distinctive Banyumas versions have developed, these pieces are not thought to be as thoroughly indigenous as the *lancaran*. This may explain why both sources of notation mentioned above (Departemen PDK 1980 and Soebiyatno 1979) exclude the *wayang* pieces.

Calung

Although the *calung* can be seen as a substitute for the larger gamelan, the playing techniques do not simply duplicate those of the gamelan instruments. The use of bamboo, which has a very fast sound decay in comparison with metal, requires that the tones which are to be sustained must be reiterated in *calung* playing. Thus, for example, the *calung slenthem* normally sounds each *balungan* tone two, four, or eight times in succession, depending on the *irama* level. Rather than anticipate the *balungan*, it sounds with the beat and afterwards, in order to keep the tone sounding after the beat, just as it does in a metal gamelan. Sometimes for *gongan* in expanded *irama* levels, the *calung slenthem* plays in alternating anticipation, sounding what the *peking* would play in Solonese style.

A variety of techniques characterize playing on the two multi-octave *calung* (here *gambang barung* and *gambang panerus*). For the few Banyumas *ladrang* and *ketawang*, for pieces in the expanded *irama* levels, and for the pieces borrowed from the Yogyanese and Solonese repertories, the *gambang barung* plays like the Solonese and Yogyanese *gambang* – in the continuous, rapid succession of tones, mostly doubled at the octave (*banyumili*). The *gambang panerus* plays patterns in imitation of the *gendèr panerus*. While both parts are related to the *balungan* and to the vocal melody, they are not directly coordinated with one another. For the usual performance of Banyumas *lancaran*, however, the two *calung* play interlocking patterns which often resemble the *bonang* interlocking discussed above. The terminology for the interlocking techniques on *calung* is not standardized. At the local SMKI conservatory I encountered the same terms as used for Banyumas *bonang* playing, with the addition of one (*nglagu*).

Drumming

Banyumas musicians pride themselves on their lively drumming, related to Solonese *ciblon* or Yogyanese *batangan* playing, both in variety of timbres and in vocabulary of patterns, but with some uniquely local elements. Whereas the lively drumming in Solo and Yogya employs only the *ciblon* (middle sized drum), in Banyumas this drum is combined with the *ketipung*. Like the small *kulanter* drums in Sunda, the *ketipung* in Banyumas are usually placed standing on one head, allowing only the smaller head to be played. For especially small *ketipung*, it is the larger head that is struck. The high pitched one-finger stroke ("thung"), one finger rim-shot ("tong"), and the slap ("tak") sound noticeably higher in pitch on the *ketipung* than they do on the *ciblon*, yielding a wider variety of timbres than is available in Solonese or Yogyanese drumming.

The patterns played on the *ketipung* and *ciblon* in Banyumas derive from the dance of the *lènggèr* (singer–dancer), whom they often accompany. The *lènggèr* is the Banyumas counter-part to the singer–dancers known as *talèdhèk* in the areas of Yogya and Solo, and to the somewhat more refined, but still flirtatious, *gambyong* dancer of Solo. The *ciblon* drumming patterns used most often in Yogya and Solo essentially accompany the dancing of the *talèdhèk* or *gambyong* (a female dance derived from *talèdhèk* dancing, but in which the dancer does not sing). The process has been the same in all three regions whereby in concert situations with no dancer, the drummer, as it were, accompanies an imagined choreography.

Though drummers may exercise a measure of freedom, they share in common a basic vocabulary of patterns and several paradigms for the sequence of these patterns, coordinating with the dance choreography. One of the most common in Yogyanese and Solonese practice is the *ciblon* drumming for *ladrang* pieces in *irama* level III (= *irama wilet*), which follows essentially the same paradigm in all but the first, third, and final *gongan*.[10] In Banyumas style, no single paradigm prevails for a given formal structure. However, since most Banyumas pieces comprise short *gongan* (the eight or sixteen beats of *lancaran*), the drumming sequence usually fills several (two or four) *gongan* before repeating.

Though the arrangement of patterns within the framework of a *gendhing* is different in Banyumas than in Solo (or Yogya), some of the principles are the same. Each cycle is identified by a basic pattern, a *sekaran*, which is played in whole or in part before and after several boundary markers. And following a major boundary marker – called in Solonese tradition *ngaplak* (literally, "slap," "make the sound of the drumstroke *plak*" = tak), in Yogyanese tradition *nyamber* (literally, "swoop like a bird"), and in Banyumas *kèwèran* (literally, "dangling"), but sounding similar in the three styles – a new *sekaran* is played leading to the *gong* and then continued in the following *gongan*. It is also the practice in Banyumas as well as Solo and Yogya that the choice of *sekaran* alternates between *mlaku* ("moving") patterns (1st, 3rd, 5th, and so on) and *mandheg* ("stopping") patterns (2nd, 4th, 6th, and so on).

It cannot be readily shown in notation, but one of the essential elements in Banyumas drumming is its especially lively and even mischievous nature. While *ciblon* in Solo or Yogya can become fairly lively, it is still more subdued than some Banyumas drumming. And it is not just a few pieces for which such drumming is appropriate, but every piece. Even in the *wayang* pieces, though close in many ways to the *wayang* pieces in Yogya and Solo, the drumming strikes visitors familiar with *wayang* from the court areas as especially lively. Whereas the opening pieces in Yogya and Solo tend to present a calm mood, as befits *pathet nem*, in Banyumas even Gendhing *Bondhèt* is played with spirited drumming. The tempi in Banyumas are faster, as will be discussed below. The drummer may opt to play a few strokes much louder than the others, or otherwise surprise and delight the listener.

Drumming is one of the main elements that helps maintain the popularity of this tradition. In many of the newly composed pieces, drumming patterns are borrowed from the popular Sundanese social dance music (*jaipongan*) and from Indonesian popular music (*dangdut*). In Banyumas, more than any other central Javanese region, *kendhang* playing can become quite virtuosic, and the best drummers gain reputations and rather handsome recompense in comparison to all other musicians except the ever-essential vocalists.

Vocal parts

The basis of Banyumas music is vocal. Not only the new *lagu dolanan*, but all the older pieces, other than those of the *wayang* repertory, place clear emphasis on the vocal parts. Rasito points out that it is not unusual for two distinct pieces to share similar *balungan* and to be distinguished primarily by the vocal melody (e.g., *Béndrong Kulon*, *Yaksan*, and *Kunang Mabur*, all of which consist of two *gongan*, one with *gatra* ending on 5 and 6, the other with *gatra* ending on 6 and 5). Even the *gendhing lampah* are characterized by a variety of vocal phrases (known as *senggakan*) constructed in relation to the instrumental melody. Though Yogyanese and Solonese performance styles include *senggakan* in some pieces, they are only rarely heard in the *gendhing lampah* of either.

Good Banyumas vocal performance is generally described as *ramé*, a term indicating lots of activity, "busy" or "noisy" in a positive sense. *Senggakan* frequently enliven the Banyumas *gendhing* in regular forms, in addition to the *gendhing lampah*. Short cries or calls by the male singers (*alok*) are also prevalent in Banyumas performance, usually in an interlocking alternation reminiscent of some of the livelier forms of Sundanese music, such as *ketuk tilu* (literally "three *ketuk*" – a small ensemble genre featuring a singer–dancer) and the more recent *jaipongan*.

A number of features characterizing Banyumas vocal style are exhibited in the well-loved Lancaran *Grombol Kethèk*. Banyumas singing by a solo *pesindhèn* can at times be florid, but it more often involves reinforcement of the steady beat than is typical in the solo singing for Solonese or Yogyanese *gendhing*. For example, the part notated below, with regular durational values, is essentially what is realized in performance by a Banyumas *pesindhèn*. Though a slight rubato is not uncommon, it only involves a very subtle lagging behind the beat – in contrast to the seemingly free rhythm in other styles, in which the *pesindhèn* may reach the final tone of her phrase as much as three or four slow *balungan* beats after the end of the corresponding *balungan* phrase (see Sutton 1987:121–29).

Also notable is the slightly higher tessitura than is found elsewhere in Java. Banyumas vocal parts may emphasize high pitch 5, and some of the *sulukan* even touch on high pitch 6. Elsewhere in Java high pitch 5 appears only occasionally, as a neighbor tone, touched momentarily from high pitch 3 and never sustained. But in the last line of Lancaran *Grombol Kethèk*, for example, the *senggakan* climbs from high 2 to high 5, which is articulated on a strong beat and held before descending an entire octave to the gong tone middle 5.

Two basic varieties of text are used by the *pesindhèn* in most Banyumas *gendhing*: *wangsalan* and *parikan*. Both are usually interspersed in performance with *abon-abon* (interpolated words or short phrases) added by the solo vocalist as fillers that provide for a direct and often flirtatious communication between the singer and her male audience, for example "ya rama" (literally, "yes, mister"). The verse which appears in Figure 3.18 is one of many popular

```
balungan:    6       2       6       2       6       5       3       2
                     ___             ___                             __
pesindhèn: .  6 i 2   .   .  6 i 2   .   .   6   5   .  5 653   2
              Ya rama         Ya rama           Ja- nur  gu-   nung


balungan:    3       5       6       2       3       5       2       3
                                              ___
pesindhèn: .  .  .  6  6  6  6  . 66  2  i 2 6   6  165 3
              Ja- nur gu- nung saku-lon  ban-jar pa- to- man
senggakan: .  .  .  .  .  .  .  3  2  3  6  2  i  6  3
                               é  o  é  a  i  o  o  ing


balungan:    5       3       5       3       6       5       3       2
              ___             ___                  ___     ___
pesindhèn: .  2 5 3   .   .  2 5 3   .   .   6  i 2i6  3 5 3   2
              Ya rama        ya rama        ka- di-  nga-  rèn


balungan:    3       2       1       6       5       2       3       5G
                                              ___     ___
pesindhèn: .  .  .  2 2 2 2  . 2 2  2 3 i 2 6  5 6 3  5
              ka- di- nga-rèn wong ba-gus ga- sik te- ka- né
senggakan: .  .  .  2 2 3 5  . 3 2  6 i 6  .  5
              Du- a  lo- lo      lo-           ing
```

3.18   Vocal parts for Lancaran *Grombol Kethèk*

wangsalan that may be used in all but the few *pamijèn* pieces. Words in the first portion (here the first two lines) suggest a key word or two in the second (here the last two lines). "Janur gunung" is an expression of surprise, but its more literal meaning suggests the areca palm (*arèn*). *Janur* is the pale green leaf of a young coconut palm; *gunung* is "mountain." This phrase hints at the first word of the second portion (*kadingarèn*), also an expression of surprise ("isn't it strange," "what a surprise") whose last two syllables are the word *arèn*. "Sakulon Banjar patoman" translates as "west of the Banjar indigo plantation." To those familiar with the geography of western Central Java and neighboring Sunda, the area referred to is Tasikmalaya. In the *wangsalan* this suggests the word *gasik* (literally, "early"), which rhymes with Tasik. As in most *wangsalan*, the elements of the first portion are not connected, either by rhyme or by meaning. Rather they each suggest a part of the second portion, which coheres as a single sentence – in this case, "What a surprise, the good looking man has come early."

This and other popular Banyumas *wangsalan* are heard in many pieces, not just Lancaran *Grombol Kethèk*. The mood of most of the Banyumas *wangsalan* is light. Those from Solo and Yogya often tend to be didactic, with a moralistic message. Nowadays, Banyumas singers may use these more serious *wangsalan* in some Banyumas pieces, but the Banyumas *wangsalan* continue to be quite popular.

The other popular category of text is *parikan*, which involves rhymes and is considered less sophisticated than *wangsalan*, since no puzzle is presented. They are also more consistently humorous than *wangsalan*. In the performance of Lancaran *Grombol Kethèk*, the drummer usually signals a sudden halt to the instrumental playing midway through the third line – known as *andhegan* (literally, "stopping") in Yogya and Solo, and called *pedhotan* (literally "broken off," "interrupted") in Banyumas. The solo *pesindhèn* then sings a short *parikan* and is joined by the instrumentalists as she completes the rhyme. Several of the *parikan* are given below:

```
first half:   6     6     6     6   6 3 6   i   2   6   i 2
           a. Grom-bol ke- thèk manuk si-  ka- tan (ra- ma)
           b. Ma-  nuk sri- ti kecemplung ba- nyu (ra- ma)
           c. Ma- ngan ke- tan la-wu-hé  pe- da (ra- ma)


second half:  5     5     5     5   .   5   6   2   .   3   5   5
           a. E-  suk go- tèk       so- ré  pe-     ga-     tan.
           b. Mbe- ngi ngim- pi     a-  wan ke-     te-     mu.
           c. A-  rep pe- ga-       tan o-  ra      si-     da.


Translations:
           a. Group of monkeys, little brown wagtail bird
              Search in the morning, divorce in the afternoon.

           b. Little black swallow, falls into the water
              Dream at night, meet in the daytime.

           c. Eat sticky rice, with dried salty fish
              Going to divorce, but it didn't happen.
```

3.19   *Parikan* for *pedhotan* (*andhegan*) in Lancaran *Grombol Kethèk*

In Banyumas the second half of the *parikan* usually pokes fun at the tensions associated with sexual attraction. The first half sets up the rhyme, but may otherwise be unrelated or only indirectly related to the second half. The humor arises partly from the element of surprise in the leap from one topic in the first half to another in the second half. Also humorous is the blunt mention of topics such as divorce; and the bluntness is reinforced musically by singing in regular rhythm, in contrast to the unmeasured parlando style of most *andhegan* elsewhere in Java.

Several other musical characteristics distinguish some vocal parts in Banyumas. One is the imitation in the vocal contour of the composite pattern formed by the two *bonang* in Banyumas style interlocking. Approaching tone 6, for example, the usual *bonang* parts would sound as follows: 6 i 6 i 6 i 6 6. In many versions of Lancaran *Éling-éling*, one hears the *pesindhèn* sing the following:

```
balungan:     1     6     1     5     1     5     1     6G

pesindhèn:              2 5   5 5   6 5   6 5 6   i 6 i 6 6
                        É-ling é-ling sapa é-ling balia maring
```

3.20   Lancaran *Éling-éling*, excerpt

The melody for the last two words of the line ("balia maring") is identical to the composite *bonang* or *gambang* melody, with the upper neighbor tone (1) sounding on the beats in alternation with the main tone (6) in between the beats, until the last beat, where the main tone appears, rather than the upper neighbor.

Another important aspect of Banyumas vocal style is the use in some pieces of a vocal scale which departs from the instrumental (*sléndro*) scale. In many pieces the vocal part includes intermediary tones between tones 3 and 5 of the instrumental scale and between tones 1 and 2. Sometimes the intermediary tone may substitute as a flatted alternate (e.g., 3 – lowered 5 – 6), but it may also appear in a single passage with both surrounding tones (e.g., 3 – lowered 5 – 5). In Banyumas solo *tembang* (sung verse forms), such as *Pangkur* and *Asmaradana*, the scale is essentially a gapped pentatonic, with several alternate tones, often interpreted as a version of *pélog*. This is similar to the *miring* or *barang miring* scale in Solonese and Yogyanese vocal and *rebab* melodies, but is less independent of the *sléndro* scale. Some musicians characterize this Banyumas vocal scale as a combination of *sléndro* and *pélog*. Many of the tones coincide with tones of the instrumental *sléndro* scale. Yet this vocal scale is complicated by the use of high and low variants for several tones: those notated below in the *pélog* interpretation as 2 and 6. This scale resembles the *madenda* scale heard in Sundanese vocal and instrumental music (see Kunst 1973 1:64–66).

```
sléndro scale:        1      2    3      5      6      i    2    3

vocal scale:                 x    x  x (x)      x    x (x)    x    x  x
             or:       x      x    x (x)      x  x   (x)      x    x    x

pélog interpretation: 1      2    3  (4)      5    6 (7)    i    2  3
             or:  1      2    3  (4)      5    6   (7)    i    2    3

Western approximation: E      F#   G    A      B    c+ d      e    f# g
                       E      F+   G    A      B    c  d      e    f+ g
```

3.21   Vocal scale used in some Banyumas *tembang*, such as *Pangkur Banyumasan*

In performance, the vocalist may not always coincide exactly with the instrumental scale even on the more stable tones. Yet she (or he) is usually close enough for an instrumentalist, playing a *sléndro gendèr*, to anticipate and confirm pitches in the vocal melody as is usual in *tembang* singing in the context of a gamelan performance.

The repertory of Banyumas gamelan pieces includes several special pieces (*pamijèn*) characterized by extended passages of unaccompanied singing, often with male and female voices in alternation.[11] In *Kembang Lepang* (= *Kembang Glepang*), a *pesindhèn* sings an extended solo introduction in which a male comments, either in singing or speaking voice. Clearly influenced by the Javanese genres of Islamic singing accompanied by frame drums (*terbang*), such as *slawatan* and *jani-janèn*, is the unusual *Randha Nunut*, in which a female vocalist alternates with a male chorus (in Banyumas, usually the instrumentalists, rather than a separate *gérong* section). The singing is sometimes in parlando rhythm, but more often in steady durations, with little melodic motion – much like the style of singing in *slawatan*. The instrumentation for the accompanied portion is often sparse, with only drum and *gong* punctuation. If played at all, the *bonang* may simply execute an ostinato independent of the melody. While not an exact replication of *slawatan* accompaniment, the use of the gamelan for this piece is, I am told, intended to approximate it. A second section of the piece, with a *balungan* and full gamelan (or *calung*) instrumentation, conforms more closely to other

Banyumas *lancaran* style. Shown in Figure 3.22 is the first section, usually repeated four or five times, with a different text after the first line.

```
UNACCOMPANIED:
  parlando          6  i  2    6 3    5 6  53
   (female)         Randhané nu     nut

  parlando or steady  1  2  3  3    1   2  3  3
   (female)           o- ra nginang o-  ra ngemut

  steady rhythm     i  i  i  i    i   i  i  2
   (male or female) o- ra ngi-nang o-  ra nge- mut

  parlando          i  6  3  1    2   3  5  6
   (female)         Lam-bé- né  di- gru-mut se- mut

  steady rhythm     .  .  3  3   .  .  3  3   .  .  3  5  3  2  .  1G
   (male)                Lambé-       né di-       grumut   se-   mut


GAMELAN (or CALUNG) ACCOMPANIMENT (all singing in steady rhythm):

.    .   i   i   i   i   i   i   i   i   i   i   i   2   3   3
        Pin-dhang pin-dhang pi- thik bum- bu- né sar- wa  sa- thi-thik


2   2   2   2   2   2   2   2   i   i   6   6   5   3   5   6G
A-  ja  ngum-bar pra-wan ci- lik a-  kèh bu- jang pa- ting sli-dhik
```

Translation:

```
The widow (divorcée) follows along
Does not eat betel, does not look longingly (x2)
Ants are creeping up to her lips (x2)
Salty chicken dish, just a little bit of spice
Don't leave a little young maiden alone, lots of bachelors will investigate.
```

3.22 *Randha Nunut*, vocal part (excerpt)

The use of *parikan* gives the piece a humorous tone. Later verses talk of the widow/divorcée following various members of the gamelan, giving a humorous immediacy to the issue of sexual attraction. In the performance both of this piece and of *Kembang Glepang* (mentioned above), the unaccompanied portion may include overtly humorous spoken commentary between the lines of singing.

In general, the vocal part in Banyumas is not only the dominant part, but is the one which defines the piece. Through its textual and musical structure, the vocal part contributes to the lively and humorous nature that infuses so much of the Banyumas tradition. And with the trend towards emphasis on the human voice in gamelan music throughout Java in recent years, it is not surprising that some of these Banyumas pieces have become widely known and enjoyed outside their own area.

Tempo treatment

In the previous chapter we noted that Yogyanese style performance shows a preference for slower tempi than Solonese style. One of the distinguishing features of Banyumas style, contributing to its lively feel, is the use of especially fast tempi in some instruments. Comparison with Solonese and Yogyanese styles is somewhat problematic because in Banyumas some instruments may be playing at tempi comparable to or even slower than those in Solonese and Yogyanese style, while others are playing at twice that rate.[12] As in the discussion of tempo in the court-derived traditions, I refer to the tempo of the fastest pulse, represented by passages in the drumming. In Banyumas *calung* playing the composite pulse of the two interlocking *gambang* (*barung* on the beats, *panerus* between beats) is often extremely fast. In the larger gamelan the two *bonang* may produce a very fast pulse through interlocking. In the settled vocal sections, the two *bonang*, though still interlocking, are likely to play at only half the fastest pulse, which then manifests in the *celempung/siter* part. The tempo is often too fast for the one *gambang* in the larger gamelan to play the fastest pulse the way it does in Yogyanese and Solonese styles; instead it often sounds at only half this tempo. Figure 3.23 gives tempo readings for the popular Lancaran *Éling-éling* from four cassette recordings (two of *calung*, two of full gamelan).

Fastest Pulse		Type	Name	Source
1st Section (irama I)	2nd Section (Irama II)	of Ensemble	of Group	(Cassette Recording)
504–528	448	large gamelan	Purba Kencana (dir. by Rasito)	Blenderan Kusuma KGD–033
552	432	large gamelan	RRI Purwokerto (dir. by Hadisucipto)	Waru Dhoyong Lokananta ACD–160
552–576	416–432	calung	Budi Makarya (dir. by Madiyono)	Ebeg-ebegan Borobudur
592–608	504	calung	Sekar Budhaya (dir. Tawiasa)	Senggot Lokananta ACD–159

3.23   Banyumas tempi in four performances of Lancaran *Éling-éling*

It is not surprising that the fastest tempi are found in the *calung*, where the interlocking *gambang* can reach dizzying speeds. Playing fast off-beat is easier with light *gambang* beaters than with the heavier *bonang* beaters of the larger gamelan. It is also in *calung* playing that we find the greatest difference between the tempo of the opening instrumental section and the slower, settled section in which the *pesindhèn* sings. Still, even the slowest tempo shown is significantly faster than any of the tempi listed for the Solonese or Yogyanese pieces (in Figure 2.41). Tempo, then, is a significant factor in regional style, contributing in Banyumas music to the sense of *ramé* exuberance that makes this music so popular.

Banyumas tradition and regionalism

A distinctive Banyumas musical tradition would appear to be flourishing today throughout the region. Though the older repertory is quite small, numbering only fifty or sixty pieces, many new pieces are being added to the repertory by productive and talented young Banyumas composers. New *calung* groups abound, providing ample opportunity for residents of the region to hear the old and new Banyumas pieces. The top puppeteers and their gamelan musicians are kept busy to the point of near exhaustion with engagements during much of the year. The founding of a local performing arts conservatory (SMKI Banyumas), the publication of several books on Banyumas traditions, and the rapid growth of the local cassette industry have all combined to give Banyumas tradition a greater visibility and legitimacy in the world of Javanese music than it had known previously.

Yet, as I have pointed out from time to time in the preceding discussion, influences from "the east" (i.e., Yogya and Solo) abound. It would be unusual to attend any performance – other than *èbèg*, perhaps – in which no pieces from the Yogyanese or Solonese repertories were played.[13] An all-night performance of *lènggèr* with *calung* or *angklung* usually begins with an hour or more of "eastern" pieces. Only after the *lènggèr* appear in costume are the Banyumas pieces played. And for the remainder of the night the audience is treated not only to Banyumas pieces, but also to songs from popular Indonesian genres such as *dangdut* and "pop." In *wayang kulit*, many Banyumas groups use standard *wayang* pieces from Solonese and Yogyanese traditions (see Lysloff's transcription of "Srikandhi Mbarang Lènggèr" in Lysloff 1990). The recent publication on Banyumas *wayang*, whose stated purpose is to set guidelines for maintaining the distinguishing features of Banyumas *wayang* tradition, lists many Solonese pieces as the proper choice in Banyumas *wayang* performance (Sekretariat Nasional 1983:161–64). And, as we have seen, even the Banyumas versions of the *gendhing lampah* may bear close resemblance to those of Solo and Yogya. The Banyumas *gendhing* in regular forms are heard only during the lighter moments. In *jemblung* performance, despite its emphasis on humor and its close association with the Banyumas region, one is likely to hear more pieces from the Solonese repertory than from Banyumas.

If these musical genres are so heavily infused with music generally acknowledged to come from outside the Banyumas region, it might seem that a Banyumas tradition is eroding, rather than flourishing. But I would contend that no genre needs to isolate itself from other influences in order to maintain vitality. The Banyumas repertory, both old and new, continues to be performed. No musician I spoke to indicated that any major repertory item or performance style has fallen into disuse. Rather, the changes they speak of are the additions of pieces to the repertory, of *pathet nem* to the *wayang*, and of Indonesian popular songs to the *lènggèr-calung* performances.

I have taken the stance in this study, based on indigenous understanding, that Banyumas tradition consists of what is unique to Banyumas. Thus, a *calung* playing Ladrang *Pangkur* is a Banyumas rendition of something generally acknowledged as originating from outside the region – the instruments are indigenous to the region, the piece is not. If we take a different perspective, we might say performance tradition in Banyumas, based on current standards of performance, consists of pieces and playing techniques originating not only within the Banyumas region, but from the court areas to the east, from Sunda (especially the recent *jaipongan* influences), and from popular Indonesian national culture (pop, *dangdut*, and so on). We can see a parallel between musical taste and the complex conceptions of cultural identity characteristic of this region. The people of Banyumas are keenly aware of their particular regional identity as "*orang Banyumas*" (literally, Banyumas people), reflected in the local pieces and performance style. Yet they also view themselves as "central Javanese" and "Indonesian." Thus, they can play and enjoy a Solonese *gendhing* or an Indonesian *dangdut* song – not as exotic borrowings, but as forms of expression of their own cultural identity. And while *jaipongan* has become popular throughout much of Java, it finds a special niche in Banyumas, where the people's conception of local cultural identity is often defined as marginal – on the Sundanese edge of central Java (see Departemen PDK 1980:4).

Nevertheless, performances in Banyumas are distinctive. Despite extensive use of Solonese repertory in *wayang*, for example, the feeling from the lively opening scene is unmistakably Banyumasan. The propensity for humor and *ramé* is evident in all genres of traditional Banyumas performance that involve gamelan or related ensembles. It is a mark of the strength of Banyumas regional culture that the indigenous pieces and style thrive in the contemporary environment alongside pieces associated with more powerful centers of culture (the courts and the national capital). We have already seen some of the influences of the courts on local *wayang* repertory. The new compositions by Banyumas musicians also show influences from the highly regarded composer Ki Nartosabdho and from Indonesian popular music, but maintain distinctive features that ensure the continuity of an identifiable Banyumas tradition. As we will see in later chapters, Banyumas tradition has also exerted important influence outside the region, capturing the fancy of many central Javanese musicians, including Ki Nartosabdho himself.

4 *Partial survival of a tradition in north central Java: gamelan music of Semarang*

Semarang is a bustling port city, better known for its commerce and industry than for its performing arts. For many centuries Semarang has known traders from China and the Middle East. And during much of the colonial period, Semarang was the main center of Dutch government over Central Java. The city lies in the heart of the *Pasisir* region, which, as mentioned in the introduction, is seen as a more devoutly Islamic region than other parts of Java. In areas of Java where Islam is strong, arts with overt connections to Islamic religion, such as *slawatan*, are usually favored over those without these connections, such as gamelan or *wayang kulit*. Yet even in the smaller and more isolated *Pasisir* towns of Demak and Kudus, one finds *wayang kulit* and gamelan enjoyed by at least some segments of the population.[1] Semarang is a large and cosmopolitan city today, the third most populous in Java (after Jakarta and Surabaya), and supports a number of fine gamelan groups, along with several commercial *wayang orang* theaters. Semarang was the home of the famous drummer, composer, and puppeteer Ki Nartosabdho until his death in 1985 and is still the home of his famous gamelan group Condhong Raos (see Sutton and Choy 1986).

Today the gamelan music played in this city and the rural areas surrounding it is almost entirely of Solonese origin. Though both Semarang and Banyumas lie at some distance from the cultural center of Surakarta, musicians in Semarang see themselves more in the mainstream of central Javanese culture than those in Banyumas. Semarang is, in fact, nearer to Surakarta geographically, and it is the provincial capital of Central Java. More importantly, both Semarang and Surakarta are east of the *ngapak–mbandhèk* line, and share essentially the same language. It is difficult to determine to what extent Semarang has supported a distinctive regional tradition of gamelan music in the past. Influence from the Javanese heartland (especially Solo) may have been strong for centuries. Yet a small repertory of pieces and certain performance techniques identified as "Semarangan" survive today and suggest the existence of a more significant Semarang regional tradition in the past.

In contrast to the residents of Banyumas, who indicate a clear sense of regional identity, those I spoke with in Semarang, including a number of musicians, do not express any notion of distinctive regional identity other than as central Javanese. They distinguish themselves from the Solonese primarily as being less refined. Some mention the phrase "*gretak* Semarang," which translates literally as "Semarang snarl" and refers to the brusque manner characteristic of this port city. But they do not feel that this characteristic is reflected in the gamelan music or other performing arts associated with Semarang. Instead, it is the mix of cultures that is most often cited as characteristic of Semarang's gamelan music. In his introduction to W. S. Hardjo's study of Semarang vocal music, Iman Prakosa writes:

Semarang is a region or locale. . . whose population has always undergone change. From former times down to the present, this region has grown continuously with various kinds of inhabitants. They come

101

from various regions, both from within the country and from foreign lands. Semarang's society is, thus, a mixed society. Various styles/special traits of the population then mix and form a new style/trait – "mixed style/trait."

Semarang adalah salah satu daerah atau tempat yang dalam hal ini kepenghuniannya selalu mengalami perubahan. Pada setiap waktu, sejak dahulu sampai saat ini selalu berjalan terus, daerah ini selalu ditambah dengan berbagai warna penghuninya. Mereka datang dari berbagai daerah, baik dari dalam maupun dari luar negeri. Masyarakat Semarang adalah masyarakat campuran jadinya. Berbagai gaya/ ciri masyarakat penghuninya kemudian bercampur dan akan membentuk gaya/ciri yang baru ialah "gaya/ciri campuran."   (Iman Prakosa in Hardjo 1982:1)

This mixture is apparent in the several contrasting scalar orientations in Semarang vocal music and the special Semarang tempo treatment of standard central Javanese instrumental forms (*ladrang*, and so on), described below.

Instrumentation and tuning system

Gamelan musicians in the Semarang area play on gamelan of the standard Solonese type described in chapter 2. All of the gamelan I have seen in the Semarang area – at RRI, at the several *wayang orang* theaters, at government offices, and in private homes – conform to this standard, not only in pitch vocabulary, but even in the design of the wooden cases for the *saron*, *bonang*, and *gambang*. In fact, I am told, many of these gamelan were manufactured in the Surakarta region and brought to Semarang. Once famous as a center of *gong* making, Semarang now looks to the few makers in Surakarta for the best new instruments.[2] The only distinguishing feature of older Semarang gamelan, I am told, is the preference there for relatively small *gongs*. While in Yogya and Solo the pitch of the large *gongs* is almost always 5 or lower, a "*gong* Semarang" is tuned to pitch 6, the same pitch of the lowest *gong siyem* in some of the larger Yogyanese and Solonese ensembles. Yogyanese and Solonese tend to find this undesirable for *gendhing* that end on pitch 5 or 3, as it seems to suggest further tonal motion, ascending from the 5 or 3. (Use of gong 5 with a piece that ends on pitch 6 poses no problem, they say, since the low sound of the *gong* simply adds weight and finality to the final focused pitch in the melody.) Otherwise, the instrumentation does not contribute to a distinctive Semarang style.

Elsewhere on the north coast, in the area west of Semarang to around Pekalongan, one finds an ensemble known as gamelan *jengglong* (also known as gamelan *penthung*) used to accompany a version of *wayang kulit* known as *wayang jengglong*. The instrumentation suggests Sundanese/Cirebon influence, with a double-reed (*terompèt*) and several single-row gong chimes (*jengglong*), as well as two *kendhang*, two *bonang*, *gambang*, *saron barung*, *demung*, *gong*, *kempul*, *kenong*, and a large drum with tacked heads (*bedhug* or *jidhor*) (Soekarno 1979:3–4). This genre of *wayang* is a variant of *wayang purwa* (with stories from the Mahabharata and Ramayana) infused with important Islamic teachings (Soekarno 1979:1–2).

Tuning system and tuning

Semarang now shows no marked preference for one tuning system over the other in gamelan instruments. The gamelan ensembles I saw were all *sléndro-pélog* combinations; musicians play the Surakarta repertory, which requires both *sléndro* and *pélog*. Even the small repertory of Semarang *gendhing* includes pieces played in both tuning systems, though here *pélog* predominates. Kunst notes slight preference in Semarang for *pélog* ensembles in the early twentieth century, and a strong preference there for *pélog* in the vocal music (Kunst 1973: Appendix 58A and 58B).[3] Kunst posts a blend along the north coast of *pélog* from Cirebon and *sléndro* from Mataram influences (Kunst 1973 I:21). Yet it is curious that he notes of Semarang in particular that the *sléndro* ensembles were found mostly in "the larger places," and the *pélog* gamelans in the villages (Kunst 1973 II:554). It may be, then, that the area strongly favored *pélog* before influences from the south central Javanese heartland brought *sléndro*.

Semarang gamelan conform to Solonese standards not only in instrumentation, but also in tuning. That is, the fixed instrumental tuning does not present any marked deviation from the range of acceptable variants found in Surakarta. Yet the most distinctive feature of Semarang vocal music is the use of a seven-tone scale that approximates very closely the Western tempered scale. It is possible, before the heavy Solonese influence that has characterized gamelan musical development in Semarang for at least the last fifty years, that the seven tones of the *pélog* scale might have also approximated this Western tuning. During a visit to the region in 1974, I heard a small, itinerant *pélog* ensemble playing instruments which appeared to be quite old. The intervallic structure was close to that of a Western scale, starting with pitch 1 as mi (1=mi, 2=fa, 3=so, 4=la, 5=ti, 6=do, 7=re). In more standard *pélog*, the interval between 3 and 4 is greater than a whole tone, and others are less than a whole tone (2 to 3, 4 to 5, 6 to 7).

Though I speak of the Western tempered scale – and Javanese musicians speak of *laras* "*diatonis*" – it cannot be shown conclusively that the prevalence of this scale in Semarang is due to Western influence. Musicians both from Semarang and from elsewhere suggest that this scale is derived from the Arab presence in the region and that Semarang singing sounds like reading or reciting of the Koran (*ngaji*).[4] Such an opinion may be based more on the knowledge that Islam is relatively strong on the north coast, than on specific similarities in intervallic structure. Demonstration of Islamic connections can enhance status and legitimacy in contemporary Indonesia, particularly for arts that the more devout Muslims (*santri*) have generally condemned, such as *wayang kulit* and gamelan.

Chinese influence, on the other hand, is usually denied unless the evidence is overwhelming. No Javanese suggested Chinese influence in Semarang singing, but it seems possible. Not only has there been a strong Chinese presence in the region for many centuries, but the singing style itself incorporates intervals found also in Chinese singing, and can be seen to use a pentatonic core in some passages, with exchange tones. At any rate, Chinese intervals are much closer to those of the Western scale than those of Islamic Koranic recitation. The ways in which Semarang singing is incorporated into gamelan playing will be dealt with below.

Repertory

The extant Semarang repertory is so small that one hesitates to speak of a Semarang "tradition." It is my contention that such a tradition once existed, and that it has left us a few pieces, along with some special techniques of performance identified with the region. To these have been added a few recent pieces that combine Semarang vocal melodies with full gamelan ensemble. Some of these may also incorporate the special performance techniques which characterize the older repertory. Best known and most widely recognized as unique to Semarang are the *gendhing bonang* Semarangan: two large *gendhing* and seven *ladrang*, as listed below.

Formal Structure	Gendhing Title	Tuning System(s)	Pathet(s)
Gendhing, kethuk 2 kerep, minggah 4	Kutut Manggung	pélog	nem
Gendhing, kethuk 2 kerep, minggah 4	Jati Kendhang	pélog	nem
Ladrang	Agun-agun	pélog sléndro	barang manyura
"	Bima Kurda	pélog	lima
"	Babat Kenceng	pélog	barang
"	Cepaka Mulya	pélog	barang
"	Éling-éling	pélog	nem
"	Gonjang Pati	pélog sléndro	barang manyura
"	Kombang Mara	pélog	lima

Sources: commercial cassettes Lokananta ACD–049 and ACD–050, recorded in 1974, and dubs made in 1986 by Ponidi from archive reel-to-reel tapes at RRI Semarang dating from the early 1970s.

4.1   *Gendhing bonang* Semarangan

The predominance of *pélog* is clear, reminiscent of the Solonese *gendhing bonang* repertory, which consists of twenty-seven *gendhing* in *pélog* and only five or six in *sléndro*.[5] Although the Solonese *gendhing bonang* are all large *gendhing*, the Semarang *bonang* repertory consists mostly of *ladrang*. Still, it should be noted that these *ladrang* are often played in a very slow tempo and, like the Solonese *gendhing*, normally proceed through a transition and change in drumming and *balungan* styles (*mérong* and *minggah*).

Other pieces identified with Semarang involve vocal parts. One anonymous piece, *Dhendhang Semarangan*, employs a modified *ladrang* formal structure and combines the heptatonic singing (*diatonis* or *sléndro miring*) with a full *sléndro* instrumental ensemble. Though identified in the title as a Semarang piece, some musicians, including Ponidi, suggest that this piece derives from *kroncong* (an acculturated genre using Western instruments and scales).[6] Other *gendhing* are recent compositions by the director of the RRI Semarang studio gamelan musicians, Ponidi, who has lived in Semarang for over thirty years, but grew up in Solo and learned Solonese gamelan tradition first. (Because of Ki Nartosabdho's greater prominence as a composer and the knowledge that he resided in Semarang, these pieces are sometimes attributed to him.) The pieces incorporate traditional Semarang vocal melodies (*tembang macapat*) in several common central Javanese formal structures.

In Hardjo's brief study of Semarang solo vocal music, he identifies several versions of the

Formal Structure	Title	Tuning System	Pathet	Vocal Scale
(Ladrang)	Dhendhang Semarangan	sléndro	sanga	diatonis
Ladrang	Pangkur (Semarangan)	pélog	barang	6-tone pélog
Ladrang	Sinom (Semarangan)	sléndro	manyura	diatonis
Ketawang	Mijil (Semarangan)	pélog	nem	pélog
Lancaran	Asmaradana (Semarangan)	pélog	nem	7-tone pélog
Srepegan	Durma (Semarangan)	sléndro	manyura	sléndro

4.2   Semarang *gendhing* with vocal parts

following *macapat*: *Asmaradana* (2 *sléndro*, 1 *pélog*), *Sinom* (1 *sléndro*; 1 *sléndro miring*, also notated *diatonis*), *Pangkur* (1 *sléndro*, 1 *pélog*; notated in both *bem* and in *barang* scales), *Durma* (1 *sléndro*, 1 *pélog*), *Mijil* (1 *pélog*), *Kinanthi* (1 *sléndro*), and *Dhandhanggula* (two *sléndro miring*, both notated as *sléndro*, with slashes for non-instrumental tones, and as *diatonis*). Despite the fact that the heptatonic *diatonis* singing more closely resembles *pélog* than it does *sléndro*, Ponidi's Ladrang *Sinom*, like *Dhendhang Semarangan*, uses *sléndro* instruments, rather than *pélog*. The effect is less dissonant than one might imagine, since the vocal and instrumental scales meet on certain pitches (usually 6, with 2 and 3 very close). And it is easier for singers to maintain the *diatonis* scale with the contrastive *sléndro* than with *pélog*, which could very well draw the singer to modify the vocal scale to a seven-tone *pélog*. One also finds extensive use of contrasting vocal scales, such as *pélog*, with *sléndro* instrumental playing in Sundanese (and Cirebon) traditions.

Ponidi's other pieces match vocal and instrumental scale (*pélog* with *pélog*, *sléndro* with *sléndro*), though some *pélog* passages involve what would be unusual combinations in any other Javanese tradition – particularly the use of tones 7 and 1 in juxtaposition, also 3, 4, and 5.[7] Even the vocal melodies of the *pélog macapat* that Ponidi uses in his vocally-oriented *gendhing* are characterized by contours unique to Semarang tradition and often resemble closely the contours found in the *diatonis* melodies. Thus, although each of Ponidi's pieces is assigned to one of the six standard central Javanese *pathet*, it may involve pitch vocabulary or contours that are not found in the much larger repertories of other regions.

It seems likely that there has been some flexibility in the intervallic structure of the solo *macapat* such that a melody might be sung as *pélog* by some performers, as *diatonis* by others, and as a modified *sléndro* (*sléndro miring*) by still others. As will be shown below, certain characteristic contours are found in both the melodies now given as *pélog* (such as *Pangkur*) and those given as *diatonis* (*Sinom* and *Dhandhanggula*).

Ponidi's few pieces make use not only of the most popular Solonese and Yogyanese "small *gendhing*" forms (*ladrang*, *ketawang*, and *lancaran*), but also of the *gendhing lampah* form *srepegan*. According to A. Salim, who often performed for *wayang kulit* performances utilizing Semarang gamelan music, the repertory included a set of *sléndro gendhing wayang* (i.e., *gendhing lampah*) Semarangan. I was unable to obtain notation for these pieces, though I am told they are closely related to Solonese *ayak-ayakan*, *srepegan*, and *sampak* as we know them today. A. Salim also mentioned that the Semarang *wayang* performances usually began with Gendhing *Bondhèt* for the first major scene, the same piece used in Banyumas tradition in this context. Figure 4.3 gives a Semarang version of this dictated to Marc Perlman by A. Salim in 1986:

```
Buka:   5 5 3   5 6 5 3   2 1 2 6   3 2 3 5N/G

mérong:          t                    t          N
         2 2 . .   2 3 6 5   1 6 3 2   3 6 3 5
         2 1 2 1   2 1 6 5   1 6 3 2   3 6 3 5
         2 3 5 6   2 1 2 6   2 1 2 6   3 5 2 3
         .5.3.5.3  .56 5 3   2 1 2 6   3 2 3 5G

inggah:  t          t          t          t     N
         3 2 3 1   3 6 3 5   3 6 3 2   3 6 3 5
         3 2 3 1   3 6 3 5   3 6 3 2   3 6 3 5
         3 1 3 6   3 1 3 6   3 1 3 6   2 5 2 3
         2 5 2 6   2 5 2 3   2 1 2 6   3 2 3 5G
```

4.3   Gendhing *Bondhèt Semarangan, sléndro pathet nem* ("sepuluh"?)

Comparison of this version with those of Banyumas, Surakarta, and Yogyakarta (see Figure 3.10 in the previous chapter) reveals similarities at various levels, from *kenong* and *gong* tones to the identity of some corresponding *gatra* in the third and fourth *kenongan* of the *mérong*. Like the Yogyanese and Solonese versions, the *mérong* here is sixty-four beats. Yet, according to Ponidi, this used to be played at a very slow tempo, stretching the *kenongan* to the same length as is now found in Banyumas. The *inggah* section, even stripped of the *pancer* tones (3 in the first eleven *gatra* and the last, and 2 in the twelfth to fifteenth *gátra*), is markedly different from all the other regional versions, though it can be seen to follow the same overall contour.

Other pieces that were formerly part of the Semarang repertory may have shared titles with those of other traditions but been known in distinctive Semarangan versions. A. Salim recalled that during the 1920s a Semarang variant of Gendhing *Gambir Sawit* was played for female singer–dancers (he used the central Javanese term *talèdhèk*). Pigeaud mentions the use further west along the north coast of the following *pélog* pieces, without listing formal structure or *pathet*: *Gagah-Sétra, Génjong, Jemparing, Clunthang, Sumyar, Gunungsari,* and *Wani-wani* (Pigeaud 1938:107). Most of these titles are widely known elsewhere in Java.[8] Yet it should be noted that *Wani-wani* is apparently a favorite in Semarang, since Nartosabdho includes it on a tape devoted to pieces associated with Semarang, and his group performs it with Semarang style tempo changes (*Sarwa-sarwi Semarangan*, Fajar Cassette No. 980).

Pathet

Nowadays, the *pathet* categories for gamelan music in Semarang are identical to those of Surakarta. And it is quite possible that these categories have long been known in the region. In an interview with A. Salim, a senior musician from Semarang, in poor health during my interview (1983), I was told that *wayang kulit* in Semarang tradition began with the Semarang version of Gendhing *Bondhèt*, which used to be classified as *pathet sepuluh* (literally, "ten"). More recently it has been classified as *pathet nem*, and the progression of *pathet* in the *wayang* has been the same as that found elsewhere in central Java (*nem–sanga–manyura*). Though it is otherwise unknown in central Java, *pathet sepuluh* is one of the three main *sléndro pathet* in the east Javanese tradition of the Surabaya-Mojokerto-Malang triangle.

All three *pélog pathet* are represented in Semarang. Outside of *wayang*, one does not find any Semarang pieces designated *sléndro pathet nem*, and only *Dhendhang Semarangan* as *pathet sanga*. The absence of *nem* and the emphasis on *manyura* recalls the pattern of distribution in Banyumas prior to the recent reassignment there of some pieces as *sléndro pathet nem*. Indeed, the evidence from Semarang and Banyumas suggests that *pathet* categories may have been applied only recently to non-*wayang sléndro* repertory in areas far from the courts.

Semarang *gendhing* and the Solonese and Yogyanese repertories

Most of the Semarang titles are known also in Solonese and Yogyanese tradition, but the Semarang versions have distinctive *balungan* as well as treatment. The two titles *Cepaka Mulya* and *Gonjang Pati* are not found in any repertory lists of Solo or Yogya. The title *Jati Kendhang* suggests relationship with the *gendhing* entitled *Jati Kondhang*, yet while the Solonese and Yogyanese versions of this piece are similar to one another, neither bears any likeness to the Semarang *Jati Kendhang*. The six other pieces are related in varying degrees to the Solonese and Yogyanese pieces whose titles they share in common.

The Semarang version of Gendhing *Kutut Manggung* follows very closely the contour of the more widely known central Javanese versions (Yogyanese and Solonese), though the latter are normally played in either *sléndro pathet manyura* or *pélog pathet barang*. And while the *inggah* section of the other versions is usually a *ladrang*, in the Semarang version it is the larger *kethuk* 4 form, with a *pancer* 1 on all the weak beats. Figure 4.4 gives the Semarang version, with a Solonese version in *sléndro*. (In *pélog pathet barang*, pitch 7 would replace pitch 1.)

```
       SEMARANGAN VERSION                    SOLONESE VERSION

mérong:                              mérong:
       t               t        N           t              t        N
 2 1 2 1   2 1 2 3   5 6 5 3   5 3 2 1      . . 1 .   1 1 2 3   5 6 5 3   2 1 2 1
 2 1 2 1   2 1 2 3   5 6 5 3   5 3 2 1      . . 1 .   1 1 2 3   5 6 5 3   2 1 2 1
 . 3 . 2   . 1 . 6   . 2 . 1   . 5 . 3     3 2 1 2   . 1 2 6   3 5 6 1   6 5 2 3
 . 1 . 6   . 2 . 1* 6 5 3 .   3 5 6 1G     2 1 2 .   2 1 6 5   3 3 . 5   6 1 2 1

to proceed to inggah, substitute:   inggah ladrang:
                *5 6 5 3   5 2 5 1G        t   (P)  t   N   t   P   t   N
inggah:                                   3 2 5 3   6 2 6 1   3 2 5 3   6 2 6 1
       t       t       t       t    N     3 2 1 6   5 1 5 6   3 2 5 3   6 2 6 1G
 5 2 5 1   5 6 5 3   5 6 5 3   5 2 5 1
 5 2 5 1   5 6 5 3   5 6 5 3   5 2 5 1     an expanded version of the ladrang
 5 3 5 2   5 1 5 6   5 2 5 1   5 6 5 3       (played only in irama III & IV):
 5 1 5 6   5 2 5 1   5 6 5 3   5 2 5 1G         t          (P)       t        N
                                          3 6 3 2   5 6 5 3   6 1 3 2   6 3 2 1
(Semarang version, transcribed           3 6 3 2   5 6 5 3   6 1 3 2   6 3 2 1
   from Lokananta cassette ACD-050)       3 6 3 2   6 3 5 6   3 5 6 1   6 5 1 6
                                          3 2 3 2   5 6 5 3   6 1 3 2   6 3 2 1G

(Solonese version, based on               (a rarely played inggah kethuk 4:
  notation from Suhardi,                        t        t        t        N
  and Mloyowidodo 1976I:131)               . 2 . 1   . 2 . 3   . 5 . 3   . 2 . 1
                                           . 2 . 1   . 2 . 3   . 5 . 3   . 2 . 1
                                           . 3 . 2   . 1 . 6   . 2 . 1   . 5 . 3
                                           . 2 . 1   . 6 . 5   . 6 . 5   . 2 . 1G)
```

4.4   Semarang and Solonese versions of Gendhing *Kutut Manggung*

Though these are closely related structurally, the Semarang version is purely instrumental, whereas the Solonese (and Yogyanese) versions feature the solo *pesindhèn* and the soft instruments.

The Semarang version of Ladrang *Bima Kurda* gives a very different impression than either the Yogyanese or Solonese versions (see Figure 2.12). Yet it bears a general resemblance, particularly to the Solonese version, only transposed such that the prominent tones of the Solonese version – 5, 7, and 2 – become 1, 3, and 5 in the Semarang version. As in the Solonese version, each of the three *gongan* is played twice before the whole cycle is repeated.

```
SEMARANG VERSION (pélog pt. lima)        SOLONESE VERSION (pélog pt. barang)


   t  P   t  N                              t  (P)  t  N
  2 1 2 1  2 5 6 1                          . . . 5  . 2 3 5
  2 1 2 1  2 5 6 1      (x2)                . . . 5  . 2 3 5      (x2)
  2 1 2 1  2 5 6 1                          . . . 5  . 2 3 5
  5 6 1 2  5 3 2 1G                         . 3 5 .  6 7 6 5G

  3 3 . .  1 2 3 2                          . 7 7 .  7 6 5 6
  3 1 2 .  3 2 1 2      (x2)                5 6 7 .  7 6 5 6      (x2)
  3 1 2 .  3 2 1 2                          5 6 7 .  7 6 5 6
  . 1 6 .  5 6 2 1G                         . 5 3 .  2 3 6 5G

  5 5 . .  1 6 5 3                          . 2 2 .  2 3 2 7
  2 3 5 .  1 6 5 3      (x2)                6 7 2 .  2 3 2 7      (x2)
  2 3 5 .  1 6 5 3                          6 7 3 2  . 7 5 6
  . 2 1 .  5 6 2 1G                         . 5 3 .  2 3 6 5G
```

4.5   Semarang and Solonese Versions of Ladrang *Bima Kurda*

Also preserved is the characteristic rhythm in the penultimate *gatra* of the *gongan* (. x y .). Though not a *gendhing bonang* in Solonese tradition, it is framed there by a loud-playing *lancaran* (*Singa Nebah*). In Yogyanese tradition it is one of the favorite loud-playing pieces, used to accompany the martial *lawung* dance.

The other *gendhing bonang* only bear slight resemblance to the *gendhing* in Solonese and Yogyanese tradition with the same titles. *Kombang Mara* in Solonese tradition is a long and stately "large" *gendhing*, played only in soft style. Its emphasis on pitches 1 and 5, its use of 4 and 3 in complementary distribution, and its classification as *pathet lima* are the only features it shares with the Semarang version. The other pieces share formal structure (*ladrang*), occasional passages of *balungan* and some *gong* or *kenong* tones. Otherwise they are distinctive items of repertory.

Semarangan musical style

Though the extant repertory is small, performance style in Semarang gamelan music is distinctive in a number of ways. Associated with the *gendhing bonang* Semarangan are special techniques for playing *bonang*, special drumming patterns, and special tempo treatment. These are sometimes employed in other pieces, such as Ponidi's Ladrang *Pangkur*, or in pieces not exclusively associated with Semarang, such as Ladrang *Gégot* and Ladrang *Wani-wani*. The vocal style associated with Semarang, as mentioned above, is the use of the *diatonis* or *sléndro miring* scale. The way this scale fits with *sléndro* instrumental playing and the contours that characterize Semarang singing both in *diatonis* and in *pélog* will be elaborated below, following the coverage of instrumental style.

Gong punctuation

Though the standard forms of the other central Javanese traditions are used in Semarang, the *kempul* in Semarang style *ladrang* (and Ponidi's Ketawang *Mijil*) is played in the middle of each *kenongan*, including the first. In Yogyanese- and Solonese-style *ladrang* and in Solonese-style *ketawang*, the *kempul* is silent in the first *kenong*. The "rest" (*wela*) is maintained in Ponidi's *lancaran* (no *kempul* between *gong* and first *kenong*). In some versions of *Dhendhang Semarangan*, the small *gong* (*siyem*) plays every other beat in the first half of the first two *kenongan*:

```
Vocal introduction (from Dhandhanggula Semarangan):    ...2N/G

        S   S   S   S                         N
     [: 5 2 5 2  5 6 1 2*  (stop, vocal solo)... 2S

        S   S   S   P         t       N
     5 2 5 2  5 5 6 1  2 1 6 5  2 3 5 6

          t       P       t       N
     2 1 2 6  2 1 6 5  3 2 3 2  3 5 6 5
     . 2 2 .  2 5 2 3  . 6 . 5  6 5 3 2G :]
```

              (from Lokananta cassette Rujak Sentul, ACD-058)
4.6   *Dhendhang Semarangan, sléndro pathet sanga, balungan* and gong punctuation

Otherwise the gong punctuation in Semarang is identical to that found in the court-derived traditions of central Java.

Balungan

While one finds considerable variety in the *balungan* of the few Semarang *gendhing*, several features can be distinguished. The *gendhing bonang* are all characterized by the playing of two sections, very closely related melodically, but not identical. Drumming and *bonang* styles change as one makes the transition from one section to the other. Though a variety of rhythmic configurations are possible in the *balungan* during the first section, the *balungan* rhythm in the second section is a regular four tones per *gatra*. In five of the nine *gendhing* the second section adopts a *pancer* orientation, sounding the same tone on all the weak beats. The contrast between the two sections in two *gendhing* is given in Figure 4.7.

A second feature to be noted is the use in some pieces of six or even seven *pélog* tones and, in several of Ponidi's pieces, unusual juxtapositions of tones. *Gendhing* with six or seven *pélog* tones are found in the Solonese and Yogyanese repertories as well, but in Semarang appear to be somewhat more prominent. In the seven traditional *gendhing bonang* of Semarang, all of which can be played in *pélog*, three have six *pélog* tones and one has seven. In Ponidi's Ladrang *Pangkur*, we find the highly unusual *gatra* 7176 and 1765; tones 7 and 1 are usually in complementary distribution and would not appear in the same passage. His Ketawang *Mijil Semarangan* contains the unusual .234 1232, and in his Lancaran *Asmaradana* the unusual

```
            FIRST SECTION                      SECOND SECTION

Ladrang Gonjang Pati, sléndro pathet manyura:

      t       t  N                       t       t  N
    . 1 . 6  . 1 . 6                   5 1 5 6  5 1 5 6
    . 1 . 6  . 5 . 3                   5 1 5 6  5 1 5 6    (Pancer 5)
    6 1 3 2  6 5 2 3                   5 6 5 2  5 6 5 3
    6 5 3 2  . 1 . 6G                  5 6 5 2  5 1 5 6G


Ladrang Kombang Mara, pélog pathet lima (excerpt):

      t       t  N                       t       t  N
    5 5 . .  4 4 2 5                   5 5 6 5  4 4 2 5
    . . 1 6  5 4 2 5                   6 5 1 6  5 4 2 5    (Non-pancer)
    . . 1 6  5 4 2 5                   6 5 1 6  5 4 2 1
    6 1 2 3  5 3 2 1G                  6 1 2 3  5 3 2 1G
```

4.7   First and second sections in two Semarang *gendhing*

passage ..6. 5.4. 2124 5321G. These contours break with the norms of instrumental melodic structure in Yogyanese and Solonese traditions and are most likely related to the Semarang vocal style.

Bonang

Two orientations are found in Semarang *bonang* playing, contributing to the contrast between the two sections in the *gendhing bonang*. In the first section, *bonang* playing involves two techniques frequently used in Solonese and Yogyanese traditions: *mipil* (or walking) and *nduduk gembyang* (octaves, usually combined with reiterated single tones). Sometimes both *bonang barung* and *panerus* play *mipil*, as they do in Solonese and Yogyanese style. But more often the *barung* plays *nduduk gembyang*, while the *panerus* plays *mipil*. In the slow, settled tempo characteristic of the first section of *gendhing bonang* Semarangan, the *bonang* play to each tone of the *balungan*, not just to the strong beats. The *panerus* makes a *mipil* alternation between each tone and the upper neighbor, as shown in Figure 4.8.

```
                                    t                         N
balungan:                6         5           2          3

bonang          6. 6 . .    5 . 5 . .    2 . 2 . .    3 . 3 . .
  barung       6 6̣ 6̣  6 6̣    5̣ 5̣ 5̣  5 5̣    2̣ 2̣ 2̣  2 2̣   3̣ 3̣ 3̣  3̣ 3̣

bonang     .6̇1̇.1̇6̇1̇.1̇6̇1̇.1̇6̇1̇..56.656.656.656..23.323.323.323..35.535.535.535.
panerus
```

(based on notation furnished by Djoko Soejono)

4.8   *Bonang* playing in Ladrang *Gonjang Pati*, excerpt of first section

Variations on this basic paradigm include the substitution of lower neighbor tones in the *panerus* part, the use of a sparser *barung* part, sounding octaves on the second and fifth subdivision, as in Figure 4.9. In some cases the octave playing may lead to every second tone, rather than to every tone, particularly when the *balungan* is played at a faster tempo. In the *mérong* of the two large *gendhing* (*Kutut Manggung* and *Jati Kendhang*), the *bonang* play in normal Solonese style – *mipil* for *gatra* with four *balungan* tones (*balungan mlaku*), and

```
balungan                    7               5              7           6

bonang     . 7 . . 7 . . . . 5 . . 5 . . . . 7 . . 7 . . . . 6 . . 6 . . .
barung       7   7         5   5         7   7         6   6

bonang
panerus    272.272.272.272.653.653.6535653..72.272.272.272.767.765.76575676
```

(transcribed from Lokananta cassette ACD-049)

4.9   *Bonang* playing in Ladrang *Cepaka Mulya*, excerpt of first section

both play *nduduk gembyang* for sustained tones (*gantungan*) or *gatra* with two *balungan* (*nibani*).

In the second section, regardless of the formal structure, the *bonang* play an interlocking pattern unique to Semarang. The pitch choice in the *bonang* parts is here determined only by the tones on the strong (i.e., even) beats of the *balungan*. The *barung* sounds the stressed tones (those sounded on the strong/even beats) between the *balungan* beats, and the *barung* sounds the upper neighbor of these stressed tones between the *barung* beats and the *balungan* beats. On the weaker *balungan* beat, in slower tempi, the *panerus* may also play a tone two steps above the stressed tone, shown in parentheses in Figure 4.10.

```
balungan        1       3       1       5P      1       2       1       6N

bonang      3 . 3 . 5 . 5 . 2 . 2 . 6 . 6 .
barung      3   3   5   5   2   2   6   6

bonang      5 . 5(6)5 . 5 . 6 . 6(1)6 . 6 . 3 . 3(5)3 . 3 . 1 . 1(2)1 . 1 .
panerus     5   5(6)5   5   6   6(1)6   6   3   3(5)3   3   1   1(2)1   1
```

4.10   *Bonang* playing in Ladrang *Éling-éling Semarangan*, *pélog pathet lima*, second section

In most Javanese gamelan playing, the *bonang* part maintains a more or less constant tempo, changing its density in relation to changes in the tempo of the *balungan*. However, the *bonang–balungan* relationship in Semarang style remains constant, regardless of tempo. This means that at slow tempo (*irama* II) the *bonang* playing is relatively sparse, but at fast tempo (*irama* I) it can be dazzlingly fast. (See further the discussion of tempo and treatment below.)

Peking

It is curious that, despite Semarang's greater proximity to Solo, the Semarang style for *peking* playing is essentially the same as in Yogyanese tradition. Regardless of the *irama* level, the *peking* anticipates the tones of the *balungan*, rather than echoing them or oscillating back and forth between two successive *balungan* tones (as in Solonese tradition). And the *peking* plays in both sections at a constant ratio with the *balungan* beats (2 per *balungan* beat), regardless of the tempo or the *irama* level, like the *bonang* in the second section. Though several styles of *peking* playing are currently associated with Yogyanese style, the older palace musicians in particular tend to identify the simple anticipation and maintenance of the constant 2:1 ratio with the *balungan* as the most "authentic" Yogyanese *peking* style. And this is precisely the style used in the Semarang *gendhing*.

Drumming

Semarang-style drumming contributes much to the special flavor of Semarang *gendhing*. Not only are the standard patterns for the large *gendhing* and the *ladrang* easily distinguished from those of Yogyakarta and Surakarta, but the drummer in Semarang style is likely to use a beater to strike the large head of the large drum. As in Yogyanese and Solonese tradition, the *gendhing bonang* never involve the *ciblon* drum. Yet in Semarang, a single drummer plays the large and small drums not only in *ladrang*, but also in the second section (*inggah*) of the large *gendhing*. Only in the first section (*mérong*) of the large *gendhing* is the drum pattern restricted to the large drum. For Ponidi's vocal pieces in other forms (*ketawang*, *lancaran*, *srepegan*) standard Solonese drumming style is chosen, as no Semarang version for these forms is known today.

What strikes most listeners in comparing Semarang drumming style to that of other traditions is the extensive use of the drum stroke "dhung" and, particularly in the first section, the high density of drum strokes. Compare, for example, the drum patterns for the slow, settled tempo in the first and second sections of *ladrang* in Semarang style with that of the slow, settled tempo *ladrang* in Solonese style, shown in Figure 4.11. The softer strokes ("ket," "tok") used by the drummer to keep time and mark subdivision are not considered to be part of the pattern and are usually not notated. The pattern for the second section in Semarang *ladrang* is clearly less dense than for the first, since it is essentially the same pattern that is played at fast as well as slow tempi, but the emphasis on the *dhung* stroke is still apparent. No less apparent is the contrast with the Solonese pattern. Javanese musicians, it should be noted, sense an underlying relationship between the Solonese and Semarang patterns by nature of the strokes heard at important structural points (*kethuk*, *kempul*, *kenong*). Yet even here, there is considerable contrast. For the sixteen such points in a *gongan* of *ladrang* form, the Solonese pattern shares ten strokes with the Semarang first section and eight strokes with the second section.

Solonese *ladrang* do not consist of two contrasting repeated sections the way Semarang *ladrang* do. A Solonese *ladrang* may change *irama* levels and undergo a shift from "two-drum" style to *ciblon* drumming, but does not move irrevocably from a first section to a second section. In Solonese and Yogyanese traditions, it is only the larger *gendhing* which progress from a repeatable first section (*mérong*) to a repeatable second section (*inggah/dhawah*). In some cases, however, a *ladrang* in Semarang style may open with a few *gongan* played fast, rather than settling immediately to the slow tempo. The drumming used for the fast *gongan* is that which I am calling "second section" drumming. Examples of these fast beginnings can be heard in Ladrang *Cepaka Mulya*, Ladrang *Kombang Mara* and Ladrang *Bima Kurda* (on Lokananta cassette ACD–049).

For the first section (*mérong*) in the two large *gendhing*, the Semarang drum pattern is like the Solonese or Yogyanese both in its sparseness and, for the first and fourth *kenongan*, in the actual sequence of strokes, as shown in Figure 4.12. Does the Semarang version represent a relatively recent variation of the Solonese or Yogyanese versions introduced into the region and altered by Semarang gamelan musicians? Or have all three versions developed from older

SOLONESE STYLE: (Martopangrawit 1972b:31)

(irama II/dadi):
```
                     t                    (P)                        t                      N
. . . . . . . . . . . . . . . . . d  . d . . D d . D . . . . . . . . . .

. . . d . . . d . . d D . . D d . . . . . . . . d . D . . . d . D

. d . D . . . d . . d D . . . T . d . d . d . D . d . . d D . d

. . d D . d D . d D d . D . d D . . . . . . . . d . . d D . d . D
```

SEMARANG STYLE: (Transcribed from Lokananta cassette ACD–050 by the author)

1st section (irama III/wilet):
```
          _____ t                    ___ P ___          _____ t            ___ N
                                     ‾‾‾                                    ‾‾
. . . dD ddd d dD . . . . . d .d. dd  ddd d dd dddd  dD ddd d dD . . . . . d .d. dd  dd

_____ _____
dd dd dd dd  dD ddd d dD . . . . . d .d. dd  ddd d dd dddd D . . dD d .d. d D . dd.dD .d. d dd D

___ _____
dD d D  d  D  dD ddd d dD . . . . . d .d. dd  ddd d dd dddd dd  dD ddd d dD . . . . . d .d. dd d

_____ ___ ‾‾‾              ‾‾‾  _____  _____    ‾‾‾ ‾‾‾‾‾ ‾‾‾‾
dd dd dd dd D . . . dD d .d. d  D . dd.dD .d. ddd d D . d .d. d dd.d. d .d.dD  .dd ddd ddd dD.D.d.dd d .dd D d .
```

2nd section (irama II/dadi and I/tanggung):
```
            t                        P                        t                      N
. . . d . d . D . . . d . d dd . d . . d . d . D . . . d . dd .

d . . d . d . D . . . d . d dd . d . dD . . . d . D .‾d. d ddd D

. dD . dD . dD . dD . D . d dd . d . d . D . . . d d d Dd

dd D dd d D d d d d .‾dd d dD . dD . dD d . D . dD . D . .
```

D = Ɗ = "dhang" ("bem"); d = ɖ = "dhung"; T = "tak";
. . . . = one gatra (four balungan beats)
⌣ = triplet subdivision

4.11 *Ladrang* drum patterns in Semarang and Solonese styles

drum patterns, practiced prior to the division of Mataram in 1755? We know of an influx of Solonese musical influence in Semarang during the 1920s and 1930s, but the *gendhing bonang* Semarangan are said to have existed well before then (A. Salim, personal communication 1983; and Ponidi, personal communication, 1983 and 1986).

Little is known about the former contexts of performance of the *gendhing bonang* Semarangan. In Solonese tradition the *gendhing bonang* never accompany dance, nor do they in Semarang, at least in recent memory. In fact, the only mention of anything relating to a Semarang tradition in dance was A. Salim's comment about a Semarang version of Gendhing *Gambir Sawit*, which accompanied the singer–dancers (*talèdhèk*) in the 1920s. It is curious, nevertheless, that immediately following the last *kempul* beat in the Semarang *ladrang*, first

```
       KETHUK 2 KEREP SEMARANGAN              KETHUK 2 KEREP, PELOG (SOLONESE)
        (transcribed from Lokananta                (from Martopangrawit 1972b:50)
             cassette ACD-050)
mérong:                                      mérong:
        t           t       N                       t         :   t       N
  . . . D . . . . . d . D . . . d              . . . D . . . T . d . D . . . d

  . . . D . . . . . d . D . . . T̄d            . . . d . . . D ⌐. . . . d . . D

  d d d D . . . d . . . d . . . D              . . . D . . . d . . d . . d . .

  d D d D . d . D . d . . D d . .              . d . . . . d . D . d . . D d . .


                     SARAYUDA (YOGYANESE)
                      (from Susilo 1967:270)
        dados (mérong):
                    t               t       N
             . d . D . . . T D d . D . . . d

             . . . d . d . D . . . T d . . D

             . d . D . . . T D d . D d . D d

             d . d . . D . D . d . T D o o͞D.


D = "dhang" ("bem"); d = "dhung"; T = "tak"
. . . . = one gatra
```

4.12   Drum patterns for first section (*mérong*) in large *gendhing* (with 64 beats per gong), Semarang, Surakarta, and Yogyakarta versions

section, leading up to the gong stroke, the drummer plays a triplet pattern. This is precisely where Solonese and Yogyanese *ciblon* drumming often plays the triplet *ngaplak* pattern (in Yogya, often called *nyamber* – literally, "swoop"), corresponding to the dance pattern *trisig* (= *nyamber*), in which the dancer moves briskly on tiptoe. Not only is this pattern used in dance dramas for the "flying" of birds and supernatural characters able to fly, but it also serves as a transitional marker, separating one repeatable movement from the next. Whether or not the entire *ladrang* pattern in Semarang style derives from dance accompaniment, it seems likely that the approach to the *gong*, at least indirectly, shows the influence of dance drumming.

Current performance of *Dhendhang Semarangan*, which appears to be more popular outside Semarang than the *gendhing bonang*, requires *ciblon* accompaniment throughout. The versions I have heard have consisted of standard Solonese-style *ciblon* patterns. In this case, it is the vocal style that distinguishes the piece from other light, vocally oriented *gendhing* (especially *jineman*) in the Solonese repertory.

Vocal style

One cannot discuss Semarang repertory, tuning, or *pathet* without addressing certain aspects of the vocal style, as I have above. Here we can investigate in more detail both the coordination between vocal and instrumental scales and the vocal melodic contours that are unmistakably "Semarangan."

In *Dhendhang Semarangan* and Ponidi's Ladrang *Sinom*, the *diatonis* or *sléndro miring* vocal part is sung with *sléndro* instrumental parts. In Figure 4.14 is given the first of three *gongan* in Ladrang *Sinom*, transcribed from an archive recording from RRI Semarang. Notation of these pieces presents some problems because of the use of two different scale systems. Cipher notation for *sléndro* or *pélog* in Java is based on instruments, which usually have pitch 6 around A or B-flat. The use of cipher notation in Java for Western tunes and for *diatonis* Javanese tunes, however, is not necessarily intended to suggest pitch level. Rather, like ciphers and *solfège* in the West, the Javanese *diatonis* notation presents intervallic relationships. Yet while we expect a piece to end on a tonic (1, or "do"), Javanese melodies, including the Semarang *diatonis* melodies, do not. In the two versions of *diatonis* notation for the Sinom vocal melody available to me (Hardjo 1982:13 and a manuscript from Ponidi), different choices are made with respect to the pitch level of tone 1. In Hardjo's version, tone 1 sounds to Western ears like the "do," although the tune then ends on "so" (5), which corresponds (or nearly does) with instrumental tone 2. Ponidi's version attempts to show more readily the relationship with the *sléndro* instrumental scale, which intersect at *sléndro* 6 and, very nearly, at *sléndro* 2 and 3. The alignment of the *diatonis* scales with an equidistant *sléndro* are shown in Figure 4.13. The actual *sléndro* intervals will vary slightly from one ensemble to another; and it is quite possible that the vocal *diatonis* scale is modified slightly to fit with the particular ensemble being used.

Hardjo's diatonis:

3....4.........5.........6.........7....1.........2.........3....4.........5̇

Ponidi's diatonis:

7̣....1.........2.........3.........4....5.........6.........7....1̇.........2̇

sléndro:

..1..........2..........3..........5..........6..........1̇..........2̇.

4.13   Relationship between vocal "diatonis" and instrumental *sléndro* scales

In Ponidi's version, tone 4 is a whole tone above 3 – a "fis" rather than "fa." Though Hardjo's version conforms to Western expectations of intervallic structure (with 4 a half tone above 3), it is more confusing to read his versions with the *sléndro* cipher notation. Thus, the notation in Figure 4.14 uses Ponidi's system, but with a sharp sign by the 4.

Of course, the combination of the *sléndro* instrumental scale with a different instrumental scale is not unique to Semarang. Its occurrence in Banyumas has been discussed in the previous chapter, and the use of *barang miring* in Solo and Yogya has been mentioned as well. But the two scales sound more independent of one another in Semarang tradition, representing what is generally agreed to be a greater mix of cultural influences than one finds, or would expect to find, in the other regions.

Several other important characteristics of Semarang vocal style are apparent in this example. One is the extended melisma, found in the fourth line. Another is the tendency to employ a different set of tones in ascent than in descent, as in the make-up of certain *raga*s in Indian art music. At the end of the first line, we find the tones 7–2̇–3̇ in ascent and 1̇–7–6 in descent. Throughout the portion notated and, indeed, throughout the entire piece, tone 1 is

```
balungan:          .    3    .    2P    .    3    .    6N
vocal:     .    .    .    .    7  2̇  7  2̇   .    .  7  2̇   .    .  2̇ 3̇ 1̇ 7 6
                            Ca- ri- ta nggon        ing-sun         nu  lar
```

```
balungan:          .    2    .    1P    .    2    .    6N
vocal:     .    .    .    .    6  1̇  6   7   .    .  5  3 2   .   3  5  6
                            Wong tu- wa kang        mo- mong        dhi-ngin
```

```
balungan:          .    5    .    6P    .    3    .    2N
vocal:     .    .    .    .    .    .    .    .    2̇  7   .    .  2̇ 3̇ 2̇
                                                   A- kèh        kang su-
```

```
balungan:          .    5    .    3P    .    6    .    2N/G
vocal:     .    .  7  6  .  .  5  3   .    .  4# 5  6  4#  3  2
                   gih ca-       ri- ta
```

4.14 Ladrang *Sinom Semarangan, sléndro pathet manyura*, first *gongan*. (Semarang *macapat* adapted to *sléndro* gamelan by Ponidi)

never used in ascent from 7 to 2. And, while we find the ascending passage 3–4#–5–6, we do not find the reverse. The descent (on the melisma in the fourth line, above) skips from 6 to 4#, omitting 5.

The extended melisma and the contrast in ascent and descent are also typical of Semarang vocal melodies normally performed and conceived of as *pélog*. Figure 4.15 is an excerpt from Ponidi's Ladrang *Pangkur* in which these traits are evident.

```
balungan:        2    2    .    .    2    3    2    7P
vocal:     .    .    .    .  7̣  2  2  2   .  2 3  7̣  .    .  7̣  7̣
                          Ka- la- mun a-    na   ma-        nungsa
```

```
balungan:        .    6    2    7    6    5    3    5N
vocal:     .    .  7̣  6  .  5̣ 6  7̣  5̣  3   .  2 3 1  1 2 7  6   5
                   a- nying-   gah-i du-    gi la- wan pra-yo- gi
```

```
balungan:        .    5    6    7    2    7    6    5P
vocal:     .    .  1̇  2̇  .  .  2̇  2̇  3̇  .  6  1̇  .  .  7  2̇
                   i- ku      wa- tak-    é  tan        pa- tut
```

```
balungan:   7    6    7    5    3    2    1    2N
vocal:    .  7  6  5  .  .  7  6  5  3  2  3  2  3  1  2
          (-ut)
```

4.15 Ladrang *Pangkur Semarangan, pélog pathet barang*, excerpt. (Semarang *macapat* adapted to *pélog* gamelan by Ponidi)

The vocal melody here extends the syllable "*ut*" (of "*patut*") in a fourteen-tone melisma, with a range of more than one octave and filling two full *gatra* of *balungan*. And any descending passages following the use of tone 1 always rise to tone 2 and then skip over tone 1 to tone 7 (or a lower tone), as in the few beats at the end of the second line and, an octave higher, in the third and fourth lines.

One can find occasional passages in other Javanese vocal music which contain melismas or contours with contrasting tonal orientations in ascent and descent. Yet these are prominent in Semarang style and are integral to the special sound of the solo *macapat* and of the adaptations of these *macapat* to the gamelan tradition; and they characterize melodies in *pélog* as well as *diatonis* or *sléndro miring*. Many Solonese *pesindhèn* reportedly came to Semarang in the 1920s and 1930s and brought with them their repertory and singing style (A. Salim, personal communication, 1983). No doubt this contributed to the demise of what was probably a much more substantial Semarang tradition, but it seems likely that they also learned some of the local music, and were perhaps particularly attracted to the unique sound of the *macapat*. At any rate, these *macapat* and their unusual melodic style survive, given new life in the *gendhing* they have inspired.

Tempo and rhythmic treatment

The Semarang *gendhing bonang*, along with some of the vocally-oriented pieces, normally undergo a special Semarangan treatment with respect to rhythm. Whereas a gradual ritard usually signals a transition to another section or an ending (*suwuk*) in other Javanese styles, in Semarang style it can also serve as preparation for a sudden surge, in which the tempo of all the instruments doubles near the end of the *gongan* – where one would expect the piece to end. To establish the new tempo, the drummer signals a slight acceleration before the gong beat and the *balungan* instruments play the penultimate tone three times, effectively turning the last two beats of the *gongan* into four, as shown in Figure 4.16 (5 1 becomes 5551). If the piece is to end, the acceleration signal is not given and the piece continues to slow to the final gong beat, with the *bonang* playing a special, sparser pattern, reserved for *suwuk*.

Slowing the tempo in Semarang style creates tension for the experienced listener, for it is only the drummer who knows more than a few beats in advance of the gong stroke whether the piece is to continue toward a slow ending or suddenly come back to life. It is not unusual to go through four or five ritards before actually ending. The tempo doubling, as it were, frustrates the expectation of an imminent ending and represents a kind of musical mischievousness that most performers and listeners, nowadays anyway, find humorous. This is in contrast to the *gendhing bonang* of Solonese tradition, or *soran* performance in Yogyanese tradition, where a light or humorous element is not routinely found.

Aside from this special treatment of tempo, one does not normally hear musicians characterizing Semarang style as exceptionally fast (like Banyumas style) or slow (like Yogyanese style). Yet one encounters an unusually broad range of tempi for the fastest pulse (density referent) in Semarang performance. The spectrum is so broad as to contradict the general tendency for a more or less constant tempo for the fastest pulse in other central Javanese gamelan traditions. The first section of the Semarang *gendhing bonang* in *ladrang* form usually settles at a tempo considerably slower than the normal range of *irama dadi* (= *irama* II) in Solonese and Yogyanese traditions.[9] This allows the *bonang* to subdivide at what would be called *irama wilet* (= *irama* III), albeit with a relatively fast density referent tempo.

```
Ritard with doubling of tempo (at *)
                                        t*              N/G       t
balungan        5       3       5       2  5  5  5   1  5  2  5  1
                                                                    etc.

bonang      3 . 3 . 2 . 2  .i .i .i .i .2 .2 .i .i .
barung      3̣   3̣   2̣   2̣   1  1  1  1  2̣  2̣  1  1


bonang      5 . 5 6 5 . 5 . 3 . 3 5 3 . 3 .2.2.2.2.2.2.2.2.3.3.3.3.2.2.2.2.
panerus     5̣   5̣ 6 5̣  5̣   3̣   3̣5̣3̣   3̣  2̣2̣2̣2̣2̣2̣2̣2̣3̣3̣3̣3̣2̣2̣2̣2̣


Ritard for suwuk (ending)
                                t               N/G
balungan        5       3       5       2       5       1  (end)

bonang      3 . 3 . 2 . 2  .i .i . .
barung      3̣   3̣   2̣   2̣   1  1

bonang      5 . 5 6 5 . 5 . 3 . 3 5 3 . 3 . 2 . 2 3 . . . .
panerus     5̣   5̣ 6 5̣  5̣   3̣   3̣5̣3̣   3̣  2̣   2̣3̣
```

4.16   Excerpts from second section of Gendhing *Kutut Manggung*: ritard for tempo doubling and for *suwuk*

In the second section, due to the maintenance of a constant ratio between the *balungan* and the subdividing parts, the density referent tempo may range from extraordinarily slow to very fast. Figure 4.17 gives some readings for passages of steady tempo from recordings of *gendhing bonang* Semarangan.

Gendhing Title	Section	Irama Level	Tempo of DR (Fastest Pulse)	Source
Bima Kurda	First	III	416–448	Gending Bonang Semarangan
	Second	I	264	Lokananta cassette ACD-049 (RRI Semarang Studio
	Second	I (fast)	480	musicians, dir. by Ponidi)
Gonjang Pati	First	III	336–368	Gending Bonang
	Second	II*	132	Lokananta cassette ACD-050 (RRI Semarang Studio
	Second	I (slow)	252–276	musicians, dir. by Ponidi)
	Second	I (med)	368–400	
	Second	I (fast)	464–552	

*referred to as irama II/dadi, based on balungan tempo (44 MM), though in reference to subdivision it is a very slow irama I/tanggung.

4.17   Tempo in performance of two *gendhing bonang* Semarangan

Even in these performances by a single group, recorded in April and May of the same year (1974), one finds significant contrast between the settled tempo in the first section of these two performances. More striking is the extremely wide range in tempo in the second section (with the fastest pulse manifest in the combination of the two interlocking *bonang* parts): from a very slow 132 (much slower even than one encounters in Yogyanese style) to a rapid 552 (comparable to the faster tempi found in Banyumas). Manipulation of tempo is generally identified as an important trait of Semarang style. As attested to by the data, the style is characterized by extremes of tempo, providing an element of variety within a genre whose instrumental techniques may otherwise be quite restrictive.

Semarang tradition and regionalism

In previous chapters I have striven to keep separate the idea of a given regional gamelan tradition (e.g., Yogyakarta, Banyumas) from the kinds of gamelan music one currently encounters within a single region. In no case is this distinction so crucial as in Semarang, where almost all gamelan music performance today is Solonese style. Though musicians there identify certain repertory and style as "Semarangan," they do not incorporate it very regularly into their performances. At the commercial *wayang wong* theaters and at privately sponsored *wayang kulit* and gamelan concerts, one expects to hear Solonese gamelan music almost exclusively. For stylistic variety, a Yogyanese piece or even a Banyumas piece will more usually crop up than a Semarang piece.

The only place one can expect to find Semarang pieces performed with some regularity is at the RRI studio in Semarang, where the *gendhing bonang* are broadcast once a month in the early morning. Indeed, given the tiny size of the repertory, one could not expect more frequent representation on the radio. But neither these nor the vocal pieces are very much in evidence elsewhere. During July 1983, an elderly Semarang puppeteer presented a full-length *wayang kulit*, with gamelan accompaniment provided by a few of the oldest musicians in Semarang, who struggled to remember some of the distinctive local versions of the *wayang* repertory. A. Salim was one of the participating musicians and complained to me in an interview several days later that the *wayang* music was truly lost, since even these older musicians had experienced great difficulty in attempting to resurrect the style. Musical influences from Surakarta, he said, had been strong for over fifty years.[10] Solonese musicians, particularly *pesindhèn*, came to Semarang in large numbers. Radio broadcasts and early recordings have featured Solonese style there since their inception.[11] Performing artists do not seem to feel a sense of Semarang identity, nor is there any institution, such as a conservatory, to give visibility or focus to any notion of Semarang artistic identity.

Of the three most highly regarded gamelan musicians in Semarang, only one, A. Salim, grew up in Semarang. Ponidi moved to Semarang in the 1950s and only learned about Semarang gamelan and vocal tradition after that time. It is to his credit that he has created new pieces by adapting traditional Semarang solo vocal music to gamelan, but the results show a clear debt to Solonese tradition. Ki Nartosabdho, an extraordinary artist who is discussed further in chapter 8, resided in Semarang for nearly forty years. He, too, made use of some Semarang techniques in his compositions. Yet his eclectic style, based – as he himself acknowledged – on Solonese style, drew more on Banyumas and other styles than on Semarang style. Were the current musical climate not so conscious of individual stars, his accomplishments might all be subsumed under a new branch of Semarang tradition, but his music is identified with him and a modern Javanese style (or "central Javanese" style), rather than as "Semarangan."

Looking only at what persists as uniquely Semarangan and is generally recognized as such, we find today two seemingly unrelated genres: the *gendhing bonang*, on the one hand, and the *gendhing* featuring vocal parts, often with unusual scalar orientation, on the other. Some of the vocal music suggests outside influence (Western, or perhaps Chinese or Arab). Yet several vocal pieces that incorporate *sléndro* or *pélog* melodies, though not found in other regional repertories, do not sound any different from similar pieces in Solonese tradition. The *wayang* repertory has all but disappeared, but represented a third component to the Semarang tradition.

And thus we are somewhat at a loss to construct a coherent view of a Semarang local culture, with its own performing arts tradition, though evidence suggests that such a tradition once existed. Instead, the gamelan music heard today that is identified as Semarangan bears witness to the complex and in some ways incongruous cultural make-up of the region.

Reflecting on the waning of this tradition, we must remember that musical repertories and styles of performance cannot persist without some viable form of ongoing patronage. Were *wayang kulit* puppeteers still performing in Semarang style, making live appearances and commercial cassette recordings, it seems very likely that musicians would have retained a Semarang *wayang kulit* repertory of *gendhing*, *sulukan*, playing techniques, and theoretical conceptions (e.g., concerning *pathet*). Those who have sponsored *wayang kulit* there in recent years have reportedly favored puppeteers who perform in Solonese style. Thus, whatever preferences individual musicians (such as A. Salim) might have had for a distinctive local gamelan music have here encountered strong challenge from the prevailing tastes in the market-place. As a result, the Semarang *wayang* music is practically never performed, and younger musicians simply do not have the chance to hear it.

The presence of the RRI Semarang studio and the extraordinary popularity of Ki Narto-sabdho have both provided opportunities for the continued performance of some Semarang *gendhing* and the unique vocal and instrumental styles identified with Semarang. From what I gather, Semarang gamelan music serves primarily as a change of pace – musical variety in an environment dominated by Solonese tradition – more than it does an expression of regional identity for performers or listeners. In the other regions in which I conducted research, musicians often spoke with a sense of regional pride about the local music, indicating a strong link between the feeling of the music and their own identities as *orang Banyumas* (Banyuma-san), *orang Yogya* (Yogyanese), *orang Jawa timur* (east Javanese). Musicians I spoke with in Semarang did not express a comparable sense of pride about Semarang.

Nevertheless, musicians at the radio station and in Nartosabdho's group, who are largely from the Semarang area, play the surviving Semarang *gendhing* with greater frequency and – I am convinced – a greater sense of "natural-ness" than musicians in other regions who also sometimes insert an occasional Semarang *gendhing* into their performances nowadays. For Yogyanese, Solonese, and Banyumas musicians, these *gendhing* still represent something of an interesting oddity: at times awkward or challenging in comparison to the music they more often perform. Musicians from other areas generally learn these *gendhing* either from recordings of Semarang musicians or, in the case of RRI studio musicians, from direct observation of performance at the occasional *Catur Tunggal* ("Four [in] One") broadcast sessions with musicians from the four main RRI studios in central Java (Yogya, Solo, Semarang, Purwokerto). However weak the sense of regional identity is in Semarang, then, something of a Semarang identity is at least imagined by musicians and listeners from other regions, and this is reinforced by the ongoing authority Semarang musicians have in the larger world of Javanese music as the most legitimate source of Semarang gamelan music.

5 A major East Javanese tradition: gamelan music of Surabaya-Mojokerto-Malang

East Java is a province with a wealth of indigenous genres of performing arts which have developed and proliferated without any powerful centralizing institutions since the fall of the last great Hindu–Javanese kingdom, Majapahit around 1500 A.D. Those with whom I spoke about East Javanese cultural geography invariably stressed its heterogeneity in contrast to that of central Java (i.e., the province of Central Java and the Special Region of Yogyakarta). They usually mention five regional groups or "ethnic areas" (*wilayah etnis*): the Madurese on the island of Madura and along the north coast from Pasuruan eastwards; the Osing in Banyuwangi; the Tengger in the upland areas around Mount Bromo; the "east Javanese" (*Jawa timuran*) in the central part of the province (primarily in the triangular area marked by Surabaya, Mojokerto [or Jombang], and the coast south of Malang); and the "central Javanese" (*Jawa tengahan*) in the area west of the Brantas river (Kediri). Some mention a sixth group, the "northern coastal Javanese" (*Jawa pesisiran utara*) along the coast from Tuban east to Surabaya, though it is generally noted that this area lacks a distinctive performing arts tradition (Munardi *et al.* 1983:6). Hatley writes of the "*arèk* Javanese," which include the second, third, and fourth groups mentioned above, though he too distinguishes these three subdivisions within this larger grouping (Hatley 1984).

In this chapter I will focus primarily on the "east Javanese" of the central area, and it is to this region and its culture that I refer with the lower case "east." Though Madurese gamelan music is clearly indebted to influences from both eastern and central Java, my concern with Javanese gamelan precludes coverage of Madurese traditions. The Tengger do not, to my knowledge, maintain a distinctive gamelan tradition. Though some Tenggerese own and play gamelan, the repertory performed consists mostly of pieces from other, lowland Javanese traditions. And by all accounts, for important ceremonies, the Tengger generally invite visiting troupes from the neighboring east Javanese region, particularly Malang (Munardi *et al.* 1983:8; Hefner and Smith-Hefner, personal communication, 1981, 1987). In his fine study of the Tengger, Hefner takes pains to dispel both the notion of the Tengger as a distinct ethnic group (Hefner 1985:41) and the view of the Tengger highlands as "a distinct social region" (Hefner 1985:44).

The region of Banyuwangi is rich, with its own genres of performance that clearly represent a distinctive tradition, exhibiting obvious similarities with some forms of Balinese music.[1] The Osing identify themselves as Javanese, although they are seen by most other Javanese as somewhat exotic. This is a region whose music is only sometimes identified as "gamelan" music, and whose style and repertory stand further from the court traditions than any other. It is this very distinctiveness which, as we shall see, makes Banyuwangi music especially attractive as a symbol of province-wide "East Javaneseness." My concern with this tradition, however, will be less in its description – for it is only marginally "gamelan" music and has been well described elsewhere – than in its role in the politics of regionalism.

In the "central Javanese" region of the province one finds a continuum in musical style from very nearly Solonese, around Madiun, to something more of a mix between Solonese and "east Javanese" further east. In particular, the drumming seems to become increasingly loud and coarse as one moves eastwards. The well-known Justisi Laras group in Madiun, for example, uses Solonese drum patterns, but played louder than is normal in Solonese concert music (*klenèngan*). Recordings of Solonese pieces from towns such as Trenggalek, Tulungagung, and Blitar exhibit greater deviation from Solonese norms than the Madiun groups.[2] Trenggalek and Tulungagung are known for their own styles of social dance music (*tayuban*) in which pieces normally associated with Solonese tradition are performed with unique local drumming styles.[3]

Just as one finds changes in style moving eastwards through the "central Javanese" portion of the province, one finds some variation within the central portion of the province as one moves from the Surabaya-Mojokerto area south to the Malang area. Indeed, the whole notion of regional identity becomes rather more complex here than in central Java. The Javanese I spoke with in Malang, including a number of musicians and other performing artists, indicate a shared identity with the Javanese from Surabaya and elsewhere in central east Java as *orang Jawa timuran*. Yet there is also clearly a shared sense of being *orang Malang* in particular. For the performing artists, this means a special pride in certain practices and items of repertory associated with Malang, rather than with Jawa Timur as a whole.

But does one speak of a Malang tradition or merely of a Malang variant of a larger east Javanese tradition? My sense is that the latter more accurately reflects indigenous conceptions and is consistent with the identification of traditions throughout this study. In his study of masked dance-drama (*wayang topèng*, also called *topèng dhalang*), Soleh Adi Pramono refers to pieces as East Javanese in "form and style" (i.e., tradition), with "ways of striking" (i.e., details of melodic contour) characteristic of Malang: "bentuk dan gaya gending Jawa Timuran cara pukulan Malangan" (Soleh Adi Pramono 1984:95). Murgiyanto and Munardi, scholars and performers from central Java with extensive experience in the province of East Java, also consider the Surabaya-Mojokerto-Malang triangle as a distinctive region, whose people share the dialect of Javanese language identified as "east Javanese" (*Jawa cara wétanan* or *Jawa Timuran*) along with their own musical style (Murigiyanto and Munardi 1979:16, 72).

Asked to characterize the people of east Java, the central Javanese will usually respond that they are more *kasar* – coarse and direct, without the taste for refinement in manners, language, and arts associated with the courts. To a large extent, the people of east Java would agree, though they seem less apologetic about their lack of refinement than some central Javanese might expect. Within the province, one finds a spectrum of evaluations. Those of the "central Javanese" region view those further east as more *kasar* than themselves. The east Javanese (*orang Jawa timuran*) view the Tengger and Osing as more *kasar* than themselves. And the ethnic Javanese in the province generally view the Madurese as excessively *kasar* and harbor fears of the Madurese as vicious and prone to crime. My own experience with Madurese has certainly not supported this Javanese stereotyping of them. Yet it is not my intent here to evaluate the accuracy of these stereotypical images, but rather to point out that they exist and that the key variable in the minds of many Javanese is the degree of refinement or coarseness. No one would deny that the language and arts of Yogya and Solo are more refined than those of east Java. But in east Java one finds an ambivalent attitude toward the whole notion of courtly refinement and all that it encompasses. In some ways east Java has tried to partake of it, yet in many ways it rejects it as alien. In our discussion below, we will see this struggle as it manifests itself in gamelan music and the related performing arts.

One of the crucial factors in east Java's current dilemma is the awareness that it was once a center of mighty court culture. The capital of the Majapahit empire, which fell around the beginning of the sixteenth century, was located just outside present-day Mojokerto, in what is now the small farming town of Trowulan. Architectural ruins attesting to this and other earlier kingdoms are scattered throughout the east Javanese countryside and stand as reminders of the courtly culture that once existed there. For the last four centuries, however, the powerful centers of culture have been further west – in central Java and now also Jakarta.

Ironically, it is only on the island of Madura that more recent courts have existed.[4] But these could not represent cultural centers for the Javanese of the province. Instead, the Javanese there have looked to Yogya and Solo with some envy, and at the same time have developed a sense of identity distinct from the central Javanese. As we shall see below, the gamelan music and related performing arts of central Java enjoy considerable popularity throughout East Java province, providing a direct aesthetic connection with the more prestigious neighbor regions to the west.

In some ways, the situation is comparable to that of Banyumas, where Solonese gamelan music is no less familiar than the indigenous regional tradition. But East Java is a separate province with indigenous traditions differing more sharply from Solonese than does the indigenous tradition of Banyumas. And actions performed at the official level, both by national and by provincial governments, tend to promote the notion of cultural boundaries conforming to contemporary political boundaries. A full understanding of the dynamics of any regional tradition in East Java today, then, requires taking into account the large context – not only the other regional traditions of East Java, but those of central Java as well.

The focus of this chapter is the gamelan music known generally as *Jawa Timuran*, and it is my task to identify the repertory and performance styles it comprises. First we should be cognizant of the major contexts of performance in this region of East Java, as they are not identical to those in central Java. (Though it has been my intention in previous chapters to portray the diversity of gamelan traditions in central Java, it will be expedient to refer to all of these in the present chapter as "central Javanese.")

One hears east Javanese gamelan music today mostly in performances of *wayang kulit*, *tayuban*, *wayang topèng* (masked dance-drama), and *ludruk* (popular theater). East Java's *wayang kulit* tradition is closely related to those of central Java, but the sequence of *pathet* in east Javanese *wayang kulit*, and the repertory and style of the music, are unique to east Java. Many puppeteers in east Java have adopted Solonese tradition for *wayang* performances, and others have blended Solonese and east Javanese styles and repertories. Due to the absence of any single authoritative center for the tradition, the *wayang* tradition is less standardized than either Yogyanese or Solonese traditions. Often one finds an overall sequence of scenes and *pathet* which conforms fairly closely to an east Javanese norm, but which may incorporate central Javanese gamelan pieces. Yet the work-horses of the *wayang* repertory (comparable to *Ayak-ayakan*, *Srepegan*, and *Sampak* in central Java) bear remarkably little likeness to their central Javanese counterparts.

Tayuban is a genre that was once widespread throughout Java, but is now comparatively rare in central Java, ostensibly due to its rowdy and ribald nature. *Tayuban* are ritual celebrations – usually of a rite of passage, such as marriage or circumcision – in which men drink liquor and dance with singer–dancers known variously as *tandhak* (the usual east Javanese term), *andhong* (a term from the Malang area), or *talèdhèk* (the most widespread central Javanese term) (see plate 7). Javanese literature offers extensive poetic description of

7   Gamelan, musicians, and villagers at *tayuban* in Sumber Beji, south west of Malang, 1986.

tayuban in which the men become intoxicated and may even copulate in public view in the dance arena.[5] It is not clear whether things generally (or ever) went this far, however.[6] At the *tayuban* events I attended in rural areas around Malang, drinking was fairly heavy, but the men scarcely touched the singer–dancers. According to those I interviewed, more overt sexual expression characterized *tayuban* years ago. Today, however, a man who attempts to kiss or wrap his arms around the *tandhak* will be restrained by others present (as I witnessed on several occasions in rural Malang).

The gamelan music at *tayuban* in east Java today consists mostly of east Javanese pieces played in east Javanese style, though pieces from other repertories are often included (especially modern compositions by Ki Nartosabdho). As a rule, the pieces the male guests request for dancing with the *tandhak* are east Javanese. But the pieces a *tandhak* sings before each group of dance items are often popular *jineman* or newly composed *lagu dolanan* from central Java. These are known in *tayuban* as *ndoro-ndoro*, and are said to honor the group of men, usually situated at one table, who are about to have the opportunity to dance with the *tandhak*. Sometimes the more flirtatious *tandhak* will sit in the lap of one of the men who promises a large payment when they later get up to dance.

Both *wayang kulit* and *tayuban* are found throughout this central region of East Java. In the Tengger area, *tayuban* are held frequently, but *wayang kulit* are taboo (Murgiyanto and

Munardi 1979:28–29; Munardi *et al.* 1983:6). The genre of *wayang* that reaches the Tengger is the masked dance-drama *wayang topèng* of the nearby Malang area (see plate 8). This is a much less popular genre today than either *wayang kulit* or *tayuban*. I know of only three active troupes, and even these perform rarely.[7] Instead of the all-night performances that have typified this genre, at least in this century, one now finds brief excerpts of episodes or even single dances presented in public performances that may involve other genres of dance. So far as I could determine from personal observation and interviews, regardless of the context of performance, the gamelan accompaniment for *topèng* consists of distinctively east Javanese pieces, with little if any central Javanese influence.[8]

Ludruk (Jvn. *ludrug*) is a more recent phenomenon, associated in its early days with Jombang and Surabaya, but now enjoyed throughout most of the entire province of East Java. In the early nineteenth century, the term *ludrug* referred to the dance of two clowns, one a man in women's clothing, who performed humorous stories (Pigeaud 1938:322). This developed into a genre known as *besutan*, consisting of a few stock characters (*ludrug* Besut, his wife Jaminah, and his adversary Juragan Celep), all played by men. *Ludruk* today is a much more elaborate form of theater, with dance (see below), stand-up comedians, transvestite singers, and actors presenting plays with a high element of improvisation (see plate 9).[9] Yet all roles are still taken by men, and humor pervades most of the performance.

The musical accompaniment has also undergone considerable change. As late as 1930, the music was sometimes provided by an ensemble consisting of an *angklung*, a single-headed drum (*jidhor*), doubled-headed drum (*kendhang*), and an aerophone – probably a double-reed – sometimes with an additional group of small frame drums (*terbang*) and a gong.[10] Since the 1930s and 1940s, however, *ludruk* has usually required a *sléndro* gamelan. The music heard today consists primarily of a piece known as Gendhing *Surabayan* or as *Jula-juli.*[11] In contemporary *ludruk*, the piece is heard many times in a single performance – which generally last from eight or nine in the evening until eleven or midnight in commercial settings, and sometimes longer in cases of private sponsorship. It serves as the staple for entrances and exits, and accompanies the popular *ngrémo* dance that opens the performance.

The *ngrémo* dance, and the music that accompanies it, have now spread from *ludruk* to become an essential opening item for all genres of east Javanese performance involving gamelan – *tayuban*, *wayang topèng*, even *wayang kulit*. In radio broadcasts, the *ngrémo* music serves as the opening signature piece. Though no one actually dances in the studio, the drumming suggests a typical *ngrémo* choreography, complemented by the sounds of someone shaking the anklet bells that would normally be worn by the *ngrémo* dancer. *Ngrémo* serves as an immediately recognizable symbol of "East Javaneseness," both to the residents of East Java, and to other Indonesians, particularly other Javanese.

Contrasting male and female styles of *ngrémo* have developed; either one may be danced by male or female dancers. Perhaps because of its association with the transvestism of *ludruk*, the *ngrémo* dancers I have witnessed during several periods of field work in east Java have usually danced the style of the opposite gender (men dancing female style, women dancing male style – see plate 10). The male style is considered the more original (*asli*) and is a dynamic dance, associated with a spirit of defiance and heroism that some east Javanese proudly associate with the independence movement to rid Indonesia of the Dutch (Wibisono 1982:7–8). In both male and female styles, the dancer alternates between dance movements with relatively loud and fast music and standing still to sing with soft and slow accompaniment. One of the most

8   Pak Rasimun giving instruction to his *topèng* dance students, village of Glagah Dowo, east of Malang, 1986.

famous *ngrémo* dancers during the 1930s, Pak ("Cak") Gondo Durasim, used the singing sections as opportunities to sing clever anti-Dutch rhymes. For this he was arrested and is now recognized as an important national hero in the struggle for independence. A street is named after him in downtown Surabaya.

East Javanese music is only rarely heard as "concert music" (*klenèngan*) today, although earlier in this century such performances were not uncommon, at least in the Surabaya and Mojokerto areas. The rise of east Javanese *klenèngen* is attributed to Wongsokadi, a musician born in 1869 in Sidoarjo and who, it is said, began to include *pesindhèn* with his gamelan group in 1918 (Proyek Penelitian dan Pencatatan 1976:272–73). Beforehand, female singing with gamelan was heard only in the context of *tayuban*, and was limited to the short and lively pieces requested at these occasions. This innovation was almost certainly inspired by a similar change in the music of central Java, including that of the courts. Aside from radio broadcasts today, however, the only context in which one finds something like *klenèngan* with east Javanese gamelan music is during the daylight hours preceding a *wayang kulit* performance, but these are rare.[12]

It is important to realize that the genres I have mentioned above represent only a portion of the gamelan activity in the province of East Java. Even in the central region, one finds music, dance, and *wayang kulit* from central Java, particularly Solonese. Urban gamelan musicians are expected to be familiar with Solonese tradition. Many of the rural musicians are as well, though one does find excellent performers, old and young, who are thoroughly at home with east Javanese gamelan music and have only an elementary understanding of central Javanese. The discussion below will be concerned with the music that is identifiably east Javanese (*asli Jawa timur*), a tradition that some feel is in crisis, but which is far from extinct.

9 Transvestite singers in *ludruk* performance, Bululawang (south east of Malang), 1986.

Instrumentation

In east Java today, many of the gamelan used for the performance of east Javanese music are indistinguishable from those of central Java. Yet one can point to several features of the ensembles which are immediately apparent and identified specifically as "east Javanese." First is the middle-sized drum (*gambyak*) that may be considerably larger than the central Javanese *ciblon*. Its shell and skins are usually much thicker than other Javanese drums, and it rests on a frame which tilts it at an angle, such that the smaller head is higher than the larger. This drum is capable of a spectacular variety of sounds and can be much louder than other Javanese drums. As such it conforms to the tastes prevalent in east Java for what – by central Javanese standards – is rough, *kasar* drumming (see plate 11).

Second is the presence in some ensembles of a set of kettle gongs known as *ponggang* (also *monggang* or *panembung*), tuned one octave lower than the *kenong* (see plate 12). These are usually arranged as three sides of a rectangle, with the player sitting inside the enclosed space and striking the kettles with a padded beater resembling a *kenong* beater. The *ponggang* sounds at a slower rate than the *saron* part (*balungan*), providing an abstraction of this part, much as the *bonang panembung* does in Yogyanese tradition. Third is the presence of an

10   Daughter of puppeteer Ki Matadi performs *ngrémo* dance (male style) prior to *wayang kulit* performance by her father in Krebet, south east of Malang, 1986.

11   Pak Diyat Sariredjo, former director of RRI Surabaya gamelan musicians, laces up a *gambyak* drum at his house in Driyorejo, outside Surabaya.

12   Musicians perform east Javanese gamelan music one afternoon prior to *wayang kulit* in
Trowulan, Mojokerto, 1986. *Ponggang* in foreground.

instrument known as *slenthem*, but consisting of knobbed keys resting (not suspended by
string) over a trough or tube resonators.[13] The keys are struck on the knob, not with a mallet,
but with a beater resembling a *kenong* (or *ponggang*) beater.

Fourth, the saron resonators in many east Javanese gamelan are constructed from planks of
wood, like *gambang* resonators, rather than being carved out of a single block of wood, as is
normal in central Java. This style of resonator, known as *kijingan*, may also contain small
tubular resonators, one for each key. The *saron* in some village ensembles in central Java are
also constructed in the same manner, though rarely with tube resonators inside. To the
central Javanese, this shape has lower status and is not used in court or expensive new
ensembles. In east Java, however, some of the finest sets, including the gamelan at the RRI
studio in Surabaya, have *kijingan* resonators.

In the older ensembles of east Java, one usually finds only one *kempul*, tuned to a pitch 6 or
pitch 5, and one *gong ageng*, with no *siyem* or *gong suwukan*. I saw five or six east Javanese
gamelan with only one *kempul*, and in each case it was tuned to pitch 6. Other sources report
the use of either pitch 6 or pitch 5 (Kartamihardja 1978:32). Following the augmentation of

ensembles in central Java over the last century, however, the east Javanese have added one or two *siyem* and three or four *kempul* for each tuning system in many ensembles. But whereas the use of a single *kempul* in central Java is seen as archaic and no longer aesthetically acceptable, it is still common in the accompaniment of *wayang topèng*, for example, in east Java. It is likely that gamelan ensembles in east Java at one time included only one or two *kenong* as well. Nowadays a full complement of *kenong* – one tuned to each pitch of the scale (including *pélog* 4) is the norm. Even in the several *pélog* gamelan I encountered outside Malang, with only one *kempul* and one *gong*, the *kenong* sets consisted of six or seven *kenong*.

Some of the finest east Javanese gamelan are *sléndro-pélog* sets with the full range of loud and soft instruments in both tuning systems. More often, however, a gamelan is in one tuning only. Some of the older *pélog* ensembles consist only of loud-playing instruments, with no *gambang*, *gendèr*, *gendèr panerus*, *siter*, *celempung*, *rebab*, or *suling*. *Sléndro* gamelan, on the other hand, tend to include all or most of these soft-playing instruments. The contrast may well be due to the use of *pélog*, at least in the Malang area, for the *wayang topèng* repertory, which does not require soft instrumentation. And though the *gendhing* of the *tayuban* repertory are normally recorded with soft instruments today, they are often performed without soft instruments. The raucous nature of the performance context usually renders these instruments inaudible, particularly after the guests have consumed substantial quantities of alcohol. At the several *tayuban* I attended, the gamelan included *gendèr* and *gambang*, but these were played only in the early portion of the *tayuban*. For *wayang* accompaniment, however, the soft instruments are essential.

The *bonang* in east Javanese gamelan are identical to those of Yogyanese tradition in construction and pitch vocabulary, with ten kettles in *sléndro* (low 2 to high i on each *bonang*) and fourteen in *pélog* (low 1 to 7). The arrangement of the kettles for *pélog*, however, may vary. Solonese and Yogyanese *bonang* players may interchange the kettles tuned to 7 and to 1, since usually one or the other tone is omitted or only rarely sounded in a single piece, depending on the *pathet*. East Javanese may rearrange the lower row to situate pitch 7 in the middle position, as shown in Figure 5.1:

	Central Javanese Positions for Barang	Central Javanese Positions for Bem	East Javanese Positions
high row	4 6 5 3 2 7 1	4 6 5 3 2 1 7	4 6 5 3 2 1 7
low row	1 7 2 3 5 6 4	7 1 2 3 5 6 4	1 2 3 7 5 6 4
	(or:)	(or:)	(or:)
high row	4 6 5 3 2 7 1	4 6 5 3 2 1 7	4 6 5 3 2 1 7
low row	1 7 2 3 5 6 4	7 1 2 3 5 6 4	1 7 2 3 5 6 4

5.1   Kettle positions on *bonang* in central and east Java

The pitch range for east Javanese instruments can be slightly different from that of central Java. The *saron* and *slenthem*, which in Solonese tradition encompass low 6 to high i and in Yogyanese tradition 1 to high i, reach from 1 up to high 2 in east Javanese tradition. As in Solo, the *sléndro kenong* are tuned to 2, 3, 5, 6, and high i (sometimes without the 2 or the 3).

In *pélog*, the *saron* and *slenthem* are the same 1 to 7 found throughout Java. The *pélog kenong*, however, normally range not from 2 to high i̇ (Solo) or 3 to high 2̇ (Yogya), but from 1 to 7.

	sléndro saron	pélog kenong
Solonese:	6̣ 1 2 3 5 6 i̇	2 3 – 5 6 7 i̇
Yogyanese:	1 2 3 5 6 i̇	3 – 5 6 7 i̇ 2̇
East Javanese:	1 2 3 5 6 i̇ 2̇	1 2 3 4 5 6 7

5.2   Contrasting ranges of *saron* and *kenong* in central and east Java

In comparing the Solonese and east Javanese *sléndro saron* and *slenthem*, both of which comprise seven keys, one could suggest that musicians merely applied the cipher system differently to the same instrument in the two regions. Though now widespread throughout Java, this cipher system (*kepatihan*) developed only in the early twentieth century in Surakarta and was adopted later by east Javanese musicians, probably not until after 1950. Variant earlier terminologies existed for the tones of both the *sléndro* and *pélog* scales. Yet they all included the two numbers 5 (*lima*) and 6 (*nem*), which are retained as such in the present-day *kepatihan* system.[14] In old east Javanese terminology, the *sléndro saron* keys range from *barang* (or *sorog*) to *gulu* (= *tengah*, *tenggok*) *cilik* ("little" – or high). It is not the case, then, that tone 1 (*barang*) in Solonese gamelan coincides more or less with a tone 2 (*gulu*, *tengah*, *tenggok*) in east Javanese, even though they are both the second key from the left on the *saron*. Nevertheless, several of the older musicians I worked with distinguished a more or less normal absolute pitch level for east Javanese gamelan from a slightly higher one they called *kenceng* (literally, "tight," "taut" – higher in pitch). And they identify the pitch of most of the cassette recordings from Surakarta (RRI Solo) and Semarang (Ki Nartosabdho and Condhong Raos) as *kenceng*.

In the central region of East Java one also finds a variety of smaller ensembles that play mostly the same repertory as the larger east Javanese gamelan and are generally identified as types of gamelan. Portable ensembles which accompany the wandering *tandhak* or *andhong* have been known in a variety of formats. These are now rare, but are still met with occasionally in the rural area south of Malang, where a well-known *topèng* dancer Pak Karimum saw a small group accompanying two young girls as recently as 1986. The lead musician played a drum (a rather small *gambyak*), and was joined by a *saron* player, a *peking* player, and one other playing *kenong* and *gong*. Pak Karimun, who is well over fifty years old, remembers somewhat larger itinerant ensembles some years ago consisting of two *saron*, one *demung*, one *peking*, one *kenong*, one *kempul* and *gong*, and one *gambyak* drum. Other sources report an itinerant ensemble emphasizing the softer instruments and known as gamelan *janggrung*: drum, *gendèr*, *siter*, *suling*, *slenthem*, *peking*, and *gong kemodhong* (two metal slabs over a pot resonator) or bamboo *gong* (as in the Banyumas *calung* ensemble) (Proyek Penelitian 1976:111).

Tuning system and *pathet*

Sléndro is clearly the predominant tuning system in east Java. Only in the Malang area is *pélog* the more common tuning for gamelan ensembles. Data gathered by Kunst shows the extent of this *sléndro* predominance in the 1920s. For the east Javanese area he gives the following data:

| | complete bronze gamelan | | |
	sléndro	pélog	other complete gamelan
Surabaya:	101	16	70 iron sléndro
Mojokerto:	106	8	40 iron sléndro; 8 iron pélog
Jombang:	189	51	98 iron pélog "miring"
Lumajang:	131	42	
Malang:	106	232	54 iron sléndro; 56 iron pélog

(after Kunst 1973 II:564-566)

5.3   Distribution of *sléndro* and *pélog* gamelan in four regencies of East Java, 1920s

Pélog is the preferred tuning in the Malang area for the *wayang topèng* genre, which once enjoyed wide popularity there. Until quite recently *pélog* was also the preferred tuning in Malang for *wayang kulit purwa*, the shadow plays based on the characters and stories of the *Mahabharata* and *Ramayana*. Elsewhere in central and east Java, these *purwa* plays – by far the most widely performed – are accompanied wholly or primarily by *sléndro* gamelan. The preference for *pélog* in Malang is one of the strongest points in favor of positing a distinct Malang tradition. But the repertory and performance style, at least today, do not differ substantially from that of the rest of east Java.

Although most of east Java shares with central Java the use of *sléndro* with *wayang kulit purwa*, it does not share the same *pathet* system. The east Javanese know a different set of *pathet* terms and a different sequence of *pathet* in their *wayang*. The question of *pathet* assignment is at times problematic in all Javanese traditions. On the whole, it seems to be less generally agreed upon in east Java than elsewhere, perhaps because *pathet* has been less often mentioned there than in central Java. The publication of books of notation and the production of cassettes in east Java have both tended to follow the central Javanese custom of listing *pathet*. Yet one finds not only a lack of consensus concerning which *pathet* a piece belongs to, but also a lack of agreement as to which system of terms should be used – central Javanese or east Javanese. Though correspondence is not always exact, one can compare the two *pathet* systems as follows:

Central Java	East Java	Prominent Tones	Avoided Tones
slÉndro:			
nem ("6")	sepuluh ("10")	2, 6, 5	1
sanga ("9")	wolu ("8")	5, 1	3
manyura ("peacock")	sanga ("9")	6, 3, 2	5
[galong ("clay")]*	serang ("attack")	3	2
pÉlog:			
lima ("5")	bem (= sorog, pengasih)	---**	7
nem ("6")	" " "	---**	7
barang ("thing")	barang (= miring)	---**	1

*limited category, Yogya only
**difficult to delimit "prominent tones" in pélog

5.4   *Pathet* categories in central and east Java

In his article in *The New Grove*, Crawford notes that the tones chosen for *pancer* (sounded on weak beats, or between beats, as a means of filling in a sparse *balungan*) are usually the very tones otherwise avoided in the *pathet*: 1 for *sepuluh*, 3 for *wolu*, 5 for *sanga*, and 2 (but also 6) for *serang* (Crawford 1980:203).

East Javanese do not normally distinguish two separate *pathet* categories for *pélog bem* (the scale which excludes pitch 7), despite the fact that some gamelan *pélog* consist only of the *bem* scale. Kunst reports "ancient East Javanese gamelans" known as *pélog pengasih* (*pélog bem* scale) and others known as *pélog miring* (*pélog barang* scale). The full seven-tone *pélog* in east Java was known as *Mataraman* (also *Mentaraman*) and represents, in Kunst's estimation, an introduction from the Mataram kingdom of central Java (Kunst 1973 1:12–13). In Malang, where *pélog* is predominant, one finds the *sléndro* terms applied to distinguish pathet: *wolu*, *sanga*, and *sepuluh* in *pélog bem/sorog*; *sanga*, *sepuluh*, and *serang* in *pélog barang/miring*.

The *pathet* sequence in east Javanese *wayang kulit* is somewhat more complex than that of any central Javanese tradition. Figure 5.5 shows the sequences and approximate times given by Crawford for *wayang* in Mojokerto (Ki Piet Asmoro and his followers) and by Timoer for *wayang* in Gempol (south of Surabaya, as performed by Ki Suléman and his followers).

Mojokerto (Crawford 1980:202)		Gempol (Timoer 1988 I:139)	
pathet sepuluh	7:30 – 10:00	pathet wolu then sepuluh	8:00 – 9:00
pathet wolu	10:00 – 1:00	pathet sepuluh back to wolu	9:00 – 2:00
pathet sanga	1:00 – 3:30	pathet sanga	2:00 – 4:00
pathet serang	3:30 – 5:00	pathet serang	4:00 – 6:00

5.5   *Pathet* sequence in east Javanese *wayang kulit*

Crawford explains that during the *sepuluh* section, dance pieces in *pathet* "other than *sepuluh*" are used. In my experience it has been *pathet wolu*, as indicated in Timoer's list. And in both cases, the actual shadow puppet performance does not begin until around nine-thirty or ten when the puppeteer begins to move the puppets. A variety of pieces in *pathet supuluh* are played first and enjoyed as a long prelude to the puppet play.

In Malang, as far as I could determine, the sequence in *pélog* is comparable. The performances I heard in the Malang area happened to use *sléndro* and followed the same general progression as indicated above. In several cassette recordings of the most popular Malang-area *dhalang*, Ki Matadi, a *pélog* gamelan is used, but only for the first hour or two. The first cassette begins with only a short piece, followed by the opening of the play with Gendhing *Gandakusuma* – normally classified as *pathet supuluh* in *sléndro*, but orally designated *pélog pathet wolu* by the puppeteer on the recording (Ki Matadi). I was told that the normal sequence in *pélog* would be *pathet wolu* for three hours, *pathet sanga* for three hours, and then *pathet serang* (*pélog barang*) for two hours. Yet I suspect there is considerable variation in the timing and perhaps in the actual scale (*bem* or *barang*) and *pathet* used.

Repertory

The repertory of east Javanese *gendhing*, while substantial, is not nearly as large as those associated with either Yogyanese or Solonese traditions. From all the sources available to me, including published and unpublished books of notation, cassettes, and personal communication, I count 347 east Javanese *gendhing*. And as one would expect, a vast majority of these are notated and played in *sléndro*. Older musicians complain of the loss of pieces they played and heard frequently when they were younger, but which now are rarely or never performed. Many of these have been notated in two collections of east Javanese pieces from the Surabaya and Mojokerto areas: Asmoro 1971 and the more comprehensive Ronoatmodjo 1981a. But notation does not insure a continued place in the active repertory. It is primarily the shorter and livelier pieces associated with *tayuban* that are still widely performed. One also hears a few of the more subdued and longer pieces in *wayang kulit* performances. Though less active than either *tayuban* or *wayang kulit*, the *wayang topèng* tradition persists, along with its repertory of *gendhing* – the only east Javanese pieces normally played in *pélog*. In *ludruk*, one hears the ever-popular east Javanese signature piece *Jula-juli*, along with assorted modern pieces borrowed from various other genres.

As in Banyumas, performances of gamelan music in east Java often involve a mixture of local and Solonese repertories and performance styles. Many of the commercial cassettes identified explicitly as east Javanese contain one or more pieces normally associated with the mainstream central Javanese tradition, especially the *lagu dolanan* of Ki Nartosabdho and others. While it might seem justifiable to include all these pieces in our discussion of east Javanese repertory, it would not reflect the conceptions of the musicians themselves. While central Javanese pieces are a staple in *tayuban* performances and are increasingly evident in all but the most conservative *wayang* performances, the performers readily identify some pieces as *Jawa tengahan* and others as *Jawa timuran*, even if the cassette companies do not.

The central Javanese presence is felt not only in the repertory performed but also in the way some musicians are now beginning to classify the east Javanese *gendhing*. One can identify formal structures in east Javanese gendhing comparable to those of central Java, but the many east Javanese musicians with whom I spoke did not generally identify pieces by formal structure, nor did they have a set of terms for the formal structures. It is only very recently, since the founding of the SMKI conservatory in Surabaya in 1973 (originally Kokari), that an east Javanese system of terms for formal structure has been developed. This system clearly represents a response to the standard established by central Java – a wish to lend greater prestige to east Javanese gamelan music by developing comparable, yet distinctly east Javanese technical terms. Those without close connections to the conservatory are either unaware of these terms or choose not to use them, complaining that they are confusing. For while the claim is made that the terms refer to *bentuk* ("form"; i.e., formal gong structure), several of the categories seem to overlap and to be based on other criteria.

Despite the problems this system poses, it is the most comprehensive attempt I know to classify the east Javanese repertory, and it is likely to gain a firmer foothold in the future, as SMKI graduates encourage its use throughout the region. The system is explained and illustrated in Soenarto R.P. 1980; and with several added categories it is used to group the repertory presented in Ronoatmodjo 1981a. For the most part, it derives the name for a particular formal structure from the title of a well-known east Javanese piece within that formal structure (e.g., *Cakranegara, Samirah, Luwung*). Figure 5.6 gives the categories used in Ronoatmodjo 1981a, with gong structures and relevant commentary.

The first section in the "larger" forms (*lambang, titipati, gambir sawit*), like the *mérong* in large central Javanese *gendhing*, is calmer in mood than the second and is generally less expanded. But unlike central Javanese *gendhing* of this type, the gong structure of the two sections is the same. Though some east Javanese refer to the two sections with the Solonese terms *mérong* and *inggah* (= *minggah*), Soenarto R.P. (1980) gives the following as east Javanese equivalents: first section as *mbok-mbokan* ("like mother," from *mbok*) and second section as *anak-anakan* ("like child," from *anak*).

Musicians speak of *Ayak kempul kerep* (frequent *kempul*) and *Ayak kempul arang* (sparse *kempul*). The former indicates a 1:1 ratio between *kempul* and *balungan* beat, as shown in Figure 5.6, or even a 2:1 ratio. The latter indicates a *kempul* stroke every second *balungan* beat. The same two formal structures are used for pieces known as *Krucilan*, a term used by some musicians as a category synonymous with *Ayak*. However, the term can also refer both to specific pieces (identified by *balungan*) and to the fast interlocking between two *saron* for such pieces. The term derives from the nearly obsolete *wayang krucil* (= *klithik*), involving flat wooden puppets. Other pieces known as *Srepeg* (or *Srempeg*) have one or two *balungan* beats per kenong, and kempul every second *balungan* beat. Yet some musicians use this term to refer to pieces with *Ayak* structure, as described in item 11, Figure 5.6.

As is evident from the description in Figure 5.6, the formal gong structures used in east Javanese *gendhing* are similar in principle to those of central Java, but with some important distinguishing differences. Most striking to those familiar with central Javanese music are the pieces associated with *wayang* (*Ayak*, *Srepeg*, *Gedhog*, *Krucilan*), particularly the use of *kempul* more frequently than the *kenong*. Though the *gambir sawit* form resembles the *kethuk 2 kerep* form used for Gendhing *Gambir Sawit* in Solonese tradition, in east Java it includes *kempul*. And in the smaller forms, *kempul* occurs in the middle of every *kenongan*, including the *kenongan* immediately following the *gong* – hence with no *wela* (*kempul* rest) as in Solonese *ketawang* and Yogyanese and Solonese *ladrang* and *lancaran*.

The first problem the SMKI system presents, as many musicians will readily point out, is that the identity of many of the pieces in the east Javanese repertory depend on melody (*balungan* and vocal), rather than formal structure. One often hears the same *gendhing* performed on different occasions with two or three different formal structures. This is the rare exception in any of the central Javanese traditions.

Second, in an attempt to incorporate the few categorical terms that do enjoy wide usage among east Javanese musicians, the system has several terms for what appear to be the same formal structure. East Javanese generally refer to *gendhing* with eight- or sixteen-beat *gongan*, four *kenongan* per *gongan*, as *giro* – an apparent synonym for the central Javanese *lancaran*. Yet some *gendhing* with this formal structure are classified in Ronoatmodjo 1981a as *bentuk jula-juli*. Used as a category of *gendhing* formal structure, I was told by musicians at SMKI Surabaya, *jula-juli* is supposed to suggest *lancaran* pieces which incorporate singing and soft instrument parts. Perhaps this is what was intended, but in Ronoatmodjo some of the pieces classified as *giro* may involve singing (e.g., *Jamong*, *Blèndèran*) and others classified as *jula-juli* are usually only played in loud style (e.g., *Tropongan*).

East Javanese generally refer to *gendhing* played in loud style with longer *gongan* than *giro* as *gendhing gagahan* – comparable to the category *gendhing bonang* in Solonese tradition. This category, however, is given as one of the formal structures by Soenarto R.P. (1980:1) and by Ronoatmodjo (1981a:3–10). Soenarto offers a diagram that shows *gagahan* to have the same structure as *luwung* – an east Javanese counterpart to the *ladrang* of central Java. Yet the pieces notated by Ronoatmodjo under the heading *gagahan* display a variety of structures, some beginning, at least, like *giro*.

Also problematic are the forms associated with *wayang kulit*: *ayak* and *srepeg* in Ronoat-

1. Giro (8 or 16 beats per gongan):

```
          t p t N t P t N t P t N t P t N/G
          . . . . . . . . . . . . . . . .
   or:    . . . . . . . . . . . . . . . .
```

2. Gagahan (loud-style pieces, often but not always with the following
   gong structure):   t   P   t   N   t   P   t   N
```
                       . . . . . . . . . . . . . . . .
                       t     P     t     N     t     P     t     N/G
                       . . . . . . . . . . . . . . . .
```

3. Cakranegara: t   P   t   N   t   P   t   N/G
   (= Cokronegoro)
```
                        . . . . . . . . . . . . . . . .
```

4. Samirah: t   P   t   N
```
                        . . . . . . . . . . . . . . . .
                        t           P           t           N/G
                        . . . . . . . . . . . . . . . .
```

5. Luwung (pieces with vocal and soft instruments, same gong structure as
   given for Gagahan):
```
                        t     P     t     N     t     P     t     N
                        . . . . . . . . . . . . . . . .
                        t     P     t     N     t     P     t     N/G
                        . . . . . . . . . . . . . . . .
```

6. Lambang: same as Samirah, but with two sections (mbok-mbokan and anak-
   anakan) – with change in drumming style, but same gong structure.

7. Titipati: same as Luwung, but with two sections (mbok-mbokan and anak-
   anakan) – with change in drumming style, but same gong structure.

8. Gambirsawit: largest structure, with two sections (mbok-mbokan and anak-
   anakan) – with change in drumming style, but same gong structure:
```
                        t           P           t           N
                        . . . . . . . . . . . . . . . . . (x3)
                        t           P           t           N/G
                        . . . . . . . . . . . . . . . .
```

9. Jula-juli: same as Giro, but (usually?) with soft instruments and singing.

5.6   Formal structure in east Javanese *gendhing*

modjo 1981a, also *gedhog* and *krucilan*. Each of these implies not one but several formal structures and is identified by specific *balungan* melody, performance technique (*saron imbal*, drumming, and so on), and dramatic function as well as gong structure.

In short, we find a tradition whose repertory has been categorized sometimes by instrumentation (*gagahan*), sometimes by formal structure (*giro*), sometimes by a combination of factors (the *wayang* pieces). It becomes problematic to compare the east Javanese and central Javanese repertories based on formal structure alone, particularly since the level of distinction applied in Ronoatmodjo's collection of *gendhing* notation is never evident on commercial

10. Goyang-goyang (kempul, kethuk, and gong pattern as shown, but kenong not
    notated in Ronoatmodjo 1981a):

```
          t  P  t  P  t  P  t  G
          .  .  .  .  .  .  .  .
```

In performances of pieces in this category, however, the formal structure is
usually the same as Solonese srepegan: 1 beat per kenong, 2 kenong per kempul.

11. Ayak: irregular, formal structure not notated in Ronoatmodjo; usually
    performed with steady kempul beats and only occasional kenong and gong
    beats, for example:

```
                           N                   N
    P t P t P t P t P t P t P t P t P t P t P t G
    .  .  .  .  .  .  .  .  .  .  .  .  .  .
```

12. Srepeg: irregular; formal structure not notated in Ronoatmodjo 1981a.
    The only pieces in this category in Ronoatmodjo are Gedhog and Gedhog
    Rancak, with no kempul and no kethuk. These and other gedhog pieces are
    usually performed with two or four balungan beats per kenong and two
    kenong per gong:

```
                    N            N/G
                    .  .    .    .
       or .  .   .    .    .   .
```

13. Pamijèn: other irregular formal structures, including those consisting of
    three or five kenongan per gongan—a miscellaneous category, as in central
    Java.

5.6   Continued.

cassette covers. What I have done in compiling my data is to assign a formal structure where
possible, using the categories of Ronoatmodjo. For the numerous pieces whose formal
structures vary from one source to another (including all notated and recorded sources
available to me), I have listed all the structures in which the piece may be played. Thus, the
total number of items in all categories far exceeds the number of *gendhing*. We can,
nevertheless, gain a sense of the proportion of larger *gendhing* to smaller *gendhing* and the
correlation between *gendhing* structure and *pathet*. I combine the two categories *giro* and *jula-
juli* here, since the distinction is unclear in Ronoatmodjo 1981a. *Lagu dolanan* are not usually
available in east Javanese sources of notation, but are prominent on the cassettes. Many of
them are borrowed from central Java and performed in Solonese style. Only those for which I
am unable to find a central Javanese source and which are played in east Javanese performance style are included in my data.

Although *pathet* is much more often indicated than formal structure in the notation and
cassette recordings of east Javanese music, it is not unusual to find one and the same *balungan*
assigned to two or even three different *pathet*. We have seen above that the *pathet* system in
east Java differs somewhat from its central Javanese counterpart. Even in the court areas,
where each piece is usually assigned to a specific *pathet* whenever it is mentioned, the nature of
pathet is still cause for much debate. In east Java, where musicians tend not to intellectualize

about music, *pathet* categories are understood primarily in relation to *wayang kulit* performance, which itself is rather more flexible than in the court traditions. East Javanese musicians assure me that *pathet* can be distinguished on musical criteria as well, but those criteria have yet to be articulated in full. The clearest distinction on musical grounds is between *pathet wolu* and *pathet sanga*, with *wolu* corresponding to central Java's *sanga* (often with a final *gong* tone 5) and *sanga* corresponding to central Java's *manyura* (often with a final gong tone 6). More importantly, in both systems the latter is thought of as a transposition up one key of the former. But we only need look at a few sources to discover divergent opinions over which pieces are to be assigned to *pathet sepuluh* and to *pathet serang*. In *pélog*, most written assignations (on cassettes and in notation books) confine themselves to *bem* and *barang*, which are easily distinguished by scale alone. Yet in oral tradition, one finds several other categories in *pélog*, as we have seen above (paralleling the *sléndro* system).

Further complicating the *pathet* issue is the extensive penetration of central Javanese *pathet* terminology in east Java. Though the books of notation use the east Javanese *pathet* terms exclusively, the commercial cassette releases are not consistent. Some may classify *gendhing* according to the better-known central Javanese system, others according to the east Javanese. In a few cases, both systems appear to be used on a single cassette. Special confusion arises in the category *sanga*, which is the only term shared by the two areas and is one of the most popular *pathet* in both central and east Javanese music. To get around this problem, I have solicited the opinions of east Javanese musicians or, in a few cases, simply decided, based on musical criteria, which *sanga* is intended. And in the data presented below, I have translated the central Javanese categories to east Javanese. Thus, a piece classified as *manyura* is listed as *sanga* below, and a piece that is clearly *sanga* in the central Javanese sense is listed as *wolu*. Similarly, *pélog lima* and *pélog nem* are listed simply as *pélog bem*. (I encountered no pieces classified as *sléndro pathet nem*.)

As we have seen, then, because formal structure and *pathet* categories are understood differently in east Java than they are in central Java, and because of the use of both central Javanese and east Javanese terminology in reference to east Javanese music, the kinds of questions that were relatively problem-free when asked of any of the central Javanese repertories can be problematic indeed when posed in east Java. Bearing this warning in mind, we can consider the distribution of east Javanese repertory by tuning system, *pathet*, and structure in Figure 5.7.

The most striking aspect of this pattern of distribution is, as we would expect, the predominance of *sléndro* in all categories (407 *sléndro* items, thirty-nine *pélog*). Nearly one quarter of the items (103) are short-*gongan* forms (*jula-juli/giro*) classified either as *sléndro wolu* or *sléndro sanga*. Both in the emphasis on short forms and in the prevalence of *sléndro*, the distribution of repertory resembles that of Banyumas. Yet the repertory here is considerably more varied, with a substantial number of loud-style pieces (the forty-seven *gagahan*). And if we combine these forty-seven, which mostly use the same formal structure as *luwung*, with the seventy pieces in *luwung* form, we have a substantial number (117) of middle-sized pieces, comparable to the large number of *ladrang* in the court traditions of Solo and Yogya. The forms identified as large forms by the east Javanese (*gambir sawit*, *titipati*, and *lambang* – the ones with two sections) comprise a small, but not insignificant, portion of the repertory, numbering forty-three items in total.

By far the most prominent *pathet* are *sléndro wolu* and *sléndro sanga*. Pieces in *sléndro sepuluh*

	SLENDRO					PELOG									Totals
	10	8	9	Ser-ang	?	Sorog/Bem	8	9	10	Miring/Barang	9	10	Ser-ang	?	
Gambir Sawit	7	4	3	–	–	–	–	–	–	–	–	–	–	–	14
Titipati	3	4	1	–	–	–	–	–	–	–	–	–	–	–	8
Lambang	5	9	5	–	–	1	–	–	–	1	–	–	–	–	21
Luwung	5	15	29	5	2	2	2	1	–	6	–	1	1	1	70
Gagahan	22	6	9	–	10	1	–	–	–	–	–	–	–	–	47
Samirah	4	10	15	–	–	1	1	–	–	1	–	–	–	–	32
Cakra-Negara	1	4	14	1	–	2	–	–	–	–	–	–	–	–	22
Jula-juli/ Giro	6	47	56	–	3	3	1	1	–	–	–	–	–	–	117
Lagu Dolanan	–	2	8	–	3	–	–	–	–	–	–	–	–	–	13
Goyang-goyang	6	6	15	–	1	–	–	–	–	–	–	–	–	–	28
Ayak/ Krucilan	2	12	11	2	–	–	3	1	1	2	–	–	2	–	36
Srepeg/ Gedhog	2	4	3	–	–	–	–	–	–	–	–	–	–	–	9
Pamijèn	3	6	16	–	1	–	–	–	–	–	2	–	–	1	29
Totals	66	130	184	8	19	10	7	3	1	10	2	1	3	2	446

5.7 Distribution of east Javanese repertory by formal structure and *pathet*

appear in all categories except *lagu dolanan*, with *gagahan* constituting the most prominent by far (twenty-two of sixty-five), due perhaps to the practice of *gagahan* performance during the *pathet sepuluh* period preceding the opening of a *wayang kulit* play. *Sléndro serang*, though it may last as long as several hours in a *wayang* performance, is represented by a much smaller number of items (eight), which may be played a number of times within a single performance. From this data, it is difficult to identify significant patterns in *pélog pathet* distribution, not only because so few items appear, but also because some sources distinguish only *bem/sorog* from *barang/miring*, while others identify two or three *pathet* within each of these scales. (Were more *wayang topèng* music and Malang *wayang kulit* notated or recorded, the number of items appearing in *pélog* would increase substantially.)

In the section below I wish to discuss, with reference to specific items, some of the distinguishing features of east Javanese repertory: the variability of gong structure, the variability of *pathet* classification, some characteristics of east Javanese *balungan* (in contrast to those of the central Javanese regional traditions), the nature of the east Javanese *wayang* pieces, and the question of *jula-juli* as piece or genre.

It would be an exaggeration to suggest that east Javanese musicians do not associate particular *gendhing* with particular formal gong structures. Indeed, some pieces are heard again and again with the same structures. Perhaps in a substantially larger sample of recordings and notation than are currently available, one would find that some of these can be varied. Yet even in my data, derived from the few known sources of notation, a large sample of commercial cassettes, and a small sample of field recordings, thirty-five pieces (10 percent of the documented repertory) occur with more than one structure: thirty-one with two structures and four with three structures. No clear pattern emerges in the application of multiple structures. Some pieces may be played with a relatively sparse gong structure in one instance and rather dense gong structure in another, including even *Samirah*, one of the pieces whose title was chosen as the term for one of the east Javanese "forms."

```
  from Ronoatmodjo 1981a:16              (from Srampat, Kencana IR-041)
  (and many cassette recordings)

    t       P       t       N        t P t N  t P t N  t P t N  t P t N
  . 3 . 2 . 1 . 6 . 1 . 6 . 5 . 3    . 3 . 2  . 1 . 6  . 1 . 6  . 5 . 3G

  . 5 . 3 . 6 . 5 . 6 . 5 . 3 . 2G   . 5 . 3  . 6 . 5  . 2 . 1  . 3 . 2G

        ("samirah" form)                 ("jula-juli" or "giro" form)
```

5.8 Gendhing *Samirah* in two formal structures

For other pieces, the nature of the *balungan* melody may vary along with the formal structure, as in the two versions of Gendhing *Ijo-ijo* given below.

```
  (from cassette Loro Pangkon,          (from cassette Pangkur Surabaya,
     Lokananta ACD-202)                    Kencana Record IR-078)

      P       N       P       N                P       N
  6 5 6 1  6 5 6 1  6 1 2 3  6 2 1 6        6 1 6 1  5 3 5 6

  3 6 2 1  6 5 2 3  2 3 5 6  2 5 3 2G       2 1 5 3  5 6 3 2G

        ("luwung" form)                       ("cakranegara" form)
```

5.9 Gendhing *Ijo-ijo* in two formal structures

In some cases, the formal structure may even change in the middle of a single performances in an intentional shift from a sparse pattern of gong punctuation to a dense reiteration of kempul strokes in the pattern associated with east Javanese *ayak* (or *krucilan*) form. Such variability gives east Javanese pieces a realm of dynamism only rarely practiced in any of the central Javanese traditions. The frequency of gong punctuation is associated throughout central and east Java with the level of excitement. The very sparsely punctuated large *gendhing* induce a calm, even meditative mood, appropriate for the more refined characters and dance movements. The densely punctuated *sampak* in central Java and *ayak* in east Java are stirring pieces, often used for moments of extreme tension in dramatic presentations. Musicians in east Java, much more than their central Javanese counterparts, may exercise some choice in determining the gong structure, based on their own feeling of what density best fits the mood of the piece and the particular context in which it is performed.

The variability in *pathet* classification is of a different order than the variability discussed above, for it is a variability in conception rather than practice. In central Java pieces may be transposed from one *pathet* to another. In east Java we find conflicting notions concerning the category to which a piece belongs without it being transposed. Even after converting the listings in central Javanese terminology to conform with east Javanese, twenty-seven of the *gendhing* in the data are listed under two *sléndro pathet* categories and three *gendhing* under three *sléndro pathet* categories. Of these, six appear as *pathet sepuluh* and *pathet wolu*, eleven as *pathet sepuluh* and *pathet sanga*, and ten as *pathet wolu* and *pathet sanga*. Those with three *pathet* assignments are all *pathet sepuluh*, *pathet wolu*, and *pathet sanga*. *Pathet serang* is a very limited category and is not generally applied to pieces other than the few played during the final hour or two of a *wayang* performance. *Pathet sepuluh*, musicians say, is somewhat difficult to characterize on strictly musical criteria. *Gendhing* classified as *sepuluh* often consist of certain passages that clearly suggest *pathet sanga* and others that clearly suggest *pathet wolu*. Hence the variability involving *pathet sepuluh* is not surprising. More remarkable are the pieces listed both as *wolu* and as *sanga*, which are supposedly easily distinguished categories. A number of these involve several *gongan*, with one ending on 6, typical of *pathet sanga*, and another on 5, typical of *pathet wolu* (e.g., Gendhing *Ricik-ricik*). Others feature melodic passages typical of both *wolu* and *sanga* and end on *gong* tone 2, but are not classified as *pathet sepuluh* (e.g., Gendhing *Cokèk*). A thorough investigation of *pathet* in east Java is beyond the scope of this study. For such an investigation not to be misleading, it should take into account the multiple listings that occur and the contexts in which *pathet* is made explicit. Outside of the *wayang* traditions, *pathet* has only recently become an issue, in response to central Javanese models in academic circles and in the commercial cassette world.

In compiling my data on east Javanese repertory I was careful to omit pieces that were played by east Javanese but were clearly attributed to central Javanese origins. Were there historical records to document the repertory heard in east Java over the past century or two, we might well posit connections between the two regions with respect to many items of repertory. Yet even where a list of pieces might appear, we would need to exercise extreme caution in drawing conclusions based on title alone. Among the 347 east Javanese pieces known to me, I find sixty-eight titles shared with one or more central Javanese repertory. Yet of these, only about one third (twenty-four) can be shown to bear a relationship to any of the central Javanese pieces with the same title and less than one quarter (fourteen) could be said to be similar (i.e., "the same piece" in different versions).

To exemplify the kinds of relationships represented in Figure 5.10, I include comparative *balungan* notation for one piece in each category (similar, related, different). As Gendhing *Bondhèt* is widely known in various central Javanese traditions, I offer an east Javanese version, with a Yogyanese version for comparison, given in Figure 5.11. The correspondence is clear. Almost every gatra, if not the same in the two versions, ends on the same tone. The second section, though performed with a double *pancer* 1 in east Java and a single *pancer* 1 in Yogya, is nearly identical in the two versions. It is performance style, discussed below, which would enable listeners readily to distinguish the regional identity of these two pieces.

TITLE OF EAST JAVANESE GENDHING	RELATIONSHIP OF EAST JAVANESE VERSIONS TO CENTRAL JAVANESE			
	YOGYAKARTA	SURAKARTA	BANYUMAS	SEMARANG
Alas Kobong		Dif.		
Alas Padhang		Dif.		
*Angleng	Rel.	Rel.	Rel.	
Arum Manis		Dif.		
Bang-bang Wetan	Dif.			
Bedhat	Dif.	Dif.		
Blenderan		Dif.	Dif.	
**Bondhèt	Sim.	Sim.	Sim.	Sim.
**Bribil	Sim.	Sim.	Dif.	
Cara Balen		Dif.		
Cèlèng Mogok	?		?	
Cina Nagih	?	Dif.		
Éling-éling	Dif.	Dif.	Dif.	Dif.
Éndhol-éndhol		Dif.		
Èsèk-èsèk		Dif.		
Gagak Sétra	Dif.	Dif.		
**Gambir Sawit	Sim.	Sim.		
*Gandakusuma	Rel.	Rel.		
**Gandariya	?	Rel.	Sim.	
*Gandariya Gandhung	Rel.			
*Gendruwo Momong		Rel.		
**Génjong	Sim.	Sim.		
*Godril		Rel.	Rel.	
Gondhèl		Dif.		
**Gonjing	Sim.	Dif.		
**Grompol	Dif.	Sim.		
*Gunungsari	Dif.	Rel.	Rel.	
**Ijo-ijo	Dif.	Sim.	Sim.	
Jangkung Kuning	Dif.	Dif.		
Jaran Képang			Dif.	
Jung Layar	?			
Kapang-kapang	?	Dif.		
Kembang Gayam			Dif.	
Kodhok Ngorèk	Dif.	Dif.		
Lambang		Dif.		
**Lambangsari	Dif.	Dif.	Sim.	
Lawung		Dif.		
Loro-loro	?	Dif.		
**Mandraguna		Sim.		
Mara Séba	?	Dif.		
Montro	Dif.	Dif.		
**Onang-onang	Sim.	Sim.		
**Ondhé-ondhé		Dif.	Sim.	
*Pacul Gowang	?	Dif.	Rel.	
Pisang Bali	Dif.	Dif.	Dif.	

5.10   Relationship of east Javanese *gendhing* to central Javanese *gendhing* sharing same titles

Though Gendhing *Bondhèt* is the standard piece for the opening scene of *wayang kulit* performances in Banyumas and Semarang traditions and may be used in Yogyanese and Solonese *wayang* performances in later scenes, it is not a *wayang* piece in east Javanese tradition. Instead, according to the highly respected musician and puppeteer Ki Piet Asmoro, it is a piece used only for *tayuban*. The standard piece for the opening scene in east Javanese *wayang* is now Gendhing *Gandakusuma*. Formerly Gendhing *Gandakusuma* was used only for plays based on the *Ramayana* or which focused on an older king from the Mahabharata, while Gendhing *Onang-onang* was chosen for plays opening in Amarta (the Pendhawa kingdom), Gendhing *Sekar Téja* for plays opening in Dwarawati (Kresna's

| TITLE OF EAST JAVANESE GENDHING | RELATIONSHIP OF EAST JAVANESE VERSIONS TO CENTRAL JAVANESE | | | |
	YOGYAKARTA	SURAKARTA	BANYUMAS	SEMARANG
Perkutut Manggung	Dif.	Dif.		
Petung Wulung		Dif.		
*Pring Padha Pring		Rel.		
Rangsang	?			
Ricik-ricik	Dif.	Dif.	Dif.	
*Rujak Sentul		Rel.		
Salatun	Dif.	Dif.		
**Samirah	?	Sim.	Sim.	
Sapu Jagad		Dif.		
Sarayuda	?	Dif.		
Sawunggaling	Dif.	Dif.		
Sekar Téja	?	Dif.		
Semèru	Dif.	Dif.		
**Sengsem		Sim.		
Sontoloyo	?	Dif.	Dif.	
Sumyar	Dif.	Dif.		
Titipati	Dif.	Dif.		
*Tropongan	Rel.	Rel.		
Turi-turi Putih		Dif.		
Udan Soré	Dif.	Dif.		

SUMMARY:

6 Sim.	10 Sim.	6 Sim.	1 Sim.
4 Rel.	9 Rel.	4 Rel.	
19 Dif.	38 Dif.	6 Dif.	1 Dif.
13 ?		1 ?	

KEY:

Sim. = similarity readily apparent between east Javanese and at least one central Javanese version (titles marked **)

Rel. = some relationship, demonstrable through analytical scrutiny, with at least one central Javanese version (titles marked *)

Dif. = different pieces, no apparent relationship

? = notation or recording of central Javanese version not available

5.10 Continued.

EAST JAVANESE VERSION
(sléndro pathet sepuluh)

YOGYANESE VERSION
(sléndro pathet nem)

Buka: 2.2. 5653 .2.1 .6.5N/G

Buka: 5353 1653 2132 55.5N/G

mbok-mbokan:

```
      t   P   t   N
   2352 3565 2353 2165
   2352 3565 2353 2126
   .126 .132 6121 6523
   3353 5653 2353 6165G
```

dados:

```
      t       t   N
   2312 .365 1653 2165
   3565 3235 2523 5616
   2126 2132 5321 6523
   5353 1653 2132 1635G
```

anak-anakan:

```
   t      t   P   t      t    N
1.16 1.15 1.13 1.12 1.13 1.12 1.16 1.15
1.16 1.15 1.13 1.12 1.13 1.12 1.12 1.16
1.12 1.16 1.13 1.12 1.15 1.16 1.15 1.13
1.16 1.16 1.13 1.12 1.13 1.12 1.16 1.15G
```

ndhawah: (played with pancer 1)

```
      t    t    t   tN
   .6.5 .3.2 .3.2 .6.5
   .6.5 .3.2 .3.2 .1.6
   .1.6 .1.6 .2.1 .5.3
   .1.6 .5.3 .2.3 .6.5G
```

5.11 Gendhing *Bondhèt*, east Javanese and Yogyanese versions

kingdom), and Gendhing *Kutut Manggung* for plays opening in Astina (the Korawa's kingdom).

Each of these pieces used for opening scenes in the *wayang* bears a title known also in central Java. Yet all of them contrast with the central Javanese pieces of the same title, with only Gendhing *Gandakusuma* showing some relationship. Below is given an east Javanese version from Timoer 1988 (I:162–63) and a Solonese version from Mloyowidodo 1976 (I:92).

```
EAST JAVANESE VERSION                        SOLONESE VERSION
(Sléndro pathet sepuluh, or wolu)            (Sléndro pathet sanga)

Buka:  .55. 2356 .2.1 .6.5N/G        Buka:   2 .356 .6.1 .2.1 .2.6 .3.5N/G

mbok-mbokan:                         mérong:
         t    P    t    N                     t              t       N
A: [[: 2312 3123 5616 2165           . 2 . 3  . 5 . 6  . 2 . 1  . 6 . 5
       3212 5321*3216 2165G :]       . 2 . 3  . 5 . 6  . 2 . 1  . 6 . 5G

(to proceed to ngelik or to          . 2 . 1  . 2 . 6  . 2 . 1  . 6 . 5
 anak-anakan:)   *3265 2321G         . 2 . 1  . 2 . 6  . 2 . 1  . 6 . 5G

ngelik:                              ngelik:
       3212 6356 2321 6535           . . 5 6  1 6 5 3  2 3 2 1  6 5 3 5
       3212 5321 3212 6356G          . . 5 6  1 6 5 3  2 3 2 1 23561.21G

       3212 6356 2321 6535           . . 3 2  . 1 6 5  . 2 . 1  . 6 . 5
       3212 5321 3216 2165G          . 2 2 3 561.61 5  . 2 . 1  . 6 . 5G

       2312 5356 3561 6535           . 2 2 3 561.61 5  . 2 . 1  . 6 . 5
       3212 5321 3216 2165G          . 2 2 . 2 3 5 6  . 2 . 1  . 6 . 5G
            (proceed to B)
                                     minggah: (normally proceeds to one of
         t    P    t    N              several ladrang, e.g., Gandasuli)
B:  [: 3.32 3.36 3.31 3.35
       ...2 ...1 ...6 ...5G

       ...2 ...6 ...1 ...5
       ...2 ...1 ...6 ...5G

ngelik:
       ...2 ...6 ...1 ...5
       ...2 ...1 ...5 ...1G  (return to A)

       ...2 ...6 ...1 ...5
       ...2 ...1 ...6 ...5G :]

anak-anakan:
         t    P    t    N
   [: 3.32 3.36 3.31 3.35
      3.32 3.31 3.32 3.36G

      3.32 3.36 3.31 3.35
      3.32 3.31 3.36 3.35G :]
```

5.12   *Gendhing Gandakusuma*, east Javanese and Solonese versions

The clear majority of east Javanese pieces sharing titles with pieces in central Java bear no apparent relationship today, though over the centuries it is conceivable that distinctive developments in disparate regions may have obscured what was once a clearer relationship. Consider, for example, the piece *Ricik-ricik*, shown in Figure 5.13 in three versions.

EAST JAVANESE	SOLONESE	BANYUMAS
sléndro sanga or wolu	sléndro manyura	sléndro manyura

buka: 2 6 2 6 1 5N/G   buka: 6.356 .532 .356N/G   buka: .3.1 .3.2 .1.6N/G

```
                                                         (P)         (P)
PN  PN  PN  PN               N  PN  PN  PN                N  PN  PN  PN
.1.5 .1.5 .2.3 .5.6G        .3.5 .6.5 .6.5 .1.6 (x2)     .1.6 .3.2 .5.3 .2.1G

.2.6 .2.6 .2.1 .6.5G        .3.2 .3.2 .3.2 .1.6 (x2)     .2.1 .2.3 .5.6 .1.6G
```

5.13   *Ricik-ricik* from east Java, Solo, and Banyumas

Although both the east Javanese and the Banyumas pieces consist of two *gongan* played in alternation without immediate repetition, and although the *gong* tones in both pieces are one step apart (the upper neighbor tone of 6 is 1), one cannot argue that these are versions of the same piece. Too many other pieces in both repertories exhibit the same characteristics.[15]

Staples of the east Javanese *wayang* repertory

East Java shares with central Java essentially the same heritage of *wayang kulit* stories and performance conventions. Yet the gamelan pieces that serve as staples for every *wayang* performance contrast markedly between these two major regions. In all the central Javanese traditions, the pieces known as *Ayak-ayakan*, *Srepegan*, and *Sampak* are united by a single relationship between *kempul* (or *gong*) and *kenong*: one *kempul* (or *gong*) beat coinciding with every second *kenong* beat. The relationship between this pattern and the *balungan* determines the particular form, though terminology varies from one central Javanese tradition to another. In east Javanese tradition, the pieces serving a comparable function (*Ayak*, *Krucilan*, *Sre(m)peg*, *Gedhog*) are characterized by a variety of relationships among the punctuating gongs and the *balungan*. In some cases it is difficult even to determine a *balungan*, since the *saron* may play a lively interlocking part, sometimes improvisatory, sometimes worked out beforehand. And in other cases the *demung* and *slenthem* each play different abstractions of the *saron barung* part. Where a clear *sarong barung* part is available (either in notation or recording), it is that part which serves as the basis for the discussion of *balungan* below. Though it is arguably more than an "outline," it is closest in spirit to the *balungan* of central Javanese pieces, as the term is used today.

The most conspicuous feature of some of these pieces – usually referred to as *Ayak* or *Krucilan*, but sometimes as *Sre(m)peg* – is the high frequency of *kempul* strokes, with *gong* and *kenong* sounded only occasionally to mark what are often asymmetrical melodic groupings. The following transcription of *Ayak Serang* exemplifies these traits (Figure 5.14). Some musicians would qualify the formal structure by referring to the *kempul* here as *kerep* ("frequent"), rather than *arang* ("sparse"). The *kempul* plays two beats for each beat of the *balungan*, at a tempo comparable to the *kempul* part for *Sampak* in Solonese tradition (about 120–180 beats per minute). And as is true for *Sampak* and related pieces in central Java, the *gong* beats are always simultaneous with a *kenong* stroke and never a *kempul* stroke. (The *kempul* and *gong* are often played by one musician both in central Java and in east Java.) The *kenong*, however, does not play at twice the density of the *kempul*, but only on certain pillar tones of the *balungan*, spaced asymmetrically: six beats, plus four beats, plus two beats, plus

(transcribed from cassette <u>Cindhe Kembang: Klenengan Jawa Timur</u>, WD-670)

```
gong:                    G                                            G

kenong:              1        3    6        1    5        6    3

kempul:    66666666111. 11111111 6666 66661111 5555 55556666 666.

balungan:   5 3 5 6 2 1  3 5 6 3  5 6  3 5 6 1  6 5  1 2 1 6  5 3
```

5.14 *Ayak Serang, sléndro pathet serang*

four beats, plus two beats, plus four beats, plus two beats. According to some musicians, the *kenong* part is flexible, in the sense that the player may decide which tones of the *balungan* melody are "weighty" enough to merit *kenong* punctuation. In a recording session I conducted in a village south of Malang, the *kenong* part for some *Ayak* pieces (there played in *pélog*) changed slightly from one repetition to the next.

The introduction and *saron* part for some *wayang* pieces behaves rather differently from anything one encounters in central Java. The drummer signals the introduction, which begins with a *gong* tone, often followed by a passage of sparse *saron* playing or a somewhat syncopated *saron* part. The *kempul* may not begin immediately to play its dense strokes, waiting instead to initiate this pattern only after the first *gongan*. And in successive renditions of a piece, which the puppeteer may require a number of times within a single performance, the *saron* melody may change markedly from one time to the next, maintaining its identity only through the introduction and the progression of pillar tones. A piece that was identified by several performers as *Krucilan* and by others as *Ayak* was performed in three versions during the *pathet wolu* section of a *wayang* performance in a village near Batu (in the mountainous region north west of Malang), as shown in Figure 5.15.

```
introduction:  (drum...)  2G . . . 5  . 1̇ 2̇ .  2̇ 1̇ 2̇ 5  . 3 2 1G

1st line, version I:    5 6 1̇ 5   6 1̇ 5 2̇   5 1̇ 2̇ 5   1̇ 5 1̇ 6

              II:       2̇ 1̇ 6 5   3 1 2 3   1 2 3 5   6 2̇ 1̇ 6

             III:       2 132 .   5 6̇1̇5 .   2 132 .   5̇1̇6̇1̇5̇1̇6̇


2nd line, version I:    5 6 1̇ 5   6 1̇ 5 2   1 2 3 1   2 3 1 5G

              II:       2̇ 1̇ 6 5   3 1 2 3   1 2 3 5   2̇ 1̇ 6 5G

             III:       561 6̇1̇2   1̇23 235   16535 35   2356535G


3rd line, version I:    5 6 1̇ 5   6 1̇ 5 2̇   1̇ 5 1̇ 6   1̇ 5 3 2G

              II:       2̇ 1̇ 6 5   3 1 2 3   1 2 3 5   6 5 3 2G

             III:       6 5 2 3   2 5 6 1̇   6 5 2 3   2 5 3 2G


4th line, version I:    5 6 1̇ 5   6 1̇ 5 2̇   3 5 6 3   5 6 3 1G

              II:       2̇ 1̇ 6 5   3 1 2 3   1 2 3 5   6 3 2 1G

             III:       6̇1̇656̇1̇2   6̇1̇65165   6 1̇ 5 2̇   6̇1̇56321G
```

5.15 *Wayang* piece (*Ayak* or *Krucilan, sléndro pathet wolu*), three versions as performed by musicians of puppeteer Ki Matadi

In each of the first two versions, the first eight or twelve beats are the same from line to line, but corresponding lines for each version bear little similarity before the final few tones. In central Java, no comparable variation occurs in any of the *wayang* pieces. Instead, variation occurs in the elaborating instruments, which may include *saron imbal*, but the *balungan* would not change within the context of a single *wayang* performance.

A second group of *wayang* pieces, more often referred to either as *Sre(m)peg* or *Gedhog*, more closely resemble the central Javanese *wayang* pieces in the regular sounding of *kenong* – often at the rate of two *kenong* per *kempul* (or *gong*). The several pieces most often called *Gedhog* are characterized by the sounding not of *kempul*, but of the large *gong* every second *kenong* stroke (with *kenong* occurring every two or four beats of the *balungan*). The result is a very frequent sounding of the large *gong*, more frequent than in any central Javanese tradition, except perhaps some of the archaic ensembles (*monggang* and *kodhok ngorèk*). In *wayang*, the *Gedhog* pieces resemble most closely the *Ayak-ayakan* of central Java, which may (in Solonese and Banyumas *wayang* overtures) have *gong siyem/suwukan* every four beats. And, like central Javanese *Ayak-ayakan*, some *Gedhog* slow down through the first several *gatra*, with the *balungan* part doubling before the tempo settles.

The application of the term *Sre(m)peg*, which some musicians call the *Ayak* pieces discussed above, is more varied than *Gedhog*. Yet in the various usage of terms for east Javanese *wayang* pieces, one does not find the terms *Sre(m)peg* and *Ayak* used to distinguish different levels of gong density or emotional intensity, as they do in all central Javanese traditions. Instead, as noted above, one often hears a single term (e.g., *Ayak*) being qualified by an indication of the *kempul* density – either "frequent" or "sparse." Thus, it is not that *Ayak* is more subdued (by sparsity of gong punctuation) than *Sre(m)peg* the way *Ayak-ayakan* is in comparison to *Srepegan* in central Javanese traditions. Rather, it is the term *Ayak* that is most consistently applied to the exciting pieces with the densest *kempul* playing, used for moments of great tension and action in *wayang* – duels and all-out battles.[16]

The *Jula-juli* "genre": the hallmark of east Java's gamelan repertory

Ask almost any east Javanese about local gamelan styles and he will respond that the quintessential *Jawa timuran* music is *jula-juli*. Yet, as I have suggested earlier, it is difficult to pinpoint precisely what is meant by this term. To some it is simply a single *gendhing*, identifiable like any other by its *balungan*. To others it is a category or genre of pieces, delimited by a particular formal structure and style of performance. To some extent a similar range of meanings exists for many musical terms in east Java. Yet this is a term familiar to many east Javanese, not just musicians; and, however it may be understood or defined, it is said to be widely known and loved throughout east Java and to represent the most immediate musical symbol of East Java, the province, as distinct from other regions of Java and Indonesia.

My inquiry into the meanings of this and related terms, which have included the consultation of published written sources, an inventory of commercial cassette contents and labels, and discussions with a number of east Javanese musicians, has yielded some rather contradictory findings. What is generally labelled *Jula-juli* on cassettes and called *Jula-juli* in performances is a particular two-*gongan* piece, with eight *balungan* beats per *gong*, four *kenong* strokes per *gong*, playable either in *pathet wolu* (with *gong* tones 5 and 1) or in *pathet sanga* (with *gong* tones 2 and 6), usually slowed down to allow for the distinctively east Javanese style of singing solo *kidungan* (a variety of sung poetry), and sometimes with variable *saron barung* part. The *pathet wolu* version usually begins on *gong* tone 5, the *pathet sanga* version on *gong* tone 2. (Thus, raised one tone, the first *gongan* of the *wolu* version is the same as the second *gongan* of the *sanga* version, and the second *gongan* of the *wolu* version the same as the first of the *sanga*.)

```
                             N P N P  N P N N
    pathet wolu:   buka... 5G  6 5 6 2  6 5 2 1G

                              2 1 2 6  2 1 6 5G


                             P N P N  P N P N
    pathet sanga:  buka... 2G  3 2 3 1  3 2 1 6G

                             i 6 i 3  i 6 3 2G
```

5.16   Balungan and formal structure for *Jula-juli*

However, some musicians say that *Jula-juli* is not a *gendhing* in the usual sense, with a certain *balungan* and formal structure, but requires the incorporation of *kidungan* singing with the particular *balungan* – in others words, that it is a vocal–instrumental piece or, given the variety found in the vocal parts and even the *saron* parts one hears, a vocal–instrumental genre.

An instrumental version, with the same *balungan* and formal structure, is heard in both *pathet wolu* and *pathet sanga* as an all-purpose accompaniment for action in *ludruk* drama, serving the same function as *Srepegan* and related pieces in central Javanese *wayang*. But in this case musicians disagree over the proper name of the piece. Some still identify it as *Jula-juli*, but others refer to it as Gendhing (or Lancaran) *Surabayan* or *Surabaya*. Especially short, fast, and loud instrumental renditions of the same *balungan* and with the same formal structure, but in *tayuban* performances, are called *Céko* or *Din Tak Tong*. Clearly, then, function rather than musical structure is for some an important criterion in the choice of term. Participants in a *tayuban* may yell out *Céko*! At this point the musicians play a very fast and loud instrumental version of *Jula-juli* as a transition for one group of male dancers to sit down and another to prepare to dance. Hence, the term is seen to refer to that transition, as well as to the music. *Din Tak Tong* is the verbal rendering of three drum sounds heard as a quick introduction to a fast rendition of this piece. *Céko* is the more prevalent term in the Malang area, and *Din Tak Tong* (or some equivalent) further north.

Though *gendhing* in east Java and central Java are usually identified by the same name regardless of the *pathet* in which they are performed, the difference between *pathet* is, for some east Javanese, an important criterion in delimiting *Jula-juli* and related pieces. Both in live *tayuban* performances and on commercial cassettes of *tayuban* music, I have only heard the fast versions (*Céko* or *Din Tak Tong*) played in *pathet sanga*. And the title "Gendhing Surabayan," though applied by some to the instrumental accompaniment for *ludruk*, regardless of *pathet*, is said by some musicians and writers to refer properly only to the *pathet wolu* version (Proyek Penelitian 1976:43–44; Hardjoprawiro 1985:23). They limit the term *Jula-juli* to the slow *pathet sanga* rendition of this piece (with *gong* tones 6 and 2, though usually beginning on tone 2). They insist that the *pathet wolu* version (with *gong* tones 5 and 1, usually beginning on tone 5), which they identify as the piece that accompanies the *ngrémo* dance, is properly called Gendhing *Surabayan*, even if it slows down and incorporates *kidungan*.[17] The same piece (with *gong* tones 5 and 1), but played in *pélog* is often referred to as Gendhing *Beskalan*, as it usually accompanies the dance known as *beskalan*, a female dance closely related to *ngrémo* and associated primarily with the Malang area.

Despite the plurality of titles and terms, it is clear to listeners and performers that these various pieces (or, depending on one's conception, these variants of the piece) all follow the same scheme – that their structure, if not their function and mood, is essentially the same. In some ways, then, the *Jula-juli* "genre" is like the "twelve-bar blues" music of America – not in its subject matter, but in the use of a basic progression (*balungan* tones, rather than chords) – in widely varying styles of realization and with or without vocal parts. Just as we find many songs using the blues chord progression, so we find many east Javanese gamelan pieces using the *Jula-juli balungan* progression, often qualified as "*Jula-juli* XX" (e.g. *Jula-juli Dol Tinuku*). Played fast and loud, the instrumental piece is usually referred to by other terms, as noted previously, but is still clearly in some senses "the same piece."

Performances of *Jula-juli* with *kidungan* almost always begin at the faster tempo (what would be called *irama* I or *irama tanggung* in central Java), and normally proceed through at least one change in *irama* level (to *irama* II or *irama dadi*). The tempo may then speed up, affecting a change back to *irama* level I, but it may also slow further to *irama* III/*irama wilet*. The singer must adjust his or her part so that, regardless of *irama* level, major vocal phrases end with – or, more often, *before* – the gong tones. At a *tayuban* performance in a village south west of Malang in August 1986, the drummer slowed the piece one level further – to *irama* IV/*irama rangkep* – to test the singer–dancer's capabilities. This has not yet become normal practice and it wound up causing difficulties for the singer, as each *gongan* became so long and the *balungan* tones came so slowly that the singer lost his way and ended his phrases in the middle of the *gongan*. Realizing the difficulty, the drummer signalled an accelerando to bring the piece back to *irama* III. Performances of *Jula-juli* usually end with a return to *irama* I, either with a ritard to a final *gong* beat or continuation to another piece.

As is carefully illustrated by Darmono Saputro in his study of *Jula-juli* (Saputro 1984), individual expression and variation abounds in *Jula-juli* performance. The vocal part will reflect the local style (e.g., Jombang or Surabaya), the individual style of the singer, and the mood of the text. Saputro identifies four kinds of mood (*rasa*) in *Jula-juli* vocal style: *pitutur* (didactic, moralistic), *prenès* (light, suggestive, flirtatious), *gecul* (humorous), and *sedih* (sad) (Saputro 1984:11). To these he adds other kinds of text content (*isi*): *kemasyarakatan* (social, dealing with contemporary Indonesia and world politics), and *keagamaan* (religious, both Islam and Kejawèn). Other sources mention that *kidungan* texts may contain advice on marital relations, love, and general social interaction, as well as government propaganda (Proyek Penelitian 1976:177).

Saputro also provides an example of the kind of elaborating part that can be played on the *saron barung* during sections of slow tempo, in this case, *irama* III/*irama wilet*. In Figure 5.17, I show the *saron* part, along with the *slenthem* and the underlying *balungan* part (which may be played on *demung*, but may also be omitted if the *demung* chooses to join the *saron*). The passage shown is one gongan of *Jula-juli*, *sléndro pathet sanga*. The *saron* part given in Figure 5.17 was transcribed by Saputro from a recorded performance. Many other variations can be heard on commercial cassette recordings from east Java, in some cases played by one *saron* and in others by several *saron* and *demung*. As in the above example, the elaborating *saron* part

```
saron:      ..16 5356 1.16 5356 .2.6 .2.3 .2.6 .2.1
slenthem:     2  .   2  .   1   .   1   .
  (or:        2 . 2 . 2 . 2 . 1 . 1 . 1 . 1 . )
balungan:     .   3   .   2N  .   3   .   1N


saron:      ..65 3235 6.65 3235 ..53 2532 1111 6216
slenthem:     2  .   2  .   6   .   6   .
  (or:        2 . 2 . 2 . 2 . 6 . 6 . 6 . 6 . )
balungan:     .   3   .   2N  .   1   .   6G
```

(saron from Saputro 1984:46)

5.17   *Saron* elaboration in *Jula-juli, sléndro pathet sanga*

is only loosely constrained by the *balungan*, coinciding with the *balungan* pitches only on the second *kenong* and the *gong* tones. *Gambang, gendèr,* and *celempung/siter* parts, normally more independent from *balungan* than would be an elaborating *saron*, are in *Jula-juli* usually more highly constrained by the *balungan* than the part shown above, as they usually coincide with every second *balungan* tone (i.e., every *kenong* tone).

The freedom in the *saron* elaboration may be a reflection of the great frequency with which this piece is performed. That is, the *balungan* is so deeply ingrained in people's minds that its identity is not in question, even when only occasionally hinted at in the *saron* part. One is reminded of the vast variety of variations, particularly by jazz musicians, of the basic I-IV-I-V-IV-I chord progression of the blues. Once a model is thoroughly established, such as the blues or *Jula-juli*, significant departures or alterations that might obscure a less well-known progression of chords or *balungan* can still be heard in relation to the model and are enjoyed because of their marked variance from it. In none of the repertories of central Java is there a single piece played with such frequency. Lancaran *Éling-éling* (*Banyumasan*) comes close to serving as a signature piece in Banyumas – one is likely to hear it at most Banyumas events involving gamelan music – and it is varied with some alternate *saron* and vocal parts, but nowhere near to the extent of *Jula-juli* in east Java. In Solo and Yogya, the only pieces heard with considerable frequency are the *wayang* pieces (*Ayak-ayakan, Srepegan,* and *Sampak*), but these are already multiple variants of several underlying models.

Musical style

Balungan

The style of east Javanese *balungan*, as notated in the available sources, and as I have heard played in live performances and on numerous cassette recordings, is remarkably similar to that of Solonese and other central Javanese repertories. In some pieces the relative density of the *balungan* changes several times within a *gongan*, but this is perhaps only slightly more prevalent in east Java than in central Java. In none of the traditions considered thus far is it the norm. The contours of *gatra* conform almost without exception to those currently used in central Java. Such similarity might represent an adjustment at some point in the past to Solonese tastes. Yet it seems just as likely that Javanese tastes throughout most of central and east Java may have long shared the same sense of melodic contour, at least at the *gatra* level.

One factor that sets at least some of the east Javanese repertory off from the central Javanese traditions is the prominent use of *pancer* and double *pancer* (*pancer rangkep*).

Whether or not to consider the *pancer* tones as belonging to the *balungan* part or as a process of *balungan* expansion is somewhat problematic. In the Yogyanese *Pakem Wirama*, dating from the late nineteenth century, directions are given to insert a *pancer* in the *saron barung* part, but the basic melody is written without the *pancer* tones shown. In some pieces, only certain passages may be constructed with a *pancer* orientation, and these would normally be shown in written form and conceived of as part of the *balungan*. The notation of east Javanese *gendhing* is, as far as I could determine, a recent phenomenon, and the *pancer* tones are usually shown.

Michael Crawford stresses the importance of *pancer* in east Java, particularly in the Mojokerto area, where, he claims, "it is used systematically in almost all *gendhing*" (1980:203). My observation of gamelan practice in Mojokerto, along with the notation of Mojokerto *gendhing* in two sources (Asmoro 1971 and Ronoatmodjo 1981a) suggest that Crawford's claim may be somewhat exaggerated. But it is certainly true of the larger pieces in the east Javanese repertory, those with two contrasting sections (*mbok-mbokan* and *anak-anakan*), that *pancer* and double *pancer* figure prominently in distinguishing the sections. While the performance of some pieces may incorporate the four episodes described by Crawford (1980:203), what is far more common is the use of a single *pancer* or no *pancer* at all in the first section and a double *pancer* in the second. Figure 5.18 gives the main (non-*ngelik*) *gongan* from both sections of the widely played Gendhing *Lambang*, *sléndro pathet wolu*.

```
                    t        P        t        N
mbok-mbokan:     . 6 . 3  . 6 . 2  . 6 . 3  . 6 . 5
                 . 6 . 2  . 6 . 1  . 6 . 3  . 6 . 5G


anak-anakan:     6 . 6 3  6 . 6 2  6 . 6 3  6 . 6 5
                 6 . 6 2  6 . 6 1  6 . 6 3  6 . 6 5G
```

5.18   Single and double *pancer* in the main *gongan* of Gendhing *Lambang*, *sléndro pathet wolu*

Instrumental techniques

Loud and complex drumming and unique *bonang* patterns are the outstanding features of east Javanese gamelan style, immediately recognizable to Javanese listeners. Beyond these, subtler contrasts with the central Javanese traditions can be identified in the playing of the punctuating gongs, the *balungan* instruments, and the elaborating instruments (though most soft instrument playing is, at least nowadays, very similar to Solonese style). Older musicians in Surabaya speak of east Javanese *suling* and *rebab* playing, but lament that only a few old players have not been significantly influenced by Solonese practice on these instruments.

Gong punctuation

Without question the most outstanding contrast between east Javanese gong playing and any of the central Javanese is the fast *kempul*, punctuated only sparsely by *kenong* and *gong*, in the *wayang* pieces. Earlier in this chapter I have also provided schema for the standard formal structures of the east Javanese repertory. The most notable contrast between east Javanese and Solonese traditions in the pieces of regular *gongan* length is the sounding of *kempul* at the midpoint of every *kenongan*, even in the forms with short *gongan* (*jula-juli, giro*). I find no indication – either from personal observation or from written sources – that east Javanese *kempul* players vary the part as may occur in Banyumas (sometimes three, sometimes as many as five *kempul* per *gongan* in a *lancaran*). And, since many east Javanese gamelan have only one *kempul* (tuned to 6), the kempul part may not vary in pitch as it almost always does in the central Javanese traditions. East Javanese tastes seem to be following those of central Java in the addition of *kempul* (and sometimes *kenong*) to allow for pitch choice on this instrument. The *gong suwukan* (*siyem*) is also not present in many gamelan; and thus, one may hear large *gong* sounded at the end of short phrases which, in central Java, would be marked by the *suwukan* (*siyem*).

The *ponggang*, though present in only a few of the ensembles I saw, plays a part very similar in principle and in density to the *bonang panembung* of Yogyakarta – sounding every two or four *saron* beats. In *sléndro*, with both 1 and high 1 as pitch options, players usually choose to play both simultaneously, rather than either one, even though all other pitch choices can only be realized as single tones. This practice gives special emphasis to tone 1, but apparently without any implications for *pathet*. Combinations other than this one possible octave (such as *kempyung*, e.g., 2 and 6) are, as far as I could tell, never played on this instrument.

Balungan instruments

Although the *ponggang* could be classified as a *balungan* instrument, like the *bonang panembung* in Yogyakarta, it is the *slenthem* and *saron* instruments that east Javanese normally identify as *balungan* instruments today – those that carry the instrumental melody that sets one *gendhing* off from another. It is not clear how long this term has been used in this sense in east Java. But this is the part chosen for notation by musicians in east Java, just as it is in central Java. In many pieces, the *saron* (*barung* and *demung*) and *slenthem* simply sound this part in unison. In some, particularly when the *balungan* tones are sparse, the *slenthem* may anticipate only the stronger tones of the *balungan*, sounding them on the weak beats or in between the beats (*gemakan*), as shown in Figure 5.17. Also, the *saron barung* may play a fast interlocking elaboration of the *balungan*. Though found in Solonese, Yogyanese, and Banyumas styles, it is in east Javanese gamelan playing that one most often hears the *imbal* style known sometimes as *kinthilan* (from *inthil*, literally "goat droppings"), in which two *saron* play the same (or nearly the same) melody, one trailing the other by one beat of the fastest pulse (density referent). Figure 5.19 shows an excerpt from a piece identified as Gendhing *Krucilan*, with fast *saron imbal kinthilan* that is often played at breakneck speed.

```
balungan:      .  1  .  6  .  1  .  2  .  1  .  6  .  1  .  5G
 saron I:    . i 6 5 6 i 5 6 2 i 5 3 2 5 3 2  5 3 2 3 2 3 5 6 5 6 2 i 6 2 3 5
 saron II:   . i 6 5 6 i 5 6 2 i 5 3 2 5 3 2  5 3 2 3 2 3 5 6 5 6 2 i 6 2 3 5
```
5.19   *Saron imbal kinthilan* in Gendhing *Krucilan, sléndro pathet wolu*

One of my most memorable evenings in east Java was a night spent in 1986 listening to Ki Piet Asmoro's gamelan group accompany him in a *wayang* performance in his native Trowulan, Mojokerto. The *saron imbal*, fast and light, sounded throughout the night and echoed in my mind for days afterward. It was both spirited and controlled, virtuosic and subtle and, for lack of a better term, magical.

Bonang and saron peking

Bonang playing style is the musical element most consistently and immediately recognizable as east Javanese in the performance of the *gendhing* repertory. Though the two *bonang* anticipate and emphasize tones on the stronger beats of the *balungan*, as they often do in the several central Javanese traditions, the patterns by which they do so are uniquely east Javanese. Three basic techniques can be identified for the *bonang barung* – in east Java often called *bonang babok*. Terms for these techniques are not standardized, but the constraints on the use of the techniques are widely shared. For the present discussion I use the terms taught at the SMKI conservatory in Surabaya and explained by Diyat Sariredjo (retired leader of the national radio station gamelan musicians in Surabaya) and Soenarto R.P. (in his introductory booklet on east Javanese *karawitan*, Soenarto R.P. 1980): *panceran* (*pancer* and *pancer nibani*), *ngracik*, and *bandrèk*. The *bonang panerus* plays mostly in octaves, often interlocking with the *saron peking*.

The choice of *bonang* technique is constrained by the category of piece and the style of drumming. In almost all pieces with shorter *gong* phrases (by far the most frequently performed today), and in the livelier second sections (*anak-anakan*) of pieces with longer *gong* phrases, the *bonang babok* plays between the beats of the *balungan* (*pancer*) and sometimes together with the *balungan* tones as well (*pancer nibani*). The *pancer* tone, in other words the one played between the beats, is usually either the upper neighbor tone to the next strong tone in the *balungan*, or it is a tone avoided in the *balungan* and played consistently, regardless of the *balungan* contours, in the lower register. In many cases, the latter practice results in the *bonang* sounding like a central Javanese *kethuk*, though the pitch in central Javanese *sléndro* is 2, whereas in east Java it can be another pitch (often 3 in *pathet wolu*, or 5 in *pathet sanga*). In *pancer* style, the *bonang babok* normally sounds only single tones (not octaves) and only between beats.

Pancer nibani is similar, but is characterized by greater density of playing. In addition to the *pancer* tones(s) between beats, the weaker tones of the *balungan* are sounded simultaneously on the *bonang* in the lower octave and the stronger tones are sounded in octaves, as shown in the figure below. Soenarto R.P. explains the term "*nibani*" (literally, "to fall on intentionally") to mean that the *bonang* tones "fall on" the *balungan* beats, coinciding both in rhythm and in pitch.

While the *bonang babok* plays one version of the *panceran* technique, the *bonang panerus* plays octaves (*gembyang*) between the beats of the *bonang babok* and the beats of the *balungan*, anticipating the stronger tones of the *balungan* – that is, those falling on even-numbered beats. Simultaneously with the *bonang babok* and *balungan* beats, the *saron peking* plays the upper neighbor tone of the *bonang panerus* tone, except on the strong beats of the *balungan*, where the *peking* either is silent or steps down to coincide with the *balungan* tone. This

```
                        P     N     P     N     P     N     P    N/G
balungan:               1     6     1     3     1     6     3     2

bonang babok, pancer:
(upper neighbor)  i̇ . i̇ .  5 . 5 .  i̇ . i̇ .  3 . 3 .
(like kethuk)     5̣ . 5̣ .  5̣ . 5̣ .  5̣ . 5̣ .  5̣ . 5̣ .


bonang babok, pancer nibani:
(upper neighbor)  i̇   i̇ 6 5   5 3 i̇   i̇ 6 3   3 2
                  1      6̣  5̣   3̣  1    6̣  3̣   3̣ 2̣

                         6         3          6            2
(like kethuk)     5̣ 1 5̣ 6 5̣ 1 5̣ 3 5̣ 1 5̣ 6 5̣ 3 5̣ 2̣
```

5.20 *Panceran* technique on *bonang babok* (excerpt from Gendhing *Surabayan*, *sléndro pathet sanga*)

technique of *peking* playing is known as *tetegan* (literally, "small beat") or *timbangan* (literally, "even," "balance") (Soenarto R.P. 1980:8) and is unique to east Javanese gamelan style.

```
                 P        N        P        N        P        N        P       N/G
balungan:        1        6        1        3        1        6        3        2

peking:      i̇ i̇ i̇ (6)  5 5 5 (3)  i̇ i̇ i̇ (6)  3 3 3 (2)

bonang       6 . 6 . 6 . 3 . 3 . 3 . 3 . 6 . 6 . 6 . 6 . 2 . 2 . 2 . 2 .
panerus:     6̣ 6̣ 6̣ 6̣ 3̣ 3̣ 3̣ 3̣ 6̣ 6̣ 6̣ 6̣ 2̣ 2̣ 2̣ 2̣
```

5.21 *Bonang panerus* and *saron peking* interlocking (excerpt from Gendhing *Surabayan*, *sléndro pathet sanga*)

When the *balungan* tempo is slowed and the *bonang* and *peking* double (or quadruple) their ratio with the *balungan* beat, the *peking* normally provides a sense of quadratic phrasing, resting every fourth *peking* beat until the *balungan* beat it is anticipating, as shown in Figure 5.22.

```
                  P                 N                 P                 N
balungan:         1                 6                 1    .            3

peking:      i̇ i̇ i̇ .  i̇ i̇ i̇ 6  5 5 5 .  5 5 5 3
             ------------  ------------  ------------  ------------
    (or:     i̇ i̇ i̇ .  i̇ i̇ i̇ .  5 5 5 .  5 5 5 .)
```

5.22 *Saron peking* phrasing in *tetegan* (= *timbangan*) technique (excerpt from Gendhing *Surabayan*, *sléndro pathet sanga*, *irama II*)

The interlocking between *bonang panerus* and *peking* in east Java and the way it relates to the *balungan* part is structurally nearly identical to the basic paradigm for interlocking between the two *bonang* in Banyumas playing and the two *demung* in Yogyanese *demung imbal*. This paradigm is characterized by one instrument playing "on beat" and sounding the upper neighbor tone of a *balungan* tone, and a second instrument playing "off beat" (between the beats of the first), sounding the *balungan* tone itself (rather than its neighbor). And in all three traditions, this kind of playing is felt to be lively and spirited, and therefore inappropriate for the pieces or sections of pieces within each repertory that require a calm or serious mood.

What, then, gives the east Javanese playing its distinctive sound? To some extent it is the timbre and register of the instruments involved, particularly the contrast between the low and ponderous *demung* and the much higher *peking* and *bonang panerus*. Yet it is also the degree to which the paradigm is varied. In both Banyumas and Yogyakarta traditions, the two interlocking instruments are more involved in a game of some spontaneity in which other tones, usually conjunct with the immediately previous one, can be chosen. And in Yogyanese *demung imbal* the whole pattern can shift in relation to the *balungan* so that it is the on-beat instrument that sounds the *balungan* tone, not the off-beat one. Although this shift occurs occasionally in east Javanese *bonang panerus* and *peking* playing, it is rare.

Pieces or sections that are calm or serious in mood generally employ the *bonang babok* technique known as *ngracik*, which is characterized by greater melodic variety than *panceran*. Its use corresponds closely with the use of soft drumming, found primarily in the first section of pieces with two main sections, but also in certain shorter pieces, particularly those played ceremoniously to welcome guests at the beginning of a dance of shadow puppet performance (*giro* and *gagahan*). In *ngracik* technique the *bonang babok* plays mostly stepwise melodic patterns that lead to the *balungan* tones. Interspersed with these patterns are passages of *nggembyang*: reiterated single tones in the low register with rests and octave duplication that suggest rhythmic groupings of three *bonang* beats (for example, sustaining the 5 and the 2 in Figure 5.23). At slow *balungan* tempos, the *bonang babok ngracik* patterns lead to each *balungan* tone in succession, though they give greater anticipation to the stronger tones, and often sustain these tones after they have passed.

```
balungan: (5)                    6                 .              2t

bonang          5 .  5 . . .   .      2 2 . . 2 2    .        2
  babok:      5 5 5  5 5      6 1  5 6 1 6              1 6   1 6 1   6 1 2
            (nggembyang)

balungan:                      .      6             .              1P

bonang           2 .  2 . . .  .                            2 3 2   2
  babok:      2 2 2  2 2      6 1  5 6 1 6 1 1 1 . 1 1 6 5 6 1     1    1
            (nggembyang)
                             (from notation in Soenarto R.P. 1980:17-18)
```

5.23 *Ngracik* technique on *bonang babok* (excerpt from Gendhing *Lambang*, *sléndro pathet wolu* – as notated)

In performance, the *ngracik* technique may involve occasional syncopations, and rhythmic variety in the *nggembyang* passages, but is generally quite similar to that given in Soenarto R.P.'s notation. Figure 5.24 provides a transcription of a performance by musicians at the national radio station, RRI in Surabaya. One can note in both examples of *ngracik* playing the tendency to sustain the strong *balungan* tones with *nggembyang*, though it may also be used to anticipate a tone (as in the transcription in Figure 5.24, fifth system, leading to pitch 5).

The *bonang babok* player only commences *ngracik* playing after the tempo has settled. Beforehand, he may play *nggembyang* for each *gatra*. If the tempo is especially fast, as it often is in the first one or two *gatra*, he may simply play the *balungan* itself (*mbalung*).

One is tempted to equate the *ngracik* technique with *pipilan* (Solonese) or *mlaku* (Yogyanese) *bonang* playing in central Java. Each is considered to be the most refined type of *bonang* playing in its respective regional tradition. And in practice, each combines passages of mostly

```
balungan: (5)                    .              6              .              1t

bonang      5 . 5 . 5 . .              2   2 3 .2 2 .2.2 2 . 2   2
babok:    5 5   5 5   5 5   6   1 5 6 1 6    1         1        1       1 1
          (nggembyang)


balungan:                        .              6              .              5P

bonang    . i . . i . i .                          .        .
babok:    1 1     1   1   6 1 1 5 6 1 6    5 3 5   5 3 2 6 5 2 3 6 5 3 5
          (nggembyang)


balungan:                        .              2              .              3t

bonang    . 5 . 5 . 5 . 2      2   2 .   3 . 3 .   2 3 5 . 2 3 5 3
babok:    5 5   5 5   5     1 6 1   1     3 3   3 3   3
          (nggembyang)


balungan:                        .              2              .              1N

bonang    . 3 . 3 . 3 2 .   2   2 .   2 . 2        2 3 .2.2.
babok:    3 3   3 3   3   1   6 1   1     1       1 6 5 6 1     1   1
          (nggembyang)


balungan:            5              2              3              5t

bonang      5 . 5 . . .52 .2   2   2 .   3 . 3 . 3
babok:    5 5 5   5 5         6 1   1     3 3   3 3   3 6 5 2 3 6 5 3 5
          (nggembyang)


balungan:            2              1              2              6P

bonang    2 2     2   2 .   2 3 .2 2   . 2      2   2 . 1 .
babok:      1 6 1   1     1       1 1     1 6 1   1     6     5 6 1 6
```

(transcribed from field recording of RRI Surabaya
"Mana Suka" performance, June 20, 1983)

5.24   *Ngracik* technique on *bonang babok* (excerpt of Gendhing *Cindhé Laras*, *sléndro pathet wolu* – transcription)

conjunct melodic motion with the kind of reiteration discussed above (known as *nggembyang* in east Javanese and Yogyanese tradition and as *nduduk* in Solonese). Yet the central Javanese *pipilan/mlaku* playing is generally conceived today as melodic anticipation built on two successive *balungan* tones, a weak one and the strong one following it. East Javanese *ngracik* patterns, on the other hand, simply lead to single *balungan* tones, and are not constrained by the previous or following tones. One is reminded of the *bonang mlaku* playing for very slow realization of some Yogyanese *balungan*, more common forty or fifty years ago, in which case the *bonang* does indeed play a pattern to each successive *balungan* tone. Javanese musicians familiar with the two styles note the similarity, but point out that the actual contours that one hears in the two regional styles, though not completely standardized in either, are sufficiently different not to be confused.

One more frequently encounters *bonang* patterns leading to single *balungan* tones in central Javanese traditions in the context of lively *bonang imbal* playing. These patterns, referred to as *kembangan* ("flower-like"), are mostly fast-tempo (twice the normal *bonang barung* tempo). They represent the flashiest type of *bonang* playing in central Java, the furthest in mood from the calm *mlaku* playing. Consequently they do not sound or feel like the east Javanese *ngracik* patterns, despite similarity in structural function.

In these calmer musical contexts, with the *bonang babok* playing *ngracik*, the *bonang panerus* usually plays *kebyokan*: *nggembyang* in groups of threes (leading to each *balungan* tone or, in fast sections, to every other), rather than off-beat octaves anticipating only the stronger beats of the *balungan*. Yet the same off-beat octave playing described above for livelier contexts may be used in some cases. Whether the *bonang panerus* plays *kebyokan* or not, the *saron panerus* does not interlock with it in these calmer sections, but instead plays a technique known as *nintili*, anticipating each *balungan* tone in an even, continuous rhythm.

```
balungan: (5)        .      2       .      3t       .       2       .      1N

peking:        5 5 5 5.2 2 2 2 3 3 3 3 3 3 3 3  3 3 3 3 2 2 2 2 1 1 1 1 1 1 1 1


balungan:            5      2       3      5t       2       1       2      6P

peking:        5 5 5 5 2 2 2 2 3 3 3 3 5 5 5 5  2 2 2 2 1 1 1 1 2 2 2 2 6 6 6 6
```

(transcribed from field recording of RRI Surabaya
"Mana Suka" performance, June 20, 1983)

5.25 *Nintili* technique on *saron peking* (excerpt from Gendhing *Cindhé Laras*, *sléndro pathet wolu* – transcription)

When the *balungan* tones are sparse (such as the first line in Figure 5.25), the stronger tones may be sustained as well as anticipated by the *peking*, as they are by the *bonang* in *ngracik* playing. Similar playing is notated in Soenarto R.P. 1980:16.

For musical passages in which solo singing (*kidungan*) is featured, such as a *ngrémo* dancer–singer or a character in a dramatic performance, the gamelan plays quietly (*sigegan* in east Java; cf. *sirepan* in central Java) and the two *bonang* perform an interlocking technique known as *bandrèk*. Like the *bonang imbal* technique of central Java, *bandrèk* is constrained primarily by *pathet* rather than by the particular tones of the *balungan*. Whereas the two *bonang* alternate (off-beat and on-beat) in central Javanese *imbal*, in *bandrèk* the *bonang barung* plays two single tones, followed by octaves on the *bonang panerus* and a rest on the fourth (and strongest) beat. Most of the instruments are played softly, including the *bonang*. The *saron* instruments, including *peking*, may be silent. If not, the *peking* is likely to play *nintili*, rather than the livelier *tetegan/timbangan*.

```
                    Pathet Sanga              Pathet Wolu

bonang babok:       1 2 . .   1 2 . .         6̣ 1 . .   6̣ 1 . .
                                    etc.                       etc.
bonang panerus:     . . 3 . . . 3 .           . . 2 . . . 2 .
                        3̣        3̣                2̣       2̣
```

5.26 *Bandrèk* technique for *bonang babok* and *bonang panerus*

Pieces with *kidungan* singing are mostly in *sléndro pathet sanga* and *pathet wolu*, or, in the Malang area, the *pélog* equivalents. Musicians I spoke to offered no example of *bandrèk* technique for either *pathet sepuluh* or *pathet serang*.

Generally, then, one can identify three main orientations to *bonang* and *peking* playing. The first is the lively *panceran bonang babok* with interlocking *bonang panerus* (*gembyangan*) and *peking* (*tetegan/timbangan*). The second is the calm and refined *ngracik* on *bonang babok*, with *nggembyang* on *panerus*, and *nintili* on *peking*. The third is the soft *bandrèk* interlocking between the two *bonang*, with the *peking* either silent or playing *nintili*. However, in pieces with short *gongan*, with soft, refined drumming (for example, welcoming pieces), the *bonang babok* may play *ngracik*, or a combination of *ngracik* and *panceran nibani*, at the same time that the *bonang panerus* and *peking* interlock as they do in the livelier musical contexts.

No authoritative tradition has dictated a standard in east Java. The kind of *bonang* and *peking* playing helps determine the mood of the piece as it is performed. In ambiguous or borderline cases, musicians may change techniques within a single section, as I have sometimes seen them do on all three of these instruments. Still, the well-loved and immediately recognizable interlocking *bonang panerus* and *peking*, with *bonang babok panceran*, are heard in practically every piece, since even the calmest and most refined pieces normally move from a first section (*mbok-mbokan*) to a livelier second section (*anak-anakan*).

Drumming

East Javanese *karawitan* is known for its loud and coarse *gambyakan* drumming, played on the rugged *gambyak* drum, unique to east Java. Though dance and *wayang* drumming on the central Javanese *ciblon* drum can get rather loud, none can match the crackling and thunderous sounds of east Javanese *gambyakan*. The larger size of the *gambyak* drum heads and its thicker and larger wooden shell in comparison to those of the *ciblon* give the *gambyak* a capacity both for loudness and for a certain crispness or immediateness – a hard edge that seizes the listener's attention in ways that central Javanese drumming, always at least somewhat softer and subtler, does not and is not intended to. Javanese I have spoken to in both central and east Java find in this contrast an aesthetic statement of regional character or personality (*kepribadian*). No one with experience in both central and east Java could fail to notice how the east Javanese are generally more socially direct, more aggressive, and more demanding in personal encounters than most central Javanese. In its rapid-fire coarseness, *gambyakan* drumming seems the musical counterpart to east Javanese speech, which takes a somewhat faster pace than even the most lively central Javanese speech, often in rapid bursts of east Javanese *ngoko* (unrefined, familiar level) slang.

Gambyak drummers control a wide range of timbres in their drumstrokes, some say as many as sixteen or so – more than *ciblon*. Their liveliest and most technically challenging drumming occurs in the accompaniment of dance, whether a carefully choreographed *ngrémo* dance or a spontaneous *tayuban* performance. *Ngrémo* drumming is probably the most popular of all and is said by some experts to contain the basis for much *gambyakan* drumming. It juxtaposes passages of dense, rapid playing with isolated, loud strokes whose deliberate presence seems a clear musical expression of "east Javaneseness." Much of the rapid playing demonstrates a measure of independence from the steady beat of the melodic instruments, sometimes in a triplet relationship, and sometimes seeming to float over the other instruments, as if oblivious of the steady pulses and subdivision provided by the *saron* and *bonang* families. The excerpt in Figure 5.27 is a transcription from a recording of Pak Diyat Sariredjo, former director of the gamelan musicians at RRI Surabaya and probably the best known east Javanese drummer.

```
(from recording of Pak Diyat Sariredjo, Surabaya)

        P      N      P      N      P      N      P     N/G
        6      5      6      2      6      5      2      1
        +    +                             k      T      T
     .TToDoD D totlt 1 . . . T  T DT . . D D . D D . . o . .
     (iket)

        2      1      2      6      2      1      6      5

     . . . B . kT . . . . B . o . T t l tl. T .tl 1 1 . l l . . o . .
     (sabetan)


        6      5      6      2      6      5      2      1
                             T
     oDDTtTDt. TDttDTTTTTT gKT goT  t lTt lT   T
     (iket-tanjak)

        2      1      2      6      2      1      6      5
        T             T             T      T             T
     . .B . .D . . . . .Dt l o . .Dt l o . .Dt l o . .Dt l o  (etc.)
     (tindak lamba)
```

KEY:
```
T = tak (slap on larger head)                   +
o = tok, tong (rim stroke on smaller head)      D = dhak (ket and den
t = thung, dhung (ringing sound, smaller head)     simultaneous, damped)
l = lung (like t, but from larger head)
D = den (deep sound, larger head)               T
B = bah (loud den, large head or larger drum)   D = dhang (Tak and den
G = gen (soft den, large head)                     simultaneous)
K = ket (damped sound, either head)

(iket) = name of dance/drum pattern         ⌣ = triplet rhythm

_____ = rhythmic independence from quadratic subdivision of steady beat
        of other percussion instruments.

. . . . . . . . . . . . . . . = one gatra (four balungan beats)
```

5.27 *Gambyak* drumming for *ngrémo* dance (Gendhing *Surabayan*, *sléndro pathet wolu*, excerpt)

The considerable range of freedom in *tayuban* music has seen the introduction of various outside influences in recent years in *tayuban* drumming, notably the fast and loud drumming styles associated with *gandrung* (singer–dancer genre from Banyuwangi) and *jaipongan* (a social dance genre that developed from earlier West Javanese *ketuk tilu* into a genre widely popular throughout Java in the late 1970s and early 1980s; see Baier and Manuel 1986). Most of the pieces played at a *tayuban* are by request from the participating male guests, who pay the musicians for the piece they wish to have accompany their dance with the *tandhak*.

Usually the guest simply calls out the name of a piece. It is the drummer who determines the treatment, including the style(s) of drumming to be used. At the *tayuban* performances I attended in 1986 only the younger drummers incorporated *jaipongan* and *gandrung* styles into their performances.

While loud and lively *gambyakan* is unquestionably the type of drumming most frequently heard in east Javanese *karawitan* today, a calmer and sparser drumming, known as *gedhugan*, is used as well. This is most consistently encountered in contexts other than dance or drama – that is, *uyon-uyon* or *klenèngan* (both these central Javanese terms are used). *Gedhugan* is the norm for the opening section of most pieces. It is used throughout the playing of some, particularly the ceremonial pieces played on the "loud-playing" instruments: *gendhing giro* (cf. central Javanese *lancaran*) and *gendhing gagahan* (cf. Solonese *gendhing bonang*). For these ceremonial pieces, a small beater (*panggul*) made of rattan is sometimes used to signal the *buka* by knocking against the wooden shell of one of the drums, and to strike the large head of the largest drum (either *gambyak* or *kendhang gendhing*). Even with the beater, however, this drumming is nowhere near as loud as *gambyakan* drumming can be.

It should be noted that in some cases the *balungan* part is identical for both sections of a two-section piece, in which case the tempo and the drumming are what distinguish the two sections from one another. Some of the shorter pieces may begin with *gedhugan* and proceed to *gambyakan*, with no change in *balungan*. And the larger pieces, with *mbok-mbokan* and *anak-anakan* sections, may be drummed with *gedhugan* in both sections, with the option to play *gambyakan* as well. Yet in this case, it is only in the second section (*anak-anakan*) that *gambyakan* would be appropriate. Within a single piece one does not return to *gedhugan* once *gambyakan* has been introduced.

In gamelan equipped with *ketipung* and *kendhang gendhing* the drummer may use these, or only the *kendhang gendhing*, for the *gedhugan* drumming. The transition to *gambyakan*, if there is one, is then clearly marked. If the *ketipung* and *kendhang gendhing* are not present, the drummer plays the appropriate *gedhugan* patterns on the *gambyak* drum, but in a softer style that is clearly distinguishable from the animated *gambyakan* sound.

Regardless of which drum or drums are played, the east Javanese *gedhugan* patterns are fairly easily distinguishable from the patterns used in central Javanese pieces with similar formal structures. Since east Javanese drumming is generally less standardized than most central Javanese drumming, I offer below a standard Solonese pattern for *ladrang* form and, for comparison, two east Javanese patterns. The first is that given by Soenarto R.P. (1980:14) for pieces in *luwung* form, the east Javanese equivalent of *ladrang*, and the second is from my own transcription of a performance of Gendhing *Trenggalèk* (first section), classified as *luwung* form by Soenarto R.P. (1980:29) and by Ronoatmodjo (1981a).[18] In a recording I made at RRI Surabaya of Pak Jumali (Pak Diyat Sariredjo's main protégé) playing drum for this piece, he used the *gambyak* drum and played patterns nearly identical to those given in Soenarto's notation. The drumming on the commercial recording *Bonangan Jawa Timuran*, by the well known Sawunggaling *karawitan* group, was performed on *kendhang gendhing* and *ketipung* and the pattern is rather different. That Gendhing *Trenggalèk* is performed on this commercial cassette as a *gendhing gagahan* (i.e., loud playing instruments only), and labelled there as such, would account for its variance with Soenarto R.P.'s notation and the RRI performance, where it was performed in soft-ensemble style, with *pesindhèn* and soft instruments.

A comparison of other drumming patterns given by Soenarto R.P. (1980:10–27) with those

```
           t              (P)              t              N
Solo:    . . . . . . . . . . d . d . . D d . D . . . . . . . .

                                                  +   k
E.Jv (1): . . . d o . d D . . . D . D . .  o o d o d o D o d D . D . o . .

E.Jv (2): . . . . . . . d . . . d d d̄d̄d̄d̄D . . . . . . . d . . . d . d d .


           t               P              t              N
Solo:    . . . d . . . d . . d D . . D d . . . . . . . . d . D . . . d . D

                                                  +   k
E.Jv (1): . . . d o . d D . . . D . D . .  o o d o d o D o d D . D . o . .

E.Jv (2): . . . . . . . d . . . d d d̄d̄d̄d̄D . . . . d d . d D . d D . . . .


           t               P              t              N
Solo:    . d . D . . . d . . d D . . . T . d . d . d . D . d . . d D . d

                                                  +   k
E.Jv (1): . . . d o . d D . . . D . D . .  o o d o d o D o d D . D . o . .

E.Jv (2): . . . . . . . d . . . d d d̄d̄d̄d̄D . d D . d d D .d̄.d̄. d D . .d̄d d


           t               P              t              N/G
Solo:    . . d D . d D . d D d . D . d D . . . . . . . . d . . d D . d . D

E.Jv (1): d d . d o . d D . . T . d d . d . . d D . d . . d D . d . . d D

E.Jv (2): . d . d̄D. d . d d̄d. d D .d̄d̄d̄d D  d d .d̄D . .d̄d d̄d.d̄D d̄d̄d̄d̄D d̄d̄d̄d̄D
```

```
     +                                   k
D = "det" (hit and damp large drumhead); D = "dhak" (hit and damp both heads)

. . . . . . . . . . . . . . . . = one gatra
```

(Solonese pattern from Martopangrawit 1972b:31; east Javanese pattern (1) from
Soenarto R.P. 1980:14; east Javanese pattern (2) transcribed from cassette
Bonangan Jawa Timuran, WD-653)

5.28 *Gedhugan* drum patterns for *luwung* form, compared with two-drum pattern for Solonese-style *ladrang*

encountered in the various central Javanese traditions reveals occasional similarities, but nothing close to exact reduplication even for a phrase of eight beats. However, in the performance of Gendhing *Trenggalèk* on the commercial cassette, the drumming for the first half of the second section (i.e. first two eight-beat *kenongan*) resembles rather closely the standard pattern for the same passage in Semarang-style *ladrang* pieces. To a lesser extent it bears some similarity to the *gagahan* drumming given by Soenarto for Gendhing *Ricik-ricik*, though this piece, and thus the drumming pattern, consists of *kenongan* of only four, rather than eight beats (Soenarto R.P. 1980:1).

```
                        t                   P                   t                   N
Semarang      . . . d . d . D  . . . d . d d . d . . d . d . D  . . . d . d d .

E. Java       . . . d . d . D  . . . d . d . . . . . d . d . D  . . . d . d . .


Semarang      d . d . d . D  . . . d . d d . d . d D . . . d . D .d. d d d D

E. Java       . . . d . d . D  . . . d . d . . . . . d . d . D  . . . d . d . .
```

5.29 Drumming for second sections of Gendhing *Trenggalèk* (east Javanese "*gagahan*") and Semarang-style *ladrang*, excerpt

I have tried for the most part to emphasize what makes east Javanese drumming distinctive from the drumming in any of the central Javanese traditions, but some parallels suggest themselves. The use of similar patterns for loud-playing pieces (*gendhing bonang, gendhing gagahan*) in Semarang and east Java is one rather particular one. Yet the overall distribution of drumming styles through the repertories in central and east Javanese traditions reflects the same orientation towards loud and animated drumming for dance and dramatic accompaniment, refined first sections and livelier second sections in longer *uyon-uyon/klenèngan* pieces, and a progression in all *uyon-uyon/klenèngan* pieces and medleys from relatively calm, refined drumming to more animated.

Though the patterns are generally more filled in for the east Javanese than the central Javanese, the sparse *gedhugan* drumming for the opening section is played in a manner similar to that used in Yogyanese and Solonese *mérong* sections (the calm first sections of multi-section pieces). And the *gedhugan* for second sections, if it is used, is somewhat more lively – comparable to the *kosèkan* or *kosèk alus* drumming in Solonese tradition. Drummers familiar with both Solonese and east Javanese tradition note the similarity in feel between Solonese *kosèkan* and east Javanese *gedhugan*. Both involve skilful playing on a middle or large-sized drum; both combine rapid playing with sparser playing and hence suggest a kind of restraint that is absent from the livelier *ciblonan* (Solonese) or *gambyakan* (east Java). These parallels notwithstanding, the east Javanese drumming is consistently louder and livelier than the corresponding drumming in central Javanese traditions, even the most exuberant Banyumas style.

Soft instruments

East Javanese musicians, particularly in the Surabaya and Mojokerto areas, distinguish some aspects of soft-instrument playing as unique to east Javanese tradition. A generation or two ago, I have been told, the styles of playing *rebab*, *suling*, and *gendèr panerus* all stood in clear distinction to any associated with central Java.

The east Javanese *rebab*, like the *gambyak* drum, is larger than its central Javanese counterpart and produces a somewhat louder and, to some ears, harsher tone. Though less ornamented than in central Java (i.e., Solonese tradition), east Javanese *rebab* playing is often quite independent melodically from the *balungan* and may also be independent rhythmically from the steady pulse of the percussion instruments. Yet nowadays few players maintain a distinctively east Javanese *rebab* style. The *wayang kulit* puppeteer Ki Piet Asmoro is one of the few, but when I heard him play *rebab* in 1986, his bowing was weak and his playing no longer an example of east Javanese style one would wish students to emulate. Pak Diyat Sariredjo, retired from RRI Surabaya but still active there as recently as August 1986, is acknowledged to be an excellent east Javanese *rebab* player, but he claims vehemently that he is no match for what Ki Piet Asmoro was, nor for other great east Javanese musicians who are no longer living, such as the recently deceased Pak Toro (d. 1986).

Others at RRI Surabaya, and elsewhere, as far as I could determine, play *rebab* in Solonese style, even when performing an east Javanese piece. It is feared that knowledge of the multi-octave conception of many of these pieces will be lost as other older musicians die, since younger east Javanese musicians are more often drawn to other instruments, particularly drum. Thus, although a rendering of these pieces with Solonese-sounding *rebab* is already a stylistic compromise, it is seen as a more desirable alternative than the disappearance altogether of some form of *rebab* playing for east Javanese pieces. At this point, the primary concern is to pass on knowledge of the basic multi-octave conception of pieces, an effort that has resulted in one short publication (Ronoatmodjo 1981a) and some archiving work at both the high school and college-level performing arts institutions in Surabaya (SMKI and STKW).

East Javanese *suling*, whose fingering patterns are closest to those of Yogyanese rather than Solonese, used to play a prominent role in soft-ensemble pieces, sounding more continuously and at a louder volume level than does the *suling* in any central Javanese tradition.[19] This greater prominence of the *suling* suggests a relationship with the many Balinese ensembles in which a small chorus of *suling* may provide the main melody of a piece, or double it as it is played on metallophones. Yet apparently this feature of east Javanese *karawitan* has mostly disappeared. The *suling* playing I heard sounded very similar to that of Yogya and Solo, and no effort comparable to those for documenting east Javanese *rebab* playing has been initiated, to my knowledge, perhaps because the recognized experts died decades ago.

Though the *gambang* is widespread in east Java, none of the *gambang* playing I heard there stood out from what I have heard in central Java. And the *siter* or *celempung* despite evidence of its presence in east Java as early as the fifteenth century (depicted in reliefs on the Hindu–Javanese temple Candi Jago in Tumpang, east of Malang), is either played as in central Java or omitted altogether.

The *gendèr panerus*, however, which is usually the first instrument to be left silent in central Javanese *karawitan* if the musicians are short of a player or two, occupies a prominent role in east Javanese *karawitan*, at least in the Surabaya and Mojokerto areas. Most startling to those accustomed to central Javanese music is the use of *gendèr panerus* in the *pathetan* preceding and following soft-ensemble *gendhing* in *uyon-uyon/klenèngan* and sometimes in *sulukan* (*dhalang*'s mood songs) for *wayang*. *Gendèr panerus* playing in these contexts, unlike *gendèr barung* playing in central Java, is largely a single melody in parallel octaves.

In the context of *gendhing*, east Javanese and central Javanese *gendèr panerus* styles resemble one another rather closely – playing mostly rapid single note melodies, with occasional octave doubling and simultaneities. East Javanese playing might be said to stress octave doubling a bit more than is common in central Javanese, and this may make this rather soft-sounding instrument a bit more audible in the gamelan texture and account for its identification as an instrument contributing to a distinctive east Javanese sound.[20] Yet what makes east Javanese *gendèr panerus* patterns identifiable to the ear as east Javanese and not Solonese, for example, is the actual sequence of tones that make up the more commonly used formulas. It would be difficult and hazardous to suggest any overarching characteristics that set them off; it is more that a *putut gelut* pattern in east Java sounds different from any one is likely to encounter in Solonese-style performance. (See Sena'in *et al.* 1982 and Mudianto and Tasman 1983.)

The *gendèr barung* (sometimes called *gendèr "babok"* – cf. *bonang*) is said by some musicians to be a relatively recent introduction into east Javanese ensembles. While this may be true in the Surabaya and Mojokerto areas, I saw several old *sléndro* gamelan belonging to *wayang kulit* puppeteers in the Malang area that contained *gendèr babok*, but no *gendèr panerus*. And in all the east Javanese *wayang kulit* I have heard on commercial tapes or seen in performance, the *gendèr babok* is the prominent instrument for *sulukan* accompaniment. For east Javanese soft-ensemble *gendhing* the *gendèr babok* is played, albeit with some individual idiosyncrasies, in a style that one would now generally identify as Solonese. Whatever east Javanese traits may have characterized the playing of this instrument, then, they seem to have been replaced by the highly regarded *gendèr* techniques of Solonese style, which east Javanese *gendèr* players have learned through the media of radio and recordings and are expected to use in the many central Javanese pieces they perform.

Vocal style

Two basic orientations in vocal style characterize the gamelan music of east Java today. The first is the singing known as *kidungan* (or sometimes *gandhangan*),[21] which is heard most characteristically in *ngrémo* performance and is sung, by either male or female, in a style unique to east Java. The second, now referred to as *sindhènan*, is similar to central Javanese singing of the same name, and includes the singing of the *tandhak* at *tayuban*, as well as that of the solo female singers (known here, as in central Java, as *pesindhèn* or *waranggana*) that one now normally hears in east Javanese *wayang kulit* and east Javanese *klenèngan*.

Several features distinguish *kidungan* singing. First and most obvious is that it is usually performed to one or another version of *Jula-juli*, played softly on a gamelan. The melody and its rhythmic relationship to the gamelan playing enjoy a rather wide latitude of individual interpretation, but generally conform to several constraints that give it its characteristic sound. The phrases usually start with the repetition of a single high tone, on which a number of text syllables are enunciated, before falling to the phrase final. This descent can be rather sudden, at least in comparison to most solo singing in central Java, and quite precipitous – often an octave or more, as in the excerpt in Figure 5.30 from a transcription by Sri Suyamti of the well-known female singer Remu, from Surabaya.

Equally startling to those accustomed to central Javanese solo singing is the very strong tendency to arrive at the vocal phrase final before or, at the very latest, together with the prominent *balungan* tone (*sèlèh*, e.g., *kenong* or *gong* tone) that determines the vocal phrase final. This can be seen in the first and third lines in Figure 5.30. In central Javanese solo singing it is the norm to arrive at least a beat or two after the *balungan sèlèh* tone has been sounded, expressing in sound the central Javanese predilection for unhurried and subtle action. It would be stylistically incorrect in central Java for the *pesindhèn* to finish her phrase before the *balungan sèlèh* tone and nowadays it would seem pushy even for her to arrive together with the *balungan* (except in *wayang* pieces, the *gendhing lampah*). Yet in *kidungan*, as if an expression of east Javanese directness, the singer is to arrive first or at the same time.

Otherwise, the rhythmic quality of *kidungan* singing bears the same loose relationship with the steady beat of the percussion instruments that characterizes the solo singing styles associated with central Javanese traditions. The *kidungan* melody seems to float freely over

```
balungan:    5N              .         6P           .              2N

kidungan:    2̇  2̇  2̇  2̇   2̇  2̇3̇  2̇6̇1̇          5̇1̇  6   5 3 2
             Sampun dados  ta-ta lan              ca-       ra


balungan:              .         6P           .              5N

kidungan:         2̇  2̇  2̇  2̇  2̇   2̇  2̇  2̇1̇  1   1  1
                  me-na-wi le-pat     ke-pa-re-nga   pa-ring


balungan:              .         2P           .              1N/G

kidungan:         2̇  3̇  2̇      1̇  6  5    2  1
                  pa- ngak-  sa-       ma.
```

(from Sri Suyamti 1985:32-33)

5.30   East Javanese *kidungan* singing, excerpt from *Gendhing Jula-juli/Surabayan*, *sléndro pathet wolu*, as sung by Remu

the four-square and metronomic rhythm of the *balungan* and its subdividers, at times seeming almost to erase or subdue the even, steady feel of the instrumental beat.

Another prominent feature of *kidungan* singing is the vocal quality required. The singer produces what sounds like a forced vocal quality, pushing the voice, sometimes using falsetto. And particularly at the beginning of phrases, in the high register, he or she sings in a kind of *marcato*, articulating each syllable and tone with a sharp attack. As the phrase progresses, the articulations often begin more softly, then rapidly increase in volume. *Kidungan* singing requires a great deal of control to be executed correctly, and this control is greatly admired by east Javanese listeners, despite the usual central Javanese evaluation of this vocal quality as coarse and even funny.

The *kidungan* texts, as mentioned above, cover a range of topics and in *ludruk* are often improvised. They consist of verses which are catchy and often humorous rhymes of either two or four lines. The form that is most popular is a four-line poem with either an AAAA or an ABAB rhyme scheme (Hardjoprawiro 1985:xiii). *Kidungan* are primarily distinguished as such from the more general Javanese *parikan* form by the use of east Javanese dialect. Both consist of two phrases or sentences, connected by rhymes, in which the first half suggests the second; the main "message" (advice, political comment, and so on) is in the second half. Nevertheless, some scholars suggest *kidungan* be thought of as a category separate from *parikan*, since in *kidungan* one finds a greater variety in the number of syllables per line than in *parikan* (which usually have four or eight).

Sindhènan in east Java exhibits only subtle differences from that of central Java, particularly the widely popular style now identified as Solonese. The *tandhak* have apparently been active as singers and dancers in east Java for centuries, and may trace their roots back to the female singer–dancer known as Juru i Angin at the court of Majapahit in the fourteenth century (Holt 1967:114–15). But the introduction of female singing into the calmer *klenèngan* pieces occurred only in the twentieth century and into *wayang kulit* only during the last twenty-five or thirty years.[22] In the mid-1980s, with east Java as inundated as the rest of Java with commercial cassettes, there was a strong commercial imperative to include *sindhènan* in recordings of gamelan music. Though the gamelan accompaniment for *wayang topèng* in Malang still does not include *sindhènan*, commercial cassette releases labelled as *topèng* accompaniment have added *sindhènan* to make the tape, as one musician put it, "more enjoyable to listen to."[23]

In all cases this introduction of *sindhènan*, though now felt to be essential to both east Javanese *klenèngnan* and east Javanese *wayang kulit*, is readily acknowledged to have been inspired by central Javanese practice and stylistically seems to represent a direct borrowing. Sri Suyamti points out that east Javanese *pesindhèn*, like the singers of *kidungan*, tend to arrive at the *sèlèh* tone before the instruments do. And the texts they sing are often *parikan* or *parikan*-like verses, although they also make ample use of *wangsalan*, the form preferred in Solonese tradition (Sri Suyamti 1985:57).

Several prominent central Javanese musicians to whom I spoke concerning east Javanese *pesindhèn* offered enthusiastic remarks about their abilities, and indicated that the top *pesindhèn* one hears on recordings or over the radio were every bit as good at performing Solonese-style *gendhing* as the reigning stars within the ranks of central Javanese *pesindhèn*. But the *sindhènan* for east Javanese *gendhing*, and especially the *kidungan* singing that one often hears from east Java, sounded a bit strange – one musician used the term *abot* (literally, "heavy") and explained that it was a challenge for him to listen to. Certainly these and other central Javanese musicians find east Javanese singing less accessible aesthetically than the singing from different regions within central Java (e.g., the popularity of Banyumas singing now in Solo and Yogya).

One other important feature one occasionally hears in the singing of east Javanese *pesindhèn* is the use of what sounds close to a Western diatonic scale in the vocal part, as the gamelan plays in *sléndro*. We encounter this same phenomenon in Semarang, just as we find some relationship between the drumming for loud-ensemble pieces in the two regions. This may represent the residue of a style shared among peoples along the north coast of Java from Semarang as far east as Surabaya. Both Semarang and Surabaya are north coast port cities, linked by trade for some centuries. Yet it is also possible that recent contact, even through the mass media, may have led to the sharing of these traits. The Solonese musician and puppeteer Sri Djoko Rahardjo believes that the diatonic singing was prevalent in east Java before being adopted in Semarang. At any rate, while not sufficient now to speak of a Surabaya-Semarang (or Pasisiran) gamelan tradition, these similarities between the music of Semarang and east Java suggest that the powerful spread of Solonese tradition in the twentieth century has not eclipsed other interregional sharing in Java.

Tempo treatment

Tempo in east Javanese gamelan music is, in a word, varied. Within a single piece, the tempo can fluctuate considerably, particularly in pieces accompanying dance. In *ngrémo* accompaniment, for example, the drummer is almost constantly pushing or holding back the tempo. Passages within a single level of subdivision (*irama* level) may undergo temporary, and sometimes abrupt, acceleration, only to slacken a few beats later. Central Javanese, as a rule, have a hard time adjusting to this east Javanese approach to tempo. In most of the gamelan music of central Java, tempo change is more gradual. And even in the cases of sudden acceleration or ritard in central Javanese *wayang kulit* or dance accompaniment, for example, one tends to move from one steady tempo to another. As a result, some writers have found that in describing east Javanese music it is useful not only to indicate the *irama* level (*irama* I/

tanggung; *irama* II/*dadi*, and so on), but also the tempo within that level. In her thesis on *sindhènan* in Surabaya, Sri Suyamti specifies which of three tempi are employed within, for example, *irama dadi*: *tamban* (slow), *sedeng* (medium) or *seseg* (fast, literally, "tight," "squeezed together") (Sri Suyamti 1985:32–49; 55).

Tempo can be quite slow in contexts of vocal music, particularly *kidungan*, and extraordinarily fast in instrumental passages. The fastest pulse in east Javanese gamelan performance, manifest on the *gambang* in soft-playing style and on the interlocking between two *saron* or between *bonang panerus* and *peking* in loud-playing, can be as slow as about 110–120 MM (110–120 pulses per minute), but can reach tempos of 600 MM within the same performance. This fast tempo is especially remarkable when we consider that the *bonang panerus* player, or the off-beat *saron* player, must play only on weak or off-beats at this tempo. The ensemble skill required to keep this steady off-beat, where slippage of only one tenth of a second puts the off-beat playing "on" the beat, is not characteristic of gamelan playing in most of central Java, though *calung* players in Banyumas sometimes reach this tempo. Rather it suggests links with Bali, where fast interlocking is a basic feature in much ensemble music.

In east Javanese *klenèngan*, tempi more closely approximate what one finds in comparable music from central Java. Yet even in this relatively calm context, once the *gambyakan* drumming has been introduced, the tempo may surge and slacken mid-phrase in ways that give east Javanese music a kind of charge that excites east Javanese, as it upsets the more contemplative Solonese or Yogyanese.

East Javanese tradition and regionalism

Most of this chapter has been concerned with the gamelan tradition identified with the *arèk* Javanese of the central portion of the province of East Java: the Surabaya-Mojokerto-Malang triangle, an area in which great kingdoms were once centered, but which now represents no distinctive administrative unit. Indonesians today usually refer to this music, and the performing arts it often accompanies, as Jawa Timuran with an upper case "T" (East Javanese with an upper case "E"), obscuring the differences I have striven to maintain in this chapter between the particular cultural region (east) and the larger province (East). In this section I would like to consider the status of this east Javanese tradition within the larger context of East Java province and the implications of the province's musical diversity for changing conceptions and practice. In order to do so it will be necessary to introduce other genres of music and performing arts that have developed in East Java and, to varying degrees, have become emblematic – that is, as cultural practices representative of this province. Sources generally list all or most of the genres I introduce briefly in the next several pages. (See, for example, Pemerintah Daerah Jawa Timur 1975:156–81; Proyek Penelitian dan Pencatatan Kebudayaan Daerah 1976: *passim*; Team Penulisan Naskah Pengembangan Media 1977:160–77; and Munardi *et al.* 1983: *passim*.)

From what is generally identified as the "central Javanese" region of the province come two well-known genres of *reyog*. *Reyog Ponorogo*, from the town of Ponorogo, is a processional masked dance, accompanied by a small ensemble of double reed (*selomprèt*), drums, gongs, and often the shaken bamboo idiophone (*angklung*) (see Kartomi 1976 and Timoer 1978–79). The main attraction is the dancer who wears a spectacularly large head-dress and is said to represent a mythical lion (*singa barong*). The musical accompaniment is exuberant, with free–

ranging melodies played loudly on the double reed. *Reyog kendhang*, from the town of Tulungagung, is a processional dance in which all the dancers wear ankle bells and play instruments (Timoer 1978–79). One plays an ostinato on a small kettle gong, the others (about six to eight) play single-headed drums. Of these the *reyog Ponorogo* is the more popular, though both suggest humble village origins – the former in its ecstatic movement and sound, the latter in its repetitive simplicity.

The Madurese maintain their own genres of performing arts, both on the island of Madura and throughout much of the eastern most portion of Java (from Surabaya eastwards). Best known to other Indonesians is the genre associated with the court of Sumenep and known as *topèng dhalang*, a genre of masked dance-drama accompanied by larger gamelan ensembles (Soelarto 1979, Timoer 1979–80, and Sutrisno 1983). Though the style of dance and the instrumental techniques are easily distinguished from those of the central and east Javanese, this Madurese genre has clear historical connections with the Solonese tradition in much of its repertory. More widespread but less prestigious are the many ensembles known as *sronèn/srunèn Madura*, which usually accompany some form of procession or the famous Madurese bull races (*kerapan sapi*). These are small ensembles resembling those accompanying *reyog Ponorogo*: with double reed (*sroni/sruni*, *tètèt*), one or two drums, and several gongs, sometimes with a *bonang* or *saron*. Though these and other less well-known arts are indigenous to the province of East Java, they are still recognized more as "Madurese" than as "East Javanese."

In the easternmost portion of the island lives the most distinctive group that consider themselves "Javanese" – the Osing people of Banyuwangi and rural Blambangan. The performing arts from this relatively small area stand in sharp contrast to the other arts of the Javanese, some would say sharper even than the contrast between Javanese and Madurese. As Wolbers has pointed out, the culture of Banyuwangi, including the sound of its music, owes much to its proximity to Bali and a long history of animosity with Javanese further west (Wolbers 1986:74–75).

Best known is the genre called *gandrung Banyuwangi*, in which female singer–dancers dance and sing alluringly, enticing men to dance with them, rather in the spirit of *tayuban*. Yet the *gandrung* dance style, with its swaying hips and sideways shift of the torso, is more reminiscent of female Balinese dance (e.g., *jogèt*, *pèndèt*, and *légong*, among others) than the varieties of female dance known in the rest of Java. The costume worn by the dancer is unique to Banyuwangi. The *gandrung* dancers share with Malang *topèng* dancers the wearing of white socks or stockings.[24] Yet the more conspicuous sequined gold helmet (*omprok*), often decorated with frangipani flowers, resembles more closely the head-dresses worn by some Balinese dancers than those worn by other Javanese.

The accompanying musical ensemble, consisting of two Western violins (*biola*), one or two drums, several gongs (*kethuk*, *kenong*, and *kempul* or small *gong*), and a triangle (*kluncing*), also represents a configuration unique to Banyuwangi. And the vocal style, from the structure of Banyuwangi melodies and text settings to the ornamentation and vocal quality of the individual singers, is immediately recognizable as that of the *gandrung* of Banyuwangi.

No less distinctive in the Javanese context is the ensemble known as *angklung Banyuwangi*, which plays instrumental music, sometimes in accompaniment of dance. The ensemble consists of two bamboo-keyed xylophones (here called *angklung* – see plate 13), two drums, a large number of metal-keyed instruments, usually of iron, and occasionally an aerophone (flute or double-reed). The remarkable and at times fierce competitions between two *angklung*

13 *Angklung* of Banyuwangi in the Jawa Timur (East Java) pavilion, Taman Mini Indonesia Indah, Jakarta, 1986.

groups, called *angklung caruk*, know no counterpart elsewhere in Java. The music performed at contemporary *angklung caruk*, after an opening item or two from the older repertory, is very clearly inspired by the dazzling style of the Balinese *gong kebyar*.[25] The older pieces are more subdued, but otherwise do not sound "Javanese" to most other Javanese.

The most common tuning in Banyuwangi is a kind of *sléndro*, pentatonic with no small intervals. Yet Javanese musicians I have spoken to from other areas say that the intervals of Banyuwangi *sléndro* often do not fall within the acceptable limits of Javanese *sléndro* elsewhere; some intervals are too small, others too large. Some *angklung Banyuwangi* ensembles are tuned to a five-tone *pélog*, as found on many Balinese gamelans (sounding like 1 2 3 5 6 or 2 3 5 6 7 on *pélog* Javanese gamelan).

The distinctiveness and liveliness of these genres has made them probably the most popular emblems of "East Javaneseness" as opposed to "Central Javaneseness," despite their association with only one corner of the province and their marked difference from other genres of performing arts in the province.

Unquestionably the traditional arts best known in East Java, however, are those normally associated with central Java, particularly with Solo. Gamelan musicians are usually well-versed in contemporary central Javanese gamelan practice – not only in the "central Javanese" area of East Java, but throughout much of the rest of the province (except Madura). The taste for central Javanese arts is anything but new. The remarkable account of Cornets de Groot, the chief Dutch official (*resident*) of Gresik (near Surabaya) in the early nineteenth century, lists the titles of a number of gamelan pieces that, nowadays at any rate, are associated only with central Javanese and not with east Javanese tradition.[26] Reports under the *Berita Kebudajaan* (Cultural News) heading in the *Budaya* journal of the 1950s give ample evidence of Solonese dance and gamelan music being studied and performed by local residents in Surabaya (October and November 1953:47; November and December 1954:63), Malang (January 1958:51), and even as far east as Jember (December 1953:50).

These documents corroborate the accounts of musicians, who say that as long as they can remember, central Javanese influence has been strong in East Java. Radio broadcasts of central Javanese music and drama have been heard in East Java for about sixty years. And since the early 1970s, the commercial cassette industry has flooded the province with recordings of top performers of central Javanese gamelan, *wayang*, and other genres. Most of the puppeteers who profess to maintain a distinctively east Javanese style of performance are increasingly influenced by central Javanese practice. Though their *sulukan* and staple gamelan repertory remain east Javanese, central Javanese pieces and playing techniques are finding ever greater prominence throughout much of their night-long performances. Even in the Banyuwangi area one now finds gamelan played in central Javanese style.

People account for the appeal of central Javanese gamelan music (and related performing arts) in various ways. Some simply say they prefer the sound. Others say they find it more carefully conceived and sophisticated than any music of East Java, or that it represents a higher tradition, nurtured in the courts. It is orthodox, standardized, widely respected; east Javanese is heterodox and looked down upon elsewhere.

Presentations intended primarily for outsiders to the province have now a strong tendency either to combine or juxtapose several of these genres associated with particular areas of East Java. And, as will be elaborated in the following chapters, efforts at constructing a new pan-provincial East Javanese tradition are beginning to bear significant results.

It is too early to evaluate the extent to which East Java's traditional arts will merge. But it does seem clear that the genres of the central portion of the province – the *arèk* east Javanese of the Surabaya-Mojokerto-Malang triangle – represent a tradition of considerable weight at present and would likely serve as the foundation of an East Javanese tradition. Though seen to be near extinction by Western ethnomusicologists studying in the region fifteen to twenty years ago (Judith Becker and Michael Crawford), it has regained sufficient strength since then that the head of the Arts Division of the Department of Education and Culture for East Java, Dr. Sutrisno, told me in 1983 that he no longer worries about its survival and has turned the preservation efforts of his department to genres which stand on far shakier ground. The gamelan music of this region is already known to many as *karawitan Jawa Timuran* – it remains to be seen if and when it will be appropriate to call it "East" rather than "east" Javanese.

PART II

6 Gamelan music, performing arts, and government policy: formal education, contests, and festivals

While Westerners may be skeptical of any government policy on the arts as potentially threatening to a cherished artistic freedom, it is not only in socialist countries, but in many others that the government plays a substantial role in supporting, as well as suppressing, certain kinds of artistic expression (Wallis and Malm 1984:227, 234–40). The arts have long been understood by Javanese, rulers and commoners alike, to have important intrinsic powers that require the close attention of any legitimate ruler. Those in positions of power in Java have involved themselves not merely as arts "patrons," but often as determiners of style. The types and quality of arts presented at court reflected directly on the prestige of the ruler. In the early days of the nationalist movement in Java, during the first part of this century, the role of performing arts in an Indonesian nation-state was hotly debated by intellectuals in an exchange known as the *polemik kebudyaan* (cultural polemic) (Holt 1967 and Lindsay 1985). And since independence, policy makers at all levels of government, from the president in Jakarta to local "culture officers" (*penilik kebudayaan*) in rural *kecamatan* (small administrative units), have sought to nurture numerous varieties of indigenous performing arts, albeit in accord with an evolving and often ambivalent conception of Indonesian national culture.[1]

Statements of government policy

Several major axes of tension are evident in policy statements and government programs to date. One is the tension between preservation (the desire to keep things as they are, or, more often, as they are thought to have been) and creativity (the desire to experiment, combine, and change). Another is the tension between regional focus and supra-regional or national focus (in artistic vocabulary and intended participant performers and audience). A pamphlet on government cultural policy, published in 1973 in English and intended for international distribution, describes some of the goals of the government and the means of implementation.

> The broad outlines of a national and cultural policy are laid down by the Majelis Permus[ya]waratan Rakyat (People's Council). On these basic principles the government draws up plans for cultural development that imply rediscovering, preserving, developing and telling the people about their cultural heritage... Traditions and historical remains that are valuable to the nation's struggle and dignity must be preserved and handed down to new generations.
>
> (Departemen Pendidikan dan Kebudayaan 1973:10)

Evident here is the perceived need for both preservation and change (development), as well as the notion of control (in determining which traditions are "valuable").

One recurring theme in policy statements is the idea that the arts as they currently exist are imperfect, in need of improvement, and can serve at best as the foundation for something new. Specific major projects by the government include the "establishment of *conservatoires* in seven provinces ... to improve artistic standards, provide training, and awake[n] a greater popular interest in [performing] art" (Departemen Pendidikan dan Kebudayaan 1973:13), and the "establishment of regional music and dance workshops to find fresh material" (*ibid*:39).

One of the concerns that turns up repeatedly in policy statements is the need to "counteract the possible negative effects of Western pop music" (*ibid*:39). Indigenous music, traditional and regionally based, is touted as the antidote; but concern is also expressed for the problems of national cohesion that might result from too much emphasis on regional separatism. In the texts of both the 1979 and the 1984 publications of the Five Year Plans (*Rencana Pembangunan Lima Tahun*, abbreviated Repelita), it is stated that efforts should be made to do away with values that are too narrowly regional ("yang bersifat kedaerahan yang sempit"), as well as to guard against negative foreign cultural influence ("ditanggulangi pengaruh kebudayaan asing yang negatif") (Repelita 1979[III]:17; Repelita 1984[III]:17). Arts in danger of "extinction" ("yang hampir punah") are to be saved and developed "selectively" ("secara selektif") (Repelita 1979[III]:29–30). We shall examine below some of the factors determining the criteria for selection, and the extent to which some policy makers may wish to curb local heterogeneity as "too narrowly regional."

Government policy directly affects gamelan music in Java in three major realms: the public education system, the government-sponsored contests and festivals, and public media (print, radio, television, and recording). The first two of these and some publishing are administered mostly under the Department of Education and Culture, the other media under the Department of Information.[2] Our concern in the present chapter is with the first two of these – formal education and government-sponsored contests and festivals – in which governmental policy exerts the most direct control over the specifics of performance.

Public education

Programs of the Department of Education and Culture play a profound role in shaping the practices and conceptions about gamelan music and most other "traditional" arts today. In addition to requiring training in certain regional performing arts in elementary and secondary schools, the government supports a small number of secondary and tertiary institutions devoted to the training of musicians and other performers who will be equipped to teach and perform professionally.

Government schools of performing arts in Surakarta and Yogyakarta

The first of these schools of performing arts was founded in 1950, immediately after the revolution against the Dutch, in the Javanese cultural center, Surakarta. It was named *Konservatori Karawitan Indonesia*, and was usually referred to as KONSER or KOKAR until 1977–78, at which time it was changed to SMKI Surakarta, an abbreviation of *Sekolah Menengah* ("High School/Secondary School") *Karawitan Indonesia*. Translation of these names into English presents some interesting ambiguities, due both to the structure of modification in Indonesian phrases and to the somewhat slippery usage of the word *karawitan* in official circles. *Karawitan* is generally understood to refer to gamelan music, but can refer more broadly to indigenous music that does not use the Western diatonic scale. The offerings of dance and shadow puppetry at institutions bearing the name *karawitan* suggest a still broader understanding of the term as "traditional performing arts." The placement of the word "Indonesia" at the end of the name allows us to translate *Konservatori Karawitan Indonesia* as "Conservatory of Indonesian Karawitan" or "Indonesian Conservatory of Karawitan" or "Karawitan Conservatory of Indonesia" – each subtly different from the others.

It was thought at first that music from the far reaches of the archipelago would be represented, along with Western music and other Asian musics (including Chinese), and that all would combine by the nature of their presence in a single institution. Writing about this institution in the early years, Soekanto explained that "the decision of the Government to found the *Konservatori Karawitan Indonesia* was an experiment for protecting, fostering, and developing the regional musical arts" ("putusan Pemerintah mendirikan Konservatori Karawitan Indonesia adalah suatu experiment untuk memelihara, memupuk dan memper-kembang seni-seni suara daerah") (Soekanto 1953:21). He identified the many kinds of studies that were to be given at this one institution

not just on gamelan from Solo and Yogya, but from West Java, East Java, Bali, Sumatra, Sulawesi, Maluku, or all the regional musical arts that exist in all the regional cultural centers of Indonesia.

[tidaklah mengenai seni-suara gamelan dari Solo, Jogja sadja, tetapi djuga seni-suara dari Djawa Barat, Djawa-Timur, Bali, Sumatra, Sulawesi, Maluku atau segala seni-suara daerah jang ada dan berkem-bang di semua cultuur-centra daerah-daerah di Indonesia.]   (Soekanto 1953:21)

He sees these various musical arts playing a part in the growth of a national culture. Though he refrains from specifying the exact means by which such growth should take place, he does suggest that some degree of assimilation between regions is desirable.

Others were highly skeptical of either the possibility or the desirability of various regional musics blending together into a new Indonesian national music. J. A. Dungga (trained in Western music and an advocate of a Western-based Indonesian national music) warned that

The regional musical arts differ greatly in their sound and their level, and to the end of time can never meet or become one.

[Kesenian musik-musik daerah sangat berbeda-beda utjapan dan tingkatnja, sampai achir zamanpun ia tak dapat bertemu atau dipersatukan.]   (Dungga 1953:706)

And Boejoeng Saleh argued that

Rather than create a new hybrid from all kinds of regional culture in a laboratory, we should instead be providing the broadest possible guarantee of the life of Indonesia's many regional cultures. In this way, Indonesia will become a beautiful garden with flowers of many colors.

[Daripada mentjiptakan suatu hibrid baru daripada berbagai kebudajaan-daerah didalam sebuah laboratorium, kita bahkan perlu memberikan djaminan seluas-luasnja untuk hidupnja berbagai kebu-dajaan-daerah Indonesia. Dengan demikian Indonesia akan mendjadi sebuah taman indah puspa pelbagai warna.]   (Saleh 1956:248)

The problematic nature of this institution with respect to its initial goals of creating national arts became evident as the time passed (Hatch 1980, Becker 1980, Lindsay 1985). Though at first the intention was to formulate a "national culture," the idea of creating national music and dance from a melting pot proved unrealistic, at least on demand and in the short term. Indonesia's regional arts were simply too diverse for a comfortable blend. Most of the teachers hired at KONSER were Solonese gamelan musicians who, despite some early experiments – by Martopangrawit, for instance (Sutton, *Variation in Central Javanese Gamelan Music*, in press: chapter 3) – were so deeply versed in the court-derived gamelan tradition that there was little real attempt at assimilation between existing styles.

From early on, some music from West Java and from Bali has been taught at KONSER, usually by performers from these other areas; but the great diversity of the archipelago has never been thoroughly represented. With relative political stability during Suharto's New Order (at least compared to the rebellious 1950s), Indonesian government officials have seen less of a need to strive for a homogeneous national culture, at least through the arts. Government policy reflected in the curriculum of KONSER and other similar schools has shifted towards an acknowledgment of the more extreme aesthetic boundaries that exist – for example, between North Sumatran and Solonese music – and concentrated on the local tradition (Solonese) and its most widely recognized neighbors (Yogya, Sunda, Bali).

These are not generally mixed, however. Rather, they are understood in contradistinction to one another. Courses are explicitly listed as "Yogyanese gamelan, level 1" or "Solonese dance, level 4" and so forth. The precise course content is to some extent determined by the instructor, but the fact that many students receive nearly identical training does much both to reify and to standardize all of these traditions in the minds of both students and faculty. And since styles are taught separately by region, even the most natural sorts of blending, the types that very often occur outside the conservatory walls, are inhibited. Compartmentalization is encouraged. One is taught not to use Solonese *bonang* patterns, for example, in Yogyanese gamelan class, or in Yogyanese pieces in a recital. But the very fact that each student is introduced to some gamelan music outside the Solonese mainstream means that the potential for blend has been well prepared. It seems almost inevitable that a generation of musicians introduced to a variety of musical traditions in their formal education will find some way to combine them.

Given the heavy focus on Java, one might have expected some offerings on the various regional traditions discussed in previous chapters. Yogyanese gamelan music, though felt by the Solonese to be inferior in some ways to their own, has obvious claims to artistic legitimacy through its association with the royal court and has been a staple part of the curriculum. But traditions of Banyumas, Semarang, and even East Java (despite Soekanto's mention of East Java cited above) have been almost completely ignored at SMKI Surakarta. Only recently has there been a course in "East Javanese Dance," but taught by a central Javanese whose primary performance training has been Solonese. No formal courses have been offered in gamelan music of these other Javanese regions. The study of Sundanese, Balinese, and even Yogyanese arts are seen nowadays as serving a comparative function. During the first and final (fourth) years, students take courses in only Solonese arts, and sample the other offerings during their second and third years.

A second conservatory was founded in Yogyakarta in 1961 by the federal government, the *Konservatori Tari Indonesia* (literally, "Indonesian Dance Conservatory"), usually known as KONRI until the name changed in 1977–78 to SMKI Yogyakarta. For the first thirteen years, KONRI was located at the home of Prince Tejakusuma, where the first Javanese dance school (*Krida Beksa Wirama*) had also been located since its founding in 1918. The focus of the curriculum at KONRI was Yogyanese dance, with some training in gamelan music of Yogyakarta and Surakarta (see plate 14) and dance of other regions (mostly Solonese, with occasional informal study of Sundanese and Balinese dance). No other regional traditions of Javanese music or dance have been taught there.

It had been intended that KONRI would offer degrees for college-level study as well as high school; but in 1964, before anyone had graduated from the high school level, a separate college-level institution was founded, *Akademi Seni Tari Indonesia* (literally, "Academy for Indonesian Dance Arts"), known as ASTI. Under the directorship of R. M. Soedarsono, who in the years following 1964 had considerable experience studying and teaching dance overseas, the curriculum emphasized both the transmission of traditional dance and music styles and creative experimentation in choreography. By the early 1970s, the gamelan music as well as dance of Sunda and Bali were offered at ASTI, supplementing the initial offerings in gamelan music and dance of Yogyakarta and Surakarta.

Again, no courses have been offered in other Javanese regional traditions, such as Banyumas or east Java. But at this level, advanced students must present major concerts, in which creative input, including the blending of regional styles, is not only tolerated but encouraged. In 1984, for example, Supriyadi, a dance student from Purbalingga (in the Banyumas region), presented a graduation recital that required both dancers and musicians to combine elements of Banyumas, Solonese, and Yogyanese styles. In the mid-1980s ASTI was subsumed under the umbrella of the *Institut Seni Indonesia* (literally, "Indonesian Arts Institute" – known as ISI), a newly formed arts institution located in Yogyakarta and intended eventually to offer degrees up through the doctoral level in the plastic and performing arts.

During the same year of the founding of ASTI in Yogyakarta, the Department of Education and Culture made provisions for the establishment in Surakarta of *Akademi Seni Karawitan Indonesia* (literally, "Academy for Indonesian Karawitan Arts"), a college-level academy devoted primarily to gamelan music, but with majors in dance and shadow puppetry as well. Under the directorship of S. Humardani, who died in 1983, this institution has developed into a major center for musical experimentation involving gamelan. Students have been encouraged to compose new works that depart radically from traditional norms. Balinese, Sundanese, Yogyanese, and for the past five years, Banyumas gamelan music traditions are all taught at ASKI and these regional styles are frequently mixed in performances.

In 1984 I witnessed a performance of "Kilat Buwana" (a well-known *wayang* story) presented as *pakeliran padat*, a style of condensed shadow puppetry, developed at ASKI, in which whole stories that usually take an entire seven or eight hours to unfold are presented in a fraction of the time, often even less than one hour. Musicians drew on repertory and performance style from east Java and Yogyakarta to enhance their innovative renditions of what was mostly Solonese-based material. In a discussion afterwards, the musical arranger and director, S. Subono, stated explicitly that these styles were now his. I noted in my journal this fragment from his remarks: "Yogyanese style is my possession; Banyumasan is mine; Surabayan is mine; Solonese is mine" ("Gaya Yogya ya duwèku; Banyumasan ya duwèku; Surabayan ya duwèku; Solo ya duwèku") (Discussion at ASKI, Kentingan campus, June 26, 1984). This is not to say that he claims to be Yogyanese, Banyumasan and so forth, but that these various Javanese traditions are, in his estimation, not beyond his reach, either practi-

14   Students in *rebab* class taught by Pak Sastrawiryana at SMKI Yogyakarta, 1986.

cally or aesthetically. He feels a right to draw on them selectively, but would not wish to forego his Solonese basis to immerse himself in any of the others.

The structure of the curriculum at these major institutions in the prestigious court-centers of central Java, then, has encouraged an explicitly compartmentalized understanding of gamelan and related arts as regional styles and repertories, each taught in separate classes. But at the college-level institutions – after one has internalized the "correct" regional categories – experimental combinations are encouraged in certain contexts.

How do the activities at these institutions relate to government policy? The official published rhetoric concerns the building of an Indonesian identity/personality (*Kepribadian Indonesia*), rather than a Solonese, Yogyanese, Sundanese, or Banyumas identity.[3] Yet from my talks with faculty members or students at these institutions it seems abundantly clear that they do not view their attempts at perpetuating Yogya style or Solo style, for example, to be anti-Indonesia. The preservation of regional arts is, after all, called for explicitly in the recent Five Year Plans.

Those I know at these institutions have a strong sense of their own particular regional identity, usually expressed and reinforced through the style of performance in which they specialize, regardless of whatever experimental combinations they may produce. In a sense, then, when a Yogyanese performs Yogyanese music, he is being Yogyanese; when he performs Solonese, or a combination, he is being Javanese (or "central Javanese"); and when he performs Sundanese, or Balinese, or a combination, he is being Indonesian. Multiple levels of identity may be evident at different times within the same individual and do not supplant one another. Even extended involvement with music or dance of other regions will not easily erase a well-established sense of regional identity. I know of one Yogyanese dancer-musician whose main teaching assignment at SMKI Yogyakarta is Sundanese music, but he participates in dance and music concerts that are primarily in Yogyanese style and has not by any means turned his back on his Yogyanese roots. His specialty is born of economic necessity rather than aesthetic preference.

Government schools of performing arts in East Java and Banyumas

Surabaya

It was the 1970s that saw significant official recognition by the government of both Banyumas and East Javanese traditional performing arts. In 1973 the *Konservatori Karawitan Indonesia Surabaya* was founded, known as KOKARI Surabaya until it became SMKI Surabaya in 1977–78. This school has represented an evolving response to the problem of cultural identity in the arts of East Java. One of the primary forces motivating its founding was the growing perception that East Java was being dominated by outside cultural forces – Euro-American popular culture on the one hand and central Javanese culture on the other.

It was formerly assumed by administrators that regional performing arts in East Java consisted only of "folk" arts (*kesenian rakyat*) and that the only traditional Javanese music worthy of academic study was court-derived. East Javanese students were welcome at the conservatories in Surakarta and Yogyakarta, and made up a sizeable portion of the student population there. But some experts in the styles of dance and gamelan music associated with the *arèk* east Javanese impressed upon the provincial office of the Department of Education and Culture that East Java needed its own conservatory, because it had distinctive traditions in danger of extinction and worthy of study and preservation.[4] They believed that official recognition of these arts, especially in the form of an established academic institution, could help stave off the formidable encroachment of mainstream central Javanese arts and Western popular culture. The provincial government concurred with the need for a conservatory in East Java through which the region could be validated artistically. The performing artists and government officials alike were concerned that in another generation their own local tradition (especially the Surabaya variant) would disappear. But the conservatory took on a rather different shape than the artists had hoped.

KOKARI Surabaya was modelled along the lines of similar institutions elsewhere in Indonesia, with formal classes, exams, and so forth. Like other public schools, this one required teachers with degrees and the likelihood of success in a formal classroom setting. The result was that most of the teachers hired were graduates from ASKI Surakarta, ASTI Yogyakarta, or the SMKI conservatories in Surakarta and Yogyakarta. These teachers were far better versed in central Javanese traditions than in any traditions indigenous to East Java. Though some had been born and raised within the province of East Java, none could claim expertise, for example, in Madurese, Banyuwangi, Malang, or Surabaya styles of music, dance, or *wayang*. The experts in such arts have occasionally been employed as assistants, but the emphasis on notation and formal teaching methods, together with the lowly status bestowed upon them, turned them away, leaving the teaching to those less expert but holding degrees.

In recognition of the problem posed by this ironic situation, the government has funded the faculty at SMKI Surabaya to conduct field work throughout the province in order to acquaint them with the arts they are supposed to be preserving and developing. It may seem preposterous, but, in the eyes of bureaucratic administrators not especially familiar with the arts, a formally educated traditional musician is a wiser choice for a government-sponsored teaching job than someone with no formal credentials, regardless of his regional artistic expertise.

The choice of teachers from the ranks of the formally educated goes beyond the need seen for familiarity with classroom teaching and administration, however. Along with formal education in the arts and related subjects comes a rather heavy indoctrination in the national ideology, the "Five Principles" (Panca Sila). As teachers at public schools, or even as professional musicians at the national radio stations, the graduates become civil servants and are expected to join the incumbent, anti-communist party Golkar. Though every trace of the Indonesian Communist Party (PKI) appears to have been eradicated, the government still views artists, particularly those with little formal education, with some uneasiness. The PKI was strong in East Java prior to the 1965 coup, and the performing arts were thought to be one of the most effective means of spreading the communist message.

At SMKI Surabaya, the teachers themselves readily acknowledge their lack of qualifications in "East Javanese" arts, but take some comfort in viewing their job as more than merely passing on or preserving. They are to "develop" these arts, whatever that might mean, and not as isolated local genres, but rather as parts of an imagined whole tradition of East Java. What, then, determines which genres are chosen for formal recognition, transmission and "development"? In a 1983 survey, the provincial Department of Education and Culture reported 106 genres of performing arts in the province. Clearly these could not all be taught at the conservatory. A choice had to be made, identifying a few "important" genres that had the most "potential." While there is no standard hierarchical ranking for these genres, some seemed more appropriate for the conservatory than others.

In music, the genres which emphasize instrumental complexity and richness of timbre – such as the gamelan music accompanying shadow puppetry (Surabaya-Mojokerto-Malang), masked dance (Malang and Madura), and social dancing (gandrung of Banyuwangi, and tayuban elsewhere) – offer more interesting teaching material for the conservatory and higher status in interregional festivals and competitions. They are closer in many ways to central Javanese gamelan, and are more often referred to as "gamelan," in contrast to the small double-reed, drum, and gong ensembles (sronèn, reyog), frame-drum ensembles (terbangan, sandur, kentrungan), and other ensembles found throughout the province. But we should also note that genres with any overt connection with Islam, including the many genres using the terbang drums, are excluded. To the urban Indonesian bureaucrat these ensembles not only sound "primitive," they also suggest the threat of grass-roots Islamic opposition to Golkar and Suharto's New Order.

The conservatory has temporarily employed musicians specializing in one style of Madurese gamelan music (from Sumenep, a genre in fact heavily influenced by central Java) and in angklung music from Banyuwangi (which bears closer resemblance to Balinese than to any other Javanese music). Their residence at the conservatory has been intended to expose them to diverse "East Javanese" traditions as a source for "materials" (bahan) that are to be mined or "dug up" (digali). This metaphor leaves little doubt as to the evaluation of even these genres as somewhat incomplete, inferior, and old-fashioned. What is sought are "raw materials" of tone, timbre, and structure – and not the communal, rural ethos associated with many of these genres.

The result is an eclectic "East Javanese" tradition whose development is most often attributed to SMKI, but is evident at other institutions, on TVRI (television), and at tourist performance spots, especially the stage at Pandaan (located roughly half-way between Surabaya and Malang). Though Pandaan was opened in 1964, only three years after the famous Ramayana ballet at Prambanan in central Java, it was primarily central Javanese-style music and dance that was presented at Pandaan until the latter part of the 1970s. Now it is not unusual, for example, to see dance-dramas incorporating dance movement styles of Malang, Banyuwangi, and other parts of East Java, with corresponding musical styles. Groups from SMKI Surabaya perform there regularly, and their pan-East Javanese blend is now being imitated by other groups.

The reaction to these developments has been mixed. The central Javanese and other outsiders have reacted positively. That is, they tend to like the arts that East Java has singled out and are even drawing on them for their own enrichment. But in East Java, there is some resentment, particularly among the traditional artists, including those who fought for the founding of the conservatory itself. The control, they feel, is out of their hands. Much of the innovative work has been the source of bitter criticism by the older traditional artists, who see this work as unfaithful to the spirit of these arts, lacking in true feeling, and often resulting in awkward hybridization of genres from different regions. One hears complaints that the repertory is not being preserved, that some important instruments (e.g., *suling* and *rebab* in Surabaya) are being ignored, and that younger musicians dabble but show no depth of musical understanding. One of the top drummers in the Malang area, Pak Kasdu of Kedhung Monggo, complained to me that Banyuwangi music is too fast, and is more Balinese than Javanese. It strikes him as somewhat exotic and certainly not as "his own" music.

In a remarkable book entitled *Jawa Timur Menuju Kesatuan Gaya Seni* ("East Java Moves Towards a Unified Tradition in the Arts"), Djoddy Matsyachir, an outspoken East Javanese intellectual, takes a strong stand for the value of the many East Javanese arts as egalitarian, in contrast to the elitist arts inspired by the central Javanese courts ([1977]:3). Though he does not articulate the reasons why he feels East Java needs a unified tradition, he suggests – in line with the provincial government stance – that the province needs to be validated artistically in order to measure favorably with other Indonesian provinces, requiring something big and visible, rather than the many little genres scattered about the province. He clearly yearns for East Java to enjoy the artistic prestige of Central Java and Yogyakarta, especially since East Java is, in his estimation, much more deserving.

The central Javanese arts, he says, are very much out of place in contemporary democratic Indonesia. Whereas each of the arts in East Java represents a collective effort and general acceptance through *musyawarah* – a traditional village practice of reaching consensus through compromise – the court arts represent only the tastes of the supreme ruler and a few experts ([1977]:3). Through this same process of collective decision-making, the author feels, East Java can forge a unified tradition that rejects the backward and feudal elements found in central Javanese arts. Though championing the local arts, his wish for a pan-East Javanese tradition puts him at odds with traditional artists in East Java, who are more concerned about preservation of a particular local heritage than about gaining prestige for the entire province.

Matsyachir proposes a three-part plan to attain his goal: research into the history of East Java's arts, the establishment of standards from current practice, and the transmission of a unified tradition to succeeding generations. He feels strongly that SMKI (still Kokari when he wrote) has a critical role to play, but is very much disturbed by what was occurring there in the mid-1970s. Much of his book is a diatribe against one of the teachers at SMKI, A. Munardi, a central Javanese (from Yogyakarta) who combined dance movements and music he had studied in the village of Jabung (outside Malang) with those of his Yogyakarta heritage. The results he presented as "East Javanese dance." Munardi felt that such a combination elevated the Malang dance from a very local and little-known genre to something worthy of wider acceptance – something that all East Javanese presumably could be proud of. Munardi assumed that the people of East Java would view their own arts with some disdain, but he underestimated the extent to which some East Javanese people – Matsyachir and many others – looked upon central Java with suspicion and cherished their own coarseness and "folkiness."

Matsyachir's criticism has not radically altered the approach of Munardi and others at SMKI, where central Javanese arts occupy close to 60 percent of the course offerings (as opposed to the 40 percent of East Javanese and other regions, such as Bali) and where central Javanese aesthetic sensibilities still manifest themselves in matters of arrangement and production. The egalitarian ethos Matsyachir identifies as one of the main traits shared by the diverse arts of East Java is conspicuously absent.

Yet there is evidence for greater efforts at combining genres indigenous to East Java. In 1982, Soenarto A. S., who received formal training in dance in Solo and teaches at SMKI Surabaya, presented "Reog" at the Festival Penata Tari Muda (Young Choreographers' Festival) in Jakarta. The dancers and musicians were primarily students and faculty members from SMKI Surabaya. Instead of placing a village *reyog* on stage (*reyog* Ponorogo or *reyog kendhang*, for example), Soenarto choreographed a dance which combined movements from these with those found in *ngrémo* (Surabaya-Jombang), *topèng dhalang* (Madura), *wayang topèng* (Malang), *jaranan* (hobby-horse dance, in this case from Kediri), and Banyuwangi dance (Soenarto A.S. 1982:22). In the paper he prepared and delivered for discussion on the day following the performance, Soenarto argues that forms of *reyog* are found widely throughout the province, making it an appropriate "East Javanese" genre, but explains that he intended to "develop" *reyog* so that it would gain greater richness in dance movement (Soenarto A.S. 1982:19,27). And instead of the small ensemble typical of *reyog* accompaniment in East Java, he used a full gamelan playing pieces from several repertories. Some of those present, performers and scholars from around Indonesia, criticized Soenarto for the extent of his departure from traditional *reyog*, and urged him not to judge the artistic merit of the dance of one area (i.e., East Java) by the criteria of another (i.e., Central Java or Yogyakarta) (Soenarto A.S. 1982:29). Matsyachir, had he been present, would no doubt have taken issue with the slickness of production, but would have supported the effort to combine East Javanese elements. Yet he would prefer to see such efforts made by artists raised and trained in East Java, rather than central Java.

As SMKI Surabaya grows and its graduates begin to develop careers of their own, something more like Matsyachir's vision may take place. At another institution, the private, college-level conservatory Sekolah Tinggi Kesenian Wilwatikta (STKW), the focus is weighted towards arts of East Java, particularly the Surabaya-Mojokerto-Malang area, and with greater concern for documentation and preservation than development. Here some of the recognized senior experts from Surabaya and Malang teach on a regular basis, with little concern for building a larger "East Javanese" tradition. But the students who enroll here, coming with diverse backgrounds, many from SMKI, learn a variety of styles and tend in their own creative work to combine what they learn. In the STKW presentations at Pandaan, for instance, one finds the same sorts of combinations that characterize the SMKI presentations there.

Banyumas

In 1978 the provincial government of Central Java moved to establish a second SMKI in the region of Banyumas, in part to accommodate the high number of aspiring young performers who could not enroll at SMKI Surakarta, nearly 200 kilometers to the east. After a year in Purwokerto, the school moved to its current buildings in the small town of Banyumas (see plate 15). A focus on the local arts of the Banyumas region was not the original intention. At

15   Pak Rasito in front of the main classroom building of SMKI Banyumas, 1989.

the provincial level it was thought appropriate that this new conservatory, located as it was within the province of Central Java, should commence with offerings in the mainstream gamelan and dance arts of the province. The first teachers were musicians trained in the Surakarta tradition and taught Solonese gamelan music and dance. But at the urging of some local officials, who saw the opportunity for winning an unprecedented acceptability for Banyumas arts, the curriculum was soon expanded and some local musicians were hired. Within a year or so of its founding, SMKI offerings included formal courses in Banyumas gamelan music, supplemented in the succeeding years with courses in Banyumas *calung* music and the introduction of Banyumas dance movements in some of the choreographies taught.

Despite the move to offer formal studies in Banyumas arts, the vast majority of the nearly thirty teachers and assistants are graduates of the performing arts institutions in Surakarta and Yogyakarta. Some grew up in the Banyumas area and know the local arts intimately, but the majority are from other parts of Java. The director, Soeroso Daladi, does not even reside in Banyumas, but merely visits on a regular basis, and teaches Solonese singing. From its founding until my most recent visit in July 1989, most of the coursework has been in Solonese tradition, but all students are required to have at least some training in Banyumas gamelan music. Those who major in music (*karawitan*), rather than dance, are also expected to study Banyumas *calung*. Courses in Yogyanese dance constitute the only other regional tradition formally represented in beginner and advanced levels at the conservatory. When I visited in July 1989, Murdiana, a gamelan musician from Klaten and a graduate of SMKI Surakarta, was offering *pelajaran tambahan* (added study) in elementary Sundanese and Yogyanese gamelan music, but only for "comparative" purposes.

The facilities at SMKI Banyumas are quite meagre compared to the other institutions, all of which enjoy national rather than provincial sponsorship. And in fact, the provincial government provides only partial funding for this institution, paying the salaries of the senior teachers and contributing on an occasional basis to physical needs (buildings, instruments, costumes). Most of the teachers' salaries and part of the operating budget are drawn from private foundations (Yayasan Darmais and Yayasan Budaya Sendang Mas) and are combined with tuition to meet costs. Whereas the SMKIs in Surabaya, Surakarta, and Yogyakarta all have many bronze gamelan, including at least one set from Bali at each institution, SMKI Banyumas has only one bronze gamelan (Solonese), several iron gamelan, and a set of *calung*. Balinese gamelan music, of course, is not offered. Despite the proximity of Banyumas to Sunda geographically and musically, Sundanese gamelan music is not part of the regular curriculum and the institution owns no Sundanese instruments. (One of the Central Javanese gamelan is simply adapted for the "added study" in Sundanese music.)

Nevertheless, what has transpired at this small institution is having an important impact both in Banyumas and elsewhere in Java. It has helped to bring Banyumas music into sharper relief, providing it with a new legitimacy. As at other SMKIs in Java, classes are labelled explicitly as to regional tradition ("Karawitan Banyumasan," "Karawitan Solo," and so on). The juxtaposition here of the long-revered Solonese tradition with the local tradition suggests an unprecedented kind of egalitarian evaluation of the two. In the process of gaining legitimacy within a formal educational institution, however, it has also incorporated a number of theoretical notions from Surakarta, particularly as expounded by the venerated teachers at STSI/ASKI, such as the late R. Ng. Martopangrawit (see Sutton 1986b). And the extensive offerings of Solonese and Banyumas music, though they are taught separately, again provide students with great potential for combining elements from the two.

It is undeniable that the kinds of concert programs presented by SMKI Banyumas partake of many of the presentational conventions one would associate primarily with the institutions in Surakarta and Yogyakarta. These include recitals and other stage-oriented performances, which, in marked contrast to the communal ethos of *calung-lèngger* performances, for example, establish a distance between audience and performers and rely primarily on attention to sound and movement as their criteria for "success." One can easily imagine a Banyumas counterpart to Djoddy Matsyachir complaining about the dilution of these local arts; but, in my discussions with musicians and others concerned with the arts in Banyumas, at any rate, I did not encounter such an attitude. Within the few items of indigenous literature pertaining to Banyumas *karawitan*, concern is expressed over the extent to which Solonese practice has become the norm in the region (Departemen PDK 1980; Supanggah *et al.* [1981]; and Sekretariat Nasional 1983). Yet none of the activities associated with SMKI were singled out as contributing to the problem. Rather, the role of SMKI is seen as a positive step in promoting Banyumas tradition.

One of the most significant advances that musicians cite is the introduction of a new curriculum in Banyumas gamelan and *calung* music at the prestigious STSI/ASKI Surakarta. This was initiated by the director, S. Humardani, shortly before his death. Rasito, the well-known Banyumas musician and teacher at SMKI, was the first to teach Banyumas gamelan at STSI/ASKI. He now continues to visit occasionally, but the day-to-day teaching is carried on by graduates of SMKI Banyumas who are enrolled as students at STSI/ASKI.

Though the shape of the curriculum and the particular driving issues at each of these institutions helps to define each one separately from the other, they share a number of important traits. All of them contribute to an awareness of regional diversity in Javanese gamelan music. While each reflects the strong position of Solonese tradition throughout Java, each also provides strong support for the gamelan traditions local to the area in which the particular institution exists – albeit with modifications that may not be universally accepted. In the court areas, these institutions help to redefine and expand upon the traditions that developed in the courts. In Surabaya and Banyumas, the SMKIs provide an authoritative center, without recent local precedent, for the definition and crystallization of regional traditions that have developed in these areas. But with the multiplicity of regional offerings at all institutions, both students and faculty operate with the understanding that their participation in regional traditions not primarily their own, and the resulting tendency to combine and experiment, is not only legitimate but is sanctioned by government policy.

Contests and festivals

The influence of the government performing arts institutions on the general populace has been significant and promises to be pervasive in the next generation or two, as ever greater numbers of students in the public education system learn from graduates of these institutions. Already, however, Javanese in every administrative district have been touched directly or indirectly by the government sponsorship of contests and festivals. My concern in this section is primarily with the contests (*lomba, perlombaan*), which occur with considerable frequency at various administrative levels, mostly from the provincial level down to small districts (see plates 16 and 17). Festivals tend to be less frequent, occurring primarily at the national level and provincial levels, and often drawing upon successful participants in contests. When I was living in Yogyakarta in 1979, a day did not go by without the local newspaper covering one kind of contest or another – from gamelan music and dance to clean backyards. Some of these occurred with predictable regularity, others seemingly at the inspiration of some local official.

Regional "authenticity" within the arts contests seems to have come in and out of focus as a major criterion for judgement. During the late 1970s, it rather suddenly became the single most important criterion in gamelan contests in Yogyakarta – at the provincial level and

16   Dance-drama contest (Lomba Sendratari) for the *kabupaten* Yogyakarta, held at Purwo-diningratan pavilion, 1980.

17   *Muyèn* (*macapat* singing) contest, Banyumas, 1986. Photographs of President Suharto and Vice President Umar Wirahadikusumah on the wall flank the *Garuda Pancasila*, symbol of the Five Principles. Judges sit on the right and center.

within the city itself (in this case, the *kabupaten* level).[5] Judges and contestants, some of whom I knew quite well, received instructions from the local government that the performances were to be "Yogya style." Some of the pieces were chosen by the government officials, others were to be chosen by the leaders of the individual participant groups. Even at this level, questions arose as to the accepted regional identity of a particular item of repertory. The overlap between Solonese and Yogyanese repertory, as we saw in chapter 2, is extensive. Yogyanese versions of some Solonese *gendhing* are known to have been created; would these be acceptable? More problematic still was the issue of playing and singing style. How narrowly defined, in the minds of the government officials, or the judges, was "Yogyanese" *bonang* style or "Yogyanese" *pesindhèn* style?

A sufficient number of queries and complaints was received for government officials to sponsor several discussion sessions, with invitations to many of the major figures in Yogyanese gamelan performance, to help determine what precisely should be meant by "Yogyanese style." Some sessions were devoted to just one instrument, but even these failed to yield the kinds of results that could answer the contestants' questions. In one case a cassette recording of one of the required pieces was distributed to serve as a model. Close imitation of the playing style on the recording, the committee stated, would be taken as a fulfilment of the requirement to perform in Yogyanese style. This sort of arbitrary delimitation only caused further resentment among some contestants, since it rejected the more widely held conception of Yogyanese style as a set of possibilities and forced a narrowing to a single instance. One complained to me that she heard obvious errors on the recording. Were these to be slavishly reproduced?

As the debate unfolded in Yogyakarta, I was struck by the diversity of opinions among the Yogyanese about the need to nurture a distinctive Yogyanese style, the extent to which it should be defined, the extent to which regional criteria should determine contest results. Newspaper editorials attested to the plight of Yogyanese style in its own home territory and the need to bring it back to life.[6] Yogyanese nobility, with what they saw to be their family legacy at stake, echoed similar views. But a substantial number of musicians objected to contestants (whether themselves or others) being told what regional style they should use – even if such a style could be sufficiently delimited. Requiring Yogyanese repertory was one thing, but requiring a certain regional style in singing or the playing of instruments (such as *rebab*, *gambang*, even *bonang*) was both problematic with respect to definition and, even worse, an unjustifiable intrusion on what many saw as properly the realm of individual taste and habit. Some were quite open with me concerning their preference for Solonese gamelan music, feeling that it was inappropriate in the late 1970s to be so concerned over regional stylistic distinctions – implying that attempts to resurrect Yogyanese style were tinged with feudalistic overtones.

In the ten years since my extended stay in Yogyakarta, the contests have continued to require Yogyanese style, at least on some items. And discussion sessions continue to be held on an irregular basis to address questions of style. One of the ongoing concerns relating to the contests is the need to represent the region, sometimes officially as a province (Daerah Istimewa Yogyakarta – "Special Region of Yogyakarta"), in nationwide festivals. Some of these festivals – *wayang*, for example – have invited groups from several different regions within a single province (e.g., Banyumas and Solo in Central Java) and only from those provinces with an active *wayang* tradition (hence mostly Java and Bali). Others, such as dance (with live musical accompaniment), may have one participant group from each province. Implied in representation by province at the national level is a homology between the provincial unit and the cultural or subcultural unit, even though this is often not the case, as we have seen. In either sort of festival, a troupe from Yogyakarta would be expected to provide something distinctively Yogyanese, something to contrast with the other participating troupes. Yogyakarta's strong leanings towards the Solonese mainstream, particularly in gamelan music, are a potential source of embarrassment at the national level – especially for the government officials involved.

In the province of Central Java, the Solonese mainstream has been the traditional choice for most gamelan contests. In Solo itself regional "authenticity" is seldom an issue in contests, and contestants are not told explicitly that they must perform in this style. Musicians there are simply not much enamored of other regional styles – including Yogyanese, the one with which they share the most repertory. Still, some Solonese musicians like certain Yogyanese pieces and may even use Yogyanese playing style (e.g., drum patterns) in some Solonese pieces. But in a contest they would be very likely to take the safer path of choosing Solonese repertory and playing styles.

Within the city and most surrounding areas, regional stylistic definition has apparently not been an issue in Solo in recent memory.[7] In the 1950s, however, there was concern that contest participants from certain areas within the former residency of Surakarta but geographically near to Yogya (Klaten and its environs) did not seem to have sufficient grasp of the proper Solonese playing style. Musicians have told me that the model versions of *gendhing* required in contests were sometimes broadcast over the national radio station (RRI Surakarta) and that it was during this period that some of the finer points of Solonese style were standardized. More recently, notation of *balungan* and vocal parts has been provided, and other parts have been learned in accordance with a widely shared notion of what is normal within Solonese tradition as it has come to be known.

Other regions within the province of Central Java have emphasized Solonese gamelan music in their music contests, not only because this music has been well liked and widely known, but also because the winners at the local levels may go on to compete at the provincial level. Though formal policy at the provincial level does not now specify "Solonese style," it is generally understood that performance ability in this style will be a major factor in what is being judged. In the provincial contests, groups from an area such as Banyumas may present one of their local pieces, but from what I have been able to ascertain, have only done so within a larger framework of a medley that is mostly Solonese. For instance, a lively Banyumas *lancaran*, such as *Godril* or *Éling-éling*, can be performed at the end of a series of Solonese pieces, which begins with a refined *gendhing* and continues with a *ladrang* or *ketawang*. The required pieces, the ones all participant groups must perform, are always Solonese.

In Banyumas, some contests now focus on local tradition, but gamelan music contests do not. Given the new legitimacy of Banyumas gamelan music and its inclusion in the curriculum not only at SMKI Banyumas but at STSI/ASKI in Surakarta, this omission might seem difficult to explain. *Calung* and other rural arts indigenous to the region are well represented in local contests, but without the explicit goal of representing the region (or administrative district, i.e., *kabupaten*) in provincial contests. But because of Banyumas's location within the province of Central Java and the need for local gamelan contests to identify the best group to send to the provincial contests, Banyumas gamelan contests have focused almost exclusively on Solonese tradition. It is only a group that has thorough mastery of Solonese playing style that has real hope at the provincial level.[8]

Suhardi, one of the founding teachers at SMKI Banyumas and an employee of the Banyumas Department of Education and Culture Office in Purwokerto, explained to me that the two main reasons they sponsor performing arts contests are firstly, to provide support for traditions that are in danger of disappearing or in need of upgrading, and secondly, to choose representatives for provincial and national contests and festivals. He cited the contests his office had supported over the years for such genres as *bégalan* (a ritual enactment of petty robbery, with musical accompaniment), *wayang jemblung* (humorous musical drama performed without props or instruments by four or so people, seated around a table), *buncis* (male dance, accompanied by *angklung*), *gobrag lesung* (riceblock stamping music), and *muyèn* (singing of *macapat*, sometimes with framedrum accompaniment – see plate 17). These are genres that are relatively rare now and the government sought to breathe life into them. (Suhardi used the term *menghidupkan kembali* – literally, bring back to life.) *Calung* and *calung-lènggèr* contests occur with considerable regularity and are no longer seen as rescue efforts, but rather as providing incentives for improving the artistic quality, the stage presentability of this genre. It is in the *calung* contests, of course, that one hears the Banyumas *gendhing* one also finds played on bronze gamelan. And outside the contests, some of the musicians, especially the singers, perform both with *calung* and with bronze gamelan.

Any of these rural or "folk" arts (*kesenian rakyat*) might represent the region in a national folk arts festival, or even occasionally in a television special, where the best impression is made by a group whose performance has been tailored for a stage, with a passive audience, primarily interested in spectacle. Part of the "upgrading" process, then, is actually a transformation from communal rural genre to packageable artistic product.

Another intention of the upgrading, though not stated explicitly in my discussion with Suhardi in Purwokerto, is the curbing of any political potency these genres might have. Songtexts that are presented in contests and festivals often explicitly support government programs, sometimes to an almost ludicrous extent. One frequently encounters texts enumerating and interpreting the five "principles" of the pervasive *Panca Sila* doctrine. I have heard these in gamelan and *macapat* singing contests throughout Java. In Banyumas, I heard a series of texts especially saturated with government slogans that contestants sang in the *muyèn* contest I witnessed in the town of Banyumas in August 1986. *Muyèn* is usually understood to be group *macapat* singing performed just after a woman has given birth; and the texts, except in these contests, have not consisted of government propaganda.

It is also noteworthy that, despite a few isolated exceptions that I know of in Banyumas, the government has tended to avoid sponsoring contests of performing arts with close ties to Islam, such as the varieties of group singing accompanied by framedrum and known most generally as *slawatan*. Yet Koranic recitation is indeed an important contest genre, culminating in a national contest that wins front-page coverage in all the major newspapers and substantial air-time on television. However, these contests are coordinated not by the Department of Education and Culture, nor the Department of Information, but rather by the Department of Religion.

In Semarang and its environs, contests in gamelan music have not been used to support or spread knowledge of Semarang repertory or playing style. Again, the overriding concern with preparation for the provincial-level contest has made Solonese tradition the obvious choice, and the sense of a Semarangan regional cultural identity is rather weak. The selective championing of local "folk" arts is common throughout many districts of Java, and of course some genres found in rural areas outside Semarang have been represented in contests (e.g., *kendhalèn*, a kind of hobby-horse dance accompanied by small ensemble). Contests of Semarang-style *macapat* singing may have been held as well, as the government has expressed concern over rehabilitating this small repertory (Hardjo 1982), but I have no real evidence to support my suspicion.

The choice of genres and regional traditions for contests in East Java is a more complicated matter than in central Java. Presentation at the provincial level can be problematic due to the diversity of local cultural groups indigenous to the province – "central" and "east" Javanese, as well as Madurese and Banyuwangèn. Solutions have been various. I would like to consider here, as a telling example, the gamelan contests of 1981, in which contestants were asked to perform in both central and east Javanese styles.

Though much of this province is "central Javanese" culturally, it is felt that the central Javanese artistic traditions belong first and foremost to the people of Central Java province and the Special Region of Yogyakarta. In province-wide contests of gamelan music in East Java, such as that held in 1981, all performing groups were required to perform one "Jawa Tengahan" piece (i.e., central Javanese style) and one "Jawa Timuran" piece (i.e., east Javanese style). Many musicians took issue with requirements such as this, arguing that it is difficult for any but the professional musicians to perform well in two such different styles. It was a special challenge for gamelan groups from the westernmost part of the province, where the east Javanese tradition is not well-known. Several east Javanese from the Surabaya area told me that they had never heard a musician, even a professional, from west of Kediri perform an east Javanese piece with the right feeling. The drumming and subtleties of tempo were simply not right.

But the contest requirement withstood such arguments. Having gamelan musicians from all over the province play (and, if necessary, learn) the same styles, even though one of the styles is central Javanese, is one of many ways in which East Java is beginning to build a tradition that is known province-wide and is recognizably "East Javanese." I spoke to several of the government officials who set the policy. They understood well that central Javanese gamelan music is widely known in East Java and they wished to shore up the east Javanese. Limiting the competition to purely east Javanese style would have too strongly favored groups from the Surabaya-Mojokerto-Malang area, and discouraged wider participation. By setting this double requirement and providing explicit directions in the form of notation (of *balungan*, drumming, and vocal parts), they used the contest to teach at least some rudiments of east Javanese tradition to the many groups familiar only with central Javanese. The influence of SMKI is evident here as well, since the notation used has often been based on books and pamphlets of notation from SMKI faculty. With the difficulty of east Javanese *gambyak* drumming, however, it seems unlikely that drummers not already familiar with the technique would be able to learn solely from the notation, particularly since it often simplifies difficult patterns for the sake of readability.

If similar contests continue in the future, one suspects that either the groups will become increasingly skilled in east Javanese gamelan (keeping it separate from their central Javanese practice) or that something of a blend will occur. In either case, the result will be a widely shared "East Javanese" tradition, though of gamelan music in a radically different context than it has normally been performed, particularly in East Java – a formal contest, rather than a communal ritual celebration of a circumcision, wedding, or other important event. As evident from the earlier discussion of activities at SMKI Surabaya, this is clearly not the sort of blend that Djoddy Matsyachir has in mind when he speaks of a unified "East Javanese tradition."

As can be gathered from the preceding discussion, the effects of the government-sponsored contests on regional gamelan traditions vary from one locale to another, depending on the politics of culture in the particular region. Clearly these contests encourage a standardization of performance style. The requirement to perform in Solonese ("central Javanese") style in many areas helps to maintain the hegemony of this mainstream tradition. Yet in East Java and Yogyakarta, attempts are made to curtail the influence of this tradition and to support a standardized regional tradition – requiring it to be learned and performed by participants who might otherwise prefer Solonese style. As in the case of the government-sponsored institutions of formal education in the arts, the contests can bring into sharp relief the regional identity of the gamelan music that is performed. In East Java, groups have, as in 1981, been asked to perform in more than one style – much as SMKI students must take classes in gamelan music from several regions. But the impetus to experiment and combine elements from different regions finds a far more favorable environment in the performing arts schools than in the contests. At these schools students regularly participate in classes devoted to gamelan music from areas other than their own. In contests, participants more often hear and see performances by others that resemble very closely what they have prepared with their own group.

Probably the best opportunity for direct observation of performing arts from other regions are the large-scale festivals, such as those held periodically in Jakarta for *wayang* and dance. The participants are generally chosen as the best representatives of a given regional tradition, but their attendance at these festivals gives them a privileged opportunity to view top performers from other regions. Thus, again we find the juxtaposition of traditions helping to reify them as belonging to a particular region, while at the same time presenting them to people of other regions, thereby implying their value at a supraregional, national level. Participants are all urged, in accordance with government policy, both to maintain the best of regional arts and to contribute to "national culture" – as Indonesians and not just as Yogyanese, or Javanese. In a sense, then, the government policy itself helps to foster the multiple levels of cultural identity that many artists feel and which help to support new possibilities for creative combination between regional traditions. Still, there has yet to be a contest or festival in which such combination is actually encouraged by becoming one of the criteria for evaluation.

7 Regional traditions and the media: print, broadcast, recording

In Java, no less than in most of the rest of the modern world, the public media have played an increasingly prominent role in shaping artistic concept and practice during the twentieth century. A number of forces come into play in determining the representation of gamelan music in the media. The government plays a prominent role. Through various of its departments, it directly operates much of the publishing on the arts (through the Department of Education and Culture, and the national publishing house P.N. Balai Pustaka), the national radio and television stations (RRI and TVRI), and the national recording company (P.N. Lokananta). Musicians and government officials I spoke to, however, concur that the choices of genres and regional styles in these media are less directly determined by government policy or overall design than they are in the school curricula and in contests and festivals. Individual initiative, public taste, and market forces have certainly been just as important. Yet it seems that the government media, because they are partially subsidized, have concentrated more heavily on traditional performing arts, such as gamelan music, than have the private media.

A single chapter devoted to even one of the major media could not hope to provide anything more than a sense of the kinds of effects the particular medium has had. Yampolsky's book-length discography (1987) covers just one recording company. In my own writing I have dealt with some of the implications of the cassette industry for contemporary musicians, with focus on Banyumas (Sutton 1985b). My aim in this chapter, then, is to discuss some of the main characteristics of the major media as they have presented and impacted on the traditions of gamelan playing in Java, both in defining or crystallizing those traditions and in facilitating interaction between them.

Print media

In contrast to the explosion of published material on Western music of almost every variety through the course of this century, Javanese publications on music remain very few in number. Gamelan music transmission is predominantly oral, to be sure. Yet certain kinds of notation are widely used and theories about gamelan music are widely discussed. Still, the market for publications of gamelan notation or on gamelan theory is very limited. Members of gamelan performance groups I have witnessed in Yogyakarta and various parts of Central and East Java have never used published books (or sheets) of notation for playing. Those who use notation – and many do for learning pieces in rehearsals – nearly always have their own handcopied books of *balungan* notation, sometimes with drumming and shorthand indications of the *garapan* (treatment) of special passages. *Pesindhèn*, if they use written materials at all, are likely to have songtexts, but not melodic notation. Where published notation is more likely to appear is in the hands of a teacher, who may use it as an authoritative source for the *balungan* of a *gendhing*, a vocal part, or a difficult-to-remember drum pattern.

Published materials vary considerably in the level of authority they are thought to represent. A number of small booklets with gamelan notation have been published by various private (non-government) presses, but in my experience these have mostly been intended for primary or secondary school children or interested amateurs. These may serve as textbooks for students who do not plan to specialize in gamelan, not as authoritative sources for professionals or conservatory students. Instead, the publications accepted nowadays as the most authoritative are primarily those published by educational institutions, such as STSI/ASKI Surakarta. To those familiar with these institutions it may be the individual author or compiler who gives a work its special authority. For example, R. Ng. (formerly R. L.) Martopangrawit has compiled an exhaustive tome on drum patterns (1972b), and his two volumes on gamelan music theory (1969, 1972a) are major, canonical works. S. Mloyowidodo has compiled what is clearly now the most authoritative edition of *balungan* notation (1976, 3 vols.). Mloyowidodo and (until his death in 1986) Martopangrawit have been widely recognized among gamelan specialists in Solo and by others who have had some contact with STSI/ASKI as unusually knowledgable senior musicians and as skilled performers. For musicians outside Solo, who may know neither Martopangrawit nor Mloyowidodo by reputation, the fact that the publications come from STSI/ASKI is sufficient to lend them the necessary authority.

Given the hardships of budgetary restraint and the orientation of many teachers to performance, the output of both practical notation and theoretical studies has been substantial at both the SMKI level and the college level. For gamelan music, the Solonese tradition is by far the best represented in this kind of print medium. In addition to the collections of drum and *balungan* notation mentioned above, teachers have assembled extensive books of notation for *rebab* playing, *gendèr* playing, singing, and the playing of the archaic ceremonial ensembles (*monggang*, *kodhok ngorèk*, and *carabalèn*), among others (e.g., Parsana *et al.* 1972, Martopangrawit 1973 and 1976; Martopangrawit 1975, Soeroso 1975, Sosrowidagdo 1977, Suparno 1981, and Supadmi 1984). Though some publications from STSI/ASKI have dealt with other regions, even Bali, the vast majority are for Solonese style, and some are labelled explicitly as such. Even though some may only rarely be used, together they constitute a substantial outpouring and their very existence helps to reinforce the prestige of the Surakarta tradition. No other tradition is anywhere nearly as well represented in print. To the extent that these materials become available to the wider public, they also have the potential for spreading a very singular understanding of proper performance practice and ways to conceive of mainstream gamelan music. But as will be discussed further below, other media, particularly radio and cassettes, reach a much broader segment of the population and help to maintain a measure of flexibility even in this most standardized of traditions. One wonders about the situation in a generation or so, however, given the respect that these institutions and their publications now command.

Prior to the appearance of works by the respected musician-academics, however, other publications served a similar function. For example, several gamelan directors, including Mujiono and Suhardi of RRI Yogyakarta, have used Djakoeb and Wignyaroemeksa (1919), published under colonial auspices, as an authoritative source for Solonese *balungan*. The fact that the earliest publications of gamelan notation were devoted exclusively to Solonese *gendhing* has undoubtedly had some bearing on the establishment of this tradition as mainstream.

The earliest known efforts at notation of Javanese gamelan music are preserved in manuscript form, and their consultation was a privilege reserved for certain musicians and members of the nobility only. The court *bonang barung* players in Yogyakarta, for instance, sometimes played from the pages of notation collected in the *Pakem Wirama* when a rarely played or difficult piece was being rehearsed (Pustakamardawa, personal communication, 1979). As melodic leader, the *bonang* player occupied a privileged status in relation to other players for the *soran* (loud-playing) *gendhing* of the Yogyakarta repertory. Otherwise, the *gendhing* notation in manuscripts seems mostly to have been used outside the actual rehearsal or performance context by the gamelan director, and possibly by others in a leadership role (dance choreographers, for example).

The reliance of teachers and directors on authoritative published sources is not fundamentally different from a reliance on manuscripts, since the authority comes not from its mass production and dissemination but from the institution (or individuals) with which it is associated. In fact, the musicians who use these publications seem to view them, like rare manuscripts, as privileged sources, which in many ways they are. The older publications are exceedingly difficult to find for sale, though the technology of photocopying, which is a burgeoning industry in Java, provides the potential for easier access nowadays, assuming an original can be got hold of for a day or so. The publications from educational institutions are also somewhat difficult to obtain, since they are not sold in the general market-place. They are officially intended for students at these schools. Often the cover or title page carries the note 'untuk lingkungan sendiri" after the name of the publishing institution: "ASKI, for its own circle." If a title is in stock, an interested buyer can generally purchase it without official affiliation with the educational institution. (The fact that I was a foreign researcher might be seen as a special advantage in gaining access to these kinds of materials, but I know a sufficient number of Javanese who, though unknown to the particular publishing institution, have also been able to buy them.)

Gamelan traditions other than Solonese are only beginning to find representation in academic publications. Though SMKI and ASTI in Yogya have been well established for some time, the thrust of their publications has been on dance. The gamelan notation published by SMKI (e.g., Siswanta *et al.* 1974) presents *balungan* of *gendhing* for Yogyanese dance accompaniment, and does not attempt to be comprehensive with respect to the Yogyanese repertory. SMKI in Banyumas has not, to my knowledge, begun to publish. Much has been committed to writing there, however, in the form of senior recital papers. Though not reproduced for distribution, these papers record in unprecedented detail the *balungan*, vocal parts, and some of the instrumental playing for Banyumas gamelan and *calung* music.

In Surabaya, SMKI and STKW (*Sekolah Tinggi Kesenian Wilwatikta*) have published a variety of works on east Javanese gamelan music: *balungan* (Ronoatmodjo *et al.* 1981a), *rebab* (Ronoatmodjo *et al.* 1981b), *gendèr panerus* (Mudianto and Tasman [1983] and Sena'in *et al.* 1982), and a general theoretical introduction with explanation of instrumental techniques and notation for drum patterns (Soenarto R. P. 1980). It is too early to judge the extent of the impact which these will have on performance. Some have complained to me that these books reflect a Solonese bias and are marred by numerous errors. Those who are familiar with the editors and authors involved will know that the main compilers for most of these have had their training at the performing arts schools of central Java. Still, the well-respected expert in east Javanese gamelan music, Diyat Sariredjo, is credited as co-editor or assistant on several of these. Studies of music and dance from other areas in East Java have also been published by these two schools: the Solonese-influenced repertory of Sumenep, Madura (Soenarwi n.d.) and the dances and accompanying music of Banyuwangi (Proyek Rehabilitasi/Pengemban-gan 1979 and Sutojo 1981). Such publications, even more so than the curriculum itself, support the conception of distinct and separate traditions within East Java, and yet seek to facilitate a more widely shared understanding of them.

Given the authority invested in many of the works compiled and published by the performing arts schools, it might seem somewhat puzzling that both their format and their availability renders them rather ephemeral. Though most of the publications on gamelan music from other, private printing houses are typeset and fairly attractively produced, the publications by performing arts schools are almost always in stencil off-print format. Moreover, the number of copies produced is usually small (in the hundreds) and most titles sell out fairly rapidly, with no regular procedure for reprinting. It is explained that the stencil off-print format is primarily due to severe budget restraints, for it makes production cheap and thereby makes the materials available to students whose financial resources are usually extremely limited.

The limited-run, stencil off-print is the same format used by the Department of Education and Culture for many other "publications" relating to the performing arts, most of which never reach the public at all, but can sometimes be obtained at regional offices of this department. Often these are reports by employees of the particular regional office and intended not for general consumption but for the information of other civil servants in the Department of Education and Culture in preparation for a contest. I was told explicitly by employees at the provincial-level offices of this department in Surabaya that they often conduct research and produce this sort of publication in the process of considering genres for possible focus in contests or other kinds of government support (such as provision of needed materials – instruments, dance properties, and so on).

Some publications by the Department of Education and Culture, though not available in book stores, are more handsomely produced – typeset, with photographs. These include lengthy studies on particular genres and, of special interest to us in the context of the present study, a series of textbooks on regional traditions of *karawitan* (Yogyakarta, Surakarta, East Java) for SMKI students (e.g., Siswanto 1983 and Munardi *et al.* 1983). A shorter work on *karawitan* Banyumasan remains in stencil form, but may be reworked into similar format. The series on *karawitan* was commissioned not at the local level, but by the central Directorate of Primary and Secondary Education in Jakarta. The title pages indicate that all copies are the property of the Department of Education and Culture and they are not to be bought or sold. This, I was told, is to ensure that the limited number of copies remain available in the libraries of the various SMKIs and are not purchased by students, only to be sold on the second-hand market as other used textbooks often are. Clearly the intention is to assure that SMKI students become aware of the diversity of traditions in *karawitan*, and that they understand that diversity as regional.

Without going into extensive musical analysis, the books in this series outline basic characteristics of the particular tradition, identifying characteristic instrumentation, explaining theoretical terms, and describing genres unique to the region. The book on East Java incorporates material on the various cultural regions within the province, identified as *daerah etnis* (ethnic regions). Still, the emphasis is on the *arèk* Javanese (Jawa Timuran and Osing), with very little mentioned about the heavy central Javanese cultural presence in the province. Each book tends to heighten a sense of identifiable, isolated genres and traditions, with no suggestion of mixing across regional boundaries. And yet, the same individuals are expected to study the contents of each book in the series, not just the one from their own region. Thus, an egalitarian status is implied for the traditional arts, with *karawitan* Jawa Timur (and perhaps soon *karawitan* Banyumasan) given the same kind and length of coverage as the court-derived traditions of Yogya and Solo.

Also funded by the national government, although with an editorial staff that sees itself somewhat independent of particular educational policy decisions, the Balai Pustaka has contributed greatly to the corpus of published literature on Javanese culture since its founding during Dutch colonial times. Recently, some of its titles have reflected a growing interest in regional variation in Javanese performing arts.

The 1983 book on Banyumas *wayang* (Sekretariat Nasional 1983) attempted to trace the history of *wayang* in the Banyumas region and set down in writing the prominent traits that make *wayang* there distinctive from other Javanese *wayang* traditions. Some sixty local puppeteers were consulted and the result is a synthesis, complete with notation of *sulukan* and lists of preferred *gendhing* for major scenes, albeit somewhat idealized. In particular, the *wayang* tradition it describes – or, more accurately, prescribes – is one with considerably less Solonese presence than one usually finds in the varieties of "Banyumasan" *wayang* performed today.

It seems unlikely that puppeteers active now will alter their performance habits to conform with the prescriptions of this publication. It is more likely that it will influence younger puppeteers, particularly those who may seek formal education (at SMKI, for example) and be relatively receptive to the idea of learning a tradition standardized and normalized along regional lines. The more immediate impact, as I have argued elsewhere (Sutton 1986a), is in the visibility this publication provides for Banyumas tradition, both because of its recognition by a major national *wayang* organization (*Sekretariat Nasional Pewayangan Indonesia*, with the acronym "Sena Wangi") and because of the prestige of the Balai Pustaka and the relatively wide circulation of its books. Regardless of the extent to which the book actually reflects or influences performance tradition, the facts of its publication enhance the status of a Banyumas performance tradition, both in Banyumas and elsewhere in Indonesia.

Based on this model, a similar, though more ambitious publication was released in 1988 on *wayang* tradition of east Java. In addition to historical background and general performance guidelines, its two volumes contain a complete sample *lakon*, with narration and dialogue, and notation for all *gendhing* used, as well as *sulukan*. Unlike the Banyumas publication, this is largely the work of one author, Soenarto Timoer, who is acknowledged in a note from the *Sekretariat Nasional Pewayangan Indonesia* at the beginning of each volume (p. 7 in each). It is the Sekretariat name that appears on the cover and title pages, however, in order to give the publication the same legitimacy as the Banyumas volume.

I learned something about the process by which this work was compiled by speaking to Soenarto Timoer. First, he is not himself from the east Javanese heartland (Surabaya-Mojokerto-Malang), though he now lives in Surabaya. He comes, instead, from Kediri, where *wayang* style is much closer to Solonese. But as an East Javanese who has written of other performing arts traditions within the province (*reyog*, Timoer 1978–79; *topèng*, Timoer 1979–80) and who has become increasingly enamored of the many arts that are unique to East Java, he felt it important to use his abilities as a writer to help bring recognition to east Javanese *wayang*. He spoke with a number of puppeteers in the region, but rather than merely presenting a synthesis of his findings, he offers a transcription of an entire *lakon*, as performed by Ki Suléman and recorded on commercial cassette: "Lahire Ontorejo" ("The Birth of Antareja"), produced by Bumi Putra/Jayabaya cassette company, located in Malang. But rather than present the text exactly as it was performed, Soenarto Timoer decided to "upgrade" it, to make it more respectable and worthy as a model to be emulated, by translating much of the colloquial east Javanese passages in the narration into the kind of flowery high Javanese (*krama*) and "*wayang* language" (*basa pedhalangan*) characteristic of Solonese and Yogyanese *wayang*.

The musical pieces are those Suléman's gamelan group actually performed, and were transcribed for this publication by Jumiran, a gamelan musician raised and educated in Central Java who teaches at SMKI Surabaya, where his duties include teaching Yogyanese style. It should be stressed that both Soenarto Timoer and Jumiran have lived in Surabaya long enough to become quite familiar with local artistic styles. Yet it is ironic that neither of the two men most responsible for compiling this unprecedented work on east Javanese *wayang* are from the region itself. Soenarto Timoer told me that he saw this book as an important source for the younger generation, particularly those who would study at SMKI, where there is now a specialization in *wayang* puppetry. This book would help answer questions that such students might have about correct east Javanese performance, whereas before the only sources available addressed other regional styles, primarily Solonese.

Though the literature discussed above constitutes a body of printed media, rather little can actually be considered part of the mass media since it is not widely accessible. Of those mentioned, only the rather unauthoritative booklets for school children and the few publications by Balai Pustaka are even sold in retail bookstores. I am unable to judge the extent of their distribution, but do not believe it to be very substantial. The rest of the printed media on gamelan music must be sought after at government offices and educational institutions – not something the average citizen in Java is likely to feel comfortable undertaking.

Can we interpret this relative inaccessibility as a deliberate exercise of power by government officials and musicians? Based on my acquaintance with many of the individuals involved, I think this would be an exaggeration, at least to see it as a carefully implemented plan. Yet control of knowledge is certainly a kind of power. Teachers who compile books of notation do so primarily for their students, so that it is their artistic progeny that may bear the authoritative message and not just anyone who happens to be shopping at a local bookstore. Government officials who sit with cabinets full of undistributed pamphlets and studies resulting from their research can claim knowledge of many genres others may never even have heard of. In the contests they organize, then, their authority may often go unquestioned. Indeed, the belief that the path to knowledge is necessarily a difficult one and that the important is often inaccessible is deeply rooted in Javanese culture. The efforts to publish now represent a compromise between the restrictive measures of the Javanese past and the trend towards open access in the world of modern mass media.

Florida has pointed out in a carefully argued essay that the Javanese are somewhat reluctant to read even the authoritative sources to which they might have access (Florida 1987). The exact contents of many of the manuscripts in the Solonese *kraton* remain essentially unknown. It is the awareness that such a body of literature exists at all that assures an exalted status for the Solonese court tradition. Some publications on Javanese gamelan music and other performing arts may be consulted, read, even studied carefully by a few. None seem to exercise anywhere near the effects that musicological editions of works do in the West. Yet I would argue that it is the existence of these publications rather than their exact content that has the greatest impact – testifying to the existence of particular traditions more than they dictate details of performance practice. Indeed, gamelan music in all of these areas is still open to flexible interpretation and continues to be learned and understood primarily through oral transmission. It is for this reason that the other media, broadcast and recording, have had far greater impact on gamelan music than the medium of print.

Radio and television

Gamelan music has been broadcast over the airwaves in Java since the establishment of the Dutch colonial radio station NIROM (Nederlands-Indische Radio Omroep Maatschapping) in the late 1920s, with stations in Jakarta, Surabaya, and Yogyakarta.[1] Some gamelan musicians I knew in Yogyakarta had played for broadcasts on several stations (primarily on the independent MAVRO station) in the 1930s and early 1940s during Dutch times, on Hosokyoku radio under the Japanese occupation (1942–45), and then as studio musicians for Radio Republik Indonesia (RRI), which has been the official national radio station since its founding in September 1945, shortly after Indonesian independence was declared (August 17, 1945).[2] My several extended periods of residence in Yogyakarta and my close affiliation with RRI musicians there has given me a greater familiarity with the role of broadcast gamelan music in Yogyakarta and the issues surrounding it than in other places in Java. Nevertheless, I have visited RRI studios, observed broadcasts, and spoken to participating musicians and broadcasters in Surakarta, Purwokerto, Semarang, Surabaya, and Malang.

All the RRI stations are directly funded by the government through the Department of Information, and they identify what they broadcast as a combination of official news, other information programs, and entertainment. Private radio stations, financed by advertising, are also thriving in Java. The government exercises control over the type of advertising and the types of programs presented, requiring, for example, 10 percent of broadcast time to be devoted to "public service programming" (Susanto 1978:234). Still, as long as they comply with these policies and do not openly confront prevailing ideology, the programmers at these stations are free to determine what kinds of musical and dramatic entertainment they present, and many stations choose to broadcast at least some gamelan and the dramatic forms it accompanies – such as *wayang kulit*, *kethoprak*, and *ludruk* – at least in part because there is a market for these genres. Susanto's table of the most popular entertainment programs on RRI stations in Java and Madura, based on data furnished by RRI from 1972, showed *klenèngan* Banyumasan as the most popular in Purwokerto, *kethoprak* Mataram in Yogyakarta, *wayang orang* in Surakarta, *wayang kulit* in Malang, and *ludruk* in Surabaya, among others (Susanto 1978:237). (Semarang, for reasons not explained, was not included in the survey.) Each of these features gamelan music, and, in most cases, the gamelan music characteristic of the particular region in which it is being broadcast. A more recent survey might yield more complex results with respect to region. Nevertheless, the programming of regional traditional arts – gamelan music and drama – continues to occupy a prominent place in the weekly broadcast schedule on the various RRI stations. Pop music predominates on other stations, though some gamelan music is scheduled occasionally and *wayang kulit* broadcasts are fairly frequent.

As we look more closely at the role of radio in regard to the different traditions of gamelan music in Java, we find a pluralism similar to what we have encountered in the government schools. Solonese tradition is firmly established in all areas, with the appropriate local tradition also represented, although generally not as extensively as the Solonese. In a survey I conducted in 1983 of the kinds of gamelan music broadcast by the RRI stations in Java, including the many amateur groups who perform live or submit tape recordings to be broadcast, I found Solonese music to be predominant in each city. It is by far the preferred style by the amateur groups, and it is well represented in the programs of the professional musicians. Commercial cassette recordings of top groups, such as Ki Nartosabdho and Condhong Raos (discussed at length in the following chapter), are the main source of gamelan music on the private radio stations, and these are predominantly Solonese.

The larger stations of RRI (Yogyakarta, Surakarta, Purwokerto, Semarang, and Surabaya) are distinguished from the smaller RRI stations (Malang, for instance) and from the private stations in their maintenance of a group of professional studio musicians and actors. The studio gamelan musicians in each of these areas must be proficient in the mainstream Solonese tradition. At least they must know the more popular *klenèngan* pieces and (except in Yogya) the *wayang* repertory, in addition to the local tradition.

RRI Yogyakarta

Gamelan programming at RRI is determined at the local stations, and not by general dictate from Jakarta. The programming choices reflect the tastes of the musicians, the tastes of the local public, and the concerns of local officials. These have not always corresponded so neatly. A well-known example is the case of Yogyakarta, where for years (beginning even prior to the Japanese occupation) the radio station musicians drew very heavily on Solonese tradition in their choice of repertory and playing styles for such broadcasts as the popular weekly *Mana Suka* (literally, "what you like"), which lasts from nine-thirty to midnight each Monday night (with a half-hour break for news). Most of the musicians employed by the radio station from the 1930s to the 1970s were also court musicians: from the Yogyakarta *kraton*, the *kepatihan* (prime minister's residence), or the smaller rival Pakualaman located within the city, just two kilometers to the east of the *kraton*. The gamelan director from 1934 until the early 1970s was the highly respected Ki Tjokrowasito (now a resident of the United States and known as K.R.T. Wasitodiningrat). He had studied in Surakarta and, along with other members of the renowned gamelan club Daya Pradangga, did much to popularize Solonese style in the Yogyakarta area.

The same Ki Tjokrowasito was director of gamelan music at the Pakualaman, which has long maintained a preference in the arts for close imitation of Solonese music and dance, in part to set itself off from the Yogyakarta *kraton*. The *Murya Raras* concerts in honor of the Pakualaman prince have been broadcast live from the Pakualaman since about 1930, exposing Yogyanese ears to the sounds of Solonese gamelan music played by musicians highly regarded both for their skill and for their position as court musicians. Even the "Uyon-uyon Hadiluhung" concerts in honor of the Yogyanese sultan, the only *kraton* gamelan performances broadcast regularly by RRI, have been aired since about 1934 as well and have shown increasing signs of strong Solonese influence. This is not surprising when we consider that some of the most prestigious *kraton* musicians were also employed at the radio station, where they were immersed in Solonese gamelan music.

Some concerned government officials, along with members of the Yogyanese nobility, have complained periodically of the insidious penetration of Solonese tradition and the resultant decline in Yogyanese gamelan music. While I was in Yogyakarta in 1979, a directive from officials at RRI Yogya urged the then director Pak Mujiono to give greater representation to Yogyanese gamelan music by scheduling more Yogyanese *gendhing* in the weekly *Mana Suka* broadcasts than he or his predecessors had in the past. He and the other musicians resented this infringement on the artistic freedom they, and presumably most of their audience, had come to enjoy. And while RRI did begin to play more Yogyanese *gendhing*, the playing and singing styles have changed little from their basis in Solonese tradition. Under the new director, Ki Suhardi, the greater emphasis on Yogyanese repertory has continued, even though he has a strong preference for Solonese gamelan style and teaches this style to his students and the younger musicians at the radio station.

In addition to the concerts of gamelan music mentioned above, RRI Yogya broadcasts *wayang kulit*, *kethoprak* dramas, *macapat* singing, and an occasional morning concert of *gendhing soran* (loud-playing pieces), all of which feature distinctively Yogyanese repertory. And until the death in the early 1980s of the singer and director Pak Banjaransari, it also broadcast the Yogyanese sung dramatic form *langen mandrawanara*. But in contrast to the school curricula and many of the publications pertaining to gamelan, RRI has no policy to announce regional style explicitly over the air, unless a guest group is to be broadcast. Periodically the gamelan musicians from RRI Purwokerto, Surakarta, or Surabaya either visit to perform live or send recordings to be aired, in what is billed as a kind of artistic show of interregional good will. Yet these broadcasts are infrequent and evidently not anxiously awaited by the listening public. And thus most of what the public hears from RRI Yogya is performed by Yogyanese musicians – professionals and amateurs (see plate 18) – and is not explicitly identified as anything other than Yogyanese. The only mention I have heard in years of attending *Mana Suka* broadcasts in Yogya is the identification of several pieces from Banyumas that were performed by the RRI Yogya musicians (*Éling-éling Banyumasan* and *Ricik-ricik Banyumasan* are the ones I recall). Announcers do not bother to distinguish pieces individually as "Solonese" or "Yogyanese" for their listeners.

RRI Surakarta

In contrast to the mixture one hears from RRI Yogyakarta, the gamelan music broadcast by RRI Surakarta is almost entirely Solonese. A few pieces from other repertories, including Yogyanese, are played now and then, but usually identified as Yogyanese with qualifiers such as "Mataram" (e.g., Gendhing *Bondhèt Mataram*). Both *wayang kulit purwa* (with stories based on the Ramayana and Mahabharata, and primarily accompanied by *sléndro* gamelan music) and the obsolescent *wayang gedhog* (with stories of the Javanese legendary character

18 Gamelan at RRI Yogyakarta, played by members of amateur group Ngudyo Wiromo, 1974. *Slenthem* in foreground, gongs in background.

Panji, and accompanied by *pélog* gamelan music) are broadcast regularly by RRI Surakarta, bringing a variety of Solonese music to the airwaves. The commercial variety of dance-drama known as *wayang orang* (Jvn. *wayang wong* – literally, "human wayang"), which draws on the dramatic and musical repertory of the *wayang kulit purwa*, is also broadcast regularly. Probably most significant with regard to gamelan music is *Nujukarsa* (formerly *Among Karsa*) – Solo's counterpart to the Yogyanese *Mana Suka*. (In keeping with its reputation as the pinnacle of refined Javanese culture, the program titles are both polite Javanese approximations of the Indonesian *mana suka*.) These broadcasts feature a broad spectrum of Solonese *klenèngan* pieces performed by the RRI gamelan musicians and female singers whom many judge to be the best *karawitan* artists in Java.

More than any other group, these musicians have gained a reputation as the supreme representatives of Surakarta tradition. Beginning in the 1950s, those who wished to fare well in contests throughout Central Java, and others who wanted to play Solonese music "correctly," emulated what they heard from RRI Surakarta, whose signal reached far beyond the immediate vicinity (particularly at night, when most programs involving gamelan music were scheduled). Musicians for Solonese radio were hired from the ranks of the court musicians (the *kraton* Surakarta, the *kepatihan*, and the rival Mangkunegaran palace) in former times. In something of a reversal it is now the courts (the *kraton* and the Mangkunegaran) that draw on RRI Surakarta to help swell their ranks for musical needs. And in both Solo and Yogya, the palaces and RRI draw also on the local performing arts schools for dancers and musicians.

RRI Purwokerto

While the studio musicians at other RRI stations do not enjoy the same level of prestige throughout Java that the Solonese musicians do, they are well regarded in their regions – for skill as performers and for their mastery of Solonese music in addition to whatever local music they might play. In Purwokerto, RRI musicians usually present a combination of pieces in their Tuesday night *Mana Suka* broadcasts: several *gendhing* from Solo and one or two Banyumas pieces (which, as discussed in chapter 3, are mostly short *lancaran*). The director, however, is from Yogyakarta originally and does not play drum in Banyumas style. The group is more likely to devote a substantial part of the evening to Banyumas pieces if a skilled visitor, such as Rasito, sits in for the broadcast (René Lysloff, personal communication, May 1989). On the fourth Saturday evening of each month they accompany live *wayang kulit* performances, with local puppeteers who are likely to request pieces from both the Solonese and the local repertory. Occasionally they accompany other genres, such as *kethoprak*, that require Banyumas *gendhing*. And some of the RRI musicians play *calung* as well, which, as we have seen, draws on both Banyumasan and "eastern" (i.e., Solonese and Yogyanese) pieces.

RRI Surabaya

RRI musicians in Surabaya must also have facility in Solonese gamelan music as well as in east Javanese gamelan music (see plate 19). Twice a week they accompany the popular RRI *ludruk*, whose music is entirely east Javanese. Yet in their weekly *Mana Suka* broadcasts they present Solonese and east Javanese *klenèngan gendhing*, sometimes even within a single medley. Though the emphasis may vary from one *Mana Suka* to the next, these broadcasts tend to give preference to east Javanese repertory. The monthly *wayang* broadcasts involve puppeteers whose style may be primarily Solonese, primarily east Javanese, or a combination of both. Like the RRI Purwokerto musicians, the RRI musicians in Surabaya must be prepared to perform pieces that any puppeteer might request, without warning, during the performance.

A puppeteer may well bring his own drummer and a few other musicians. Yet for the other gamelan broadcasts, the RRI musicians must be competent on all instruments and singing styles in both major traditions. Pak Diyat Sariredjo (see plate 12), once gamelan director at RRI Surabaya and now retired, is regarded as perhaps the supreme master of the difficult technique of east Javanese *gambyak* drumming. Yet he is also accomplished in Solonese *ciblon* drumming. In order to help him keep the two separate, he forced himself to conform to the normal orientation of left and right hands, playing the loud "Tak" sound with his right hand for east Javanese drumming (as do almost all east Javanese drummers) and with his left hand for Solonese (as is now considered proper technique in Solonese circles). He also plays *rebab*

19   Studio musicians perform for live "Mana Suka" broadcast, RRI Surabaya. Pak Jumali plays *kendhang gambyak*, Pak Giran plays *gendèr babok*.

and tries to keep his Solonese and east Javanese *rebab* styles separate, but confesses that he is less successful in doing so on *rebab* than on drum.

RRI Semarang

At RRI Semarang, pieces from the local repertory of *gendhing bonang* are played during a short morning broadcast once a month. Otherwise the broadcasts involving gamelan music differ little from the repertory and style of RRI Surakarta. The few pieces that the RRI gamelan director Pak Ponidi composed based on Semarang *macapat* melodies, though recorded and archived, are rarely performed. And the *wayang kulit* the RRI Semarang musicians accompany monthly is almost always Solonese style. The performance I narrowly missed seeing in July 1983 by an elderly puppeteer in "Semarang style" required the assistance of older, retired musicians who did their best to recall the repertory that had been used in this tradition in earlier years.

Radio (RRI) and regionalism in gamelan music

Far more so than the medium of print, the radio in Java has had a profound impact – on the styles and repertories known and on the ways Javanese conceive of all the gamelan music they hear. While it would be difficult to substantiate this claim with hard statistics, my conversation with musicians everywhere indicated that what they learned about gamelan music came not only from witnessing and participating in live performances, but from listening to the radio, particularly RRI and its predecessors. Even the remotest villages in Java are within range of at least some RRI station. In the villages I visited in rural Central and East Java, radios were very much in evidence. The modest price of a radio puts it within reach of all but the very poorest Javanese, and the ability to operate it with a few small batteries makes it just as useful in villages with no electricity as in the cities and towns.

The performances of RRI musicians, then, have been able to reach far and wide. In all these areas, the RRI musicians have a reputation for being skilled players, and what they present over the airwaves is widely taken to be authoritative – a model to be emulated. The fact that the government has officially recognized these musicians by making them on-going employees elevates them over most other gamelan musicians in the minds of much of the population. In the era prior to the revolution, it was the court musicians who enjoyed this kind of prestige. Their reimbursement, while not luxuriant, was substantial. Nowadays those who serve as court musicians do so mostly out of a sense of duty; the income from such a position is scarcely enough to cover transportation to and from rehearsals. Instead it is the RRI musicians who, by serving the present government, draw a regular salary which, though still meagre, is for many their main source of income. The decision to make RRI performers fully-fledged civil servants, taken in the early 1980s, has further enhanced their status, providing them with higher salaries than before and with such benefits as a pension plan.[3] What these musicians perform – the pieces they play and the styles of performance they favor – have an aura of authority, a stamp of official approval from the government. Their status makes others wish to emulate them; and the radio provides the means by which this emulation can take place.

Let us review, then, what it is that listeners are likely to emulate. It is clear from the present situation and what we know about the past that the RRI stations throughout Java have provided a congenial environment for Solonese music, as well as the tradition of the particular region (though the presence of the former is often seen to be at the expense of the latter). It is difficult to know what styles of music were performed in various parts of Java before the advent of radio, but oral accounts by musicians and others I have spoken to attest to the rapid spread of music from Solo since the early days of radio. Seen by many as the center of Javanese culture at its loftiest, Solo and all that emanated from it has commanded great respect. Broadcasts of gamelan music directly from Solo have allowed musicians who might never have the opportunity even to visit Solo, to listen to its gamelan music regularly and gradually to absorb the repertory and style the Solonese musicians perform. Probably more than any other medium, the radio has helped both to standardize this music and to transform it from the regional tradition that it once was to the mainstream pan-Javanese tradition that it is today.

In a similar fashion, at the regional level, each of the major RRI stations has helped shape the regional traditions we have investigated in this study. It is, I think, not mere coincidence that we find an RRI station (with studio musicians) located in the major city of each of the regions in question. Those in search of an authoritative model of east Javanese playing, for example, are very likely to rely on RRI Surabaya, whose excellent musicians can easily be heard throughout the Surabaya-Mojokerto-Malang area.

The RRI model establishes as the norm a kind of two-tiered approach to gamelan music. The musicians must be proficient in the mainstream style, which is regional (Solonese) in origin, but pan-Javanese in its reach and popularity. And those outside the Solonese center must also be skilled performers of their own regional gamelan music. This dual orientation can be accommodated within a framework of cultural identity in which the mainstream music is Javanese (not national, but supraregional) and thus at a different level than Banyumas or even Yogyanese music, both of which, despite some occasional exposure elsewhere, remain essentially regional. A musician who may be highly skilled only in Banyumas or east Javanese style is, by contemporary evaluation, too narrow – perhaps not fully Javanese – and cannot claim the same level of musicianship as the one who knows Solonese style. Still, the RRI model implies that a musician in Banyumas ought to know the lively *lancaran* typical of the region, and the musician in east Java the varieties of *Jula-juli*, *tayuban*, and east Javanese *wayang* pieces.

It might seem that RRI practice would blur regional distinctions in the minds of listeners, and I believe it does in some instances. Pieces from different repertories are often played in the same broadcast. And in some cases, most obviously in Yogyakarta, local repertory may be performed with the playing styles associated with Surakarta. The musicians and programmers are aware of differences between regional traditions, but have been less concerned about explicit delineation of these traditions to the listening public than, for example, the government officials who set rules for contests or design curricula at the performing arts schools. Certainly it would take a knowledgable listener to sort out which *gendhing* are Yogyanese and which are Solonese in a *Mana Suka* broadcast by RRI Yogya. And the general public is undoubtedly less aware than SMKI students or *karawitan* contestants of the finer points of distinction between different regional styles of playing, but it is my strong impression that the more conspicuous differences between regional styles are widely recognized. In most cases, then, listeners have a fairly good idea of what style they are hearing and may well find aesthetic delight in the stylistic combinations and juxtapositions.

Whether the pervasive practice of broadcasting gamelan music of several traditions is primarily a reflection of public taste or has actively shaped public taste would be difficult to determine. I think it more accurate to see RRI practice and public taste as interrelated, mutually influencing one another. RRI officials cannot attract listeners to their station by decree; they must present what they think will appeal to a large number of listeners. At the same time, however, they can exert some control over the kinds of music presented, as occurred recently in Yogyakarta. Most of the RRI officials I spoke to at all these stations saw the need to help maintain regional traditions. Radio has played a critical role in this endeavor. So, too, has the commercial cassette industry, as we shall see below.

Television

Before leaving the topic of broadcast, the other major medium, Indonesian television (TVRI), deserves some mention, although its influence with respect to gamelan music has been negligible compared to that of radio. All television stations in Indonesia are directly controlled and operated by the government. In Java, stations are located in Yogyakarta and Surabaya; and the Jakarta station is strong enough to reach much of Central Java. With recent satellite facilities in operation, these stations can all be received far from their point of origin. First introduced in 1962, television is extraordinarily popular now, and is seen in many villages, where a 12-volt car battery may be used to power a set watched by scores of people crowded into a house or a village meeting center.

Broadcast time is still limited to afternoon and evening, much of that devoted to shows imported from the United States and elsewhere. In Java, *kethoprak* broadcasts occur on a regular basis, and one also sees different genres of Javanese dance with some frequency, and occasionally even a short concert of gamelan music (though usually by an amateur group). No one I have spoken to, however, claims to look to this medium for music to emulate. At best, they might pick up a new composition (*kreasi baru*) accompanying a dance. Too little music is presented on television for this medium to be anything like the authoritative source that the radio has been over the years. Still, the fact that TVRI Surabaya can be seen in many parts of Central Java, and TVRI Yogyakarta far beyond the Special Region of Yogyakarta, means that the viewing public is, from time to time, exposed to different regional styles of gamelan music, dance, and drama, further contributing to the awareness of stylistic differences and to the overlapping of cultural boundaries.

Recording

Recording, like radio, has played a critical role in the dissemination of gamelan music and in shaping conceptions about it. Since the late 1960s, which marked the birth of the cassette recording industry in Java, gamelan music and almost every other genre of music and musical drama have been recorded and sold widely. Recording in Java began at the turn of the century (in 1903 according to Philip Yampolsky, personal communication, May 1989), but for many years had only an indirect impact on the vast majority of the population, who could not afford to buy either the records or the equipment necessary to play them. Teachers I studied with in Yogyakarta remembered itinerant disc jockeys as recently as the 1950s. Each carried a phonograph with him from house to house and for a small fee would play a request from his small collection of discs. Among the choices were recordings of gamelan music, mostly from Solo. This was not, according to my teachers, a significant source of knowledge about gamelan and had negligible impact on gamelan practice.

It is not clear when recorded music began to be broadcast over the radio, though it was certainly common by the early 1930s, and it was in this way that recorded music first reached a wide audience. In the mid-1950s, the Lokananta recording company was established in Surakarta, at first to provide recordings for RRI broadcasts.[4] It was only several years later that Lokananta began to issue phonograph records for sale to the public, and in 1961 it became a national company separate from RRI whose primary business was the sale of phonograph records (Yampolsky 1987:2).

Around this time a few other private companies, including Serimpi, Indah Record, Aneka Record, and Elshinta, and others, began to issue recordings of gamelan music and other genres, but their releases do not seem to have enjoyed the same status as the Lokananta discs. One of the main reasons, I suspect, is that Lokananta, although no longer officially connected to RRI, drew primarily on the RRI performers, already widely known from their exposure over the airwaves, or on other famous musicians, such as Nartosabdho, for their recordings. Also, the quality of both the recordings and the phonograph discs themselves tended to be higher than in the releases of the other companies. But Lokananta did not have a monopoly on RRI performers. Serimpi, for example, released recordings of *gendhing* performed by the RRI Solo musicians, and even of *ludruk* by the actors and musicians of RRI Surabaya. Repertory from other regions was recorded as well, sometimes in a pot-pourri format. For example, the gamelan group Karya Waditra and a *pesindhèn* with the unlikely professional name of Suratmi B-29 (after the B-29 bomber) recorded several discs with pieces from

Banyumas (*Kembang Glepang* and *Getuk Gorèng*). The *Getuk Gorèng* album includes the *macapat Dhandhanggula Semarangan* and *Dhendhang Semarangan*, as well as pieces from the mainstream repertory (*Kembang Kates* and Ladrang *Pangkur*). The regional origin of these pieces is listed plainly in the liner notes. The notes to the Lokananta recordings of RRI musicians identify the RRI station with which the musicians are affiliated but do not elaborate further on regional style. Groups from Yogyakarta, Surakarta, and even Jakarta all recorded Solonese *gendhing*, though some local nuance is evident in the Yogyakarta recordings.

Though both live musical performance and recorded music were broadcast over the radio, the recordings – usually of RRI musicians – began to take on a special significance as permanent documents that avid listeners would hear again and again over the years. Suhardi, my main teacher in Yogyakarta, vividly remembers listening to radio broadcasts during the late 1950s and the 1960s and paying special heed to the recordings, which he could study in depth because he heard the same few recordings many times. From these he absorbed not only the general traits of playing and singing style, but precise patterns. For example, he followed the *gendèr* playing of the late Pak Sabdosuwarno of RRI Solo with keen interest, picking up on many of the subtlest nuances in his style – not only his conception of the *gendhing* and corresponding choice of melodic pattern (*céngkok*), but the details (*wiletan*) in Sabdosuwarno's personal realization of the *céngkok* as well. Suhardi also told me that the recordings – and he identified the Lokananta recordings in particular – had a strong impact on his and other musicians' conceptions of appropriate combinations of *gendhing* in medleys, for example. Repeated hearings made them seem natural, and the knowledge that they were the choice of distinguished recording artists made them authoritative as well.

The cassette industry

By the end of the 1960s, expensive phonograph recordings were already being pirated and sold on cassette, presaging the end of the phonograph in Java and the dawn of what has grown to be a vast commercial cassette industry, with many successful private companies operating alongside Lokananta. Where phonograph records required expensive turntables and amplifiers and generally cost the equivalent of five American dollars or more per disc, commercial cassettes could be played on inexpensive equipment and cost as little as sixty American cents (and rarely more than a dollar and a half). In places with no electricity, batteries provide the necessary power. I encountered cassette players, as well as radios, in relative abundance even in small villages miles from any town. The numbers of cassettes produced soon soared above those for disc recordings. The statistics from Lokananta are telling.

According to a 1976 report, the difference in volume was enormous: in 1970, before cassette marketing began, Lokananta manufactured 41,508 discs, while in 1975 it sold 290 discs from leftover stock – and 898,459 cassettes. In 1985, Lokananta's business manager estimated the company's output of commercial (as distinguished from Penerangan [Department of Information]) cassettes as 60,000 per month.

(Yampolsky 1987:2)

Major cassette companies

Despite the official status of Lokananta as the "national" recording company, its focus in cassette production has been mostly Javanese music and dramatic forms. The fact of its location in Surakarta has no doubt contributed to the obvious preference for Solonese gamelan music over any other regional style. Yet we should also note that it is one of the stated purposes of Lokananta to earn a profit (Yampolsky 1987:2). And with Solonese gamelan music already popular throughout much of Java, the Solonese emphasis in Lokananta releases has perhaps only reinforced an existing condition, further strengthening the position of Solonese music as the preeminent Javanese music. Nevertheless, it has released some cassettes of other regional gamelan music, performed not by Solonese, but by first-rate musicians (RRI and others) from the other regions. These include east Javanese *ludruk*, *tayuban*, and *klenèngan* (beginning with *ludruk* in 1973, numerous further releases to 1988), Semarang *gendhing bonang* (1974), Banyumas gamelan and *calung* (1981, 1986, and 1988), *gandrung* Banyuwangi (1985–86), and most recently some light pieces associated with a clowning genre (*badhutan*) from Sragen, a town north east of Surakarta (1989). Yogyanese music has been released on Lokananta cassette since the early 1970s, but is conspicuously underrepresented – perhaps for market reasons, perhaps due to personal taste of the Lokananta staff. At any rate, the few recordings that contain at least some gamelan music performed by Yogyanese (usually RRI) musicians are mostly *kethoprak* or a mix of comedy and gamelan music (*jengglèng*). While Solonese music performed by Solonese groups is still dominant in Lokananta production, the representation of other Javanese regional traditions in their releases has increased markedly in the 1980s (Yampolsky 1987: esp. 8–18), including a four-cassette series of Yogyanese music in 1983 and another three-cassette series in 1988.

Other major cassette companies have followed a similar course to that of Lokananta, producing mostly Solonese or Solonese-based gamelan and dramatic forms, but with some other regional genres. Kusuma (located in Klaten) has concentrated heavily on Solonese *klenèngan* and *wayang kulit*, but has been increasingly drawn to other regional traditions. In the early 1980s, Kusuma released a few recordings of Banyumas music and *wayang kulit*, and since then has built up a substantial list of recordings of east Javanese music, along with a few recordings of Yogyanese music. Several of the Kusuma cassettes mix regional traditions: one by RRI Surakarta musicians (under the name of Riris Raras Irama), another by Nartosabdho and Condhong Raos (discussed at length in chapter 8). Fajar (located in Semarang) and Ira-Record (formerly Wisanda, with offices in Jakarta and a studio in Semarang) have recorded Ki Nartosabdho most extensively – his new compositions (*kreasi baru*), his *wayang kulit*, and his versions of Solonese *gendhing* and those of other regions. Yet both have also produced a long list of titles from other regions, including many from east Java (*tayuban* and *wayang*). Some of the best cassettes of music from Banyumas are on Ira-Record, which has recently released a few Yogyanese recordings as well. The Borobudur company (located in Semarang and formerly known as Enggal Jaya) offers recordings not only of Ki Nartosabdho, but of musicians from Banyumas and from Yogyakarta. Offerings from all these areas are now available on the Pusaka label, a relatively new company based in Semarang, whose activities in Javanese gamelan music and theatrical genres have increased dramatically in the late 1980s.[5]

The marketing strategy for these major companies no doubt varies in some detail from one to the next, and even over time within a single company. Generally, the music performed by Solonese musicians (mainly RRI Surakarta), and by Ki Nartosabdho is marketed widely: throughout Central Java, East Java, and Yogyakarta. The other music is marketed primarily in the region from which it came. True, one finds a few cassettes of Banyumas musicians playing Banyumas *gendhing* for sale as far away as Surabaya and Malang. But cassette store owners say they carry these titles mostly for people from Banyumas who might have moved to East Java.[6] Nevertheless, while this may be the main rationale, we can see that this marketing plan by the major cassette companies, including Lokananta, does place gamelan music of different regions within easy access of consumers throughout Java. More important, however, are the changes the cassette industry has wrought in conceptions of regional traditions within their areas – changes affected by smaller, regionally-based companies as well.

Smaller cassette companies

Not only has cassette technology made recorded music affordable by the less affluent masses, but it has also enabled small recording companies to crop up almost overnight. Once one has a master recording, which many of the smaller cassette companies obtain simply by hiring musicians and renting a studio at an hourly rate, duplication can be handled very easily. For example, the production at Hidup Baru cassette company in Purwokerto, until its sudden demise in 1986 on the death of its founder and owner,[7] consisted of nothing more than a few dozen cassette decks and a technician running dubs throughout the day. Though this would be inadequate to supply the kind of large market the cassettes of popular music enjoy, it was adequate for the many varieties of Banyumas genres that Hidup Baru chose to produce.

Elsewhere I have described in some detail the brief history of this and other cassette companies in Banyumas and offered my interpretation of their significance with respect to music in the region (Sutton 1985:28–40). A summary of my findings is appropriate here, as it bears directly on our understanding of the importance of the cassette industry from a regional perspective. First, small companies have been able to survive, though perhaps not with spectacular earnings, by recording regional gamelan music and other genres for dissemination primarily within the region. This has, in the estimation of many musicians, had major consequences for the more marginal traditions, such as Banyumas. It has made regional stars of certain individuals who would be unlikely to gain recognition through the national media. It has given a new legitimacy to local genres, not just gamelan music, but also the more rural genres, such as *calung* and even the hobby-horse trance dance (*èbèg*), by giving them representation in the same commercial arena as the more prestigious genres. At the same time, the presentation on cassette of these rural genres has engendered a new professionalism – what many would see as "upgrading" – in the greater coordination of tuning between singing voice and instruments in *calung* (and the less popular Banyumas *angklung* ensemble) and in the addition of the singing voice to *èbèg* music.[8]

During my research in Purwokerto in 1984, I surveyed all the cassette stores in the city and compiled a list of all available recordings of Banyumas music and related dramatic genres distinctive to the region. At that time, I found in stock and on sale 364 Banyumas titles, many of them multi-volume series (e.g., *wayang kulit*), representing a total of about 802 hours of recorded sound. In spite of a relatively small local repertory, there were 110 titles of "*karawitan* Banyumasan" (played on bronze gamelan) and 81 titles of "*calung* Banyumasan," representing multiple versions of many (though, curiously, not all) of the older Banyumas *gendhing* and many new compositions. Of the 364 titles, nearly two thirds were produced by the small local companies. I would have suspected that far fewer releases would have been sufficient to saturate the market, but apparently not so. When I returned in 1986, I counted nearly thirty additional titles, most of them apparently new releases.

In contrast to the flurry of activity in local cassette production in the Banyumas region, Yogyakarta has not been able to sustain its own local cassette industry, despite a few attempts (including production of a few cassettes by Yogyanese traditional dance clubs, Siswa Among Beksa and Pamulangan Beksa Ngayogyakarta). These groups can now be heard performing Yogyanese *gendhing* on Borobudur and Pusaka cassettes. Yogyanese gamelan music can be heard on Borobudur, Fajar, Ira-Record, Pusaka, Kusuma, and a few other labels, as well as Lokananta, but none of these companies is exclusively or even primarily Yogyanese. This relative lack of attention by the cassette industry is indicative of the narrow base of popular support for this tradition, which many find a bit stilted and old-fashioned sounding in comparison with most other commercially available gamelan music.

It should come as little surprise that we find no local cassette industry devoted to Semarang gamelan music, or any other genres of the immediate Semarang area. The very limited scope of the Semarang tradition, at least as it exists today, is clearly not enough to sustain even one small cassette company. Where we find Semarang music recorded is on two Lokananta cassettes (with RRI Semarang musicians, Lokananta ACD-049 and ACD-050) and on three Fajar cassettes (with Nartosabdho and Condhong Raos, see chapter 8).

In East Java, as in Banyumas, a number of regionally-based cassette companies have sprung up. Among others, we can cite CHGB and Nirwana of Surabaya, Bumi Putra (also known as Jayabaya) of Malang, Ria of Banyuwangi, and Semar Record of Sumenep, Madura. None of these attempts to record music from all the cultural areas within the province nor to distribute to all these areas. Semar Record produces only Madurese genres, and these are available only in the areas with a substantial Madurese population. Ria has focused on the various genres of Banyuwangi, though with considerable output of genres performed by ethnic Madurese who live in the areas north and west of Banyuwangi. Neither Ria nor Semar Record has expanded to any of the music of the Surabaya-Mojokerto-Malang region, even the profitable *tayuban* music. Bumi Putra has released at least one recording of music from Banyuwangi, but most of its cassettes consist of east Javanese *wayang* and *tayuban* music, with apparent preference for performers from the immediate vicinity of Malang. Their distribution is primarily in this vicinity as well. Among the Bumi Putra releases from the mid-1980s is a *wayang topèng* troupe which, like the *èbèg* in Banyumas, added a *pesindhèn* for the recording of a genre normally performed without female singer. CHGB and Nirwana have been more broadly East Javanese in their offerings, which have included *ludruk*, *tayuban*, *gendhing gagahan*, *wayang kulit*, *angklung* and *gandrung* from Banyuwangi, and gamelan and *sronèn* music from Madura.

On some of these, one hears evidence of cross-fertilization. East Javanese *tayuban* tapes, the most numerous of the releases in East Java, often include a piece or two from the *gandrung* Banyuwangi repertory, though sung with the usual *pesindhèn* vocal quality and accompanied by a large gamelan (central or east Javanese). *Lagu dolanan* and *jineman* vocal pieces from central Java are also prevalent and usually performed in a style essentially Solonese, though sometimes with east Javanese *gambyakan* drumming. Even an occasional Madurese song is heard, though this is still relatively rare. Perhaps one can see the cassette industry as contributing to a building of a pan-East Javanese style, but consciousness of local origin still seems high, not only on cassettes released by East Javanese companies, but on the others as well.

Cassettes and identification by region

With this overview of recording activity in the various regions of Java, let me now comment on some characteristics of the particular contents and packaging of commercial cassettes with attention to the treatment of regional issues. First, in keeping with its status as mainstream tradition, cassettes devoted wholly or mostly to *gendhing* or dramatic forms from Surakarta, or in Solonese style, almost never carry any explicit indication of this on the cassette covers (a rare exception is *Rujak Jeruk: Tayub Royal Gaya Solo*, Lokananta ACD-275). For recordings of RRI Surakarta musicians the city of origin is clear enough; but when they record under the name of Riris Raras Irama for Kusuma releases, the identity is obscure except to those who know to whom this name refers. No mention is made of style in the title of the cassette or the identification of genre. It would perhaps be to state the obvious. But even lesser known groups, if they perform in Solonese style, will not list the style by name. It is the mainstream tradition and is assumed unless otherwise indicated.

Only in rare instances are individual Solonese pieces identified by regional designation on cassette covers, whether the performers are from Solo or from elsewhere. In a cassette with various regional variants of *macapat palaran* songs performed by Ki Nartosabdho's Condhong Raos and Bagong Kussudiardjo's Sapta Mandala (*Udan Palaran*, Fajar 9057), one variant is identified as "*cengkok* Sala" (i.e., Solonese *céngkok*). And now that groups such as RRI Surakarta are beginning to play more pieces from outside the mainstream repertory, their cassettes sometimes indicate a Solonese version, as in the *Srepeg Sala* (Solonese *Srepegan*) that appears with Banyumas and Yogyanese *Srepegans* as well (*Palaran Gobyog 8*, Lokananta ACD-238).

Cassettes of Yogyanese genres, on the other hand, often provide some indication of regional identity. Direct mention is made of the name Yogyakarta (= Ngayogyakarta) on a few cassettes, including those of the *kraton* musicians themselves and other closely associated with the *kraton*, such as Siswa Among Beksa. More frequent than these, however, is the term "Mataram" or "Mataraman," whose use in reference to things Yogyanese was discussed in chapter 2. A still less direct means, which suggests Yogyanese tradition to those familiar with Yogyanese preferences in terminology, is the use of the term *uyon-uyon*, rather than *klenèngan* as the indicator of the genre – for example, Lokananta's *Uyon-uyon Gobyog* (ACD-024, from RRI Yogya), which contrasts with *Klenèngan Gobjog* (Lokananta ACD-001 and 002, from RRI Solo).

The Yogyanese identity of individual items on a cassette is generally not indicated unless the other items on the cassette are mostly not Yogyanese or a particular *gendhing* title is known in repertory from another region (e.g., Ladrang *Sri Katon Mataram*, as distinct from Ladrang *Sri Katon*). As in cassette titles, the designation of a *gendhing* as Yogyanese is most commonly made by the use of the qualifier "Mataram(an)." This term is applied whether the musicians are identified in some way as Yogyanese or not.

Banyumas cassettes almost invariably list the region as part of the indication of genre in the title or subtitle on the cassette cover: "*Gendhing-gendhing* Banyumasan," "*Wayang Kulit* Banyumasan," and so on. Names of recording groups are sometimes chosen to indicate regional identity as well. For example, S. Bono has directed a group known as Lingga Mas, from the two cities Purba*lingga* and Banyu*mas*. And the group led by Rasito and which accompanies the most popular *dhalang* in Banyumas, Ki Sugino Siswocarito, is listed on recordings as Purba Kencana, rather than their original name Mudha Budhaya. *Mudha* (young, youth) *Budhaya* (culture) suggests youthful artists, but nothing about their regional identity. Purba Kencana is another combination from the two cities *Purba*lingga and Banyumas: *kencana* is an old Javanese word meaning "gold," which in modern Javanese is *mas*.

Once a cassette is identified as "Banyumasan," the individual items generally are not. But for pieces whose titles also appear in other repertories, particularly Solonese, the qualifying regional term is usually given again: *Éling-éling Banyumasan*, *Ricik-ricik Banyumasan*, and so on. This explicit regional labelling of pieces is more likely on cassettes produced by the major companies than on those produced locally.

Other more specific geographical designations occur as well. If any piece in the Banyumas repertory represents a *tour de force*, other than the Banyumas *talu* sequence that precedes *wayang kulit* performances, it is *Gunungsari Kalibagoran*. Pieces with the name *Gunungsari* are found in Solonese, Yogyanese, and east Javanese repertories as well. The Banyumas version, however, is generally distinguished with reference not to the entire region but to one small town, built around a sugar refinery on the road between Purwokerto and the town of Banyumas. This is one example of a kind of indirect or, perhaps, in-group reference to regional identity, for there is apparently nothing particular about that town that determines the style in which this piece is usually performed. A variant performance of this piece by the RRI Solo musicians (on *Gunungsari*, Kusuma KGD-024), somewhat less spirited than most renditions by Banyumas groups, is given not as *Gunungsari Kalibagoran*, but *Gunungsari Purbolinggo*. This label identifies the piece with the Banyumas region, but perhaps suggests a more refined approach by reference to Purbalingga, which lies to the east (and thus nearer to Solo) than Kalibagor.

In East Java, cassettes are often identified explicitly with respect to regional identity. Most common is the phrase "Jawa Timur" or "Jawa Timuran," which translate literally as "East Java" or "East Javanese." This does not specify which part of the province and might be seen by those not familiar with the cultural diversity of East Java to refer to a pan-East Javanese tradition. Those more familiar generally understand this to apply to the central portion – the region of Surabaya-Mojokerto-Malang. Cassettes of *angklung* and *gandrung* generally list "Banyuwangi" or "Banyuwangèn" on the cover. Gamelan and *sronèn* from Madura are identified either as "Madura" or by reference to a major city (e.g., "Sumenep"). And *reyog* Ponorogo is identified not as East Javanese but specifically as from "Ponorogo."

If we survey the cassettes produced of *tayuban* music, however, we find a large number of references to specific cities and towns throughout much of the province, from as far west as Madiun to as far east as Lumajang, and from as far north as Tuban to as far south as Tulungagung and Blitar. I have seen *tayuban* cassettes designated as in the style of (*gaya*) Madiun, Ngawi, Trenggalek, Tulungagung, Blitar, Malang, Surabaya, Gresik, Tuban, Lamongan, Jombang, and Lumajang. Most of the musicians I consulted about this, in my search for regional differences, indicated that this was something of a marketing gimmick and that at most there were one or two pieces whose special treatment was associated with each of these cities. And indeed, this is evident in the titles of a few pieces (e.g., *Jamong Tuban*,

Godril Lumajang). Otherwise the claim of *Gaya Trenggalek*, for example, may be based merely on the fact that the performers happen to be from Trenggalek, or, if not, that they play a version of a more widely known piece (Gendhing *Gambir Sawit* was mentioned by several musicians) with a sequence of drumming patterns associated with Trenggalek. The cassette industry has latched onto the apparent resurgence of regionalism and, at least in East Java, hinted at a multitude of varied styles. Yet the *tayuban* tapes are not merely marketed in the city or town to which the cassette title refers, but instead are marketed throughout much of East Java. And much of the same repertory appears on all of these cassettes, except that those west of the *pinggir–rekso* line feature music that is central Javanese-derived, whereas those east of the line have only a little or none at all.

Though gamelan groups in East Java record music from central Java, even an occasional Yogyanese or Banyumas number (e.g., Ladrang *Clunthang Mataram* and *Éling-éling Banyu-masan*), the reverse is rare. Thus, we do not find items on cassettes of RRI Surakarta, for example, that might require identification as "Jawa Timur." Some cassettes of Nartosab-dho's and Bagong Kussudiardjo's groups contain pieces from East Java, though mostly of Banyuwangi and specifically identified as such. In recordings of music from within the province, regional style is indicated for an individual item only if it is from outside the area the cassette mostly represents – such as the occasional Madurese or Banyuwangi piece on tapes of east Javanese *tayuban*.

Regional images on cassette covers

Complementing verbal indications – or sometimes contradicting them – the images on cassette covers can also suggest the regional identity of a cassette's contents. Except for a few releases by Hidup Baru, all the commercial cassettes of gamelan music and traditional drama I have seen have some sort of photograph or, more rarely, a drawing on the cover. These can be interpreted along regional lines by knowledgeable customers, though not consistently. Many of the cassettes of Yogyanese music show the musicians dressed in the distinctive Yogyanese *surjan* (jacket with high neck) and *blangkon* (pre-wound turban – the Yogyanese with an egg-shaped protrusion in the back). These contrast with Solonese *beskap* (a somewhat more Western-style jacket) and *blangkon* (with no "egg"). East Javanese may wear several styles of *iket* (turbans hand-tied for each use) or the *péci* hat, and usually dress more informally than their Yogyanese or Solonese counterparts.

Another frequent choice is to show instruments distinctive of the region. Yogyanese cassettes often show the Yogyanese *saron*, with the upward curling wood at either end of the keys, or Yogyanese *gambang*, with wooden planks nearly upright at either end of the keys. Yet on the Lokananta cassette *Uyon-uyon Gobyog* (ACD-024) the *gambang* shown is clearly Solonese. And, because a Solonese gamelan was used for the playing of Yogyanese pieces on the Lokananta series ACD-187 to 190, the cassette covers show the RRI Yogya musicians playing that gamelan. Some Banyumas cassettes show the set of two drums, with the *ketipung* standing on one end; and, of course, *calung* (and *angklung*) cassettes often include a photograph of one or more of the instruments used. A large number of east Javanese *tayuban* cassettes show the distinctive *gambyak* drum, either in isolation or with the larger ensemble.

Other indications of regional identity are photographs of familiar sites, such as the scenes of the Yogyanese *kraton* and the *tugu* (monument) directly north of the Yogyanese *kraton* (on Lokananta tapes ACD-260 and 262). Similarly, the main *pendhapa* of the Mangkunegaran palace is shown on the covers of each of the two Lokananta recordings of the Mangkunegaran musicians (ACD-163 and 164), and scenes of the Surakarta *kraton* and the gates to the square just north of it are shown on several recent cassette releases of old Lokananta recordings of Solonese musicians (ACD-235 and 236).

Photographs of dancers can also provide clear indications of regional identity, as their costumes and often their stances are associated with a particular region. Not only do we find the singer-dancers, such as the *gandrung* of Banyuwangi and the *lènggèr* of Banyumas, but also dancers performing Solonese *gambyong* dance, Yogyanese *golèk* and *srimpi*, and different regional styles of *topèng*. *Wayang kulit* cassette covers may show puppet characters distinctive to the region, such as Bawor, the Banyumas clown-servant. Indications of regional identity, then, are abundant.

The impact of the cassette industry

In the late 1980s the cassette industry continues to flourish in Java, producing new titles of gamelan music, *wayang kulit*, and other genres from all these regions.[9] While it is difficult to assess precisely the impact this industry has had on gamelan music from a regional perspective, it is my clear impression, based on extensive discussion on this subject with musicians in all these areas, that it has been profound.

It has contributed greatly to a sharper awareness of these regional traditions in the minds of the Javanese public, helping, as I have said elsewhere, to "crystallize" them (Sutton 1986a). For example, Javanese everywhere – including local residents of Banyumas itself – are more aware now of a corpus of Banyumas *gendhing* and corresponding playing styles than they were twenty years ago. Even those who choose not to buy the cassettes they see identified as "Banyumasan," nevertheless do see them, with their regional labels, sitting on shelves beside cassettes of gamelan music from other regions. Thus, the idea of "Banyumasan" as a meaningful aesthetic category is spread beyond just those who buy the cassettes.

The combinations of the identification (explicit or otherwise) of cassettes by region and their appearance in the same format from region to region has had a clear levelling effect with respect to the relative stature of these traditions. No longer are the Yogyanese and Solonese arts so closely associated with the courts, nor Banyumas and east Javanese arts with villages. They now enjoy a more equal status, by nature of their similar patronage through the mass medium of cassette. And increasingly during the 1980s, we find *gendhing* from different regions juxtaposed on a single cassette, along with some accommodation in playing style. While it would be difficult to show a direct causal relationship, the fact that the SMKI conservatories in Surabaya and in Banyumas were both founded in the 1970s, shortly after the rise of the cassette industry in these areas, suggests a strong link, with the cassette industry as a prime initiator.

The industry not only alters relative status, it also actively redefines these traditions. The inclusion of new compositions, for instance, on cassettes identified with one region or another tends to place those new compositions within the tradition as people conceive of them, thereby expanding on older repertories. And some "traditional" pieces, the older staples of the repertory, may appear on many recordings, while others appear on none. It is the opinion of musicians I spoke to everywhere that lack of representation on cassette will very likely mean the loss of a piece from active repertory, as live performances tend to cater to the demands and expectations of the paying public.

Repertory choices can also lead to regional ambiguity on cassettes, however. The juxtaposition of Solonese and east Javanese pieces on east Javanese *tayuban* recordings – an accurate reflection of performance practice at *tayuban* today – might be easily detected by some listeners, but the audible differences might not be conceived along regional lines by others. Also, the wide popularity of *palaran* singing from the mainstream tradition has led to some regional variants in which essentially the same Solonese melodies are sung with regional inflections in ornamentation and then labelled regionally (e.g., the many volumes of "*Palaran Banyumasan*" tapes).

Style is redefined as well as repertory. Because the cassettes can be listened to any number of times, the playing techniques, singing styles, and tempo treatments of the musicians recorded are widely imitated and become authoritative models for those wishing to sound east Javanese, Yogyanese, and so forth. Older musicians in east Java recall markedly different styles of *rebab* and flute playing from what is heard today. What is recorded and emulated now is the more Solonese-based variety that younger musicians have learned. Vocal style, though still somewhat idiosyncratic and difficult to define very specifically along regional lines, has also taken a basic turn towards that of the famous *pesindhèn* of Solo and Semarang, whose voices are widely heard on cassette.

The way *gendhing* are labelled on cassettes has also represented something of a redefinition towards Solonese practice. The practice of listing formal structure, scale system, and *pathet* with the title of a *gendhing* is derived from Solo, but now found on cassettes from all these regions. The older Yogyanese practice of naming the *kendhang* pattern, which only implies formal structure without specifying it, is rarely used in cassette listings, even from the Yogyakarta palace (nor was it, for that matter, on phonograph records from Yogya).[10] In Banyumas and east Java, both formal structure and *pathet* have been variously understood. Yet the precedent set in labelling Solonese pieces is carried over to these other repertories, especially on cassettes produced by the major companies – with Lokananta leading the list. As they provide listeners with new opportunities to hear gamelan music of different regions, the cassette producers nevertheless let an impetus for consistency impinge upon the ways pieces are categorized.[11]

One of the ways the cassette industry has been able to "crystallize" or sharpen people's image of these traditions, as it contributes to defining or redefining them, is by giving unprecedented exposure to a very few star artists who are much sought after for live performances and whose styles are widely emulated. Though the industry has not replaced live performance to the extent that some feared at first, it has created a very sharp division between those who are recorded with some frequency and those who are not. Those not lucky enough to be recorded have difficulty finding sponsorship for live performances, since they offer far less prestige to the host who sponsors them than do those with reputations as professional recording artists. The fame of these few stars has been significant from the standpoint of regional diversity, however. The "super groups" – particularly Ki Nartosabdho and Condhong Raos – have incorporated various influences from different regional traditions. Through their wide exposure in the mass media – cassette recordings and radio broadcasts – these groups have contributed to the increased awareness and popularity of the gamelan music outside the mainstream, in ways that will be explored further in the following chapter.

8   Regional pluralism in the music of renowned Javanese performers: Ki Nartosabdho and his peers

Most of the performing groups that gain "superstar" status have been prone to draw rather heavily on repertory and performance styles from more than one region. While borrowing between regions has gone on for centuries, the extent to which it occurs today and the public's awareness of it has no historical precedent. This chapter is devoted almost entirely to the extraordinary efforts of Ki Nartosabdho who, more than any other, is credited by musicians everywhere with revitalizing the traditions of Javanese gamelan music – not only through his many new compositions, but in his extensive borrowing and reworking of music from all the traditions we have discussed. First, however, we should mention two other prominent Javanese performing artists whose work has been influenced by the regional diversity in Java.

Ki Wasitodiningrat and Bagong Kussudiardjo

The other major composer for Javanese gamelan during the era of Indonesian independence has been Ki Wasitodiningrat, who left Java in the early 1970s and took up permanent residence in the United States. Several of his compositions from the time prior to his departure employ instrumental techniques inspired by Balinese performance, each with a title in Indonesian, rather than Javanese (or Balinese): *Nelayan* (literally, "fisherman"); *Pulau Bali* (literally, "The island of Bali"); and *Tari Bali* (literally, "Balinese dance"), all in *pélog pathet barang*.

Ki Wasitodiningrat also drew on other Indonesian traditions for some of his gamelan compositions. For example, his *Jonjang Banyuwangèn*, *sléndro pathet sanga*, is a piece which imitates gandrung Banyuwangi in its *saron* playing and melodic style, but otherwise sounds central Javanese – with standard central Javanese instrumentation, rather than the violins, triangle, and special Banyuwangi drum. In a major concert in 1968 at the Purwodiningratan *pendhapa* in Yogyakarta, with two full gamelan ensembles and close to one hundred musicians, he presented a variety of his own compositions, including pieces inspired by *gendhing* from Banyumas and east Java (Surabaya). But these were not recorded and have, to his knowledge, not been performed since. In addition, he arranged several pieces from Banyumas (*Asmarandana Banyumasan* and *Kembang Glepang*, Becker 1980:152).

Ki Wasitodiningrat worked closely with the innovative dance choreographer Bagong Kussudiardjo in the 1960s, and both were especially drawn to the sounds of music from Banyuwangi, as well as Bali and Sunda. In more recent years, under various musical directors, Bagong's dancers and musicians have experimented with dance movements and musical styles from many parts of Indonesia, sometimes resulting in an amalgamation that appeals to some urbanites and tourists, but that many Indonesian artists find distastefully incongruous. This despite his statement early in his career that dances cannot, or should not, be created merely by combining movements from one region with those from another if their qualities differ too markedly (Kussudiardjo 1955:144). And when he presents music or dance in the style of, or primarily inspired by, a single extant regional genre, such as his east Javanese *ngrémo*, his rendition may excite his fellow central Javanese, but seems to east Javanese to be lacking the very subtleties that give east Javanese *ngrémo* its true spirit. (Certainly the musicians and dancers I spoke to in Surabaya and Malang expressed this opinion strongly and resented the appropriation of this east Javanese "treasure" by someone who struck them as incapable of capturing its essence.)

Bagong, trained in Yogyanese dance during his youth, was already showing interest in other regional styles of dance as a young man. On a visit to East Java in the 1950s he was distressed not to find formal training and "development" of dances unique to East Java (*topèng* dances from Malang and Madura, *reyog* from Ponorogo, and so on). But his concern was not so much for the survival of these arts as they had existed in the past, as it was for the stimulation of these arts to serve as sources for innovation, more appropriate for the new era of modern Indonesian nationalism.

There are many possibilities for the birth of new creations based on the original/indigenous (*asli*) dances of East Java, which can raise the standard and contribute to the development of our [Indonesia's] dance art, just as long as the authenticity of those dances is well cared for and then brought into line with the progress of the times.

[Padahal berdasarkan seni-tari-seni-tari Djawa Timur aseli tadi itu banjak kemungkinan-kemungkinan untuk lahirnja kreasi baru, dapat pula turut mendjundjung deradjat dan perkembangan seni tari kita, asal sadja seni tari tersebut dipelihara dengan sebaik-baiknja keaseliannja kemudian disesuaikan dengan kemadjuan zaman.]   (Kussudiardjo 1955:142)

He urged that the regional arts be modernized and no longer confined to their particular regions. Though he expressed concern over the state of East Javanese arts in East Java, he was encouraged that other arts – from Yogya as well as Solo – were being studied there. Like many Indonesians in the 1950s, he was caught up with the issue of nationalism and saw great potential for building national culture through creative fusion of elements from the regional arts.

In the 1980s, Bagong is one of the most powerful figures in the arts, with a strong following among some performers and a well established reputation with the government as an effective artistic diplomat – often travelling with his performing troupe to other countries in Asia and Europe. He is seen by his admirers as someone who can create new, exciting forms of dance and music while nevertheless maintaining an Indonesian (primarily Javanese) feeling. He acknowledges his debt to Indonesia's "folk dances" (*tarian rakyat*) as sources for his choreography and admires their spontaneity and ingenuousness, as well as their deep roots (Kussudiardjo 1981:34). But many feel he has gone too far, that his innovative combinations have become overly ambitious pastiches that demean the traditions from which the elements have been drawn. But at least Bagong has taken a strong and consistent stance over several decades with regard to the role of traditional regional arts. His reach has gone far beyond the different regions of central and east Java; but even when he presents material ostensibly "east Javanese," it can raise the hackles of the east Javanese, who find it hopelessly watered down.

Ki Wasitodiningrat would no doubt have had greater influence had he remained in Java and continued along the lines he was pursuing before he left. Bagong Kussudiardjo remains a major figure – primarily in dance, though cassettes of music to accompany his dances are distributed widely. His impact on gamelan music should not be underestimated, but it has clearly been surpassed by that of his peer Ki Nartosabdho.

Ki Nartosabdho and Condhong Raos

Ki Nartosabdho (1925–85) is unquestionably the person most influential in the arena of Javanese gamelan performance since Indonesian independence, known through his dominating presence in the modern media (radio, television, cassettes) from Banyumas to Banyuwangi (see plate 20). With his group Condhong Raos (literally, "harmonious/agreeable

20   Ki Nartosabdho playing *kendhang* (ca. 1971). (Photograph courtesy of Judith Becker, used by permission.)

feeling"), which he founded in the late 1960s, he has contributed much to the awareness of distinctive regional styles and repertories and to their wider acceptance in contemporary Java. He was born in Wedhi, a small town between Surakarta and Yogyakarta (and not clearly within the cultural provenance of one or the other), and resided in Semarang from about 1948 until his death. Nartosabdho publicly eschewed any regional identity other than "Javanese," and adopted musical idioms not only from many regional Javanese traditions, but also from Sunda, Bali, and Indonesian and Western popular musics. Because of his great popularity – which, in a circular argument, one could attribute in part to his championing of so many kinds of music – he was able to present music from various regions to many who would otherwise either not have heard it or, more probably, not paid much attention to it.

By his own account, Nartosabdho tried his hand at a number of arts during his childhood, including guitar.[1] But he excelled on *kendhang* and began to make his living by drumming for itinerant *kethoprak* dramatic groups in central Java. The musical tradition he came to know best was that of Solo. The famous *wayang orang* troupe he joined in the 1940s, Ngesthi Pandhawa, performed dance and music in Solonese style, but made its home in Semarang. As drummer for Ngesthi Pandhawa, Nartosabdho travelled widely in central and east Java and told me he was always eager to hear and absorb all the varieties of music he encountered. Soon after joining the troupe he became musical director and began to compose new pieces, many of them light and humorous *lagu dolanan*, intended primarily for the *punakawan* (clown-servants) in the *wayang*. Though some of these showed obvious influences from the West (e.g., rhumba rhythms), none bore the clear stamp of Javanese regions other than Surakarta.

Influences from outside mainstream Javanese gamelan

It is rather difficult to trace the development of Nartosabdho's active engagement with other regional traditions. During my interview with him in 1979 he did not mention specific instances; and my questions were directed mostly to his early background and his develop-ment as a puppeteer. One piece I believe to have been composed during the 1960s, *Lepetan*, *pélog pathet barang*, not only involves two-part singing, but employs the instrumental techniques of the Balinese gamelan *gong kebyar*, with *bonang* imitating some of the simpler patterns of the Balinese *reyong* (single-row gong chime) and the *gendèr barung* and *panerus*, played with bare wooden mallets, imitating the slower interlocking of the Balinese *gangsa* (metallophone like the Javanese *gendèr*, with keys suspended over tube resonators). Balinese music, received well internationally, has enjoyed considerable prestige in Java for some time. In the early years of the Republic of Indonesia, with much talk of building a national artistic tradition through an eclectic blend of the "highest achievements" (in the words of educator Ki Hadjar Dewantara) of Indonesia's traditional arts, Balinese gamelan music – particularly *gong kebyar* – drew much attention with its rich texture and the dazzling technical virtuosity demanded of its players.

Nartosabdho's special fascination with drumming drew him also to the dance music of Sunda, which requires great technical virtuosity on a full battery of drums. His *Nini Thowong*, whose vocal part delivers a text concerning the entranced Nini Thowong (= Nini Thowok) doll, is strongly influenced by Sundanese style, particularly in the drumming. And in his recordings of many new pieces one can hear flashes of Sundanese drumming style – the sounds of several *kulanter* (small *ketipung*-like drums set vertically, resting on the larger head) and the glissando obtained by varying the tension on the larger head of the largest drum with the heel of one foot (a technique which, to my knowledge, is not encountered in any central or east Javanese tradition).

Ki Nartosabdho and the music of Banyumas

It was during the late 1960s – he could not recall the exact year – that Nartosabdho's interest in sources outside the mainstream central Javanese tradition led him to hire Suryati, a *pesindhèn* from Purbalingga, in the region of Banyumas (see plate 21). She was, and remains today, an extraordinarily talented singer, with a voice wholly compatible with the singing of Solonese pieces in Solonese style (with Solonese vocal quality and pronunciation). Yet she also grew up hearing and learning the many spirited pieces of Banyumas, and brought

21 Nyi Suryati (middle), flanked by fellow *pesindhèn* from Banyumas, during a *wayang kulit* performance by Ki Sugino Siswocarito, 1987. (Photograph courtesy of René Lysloff, used by permission.)

knowledge of these to Nartosabdho's group. Though she maintains residence in a village outside Purbalingga, she performed frequently with Nartosabdho over the years, appearing on many of the commercial cassettes he made with Condhong Raos. Her role in Nartosabdho's appreciation and study of Banyumas gamelan music was described to me not only by Suryati in 1984, but by Nartosabdho himself, when I saw him for the last time in Semarang in 1983. He was already ailing at the time, but said he was greatly indebted to Suryati for his knowledge of Banyumas music.

This long acquaintance played a substantial role in Nartosabdho's musical career and, due to his widespread fame, in gamelan music throughout Java. Rather than compose new pieces in a style recognizably inspired by Banyumas gamelan, however, Nartosabdho began to present items of the traditional Banyumas repertory. Nartosabdho's performances of these

Banyumas Lancaran:	Banyumas Wayang Pieces:	Other Banyumas Pieces:
Eling-éling	Srepegan (manyura)	Randha Nunut
Godril	Srepegan (barang)	Kembang Glepang
Lambangsari Kenyol	Srepegan (sanga)	Ilogondhang
Ricik-ricik		
Unthuluwuk	Banyumas Ketawang:	
Waru Dhoyong	Gunungsari Kalibagoran	

8.1 Traditional Banyumas *gendhing* performed by Ki Nartosabdho and his group Condhong Raos

pieces is in a style which, though imitating Banyumas style very closely, does not duplicate it exactly. Most fundamental – and certainly most immediately recognizable to Banyumas musicians – is the drumming itself. As far as I have been able to gather from speaking to Javanese who have seen him drum these pieces, he did not use the small *ciblon/batangan* and single tiny *ketipung* that help to give Banyumas gamelan music its characteristic sound. Instead, he imitated as best he could the Banyumas drum sounds on his larger *ciblon*, occasionally using his *ketipung* set vertically as in Banyumas. Nartosabdho has been widely acknowledged as one of the most skilful drummers among central Javanese musicians, and one of the best at imitating other regional styles. Nevertheless, both the sound of the larger drum (or drums) and the fact that, as several musicians put it, "his hands were so completely at home with Solonese drumming style" resulted in a drumming style obviously inspired by Banyumas drumming, but with a Solonese feel.

The *bonang* playing techniques typical of Banyumas and described in chapter 3 are modified in Nartosabdho's performances. Though producing a pattern sounding like Banyumas interlocking, the roles of the *bonang* are actually reversed. Instead of the *bonang barung* playing off beat, as in Banyumas style (see Figure 3.15), Nartosabdho has the *bonang panerus* (the instrument that more normally plays off beat in Yogyanese and Solonese styles) perform this role, with the *bonang barung* playing on beat and alternating between two single tones (as in Solonese and Yogyanese *bonang imbal/pinjalan*) rather than playing in octaves. The pitch choices conform to Banyumas style, but the playing technique itself is essentially mainstream central Javanese, requiring only minor adjustments within idioms that are second nature for most players today.

Even though Suryati herself is very often the featured *pesindhèn* in Nartosabdho's renditions of Banyumas pieces, the singing style is also modified to sound more Solonese. It is not clear to what extent this represents Nartosabdho's own preference, as an explicit directive to his singers, rather than the choice of the individual singer. Yet it was clear to Suryati from the beginning of her association with Nartosabdho and his group that to perform with them anywhere in Java, regardless of repertory, she had to adjust her vocal quality and the ornamental nuances in her *céngkok* (melodic patterns) to sound Solonese. The older *pesindhèn* in Banyumas, those least influenced by Solonese style, sound a bit crude and unsophisticated to the ears of many Javanese today, including many residents of Banyumas. Suryati and other younger *pesindhèn* from Banyumas have accommodated these tastes by modifying their vocal style, making it sound more sophisticated and more refined – that is, more Solonese.

Pronunciation is also an aspect of Banyumas vocal style, and one that Nartosabdho was careful not to overlook. Suryati and others frequently use the distinctive *ngapak* pronunciation of Javanese in the singing of traditional Banyumas pieces in performances with Nartosabdho and his group. This strengthens the "Banyumasness" of the performance for most Javanese, regardless of whether the singer is Suryati or someone from another part of Java. But for those raised in Banyumas, conversant in Banyumas dialect and at home with the Banyumas variants of pronunciation, the attempts by *pesindhèn* from Semarang and Solo, for example, are easily spotted as imitations – just as easily as speakers of different regional variants of English (Scotsmen, Louisiana cajuns, and so forth) differentiate between the speech of someone raised in the region and all but the best imitation by an outsider. Furthermore, the texts presented by Nartosabdho's group in solo *macapat* songs leading into Banyumas *gendhing* (such as *Pangkur Banyumasan* leading into Lancaran *Éling-éling*) are in standard Javanese rather than Banyumas dialect, but pronounced in Banyumas *ngapak* style. This incongruity strikes Banyumas musicians as humorous and artificial. Those Banyumas musicians whom I questioned about these *macapat* said that local groups active in the Banyumas region do not often perform them with the Nartosabdho texts and when they do, they pronounce the words with the appropriate standard Javanese (*mbandhèk* rather than *ngapak*).

In addition to the kinds of adjustments in performance style described above, Nartosabdho has created his own versions of several Banyumas pieces through the substitution of new vocal melodies and texts he has composed himself and through the expansion of the *gongan* beyond the normal *irama* II/*dadi* typical of most traditional Banyumas versions. The new material, while exhibiting certain nuances now associated with a Nartosabdho "style," is clearly inspired in large part by traditional Banyumas practice itself. For example, Nartosabdho created an expanded version of Lancaran *Ricik-ricik* that slows from a fast introductory first *irama* level to two levels of subdivision to *irama* III/*wilet*, indigenous versions formerly expanding only to *irama* II/dadi. Yet in this new *irama* level, the singing style and alternation between male and female singers has a strong Banyumas feeling to it, albeit while retaining some of the asymmetry and syncopation that characterize much of Nartosabdho's other vocal music.

Similar kinds of vocal parts have been created for Lancaran *Éling-éling*, the *irama* II/*dadi* section of Lancaran *Ricik-ricik*, and even Banyumas *wayang* pieces (e.g., *Srepegan*, *sléndro pathet manyura*, a variant in *pélog pathet barang*, and *Srepegan*, *sléndro pathet sanga*), among others. For these pieces the new vocal parts do not fill a newly expanded *gongan*, but substitute in most cases for other vocal parts widely known in Banyumas and presumably indigenously conceived. In some senses, these changes can be said to represent a synthesis not entirely Banyumasan, but they have been adopted and popularized by Banyumas musicians, as well as other Javanese musicians, and are now generally accepted as "Banyumasan."

Before he began reworking Banyumas pieces, Nartosabdho was already famous for his reworkings of well-known Solonese pieces (Ketawang *Subakastawa*, Ladrang *Asmaradana*, Ladrang *Clunthang*, and many others) – primarily through the creation of new texts and vocal melodies. To distinguish them from the more traditional ones, his versions are often referred to as *rinengga* (literally, "decorated," "embellished"), for example, Ladrang *Clunthang Rinengga*. The reworked versions of Banyumas pieces, however, are generally not listed as such on commercial cassettes – whether recordings of performances by Nartosabdho's group itself or by Banyumas musicians who have adopted the Nartosabdho versions.[2] In some cases, Banyumas groups may perform a traditional Banyumas piece that incorporates some of Nartosabdho's innovations, but not all of them, thereby contributing to a continuum between "traditional Banyumasan" and "Banyumasan Nartosabdho" (a phrase I encountered in discussion with several musicians).

In addition to reworking or reinterpreting Banyumas pieces, Nartosabdho composed a piece entitled *Calung Banyumasan* (*sléndro pathet sanga*, on *Jungkeri*, Lokananta cassette ACD-052). The playing styles seem to mix Solonese, Banyumas and Sundanese influences, and the vocal part combines Nartosabdho's characteristic regular rhythms with ornaments clearly in imitation of Sundanese (and not Banyumas) vocal practice. Though most of the piece is rendered by full central Javanese bronze gamelan, the *gambang* is given prominence, in imitation of the sound of the *calung*, and the text describes the delightful sounds of

Banyumas *calung* music. To my knowledge, however, this piece has not been adopted by Banyumas musicians, and thus cannot be said to have entered the local repertory the way his versions of *Srepegan* have, for example.

What can be said at this point, then, about regional "authenticity"? Such a notion is becoming increasingly complicated as we look more closely at what transpires. We find a Javanese musician who, without ever having lived in Banyumas, not only learns and performs music from the region, but also arranges and reworks local pieces in such a way that his new versions are accepted and popularized in the region and enthusiastically embraced as "Banyumasan." Furthermore, composers of new gamelan pieces in Banyumas, such as Rasito and S. Bono, show clear influence from Nartosabdho in the vocal melodies they compose. At the same time, people from the Banyumas region readily distinguish the Nartosabdho renditions of Banyumas pieces, which closely imitate traditional Banyumas performance style, from more "authentic" (*asli*) performances by local groups.

The rest of Java, however, has learned most of what it knows about Banyumas gamelan music from Nartosabdho, whose cassettes are marketed widely throughout Java. Though cassette recordings of Banyumas musicians performing their regional music have been produced since the mid-1970s, they have not circulated anywhere nearly as widely as those of Nartosabdho. And even where they are available outside the region, as we noted in chapter 7, cassette retailers report that it is mainly the Javanese from Banyumas who purchase cassettes of Banyumas performers. Consumers may purchase a Nartosabdho cassette with no special interest in Banyumas *gendhing*, but discover one or two Banyumas items on the cassette. Some Nartosabdho cassettes produced in the 1980s offer *Gendhing-gendhing Banyumasan* predominantly or, in at least one case, exclusively. It is the Nartosabdho renditions of popular Banyumas *gendhing* that I have heard imitated in Yogyakarta and Malang, for example, where gamelan directors acknowledge their use of Nartosabdho recordings as the models for their own playing.

Presentation of Semarang's gamelan music

Banyumas is not the only region whose gamelan tradition intrigued Nartosabdho. Despite the small corpus of pieces and the relatively low visibility of the Semarang tradition as compared to that of Banyumas, Nartosabdho drew heavily on this tradition as well. His long residence in Semarang, he told me, contributed to both his fondness and his familiarity with Semarang gamelan music. He had not heard Semarang style performance until moving there, but was attracted particularly to the lively tempo treatment and unique drumming and *bonang* techniques that make up the Semarang sound. In 1973, shortly after the dawn of the cassette industry in Java, he recorded Ladrang *Gégot*, performed with full soft ensemble and traditional vocal parts, but with Semarang drumming, *bonang*, and tempo treatment (on the cassette *Jangkrik Genggong*, Lokananta ACD-025).[3] And the following year he recorded *Éla-éla Gandrung Semarangan*, a piece he composed and in which he combined Semarang vocal and instrumental styles with his own Solonese-based style of soft ensemble music. This piece is on the cassette *Jungkeri* (Lokananta ACD-052), along with various other regional offerings:

the traditional Banyumas piece *Randha Nunut*, Nartosabdho's *Calung Banyumasan*, and *Brajagan Surabayan* (in a modified east Javanese style). In addition to his Lokananta recordings of Semarangan music, he has released three cassettes whose titles suggest that all items on the cassette are in Semarang style: *Sarwa-sarwi Semarangan* (literally, "every bit Semarangan" – Fajar 980), *Gending-gending Semarangan* (Fajar 9265), and *Gending-gending Semarangan Vol. 2* (Fajar 9313). All of the pieces presented on *Sarwa-sarwi Semarangan* appear on one of the two other cassettes, which were released later.

Only a few of the "Semarangan" pieces Nartosabdho recorded belong to the traditional Semarang repertory. Others, like Nartosabdho's Ladrang *Gégot* (not represented on any of these Fajar cassettes) are heard frequently in Solonese style and are generally considered not to have originated in Semarang. In addition, the cassettes offer a number of original compositions by Nartosabdho, some of them with elements of Semarang performance style – though usually only in the opening and closing sections, with the main core in standard Solonese *klenèngan* style with Nartosabdho-style vocal parts. But several pieces, including the title piece *Sarwa-sarwi Semarangan*, seem to avoid any musical link to Semarang tradition altogether. Instead the texts or titles refer to Semarang or, in the case of *Candi Baru*, to a residential suburb (Candi Baru) on the hill that rims the city. One piece, *Goyang Semarang*, is part of the repertory of east Java and is, appropriately, performed in a Nartosabdho imitation of east Javanese style. This variety of connections with Semarang is summarized in Figure 8.2.

Traditional Semarang Repertory:

    Ladrang Éling-éling (bonang) Semarangan
    Dhendhang Semarangan
    Macapat Dhandhanggula Semarangan

Pieces with Semarang treatment, mixed with Solonese:

    Ladrang Gégot (Semarangan)
    Ladrang Wani-wani (Semarangan)
    Ondhé-ondhé (Semarangan)

Pieces by Nartosabdho with Semarang treatment, mixed with Solonese:

    Kagok Semarangan
    Éla-éla Gandrung Semarangan

Pieces by Nartosabdho with texts referring to Semarang and vicinity, but no
        Semarang musical traits:

    Semarang Indah
    Sarwa-sarwi Semarangan
    Candi Baru
    Simpang Lima Ria

Pieces from other regions performed with non-Semarang performance styles:

    Goyang Semarang (east Javanese)
    Télagantung (Semarangan)   (elements of Banyumas style, despite the title)

8.2   "Semarangan" and Semarang-related pieces recorded by Nartosabdho

In Java it is widely known that Nartosabdho resided in Semarang for most of his professional life. Thus, whether they incorporate elements otherwise identifiable as Semarangan or not, his many compositions and innovative interpretations of extant pieces can be seen as *de facto* "Semarangan." Some Javanese I spoke to referred to the style that pervades his many *lagu dolanan* as "Semarangan," since it could be said to have developed in that city. This despite his own identification of his gamelan music as based on Solonese style and the more general (perhaps casual) acceptance of most of his original compositions as belonging to the mainstream central Javanese (i.e., Solonese court-derived) tradition.

The reference to Nartosabdho's works and style as "Semarangan" (and hence regional) might strike Western readers as unnecessarily inexact, since it is generally known precisely which individual in Semarang is responsible for the style. Yet such imprecision is consonant with the values one generally associates with the central Javanese court culture, both in its indirection and in its avoidance of naming a specific individual. Though we do not tend to think in regional terms about orchestral performance in the West, we do hear of "the Philadelphia sound" (the "warm" string sound developed by Eugene Ormandy during his long tenure as musical director of the Philadelphia Orchestra) and find it contrasted, for example, to "the Chicago sound" (the "bright" brass sound developed by George Solti).[4] I would not wish to imply, however, that references to other regional styles – Banyumasan, Yogyanese, and so forth – represent an avoidance of naming a known individual solely or largely responsible for the development of the distinctive stylistic features. Were historical sources bearing on this question more detailed, we would likely be able to name individuals who contributed in various ways to these traditions. Yet I think it highly improbable that any single individual would emerge whom one could identify as "the" creator of any of these styles.

Influences from East Java

Nartosabdho's eclectic interest in Javanese regional traditions led him to adapt items from East Java (Banyuwangi and Madiun, as well as the east Javanese heartland) or to compose new pieces inspired by them. His *Éling-éling Banyuwangèn* has the *saron* and two *gendèr* playing a lively, fast-moving melody in Banyuwangi style, along with a vocal melody at least partially inspired by Banyuwangi singing.[5] Nevertheless, his singers maintain a central Javanese sound quality; and his performances of the piece use central Javanese gamelan, with central Javanese *sléndro* tuning, and typically central Javanese treatment on most other instruments.

As we saw in the previous chapter, many of the cassette recordings of east Javanese gamelan groups are released with titles indicating that the repertory presented is for *tayuban* from a particular town or region (Tulungagung, Trenggalek, Lumajang, etc.). Some of Nartosabdho's cassette releases in the 1980s have borne similar titles, though with locales more familiar to central Javanese: Yogyakarta, Surakarta, and Madiun. Though located within the province of East Java, Madiun is close both geographically and culturally to Surakarta. Particularly for central Javanese it can represent something "East Javanese" without seeming too remote. Cassettes claiming a Madiun orientation are, I would think, more likely to appeal to the central Javanese public than are cassettes from areas further east, for Madiun promises something a bit out of the mainstream, but not entirely. Nartosabdho never released any cassette to my knowledge designated as "Jawa Timuran" (East Javanese) or with a title referring to any area further east (e.g., Banyuwangi or Surabaya, for instance).

The Nartosabdho cassette tapes entitled *Gendhing-gendhing Tayub Madiun* (Ira-Record WD-642) and *Gendhing Tayub Madiun Volume 2* (Ira-Record WD-761) contain pieces from the Solonese repertory, as well as some generally identified with East Java (such as *Angleng*, *Godril*, *Jamong*, *Walang Kèkèk*, *Ireng-ireng*, and *Orèk-orèk*). The first of these two cassettes has the special version of *Sampak* often identified as *Sampak Madiunan*, which is distinguished from the Solonese version by the lack of repetition after the gong tones. (Though present on the recording, this item is not identified on the cassette cover; nor is the Solonese *Ayak-ayakan* played at the beginning of both sides.) The use of the Madiun version, for those

```
Sampak in Solonese Style          Sampak Madiunan
  (sléndro pathet manyura)          (sléndro pathet manyura)

2 2 2 2  3 3 3 3  1 1 1 1G          3 3 3 3  1 1 1 1G
1 1 1 1  2 2 2 2  6 6 6 6G          2 2 2 2  6 6 6 6G
6 6 6 6  3 3 3 3  2 2 2 2G          3 3 3 3  2 2 2 2G
```

8.3   Two versions of *Sampak*, *sléndro pathet manyura*: Solo and Madiun

accustomed to the far more widely known Solonese version, adds refreshing variety without challenging the listener in the way that the east Javanese *wayang* pieces discussed in chapter 5 surely would. And their mix of central and east Javanese pieces, all played with Nartosabdho's characteristic polish and spirit, makes them accessible to the widest possible Javanese audience. The central Javanese are offered something out of the ordinary mainstream, but with enough familiar material to be easily enjoyable; east Javanese are offered popular pieces from their own repertory as well as that of the prestigious central Javanese mainstream.

On several of his cassettes, including the second "Madiun" tape mentioned above, he presents his versions of *Jula-juli* (or Gendhing *Surabayan*), usually with an elaborated *saron* part reminiscent of some of those discussed in chapter 5 (though not identical to any of them). The two *bonang* and *peking* interlock in the usual east Javanese fashion, but otherwise the style of performance is something other than "east Javanese." The singing style Nartosabdho's *pesindhèn* employ is primarily Solonese in contour and nuance, and not the east Javanese singing one normally expects with this piece. The drumming and tempo treatment are also readily distinguishable from that of an east Javanese drummer, one raised in the region and familiar with the local drumming since childhood.

While the inspiration for Nartosabdho renditions may be identifiably east Javanese, they remain for many listeners an imitation: a reinterpretation for some, a dilution for others. Most of the east Javanese musicians to whom I spoke concerning Nartosabdho's involvement with their tradition expressed a strong dissatisfaction with his "Solonization" or "central Javanization" of their music, and a real disdain for what they viewed as his vain attempts at east Javanese drumming. At least, said some, he might have used an east Javanese instrument (*gambyak*). But to my knowledge, though he obviously could have afforded one, he used his central Javanese *ciblon* instead, thereby insuring a softer sound, one more palatable to the large audience already at home with the mainstream style. And the tempi, though fast at times, do not vary in the way that they do in most east Javanese performances.

Though east Javanese musicians acknowledged their debt to Nartosabdho for increasing general public awareness and appreciation of the variety of Javanese musical expression and for helping to legitimize their own tradition in contemporary Java, they sadly note the lack of a real east Javanese spirit in the pieces he has presented to the public as "east Javanese." Admittedly, the complaints of these musicians, whose pitifully small earnings from long hours of artistic endeavor contrast sharply with Nartosabdho's great wealth, might be seen to spring from resentment and jealousy, but it is my belief that their concern for their music and the elements that are lost in the transfer and adoption by Nartosabdho, or any other performers, is a genuine one.

Regional combinations in the recordings of Ki Nartosabdho

One of the curious features of Nartosabdho's musical ventures into East Javanese territory in particular is their explicitly syncretic nature. Three of his pieces that consist at least partially of the *Jula-juli* instrumental melody are given titles that combine references to two places: Ladrang *Gecul* [humorous] *Surawangi* (*Sura*baya and Banyu*wangi*); Jula-juli *Suber* (*Su*rabaya and Jem*ber*, East Java); and Lagu *Timur Mas* (Jawa *Timur* and Banyu*mas*).[6] Some Javanese I asked said they heard occasional hints of Banyuwangi vocal style in the first of these, though most of the piece sounds central Javanese until the *Jula-juli/Surabayan* melody appears near the end. It is difficult to determine what might be meant musically by the reference in the second of these to Jember, a city in the far eastern part of the province of East Java (between Malang and Banyuwangi) whose population is a mixture of speakers of Javanese, Osing Javanese (Banyuwangi), and Madurese (Adiana 1986:3; Sundoro 1986:1). I know of no reference to a distinctive musical style or repertory associated with Jember. And no obvious Madurese or Banyuwangi elements appear in Nartosabdho's piece, either in the language of the text or in the musical style. It seems likely that Nartosabdho intended in this title to suggest a familiarity with the arts of much of East Java, not just Surabaya.

The third of these, *Timur Mas*, and the context in which it is presented on the commercial cassette of the same name, demonstrate the complexity of the issue of regionalism in the hands of Nartosabdho and his musicians. Side B of the cassette begins with a rendition of the traditional Banyumas piece *Untul-Luwuk* (more often written as *Unthul-uwuk*, or *Unthu Luwuk*), with the Banyumas *pesindhèn* Suryati singing the vocal part. The performance style is as close to "authentic" Banyumas as one finds in Nartosabdho recordings. Yet the instrumental techniques and even Suryati's singing here bear the clear stamp of Solonese tastes, as discussed above. As the final tone is sounded, one of the other *pesindhèn*, Sukesi, apparently from East Java, strikes up a conversation with Suryati about their respective regional cultures, including musical style. The conversation is ostensibly impromptu, but its content has obviously been planned out for the most part:

(Conversation between the two *pesindhèn* on Nartosabdho tape *Timur Mas*.) Pronunciation of /a/ in final two syllables of words ending in open a:

"a" = aw (*mbandhèk*); "a" = a (*ngapak*)

(*end of "Untul-Luwuk"*)

SUKESI: Byuh, byuh. Gendhing kok mu énak banget. Iki mau gendhing apa sih, dhik?
   [Wow, that piece was really great. What piece was that, dhik? (dhik = "younger sister," a term of address.)]

SURYATI: Iki mau jenengé Gendhing "Unthul-uwuk Banyumasan." [That was called Gendhing "Unthul-uwuk of Banyumas."]

SUKESI: Gendhing "Kuntul Bawuk"? [Gendhing "Dull White Heron"? (Bawuk can mean dull in color, but also refers to female genitalia; the combination "Kuntul Bawuk" also suggests a popular television hand-puppet show "Kuncung and Bawuk."]

SURYATI: Dudu "Kuntul Bawuk," tapiné "Unthul-uwuk." [It's not "Kuntul Bawuk," but "Unthul-uwuk."]

SUKESI: Tak kira yèn "Kuntul Bawuk." 'Ko 'sik ta dhik, kaya-kayané aku kok kaya wis naté ketemu mbarèk pena. [I thought it was "Kuntul Bawuk." Wait a minute, it's like I have met you before.]

SURYATI: *Apa* rik*a* pangling kambé inyong? [Don't you recognize me?]

SUKESI: Sapa sih, dhik pena? [Who are you, dhik?]

SURYATI: Nyong tu lé, anu, Suryati Banyumas. Gemiyèn lagi nèng Semarang sekolah bareng karo rik*a*. [I'm, aah, Suryati Banyumas. A while ago I went to school in Semarang with you.]

SUKESI: Oh ya sih, pena dhik Suryati saka Banyumas. [Oh, yes, you are dhik Suryati from Banyumas.]

SURYATI: *apa* rik*a* lho mBak ayu Kesi, *apa* y*a*? [You're mBak Kesi, right? (mBak, or mBak ayu, or mbakyu = older sister, term of address.)]

SUKESI: Ya, aku mBak Kesi. [Yes, I'm mBak Kesi.]

SURYATI: Sukesi, rik*a* nang endi? [Sukesi, where are you from?]

SUKESI: Aku, ta? [Me?]

SURYATI: Y*a*. [Yes.]

SUKESI: Panggah nyambut ndhok Jawa Timur. [I live and work in East Java.]

SURYATI: Nyambut *apa* sih? [Say, borrow what?]

SUKESI: "Nyambut" iki ncara nggonku nyambut gawé. ["Nyambut" in my dialect means to work.]

SURYATI: Angger nèng gonku "nyambut" kuwi jenengé nyilih... Rik*a* ya bis*a* nembang k*a*ya inyong mau kaé? [But where I live "nyambut" means to borrow... Can you sing like I did just now?]

SUKESI: Ya sithik-sithik ya bisa. [Yes, I can a little bit.]

SURYATI: Tembangé, angger nèng gon rik*a* jenengé *apa*? [The song, what is it called where you live?]

SUKESI: Jenengé "Othok-Owok." [It's called "Othok-Owok."]

SURYATI: Angger nèng gonku "Unthul-uwuk"... inyong kepéngin krungu tembangané rik*a* "Othok-Owok" g*a*ya Jawa Timur k*a*ya *apa*?" [But where I live "Unthul-uwuk"... I want to hear your song East Javanese style "Othok-Owok," how does it go?]

(*Sukesi sings "Othok-Owok" – in pélog*)

SURYATI: Busat, busat. Jebulané y*a* temuné p*a*dha baé karo nggon inyong. Mung kacèké nggon rik*a* digawé pélog, nggonku sléndro. [Oh, wow. It turns out to be the same as where I live. But the difference is that they make it *pélog* where you're from, and *sléndro* where I'm from.]

SUKESI: 'Kéné dhik, upamaa Banyumas karo Jawa Timur dadèkna siji ngono, ya apa? [Okay, dhik, suppose Banyumas and East Java are combined, how about that?]

SURYATI: K*a*ya-k*a*ya luwih bagus, luwih kepénak. Jajal nènggané Banyumas karo Jawa

Timur didadèkna siji arep dijenengi *apa*, jajal? [It seems as if it would be better, more pleasing. What if Banyumas and East Java are combined, what would it be called?]

SUKESI: Upamaa dijenengna lagu "Timur Mas" ngono. [Suppose it were called "Timur Mas"? (literally, "Golden East")]

SURYATI: *Ya* apik. "Timur Mas" kuwi njikut tembung kepriwèk? [Yes, that's good. How do you get the word "Timur Mas"?]

SUKESI: Saka "Jawa *Timur*" dicampur karo "Banyu*mas*" dadi lagu: [From "*East* Java" mixed with "Banyu*mas*" (literally, "golden water").]

BOTH: "Timur Mas." ["Golden East."]

Sukesi exclaims that she liked the piece just sung and asks its name. Suryati gives her the title, which Sukesi pretends to misunderstand. Sukesi then asks Suryati who she is and Suryati replies "Suryati Banyumas" – revealing both name and regional identity in one breath. They discover that they have studied together (presumably with Nartosabdho), and then Suryati asks Sukesi her name and where she is from. Sukesi responds that she lives and works in East Java, and uses expressions that Suryati pretends to confuse due to differences in regional dialect. Eventually Suryati asks Sukesi to sing, and Sukesi says she will sing an East Javanese version of the piece Suryati has just sung.

Suryati makes generous use of Banyumas dialect (e.g., inyong, rik*a*, kepriwèk), with the appropriate *ngapak* pronunciation, obviously with the full approval of Nartosabdho. Sukesi speaks with *mbandhèk* pronunciation and uses some east Javanese (*arèk*) expressions (e.g., pena, ya apa). But in contrast to Suryati, obviously at home with Banyumas speech, Sukesi sounds rather uncomfortable with the few east Javanese-isms in her speech, indicating to the Javanese I spoke to that she may not even be from East Java (or if so, then from an area close to Central Java). Curiously enough, the point is made that the Banyumas piece is in *sléndro*, while a version from East Java – it is never made clear from what particular local repertory – is in *pélog*, and entitled *Othok-Owok* (also spelled *Othug-Owug*). None of the more salient contrasts between Banyumas and east Javanese gamelan music are mentioned. Nor is the ensuing performance style, either vocal or instrumental, anywhere near as "east Javanese" as the *Untul-Luwuk* was Banyumasan. In fact, the piece *Othok-Owok* is generally associated not with the east Javanese heartland, but more with the eastern part of Central Java, north east of Surakarta (Sragen and Blora) and may be performed in *sléndro* (e.g., *Goyang Sragen: Badhutan Sragen Kreasi Baru*, Lokananta ACD-278). Following this second piece, the two *pesindhèn* talk again and introduce the idea of a piece combining musical elements from Banyumas and East Java, appropriately entitled Timur Mas.

Rather than presenting elements from the two regional traditions simultaneously, however, the piece is in two distinct sections. The first is a close imitation of Banyumas style instrumentally, except for the prominence of *rebab* (played in a style that suggests Sundanese influence). Even the *gambang* plays in imitation of Banyumas *calung*. The vocal melody, however, sounds more like many of Nartosabdho's other pieces, and not particularly Banyumasan. The second section, signalled only by a few quick strokes on the drum, is a Nartosabdho rendition of *Jula-juli*, beginning in the fast instrumental style referred to in east Java as "Din Tak Tong" or "Céko." Though we have been told that *pélog* is typically East Javanese, this section, like most *Jula-juli* anywhere except the Malang area, is in *sléndro*. The singing here is closer than in other Nartosabdho recordings to the east Javanese *kidung* style typical of *Jula-juli*, but with a clear Nartosabdho feel nevertheless – both in rhythm and in the alternation of female voice with male chorus.

Sorting out the significance of this particular set of items and the conversation that links them is an interpretive challenge. More might be revealed were we able to question Nartosabdho today about his intentions in composing the piece and in presenting it the way he did, or to determine where Sukesi was born and raised and what might be her own conceptions of her regional identity. Yet we are not totally in the dark either. Much is feigned here in order to give the impression of real Javanese regional diversity neatly controlled and mastered by Nartosabdho and his super group.

Suryati is indeed from the Banyumas area, and speaks in "authentic" Banyumas dialect, with true Banyumas accent and intonation. But this is rendered inauthentic if we consider that she is speaking to a Javanese ostensibly from East Java. Only the most isolated members of the older generation in Banyumas today are unfamiliar with "standard" central Javanese, introduced in the schools in Banyumas during the 1920s (Sekretariat Nasional 1983:23), and heard widely on radio and television. Those who know it would unquestionably use standard Javanese, rather than the local dialect, in an encounter with Javanese from outside the region.

Suryati's singing mixes Banyumas and Solonese styles, as do the instrumental performers, but it is presented as "Banyumasan" (and thus, presumably, *not* Solonese). More complex still is her not very convincing east Javanese counterpart, Sukesi, who could have sounded much more east Javanese with a different choice of vocabulary and different accent. Perhaps this was as east Javanese as she felt she wished to allow herself to sound. At any rate, she obviously knows standard central Javanese, but chooses to sprinkle it with a few east Javanese expressions. Her "pena" and "ya apa" are sufficient for her role in this recorded conversation, for they allow the listener to identify her – though perhaps fictitiously – as east Javanese. Her singing and the instrumental accompaniment are no more east Javanese than her speaking. But because the listener is told that it *is* from east Java and because it does indeed sound different from the Banyumas version heard just beforehand, the listener accepts the opposition as indicative of real regional differences.

The culmination in the newly composed Nartosabdho piece, in which we hear neither authentic Banyumas style nor authentic east Javanese style, is wholly consistent with the tone set both in the previous musical pieces and in the conversation between the *pesindhèn*. Why such an emphasis on *rebab* in the Banyumas section when this is an instrument frequently omitted in performances by groups in Banyumas? Is it that Banyumas lies to the west, just before Sunda, where *rebab* is prominent, and therefore a prominent *rebab* might effectively suggest Banyumas to most other Javanese? Or is it intended as a Solonese element, adding refinement to the otherwise boisterous Banyumas style? And why in both sections are the vocal parts composed and sung in a style readily identified as Nartosabdho's, rather than Banyumasan or east Javanese, some elements to the contrary notwithstanding? Regional authenticity, to the extent that it is possible, would simply have been out of place. Nartosabdho might well have seen it as unoriginal, and many of his listeners might well have reacted negatively to the stranger aspects of either regional style untempered by Nartosabdho's sensibilities.

At any rate, what Nartosabdho has done here, as in other of his presentations of regional gamelan music, is to offer something akin to a "cover version" – either borrowed or inspired by specific pieces and performance styles, but modified to accommodate the tastes of a wider public. And like the cover versions by white groups in Britain and the United States of rhythm and blues pieces performed originally by black groups in the United States, Nartosabdho's renditions sell more widely and have helped to bring him fame, while the artists who inspired him, for the most part, remain relatively unknown, at least outside their own locale.

Nartosabdho and the court traditions

In addition to his extensive borrowing and modifications of gamelan music from areas far from the court centers, Nartosabdho's keen awareness of regional differences has led him to be rather more explicit than most others in differentiating Yogyanese from Solonese items in his cassette releases. Often a Yogyanese version of a piece will be labelled "... Mataram" or "... Mataraman." This same designation, as we have seen, is much preferred by other artists as well over the more explicit "Yogyakarta" to distinguish Yogyanese repertory or performance style. In Nartosabdho's releases, we find, for example, *"Pangkur Mataraman"* (on *Aneka Pangkur*, Ira-Record WD-508), "Ladrang *Cluntang Mataram"* (on *Cluntang Mataram*, Ira-Record WD-535), among many. Explicit references to Solo (= Sala) or Surakarta are rare, but do occur: *Dhandhanggula cengkok Sala* (*Udan Palaran*, Fajar 9057) and *Asmaradana macapat gagrag Surakarta* (*Asmaradana Kebar*, Ira-Record WD-512).

Those familiar with contrasts in terminology between Yogya and Solo will also note his consistency in distinguishing the vocal genre *palaran* (Solonese) from *rambangan* (Yogyanese). And in some cases the term for the genre of dance-drama in which this kind of singing is featured is the only indication of regional style: *langen driyan* (Solonese) or *langen mandrawanara(n)* (Yogyanese, often abbreviated *mandrawanaran, langen wanaran,* or simply *wanaran*). Often the designation is compounded: for example, *Pangkur wanaran Mataram,* (*Aneka Pangkur*, Ira-Record WD-508); *Kinanti Rambangan Mataraman* (*Kinanti Sandung*, Ira-Record WD-561); or even *Pangkur Rambangan Langen Wenaran Mataram* (*Pangkur Jenggleng*, Fajar 937).

Nartosabdho's frequent use of Yogyanese *gendhing* and *rambangan* has not gone unnoticed by the minority of Yogyanese who champion Yogyanese tradition and fear its decline. Nartosabdho seems to have been attracted by the vigor of the Yogyanese sound, but most musicians note that his versions of Yogyanese pieces seem to have smoothed off some of the rougher edges of Yogyanese style, even in such obvious markers of style as the *bonang*. Reacting to an editorial in the Yogyakarta newspaper in which Nartosabdho is held up as an example to others for his championing of Yogyanese gamelan music, my teacher Suhardi exclaimed how ironic this opinion was, since renderings of Yogyanese pieces by Nartosabdho's group invariably employ Solonese techniques in most of the parts.

What might we conclude about this remarkable musician, Ki Nartosabdho? First known as a daring composer of new gamelan pieces, and most famous as a *wayang kulit* puppeteer, Nartosabdho also made an enormous contribution to the various regional traditions he drew upon. Not only did he create and popularize new pieces and interpretations of traditional pieces, but, even more importantly, he established a new awareness among Javanese of the varieties of gamelan music in Java, and an openness to the artistic value of all of them. Such an openness, however, produces contradictory effects. Along with Nartosabdho himself, many of his imitators are busily melting the boundaries of regional difference, borrowing freely from whatever tradition seems to offer the most appropriate piece or technique for a desired effect.[7]

Musicians at the performing arts conservatories and academies, though keenly aware of the regional identity of the material they use, feel it appropriate now to pepper their performances with a variety of gamelan styles. At the same time, the experts in the various local traditions complain of a hybridization and dilution of their local styles, feeling that the essence of their music is lost in the transfer. We confront, then, a plurality that goes beyond neatly isolated regional differences to a situation in which elements of style and items of repertory from different regions can be juxtaposed and combined. A degree of homogenization is occurring, to be sure, but it is not, as was recently feared, that the central Javanese mainstream is simply eradicating all other regional traditions. Rather, the incorporation of diverse regional musics in the performances of Nartosabdho – combined with representation and identification of these musics in the media and in the course offerings at conservatories – institutionalizes regional differences even as some of the most distinctive aspects of style may be compromised.

9   Conclusion: regional traditions and their representations in contemporary Java

This has been a study inspired by the persistence of regional diversity in Javanese gamelan music. The near-total hegemony of Solonese-based gamelan music over other regional traditions seemed to many to be inevitable in central and east Java fifteen or twenty years ago. Our investigation of gamelan music into the late 1980s has suggested otherwise – unless the florescence of activity documented here is nothing more than a last nostalgic embrace of cultural patterns hopelessly out of pace with "modern life." My view is that for many Javanese it is not.

We have looked at the issue of pluralism not from an ethnic standpoint and not from an international or even national perspective, but at the sub-cultural level within one large ethnic group. Writers who have looked at pluralism from a broader perspective have warned of the hegemony of national and international western-based popular or mass culture.[1] Yet others see a different pattern. Moore has suggested that "many parts of the world that seemed to be moving toward homogeneity are being repluralized" (Moore 1989:26). And Hannerz states that

My sense is that the world system, rather than creating massive cultural homogeneity on a global scale, is replacing one diversity with another; and the new diversity is based relatively more on interrelations and less on autonomy.   (Hannerz, n.d., as quoted in Clifford 1988:16–17, note 6)

Though on a narrower scale, the diversity in the gamelan music of Java can be seen to be undergoing the same processes of transformation that Moore and Hannerz see developing from their more global perspective: a persistence of cultural difference both despite of and because of extensive contact and interrelationship.

Gamelan music in Java today is not a unified body of practice spread evenly throughout central and east Java. What we have found instead is a plurality of gamelan traditions, comprising distinctive regional repertories, performance styles, and conceptions, coexisting and interacting. The criteria by which these traditions are distinguished from one another has included the variation in gamelan instrumentation, preferences in tuning and *pathet*, and formal structure of gamelan pieces. In particular we have seen that *bonang* playing, drumming, vocal style, and tempo treatment are identified as important determinants of regional style by Javanese musicians and listeners.

Whatever the differences between these regions and the traditions that have developed within them, however, the strong presence of the mainstream Surakarta tradition in all these areas – discussed in each of the previous chapters – has come to constitute a shared musical heritage among the Javanese. This is additional to the unique heritage within each region, interacting with each, but (even in Yogyakarta) not replacing it altogether. Moreover, other

234

musical influences between regions have been encountered as well. Based on the evidence from oral history and written sources, some degree of borrowing and synthesis has occurred in Java over the past several centuries. Yet the latter twentieth century – the era of Indonesian independence and the era of mass media – has accelerated this borrowing and complicated the regional picture there considerably.

The notion of each area with its circumscribed set of musical practices, *batik* patterns, favorite foods, and traditional dress is one equally appealing to a Javanese sense of order as to a tourist's (and an anthropologist's) thirst for variety and "otherness." From older musicians and others of a conservative bent in all these areas, I heard again and again that each area (*daerah*) has its own arts (*kesenian*) – or culture (*kebudayaan*) or customs (*adat*). Yet many went on to qualify this by adding that it used to be this way and it should be this way, but currently is not, at least not so neatly. The conditions of modern life have contributed to and are reflected in the borrowing and blending that all would acknowledge is widespread.

These Javanese, along with many outside observers – tourist and anthropologist alike – embrace a view of regional cultures as, to use James Clifford's phrase, "endangered authenticities" (1988:5). Clifford argues rather strongly and convincingly against this view as a model of cultural process for scholars conducting ethnographic research. Yet it is widely held by the man in the street and the peasant in the rice field, and it is, thus, essential to a Javanese understanding of culture in Java. No matter that such notions of authenticity are very likely due to a Western intellectual imperialism;[2] they have now become, in Java, very much "Javanese."

While the view of certain cultural patterns as "authentic" and others as not discredits the actions and feelings of some members of the culture – that is, those who create or promote the "inauthentic" – the fact remains that a significant segment of society chooses, for various understandable reasons, to discriminate in such a way. To an outsider, such as an anthropologist, with relatively little invested emotionally in older cultural patterns that some value as "authentic," it may well seem naive or wrongminded to attribute authenticity to a certain group of cultural patterns and maudlin to express remorse over their "endangered" status. But, of course, some anthropologists lean the other way, and judge most change as degradation or decay, despite completely different evaluations by the culture members who have brought about or favored the changes. This latter case leaves the anthropologist open to accusations of condescension, assuming that s/he has a better ability than the culture bearers themselves to make such judgments. But the former, no less than the latter, involves the anthropologist in taking a stand, one with which some members of the culture will agree and others will not. Regardless of one's emotional stance, the outsider who wishes to present to others an accurate account needs to tack between the two poles these two cases represent. The previous three chapters (6–8), then, might be seen in part to serve as a corrective to the view of "authenticities" provided in the earlier chapters (2–5).

Yet most Javanese, including those who hold most tenaciously to the idea that regional cultures should remain distinctive, would not argue with Clifford's assertion that it is "increasingly hard to conceive of human diversity as inscribed in bounded, independent cultures" (1988:23) or that the twentieth century has seen "local authenticities meet and merge in transient urban and suburban settings" (*ibid.*:4). In Indonesia, the makers of government policy have wrestled with the idea of regional (or local) cultures. And despite various incentives for dismantling the boundaries fortified by regional cultural differences, the government, as we have seen, has also devoted considerable resources to maintaining those differences, albeit with some means for controlling the ways in which they are expressed.

It has been my intention in this study, particularly in chapters 6–8, to delve into the complexity that characterizes the social and political contexts that support and mold regional traditions of gamelan music today. We have been concerned with the major forces which have helped define these regional traditions in contemporary Java and contributed to their dissemination and influence upon one another. With the knowledge of particular regional traits established in chapters 2–5 as a basis, we have subsequently seen the ways in which regional traditions are maintained, circumscribed, blended, diluted, or even trivialized by Javanese musicians, cassette producers, legislators, and government officials.

Certainly today in Java one finds a consciousness about regional differences in gamelan music, as well as dance, shadow puppetry, and the whole array of readily identifiable cultural patterns (language, cuisine, dress). The high level of such awareness, compared to what must have existed in previous centuries, when population mobility and communication between these regions was more difficult and presumably less intensive than it is today, actually speaks of a heightened objectification of regional culture and new possibilities for the meaning of cultural objects, such as music, as they are apprehended by a wider public. The music of these different regions meets and interacts in the same arenas: in the performances of gamelan groups ranging from the best known professionals to village amateurs, in the classrooms of institutions devoted to formal education in the arts, on the stages of performing arts contests, on radio and television broadcasts, on the shelves of cassette stores, and on the shelves of libraries and bookstores. The modern contexts of gamelan music have brought with them various kinds of compromise, adaptation, and controversy.

The result of the increase in awareness of various regional traditions in the practice of gamelan music has not been their continued isolation. The mixture of repertory or styles even within a single performance today is, as we have seen, anything but rare. Instead it is the "purely" east Javanese, or Yogyanese, or Banyumas performance – "pure" in its exclusion of elements now identifiable primarily with another Javanese region – that is rare. The afternoon and night I spent in Trowulan, East Java, listening to Ki Piet Asmoro and his gamelan musicians came close. All the *gendhing* performed were east Javanese, and the playing styles were, in the words of the east Javanese I spoke to throughout the performance, as purely east Javanese as one finds nowadays. But even so, the younger musicians playing *gendèr barung* and *gambang* betrayed the strong influence of the Surakarta mainstream in the playing of soft instruments. The very presence of solo female singing in most east Javanese *wayang gendhing* today is attributable to influences from central Java.

At the events seen by many as best representative of Banyumas, the lengthy *lènggèr-calung* performances, it is expected that the *calung* ensemble will perform well-known gamelan pieces from Solo and Yogya prior to the appearance of the *lènggèr* in costume. And late in the evening the ensemble will do its best to accommodate requests for popular Indonesian songs with no special connection to the Banyumas region. Of course, everything sounds distinctively local because of the timbre of the bamboo *calung* instruments and their special playing techniques. Yet the regional identity of the repertory is recognized. The pieces played early are categorized by the performers as "*wétanan*" (literally, "from the east") and felt to be somewhat more restrained in mood than the Banyumas and other pieces to be played later.

Similarly the popular Indonesian songs are recognized as "pop" or "Indonesian" and are received with special enthusiasm by the younger members of the audience (which even by three-thirty in the morning may still include children as well as a large contingent of teenagers). The inclusion of such a range of repertory within a single performance insures its viability in contemporary Banyumas by simultaneously providing links with the prestigious courtly "east" (particularly Solo), the local region of Banyumas itself, and with the modern nation-state.

Cultural purists in Yogyakarta, primarily the court nobility and others affiliated with the Yogya *kraton*, decry the dilution of Yogyanese tradition with the heavy intrusion from Solo. We have seen how the dominance of Solonese style in the media of radio and recording has contributed to that "intrusion." Practice by the *kraton* musicians is taken by many to be the best representative of a Yogyanese tradition today, but it took conscious reshaping of the repertory during the past ten or fifteen years to purge that most Yogyanese of gamelan events, the regular *hadiluhung* performance, of obvious Solonese influence.[3] And today the playing techniques and some aspects of tempo treatment, derived from Solo and popularized as much in Yogya as anywhere, still give at least a Solonese nuance to these concerts performed within the Yogyanese palace itself, the symbolic center of all that is Yogyanese. As the Yogya case suggests, it is easier by decree to alter repertory choice, since it is the choice of one leader, than to alter the individual playing or singing styles musicians will use in their realization of an item of repertory. What some members of the public may hear as authoritatively Yogyanese (because of its emanation from the *kraton*, or RRI Yogya studio musicians, or a Yogyanese cassette) may incorporate many elements that others hear as Solonese.

Even in Surakarta, whose musicians tend to be the most self-assured concerning the merits and strengths of their own tradition, borrowings from other regions are increasingly evident. The situation almost everywhere, it would seem, is a musical and artistic "heteroglossia," a term Mikhail Bakhtin used in reference to the interaction of different kinds of languages that "do not exclude each other but intersect with each other in many different ways" (Bakhtin 1953:291, as quoted in Clifford 1988:23, note 6). This interaction does not negate the notion of regional distinction, but complicates it.

One approach to sorting out the complication might have been, from the very beginning of this study, to present the reader with instances of actual performances, which we could then try to unravel with respect to regional characteristics. Such an approach is taken by Lysloff in his study of music, shadow puppetry, and culture in Banyumas (Lysloff 1990). Instead, I opted for a more systematic exposition of prominent characteristics with the intention of providing the reader with a more thorough view than the "case study" approach would have allowed, followed by chapters in which the representations and interminglings of these regional traditions occupied the foreground. As we considered the representation of regional traditions in conservatories and contests sponsored by the government, in various public media, and in the activities of Ki Nartosabdho and other gamelan composers and arrangers, it has been necessary to stress the apparently contradictory roles of each in definition and reification, on the one hand, and homogenization and dissolution on the other. The following passage by Clifford would appear an apt remark on the study of gamelan music in Java in the twentieth century: "Indeed, modern ethnographic histories are perhaps condemned to oscillate between two metanarratives: one of homogenization, the other of emergence; one of loss, the other of invention" (1988:17).

We have seen various modern forces helping to redefine or "invent" the regional traditions we have looked at. And this study, as it is read and cited, may also contribute to the modification of conceptions and perhaps even musical practice – another step in the transformation process that music everywhere is constantly undergoing. A question that anthropologists and social historians have been asking recently (notably Hobsbawm and Ranger 1983, Clifford and Marcus 1986, Marcus and Fischer 1986, Clifford 1988, and Rosaldo 1989) and that ethnomusicologists have addressed as well (e.g., Gourlay 1978 and 1982, Keil 1979, Chernoff 1979) is to what extent we – the outside observers who write works such as the present study – actually create, invent, imagine the objects we describe. Especially problematic are the generalizations made in constructing such broad categories as the regional ones applied here and the normative descriptions they entail. Ranger speaks of the "ambiguous legacy ... of 'traditional' African culture; the whole body of reified 'tradition' invented by colonial administrators, missionaries, 'progressive traditionalists,' elders and anthropologists" (Ranger 1983:261–62).

Throughout the writing of this book about Javanese "traditions," I have been concerned that my inevitably incomplete view of Javanese gamelan music and its diversity will contribute to a distorted view, to a further reification of some gamelan practices as "traditions" – while ignoring others – and to a simplification or an obscuring of other interpretations perhaps more valid.[4] Yet I have relied on a variety of evidence available to me from Javanese sources in my description, and have used the categories I found to be most widely representative of indigenous perspectives, rather than inventing my own positivist categories. While it is my distinct impression that the various regional traditions I have discussed have undergone a kind of re-emergence in recent years, I have attempted throughout this study to point also to the mix of repertories, performance styles, and conceptions about gamelan music within each region I have covered.

What, then, can we say in conclusion about gamelan traditions and cultural (or subcultural) "identity" in Java? My concern with this issue is not to downgrade the importance of individual performers and composers, but to address a question often posed by ethnomusicologists and, in this case, often discussed by the Javanese themselves. I do not wish to suggest that aesthetic factors are merely subordinate to social and political factors in Java, but would certainly argue, along with most ethnomusicologists, that aesthetics cannot be fully understood in isolation from social and political realities. Of course, it is not an anonymous folk collective that acts as musical innovator. Individual musicians make choices and the repertory and performance styles result from their creative impulses. But clearly many of these individuals have at some level a concept of regional identity (other than simply "Javanese"), and those who apprehend the music are likely to attribute regional identity to what they hear.

Whether musicians limit themselves to music from their own region or borrow, they are generally aware of the regional provenance of the music they interpret. Like many Javanese, they often identify themselves explicitly with respect to their region. The regional identity looms rather large in Java, even today, particularly within the realm of the indigenous arts, for society accords far less notice to innovators as individuals there than has been customary in the West for the last three centuries. Many more east Javanese are able to distinguish east Javanese from central Javanese gamelan playing style by ear than are able to identify

Wongsokadi as an important east Javanese musician. The issue of cultural identity is, therefore, an important one.

The "juxtaposition of traditional music and cultural identity," Bohlman tells us, has been the persistent paradigm of modern ethnomusicology (Bohlman 1988:29). By labelling this well-worn approach as a paradigm, Bohlman suggests that other paradigms are possible and that a new one (historical in its orientation) may take its place, or at least gain an equal footing with it. "Both concepts [traditional music and cultural identity] can exist separately and did during a period of proto-ethnomusicology" (Bohlman 1988:27). The approach taken in the preceding pages has been situated primarily in the current paradigm Bohlman identifies. But, while not suggesting a new paradigm altogether, this study does attest to the complexity of "juxtaposing" music and cultural identity, at least to seeing them as co-variable.

Government educational programs, contests, and festivals combine with the mass media to make available an unprecedented variety of musical sounds, disengaged from their former ritual and social contexts, and to give new prestige to music from outside the courtly and urban sphere. As we encounter instances of musical borrowings between regions, are we to interpret them as a taking on of multiple regional identities by musicians and their audiences, or as the building of a new Javanese or Indonesian identity, or merely as the borrowing of musical sounds? The Javanese are conscious of these questions, and the implication music has for a shared sense of identity, as we have seen in the rationale given for the founding of the performing arts conservatories. I have suggested in the case of Banyumas *calung* music, that regional (Banyumas), ethnic (Javanese), and national (Indonesian) identities are all represented and reinforced in the choice of music and that these need not contradict one another, since they arrange themselves hierarchically. And to those most intimate with this music, more particular identities are undoubtedly also associated with subtle musical nuances (the style of a particular village, group, or individual).

Musicians are able to hear and learn music whose origins are remote, and do not limit themselves either to their own local music or to the Solonese-based mainstream. Yet when an east Javanese plays *Éling-éling Banyumasan*, he is not redefining himself as Banyumasan, or even as central Javanese. Pak Diyat Sariredjo (Surabaya) states that he is simply attracted by the sound of the piece, which he finds pleasing enough to want to imitate. He has heard it through the mass media and is aware that Nartosabdho, too, is fond of this piece. From its title he is aware of its Banyumas provenance, but he sees it along with many other *gendhing* to be enriching a constantly changing and widening repertory of Javanese gamelan music. His choice to play it does not conflict with his sense of identity as East Javanese (or east Javanese, or Surabayan), but instead is consistent with his identity as Javanese. For him there are no associations of this piece with all-night *calung-lènggèr* performances or *èbèg* trance dances or Banyumas *wayang kulit*, all of which frequently feature *Éling-éling Banyumasan* in the Banyumas region. He has not experienced the piece in any of these contexts. For him it is a lively piece with an appealing spirit, one that he wanted his musicians to perform from time to time, albeit with a different nuance than in performances by Banyumas musicians.

Like the museum artifacts described by Errington, the meanings of these sounds – including their associations and their symbolism of particular regional cultural identity – can be lost or transformed, even as their presence persists. As she reminds us,

Because meanings are not intrinsic to objects but are attributed to them in the course of human thought and practices, objects can change meanings in the course of their "lifetimes," their physical existence in the medium of duration.   (Errington 1989:49)[5]

The independence of the object (or piece, or style) from any particular meaning or cluster of meanings within its region of origin, suggests that pieces and performance styles can be recontextualized and reunderstood from one region to another. What for a Banyumas musician is a frequently heard piece, with many associations that go back to his earliest childhood, can be for a Yogyanese or an east Javanese something fresh and new, representing the spirit and humor most Javanese have learned to associate with Banyumas, but not the more specialized meaning it would have for people within the region. And, as I indicated in cases from Banyumas and east Java above, I believe that the borrowings, when they occur, are understood as consonant with a cultural identity as Javanese, subsuming but not erasing other more local senses of identity. To the extent that they internalize the sound they hear, musicians throughout Java may partake of a common Javanese tradition, then, to which all these regional traditions contribute, but this common tradition is held at a different conceptual level than regional. Still, there is also at least some feeling of otherness with respect to traditions from outside one's own region and this contributes to the appeal that music may have across boundaries: refreshing new material that is nevertheless still Javanese.

It is perhaps in considering the future of regional diversity in gamelan music that the issue of cultural identity reasserts itself most strongly and so often becomes the topic of impassioned debate among musicians and intellectuals. Several ironies present themselves. First, in many of these areas a new search for definition is being pursued, but pinning down stylistic characteristics in a comprehensive way is proving to be somewhat elusive. What is the younger generation to be taught, the teachers and government officials ask? While no one would deny the existence of musical traits unique to Yogyakarta or east Java, for example, opinions differ on the means of definition and on the value of such definition. Second, the very institutions which bolster regional traditions of gamelan music – especially the SMKI conservatories and the cassette industry – also facilitate access to other traditions, and thereby almost guarantee the demise of real regional isolation. Why does SMKI Surabaya offer so much Solonese music, for example? The directors point to practical factors: many of the teachers were trained in Solo; playing style is somewhat less standardized for east Javanese gamelan than for Solonese and therefore more difficult for students; those who know the repertory best are unable or unwilling to teach in a formal setting. And why does RRI Surabaya program so much Solonese music? Programmers and musicians alike respond that they and their listeners enjoy it.

If east Javanese students grow up fluent in Solonese tradition, even with an "understanding" of east Javanese tradition, they may be well versed in identifiably east Javanese techniques, but retain only a fraction of the repertory. What might make a young gamelan musician from Surabaya (or Malang, or Gempol) want to retain more of this repertory? I asked this of several musicians and government officials in Surabaya and Malang; the responses can be summarized as follows. Perhaps the feeling that s/he is east Javanese, and that the sophisticated Solonese will always be the best at Solonese style and never able to perform east Javanese music with all the right nuances. Or that in public multi-regional contests and festivals his/her performance of east Javanese music will be something s/he can present with a sense of full authority.

I would concur with the Javanese I interviewed that, while borrowing from one regional tradition may enhance the playing in other traditions, the survival of regional traditions, rather than isolated remnants and techniques thereof, requires a continued sense of regional identity on the part of the performers, whatever other identities are maintained simultaneously (Javanese, Indonesian). Without it the regional traditions become, in a certain sense, vestigial, as in Semarang. It has been evident that the sense of regional identity elsewhere, though still extant, is in a state of flux. And while each tradition is affected by the cassette industry, contests, festivals, and formal education, the precise configuration of problems and responses in each area is at least as distinctive as the musical styles and repertories.

This study of gamelan music from a regional perspective has been intended to underscore the diversity that most scholarly writings on gamelan music in recent years have tended to ignore. The diversity in styles and in the issues faced in each region make it clear that an informed understanding of "Javanese gamelan music" must take into account the distinctions between regional styles and repertories. By pursuing the multiple view this approach provides, we come a step closer in the written record to a representation of gamelan music in all its rich complexity.

Glossary

Ind. = Indonesian; Jvn. = Javanese. Terms are Javanese unless indicated otherwise.

abot heavy

ada-ada a type of *sulukan* for tense, emotionally charged mood in drama, accompanied by agitated *gendèr* playing

ageng see *gedhé*

alok short calls and cries of male singers

alus refined

alusan refined male dance style

anak-anakan (from *anak*, "child"), second major section in some east Javanese *gendhing*

andha "ladder"; *titilaras andha* = graphic checker notation

andhegan (= *kèndelan*, high Jvn.) "stop"; in the performance of a *gendhing*, a pause during which solo vocalist sings unaccompanied by gamelan (central Java)

andhong singer-dancer (Malang area)

angklung shaken bamboo idiophone; an ensemble featuring a set of *angklung* and several bamboo xylophones (Banyumas); see also *angklung Banyuwangi*

angklung Banyuwangi a bamboo xylophone in a frame positioned at an angle to the ground, popular in the Banyuwangi/Blambangan region of East Java; ensemble featuring these instruments; the music performed by this ensemble

angklung caruk musical competition between two rival *angklung Banyuwangi* groups

arang (= *awis*, high Jvn.) "sparse," "far apart"; for *kethuk* playing in large *gendhing*, one *kethuk* stroke on the eighth beat of each group of sixteen beats; for *kempul* playing in east Javanese *ayak* pieces, one *kempul* stroke every two beats

arèk "child"; ethnic Javanese of east Java

ASKI Akademi Seni Karawitan Indonesia: performing arts academy in Surakarta (now STSI)

asli original, indigenous, authentic

ASTI Akademi Seni Tari Indonesia: performing arts academy (ASTI Yogya now subsumed under ISI; ASTI Den Pasar now STSI)

ayak a formal structure/genre of *gendhing* for east Javanese *wayang* accompaniment

ayak-ayakan a formal structure/genre of *gendhing* for central Javanese *wayang* accompaniment

badhutan clowning, often slapstick

balungan "outline," "skeleton"; melodic outline of a *gendhing*, usually played in single-octave form on *saron demung*, *saron barung*, and *slenthem*, but usually conceived of as multi-octave

balungan beat, a regular conceptualized pulse, normally manifest on *balungan* instruments

balungan instruments, instruments that play the *balungan* in single-octave form (*saron demung*, *saron barung*, and *slenthem*)

bandrèk an interlocking *bonang* technique (east Java)

banyakan variation technique involving *saron demung*, *saron barung*, and *slenthem*

banyumili a technique of *gambang* playing, characterized by smooth, steady playing in octaves

barang name of a tone (1 in *sléndro*, 7 in *pélog*); subdivision of *pélog* tuning system (excluding pitch 1); one of three standard *pélog pathet* (central Java); see *miring*

barung see *bonang*, *gambang*, *saron*

basa pedhalangan the language used by the *dhalang*

242

batangan middle-sized *kendhang* (Yogya)

bedhaya a female court dance, performed by nine dancers (Yogya, Solo); *bedhaya ketawang* = the most sacred of the *bedhaya* dances (Solo)

bedhug large double-headed tacked drum

bem name of a tone (1 in *pélog*); subdivision of *pélog* tuning system (excluding pitch 7); in some instances, used as a category of *pélog pathet* (Yogya)

bendhé knobless gong

bentuk form, formal structure (Ind.)

besi iron (Ind.)

beskalan female-style dance genre, related to *ngrémo* (Malang area)

beskap jacket, part of men's formal dress (Solo)

besutan a genre of comic performance (east Java), all roles taken by men, predecessor to *ludruk*

biola violin (Ind.), instrument used in *gandrung Banyuwangi* ensemble

blangkon permanently wound turban, part of men's formal dress

bonang set of 10, 12, or 14 small kettle gongs arranged in two rows; usual term for the *bonang barung* (central Java) or *bonang babok* (east Java); see also *gendhing bonang*

bonang babok middle-register *bonang* (east Java), octave lower than *bonang panerus*

bonang barung middle-register *bonang* (central Java), octave lower than *bonang panerus*, octave higher than *bonang panembung*

bonang panembung lowest-register *bonang* (Yogya)

bonang panerus highest-register *bonang*

bongkel bamboo sounding device (Banyumas)

buka solo introduction

bumbung "bamboo tube"; resonators for *gendèr* and *slenthem*; gamelan *bumbung* = a small ensemble of mostly bamboo instruments (east Java)

calung bamboo xylophone (Banyumas); small ensemble featuring these instruments

cara njaba "outside manner"; performance practice outside the court (Yogya)

cara njero "inside manner"; performance practice inside the court (Yogya)

cara wangsul see *carabalèn*

carabalèn (= *cara wangsul*, high Jvn.) an archaic gamelan ensemble

cecegan (= *ngencot*) striking a *saron* key while damping it (Yogya)

celempung large zither, with twenty-two to twenty-six strings

céngkok melodic phrase, melodic formula

ciblon see *kendhang ciblon*

ciblonan drumming patterns performed on *ciblon*, usually lively

climènan (= *kemagan*) small gamelan ensemble emphasizing soft-playing instruments (Banyumas)

cocog appropriate, suitable, in agreement

dadi (= *dados*, high Jvn.) "become," "settled"; first major section of a large *gendhing*, represents a settling and expansion from the *lamba* (Yogya); see *irama dadi*

dados see *dadi*

daerah region

dangdut Indonesian popular music heavily influenced by Indian film music and Western rock

demung see *saron demung*

dhadha "chest"; third scale degree

dhagelan comedy

dhalang shadow puppeteer (*wayang kulit*); narrator and singer for dance-drama genres (*wayang wong*, *wayang topèng*, *topèng-dhalang*)

diatonis "diatonic"; seven-tone Western scale, sometimes referred to as *sléndro miring* (Semarang)

èbèg hobby-horse trance dance (Banyumas)

engkuk-kemong set of two kettle gongs, used only in *sléndro* (Solo)

gadhon small gamelan set, excluding *saron* and *bonang* instruments *gagahan* strong male dance style (central Java); a *gendhing* formal structure, usually with four eight-beat *kenongan* per *gong* (east Java); see also *gendhing gagahan*

gagrag style

galong a *pathet* category associated with last hour of all-night *wayang kulit* (Yogya)

gambang multi-octave xylophone

gambang barung one of a pair of multi-octave *calung* that interlocks with *gambang panerus* (Banyumas)

gambang gangsa "bronze *gambang*," multi-octave metal-keyed instrument

gambang panerus one of a pair of multi-octave *calung* that interlocks with *gambang barung* (Banyumas)

gambir sawit a *gendhing* formal structure with two major sections, each with four sixteen-beat *kenongan* per *gong* (east Java)

gambyak middle-sized *kendhang*, with thick heads and loud sound (east Java)

gambyakan drumming patterns performed on *gambyak*, usually lively

gandhangan see *kidungan*

gandrung "infatuated"; see *gandrung Banyuwangi*

gandrung Banyuwangi female singer-dancer; genre of music and dance featuring one or more female singer-dancers (Banyuwangi region, East Java)

gangsa "bronze"; high Jvn. for "gamelan"; Balinese metallophone like Javanese *gendèr*, with keys suspended over tube resonators

gantungan "hanging"; sustaining one tone for several beats

garapan treatment, musical variation, musical arrangement

gati (= *mares*) a repertory of *gendhing* for dance entrances and exits, often performed with gamelan augmented by Western brass, woodwinds, and snare drums (Yogya)

gatra a unit of four *balungan* beats, comparable to Western "measure"

gaya style (Ind.)

gecul naughty, mischievous, humorous

gedhé (= *ageng*, high Jvn.) "large," "great"; gamelan *gedhé* (= gamelan *lengkap*) = complete, full-sized gamelan ensemble; *gong gedhé* (= *gong ageng*, high Jvn.) = largest hanging gong

gedhog a formal structure/genre of *gendhing* for east Javanese *wayang* accompaniment; see *wayang gedhog*

gedhugan a drumming style calmer and sparser than *gambyakan* drumming (east Java)

gemakan "like [the sound of a] quail"; a type of playing on *slenthem* anticipating *balungan* tones (Yogya and east Java)

gembyakan drumming patterns performed on *batangan*, usually lively (Yogya)

gembyang octave

gembyangan nyegat a technique of *bonang* playing, sounding in octaves, on the off-beat of the *balungan*

gendèr instrument consisting of thin metal keys (usually 12–14), suspended over individual tube resonators; usual term for *gendèr barung* (central Java) or *gendèr babok* (east Java)

gendèr babok middle-register *gendèr* (east Java)

gendèr barung middle-register *gendèr* (central Java)

gendèr panembung lowest-register *gendèr*, usually called *slenthem*

gendèr panerus highest-register *gendèr*

gendhing gamelan pieces employing cyclic structure marked by gongs; "large" *gendhing* = *gendhing* with 16 or more *balungan* beats per *kenongan*; "small" *gendhing* = 8 or less *balungan* beats per *kenongan*

gendhing bonang (= *gendhing bonangan*) a repertory of gamelan pieces featuring *bonang* and *saron* instruments, performed with no singing or soft instruments (Solo)

gendhing gagahan east Javanese equivalent of Solonese *gendhing bonang*

genjring Javanese songs accompanied by tambourines and frame drums (Banyumas)

gérong male chorus

gérongan the vocal part sung by the male chorus

gesang (= *urip*, low Jvn.) "live"; a type of *imbal* playing for *saron demung* (Yogya)

geter a quick reiteration or ricochet technique in *gambang* playing

giro a *gendhing* formal structure, with four short *kenongan* per *gong* (east Java)

glebeg a technique of *gambang* playing involving damping (Yogya)

gong large hanging gong, marks major phrase boundaries (may refer to *gong gedhé* and to *gong suwukan/siyem*); term used in east Java for complete ensemble of instruments, including *gong* (i.e., synonym for "gamelan")

gong gedhé/ageng see *gedhé*

gong kebyar Balinese gamelan developed during the twentieth century, characterized by sharp contrasts in dynamic level and flashy, high-speed playing

gong kemodhong instrument with two low-pitched metal keys suspended over a wooden box, functions as a *gong*

gong suwukan (= *siyem*) medium-sized hanging gong

gongan phrase of a *gendhing* marked off by the sounding of a *gong*

gretak snarl, snap, threaten

grontolan frequent use of *geter* (Yogya)

gulu "neck"; second degree of the *sléndro* and *pélog* scales (= *tengah*, *tenggok*, east Java)

gumbeng bamboo sounding device (Banyumas)

hadiluhung "exalted"; *uyon-uyon hadiluhung* = gamelan performances to mark the sultan's Javanese "birthdays," which occur every thirty-five days, reckoned by the coincidence of the seven-day week with the Javanese five-day market week

iket hand-tied turban, part of male formal dress (east Java, also villages throughout Java)

imbal interlocking between two instruments, producing a composite melody

inggah (= *minggah*) "rise," "ascend"; second major section of a large *gendhing* (Solo)

irama dadi level of subdivision of the *balungan* beat, usually defined by a 4:1 ratio between *peking* and *balungan* beat (Solo); = *irama* II (Yogya)

irama lancar level of subdivision of the *balungan* beat, usually defined by a 1:1 ratio between *peking* and *balungan* beat (Solo)

irama rangkep level of subdivision of the *balungan* beat, usually defined by a 16:1 ratio between *peking* and *balungan* beat (Solo); = *irama* IV (Yogya)

irama tanggung level of subdivision of the *balungan* beat, usually defined by a 2:1 ratio between *peking* and *balungan* beat (Solo); = *irama* I (Yogya)

irama wilet level of subdivision of the *balungan* beat, usually defined by an 8:1 ratio between *peking* and *balungan* beat (Solo); = *irama* III (Yogya)

ISI Institut Seni Indonesia, in Yogyakarta, a university for the arts

jaipongan popular form of Sundanese music for social dance, featuring female singer-dancer, *rebab*, lively drumming, and other gamelan instruments

jani-janèn songs in Arabic accompanied by tambourines and frame drums (Banyumas)

jejer sepisan first major scene in *wayang kulit* performance

jemblung a genre of performance in which all gamelan instrument sounds are imitated by human voice (Banyumas)

jengglèng a genre of comedy and music, consisting of banter and parodied *macapat* singing by one or more comedians performing within the larger context of *gendhing/uran-uran* performance (Yogya, primarily)

jengglong a low-pitched, single-octave bamboo xylophone in *calung* ensemble (Banyumas); a Sundanese term for a gong-chime; gamelan *jengglong* (= gamelan *penthung*) = a small ensemble used for accompanying *wayang jengglong* (Semarang, Pekalongan)

jidhor single-headed tacked drum

jineman a type of *gendhing* featuring singing and soft instruments, without *rebab*

jogèt a form of Balinese social dance, accompanied by music performed on instruments mostly of bamboo

jula-juli a genre-piece closely associated with *ludruk* and the *ngrémo* dance (east Java); a *gendhing* formal structure, like *giro*, but performed with singing (east Java) *kabupaten* largest sub-provincial administrative district (Ind.; in Jvn. also written *kabupatèn*)

kadipatèn crown prince's residence

karawitan Javanese gamelan music and related vocal music (may also imply the related performing arts)

karesidenan large administrative district during Dutch period (consisted of several *kabupaten*)

kasar coarse, rough, unrefined

kasunanan the court and kingdom of the ruler (*sunan*) of Surakarta

keagamaan religious matters

kebyokan playing of *nggembyang* in groups of three (on *bonang panerus*) (east Java)

kecèr set of small cymbals, used in some archaic gamelan

kemagan see *climènan*

kemanak a small banana-shaped metal idiophone, held in hand

kemasyarakatan social matters

kembangan (= *sekaran*, high Jvn.) from *kembang/sekar* ("flower"); certain kinds of patterns for melodic instruments (esp. *bonang*) and drum

kempul small hanging gong; see *arang*, *kerep*

kempyang set of two small kettle gongs, used only in *pélog*

kempyung an interval formed between two keys on the *gendèr*, with two intervening keys (in most cases approximately a fifth)

kenceng "tight," "taut"; high in pitch

kendhalèn a kind of hobby-horse dance accompanied by small ensemble (Semarang)

kendhang double-headed laced drum

kendhang ciblon middle-sized *kendhang* (Solo)

kendhang gendhing largest *kendhang*

kendhang ketipung smallest *kendhang*

kendhang wayang medium-large *kendhang*, used for *wayang* music (Solo)

kendhangan pattern played on *kendhang*

kenong set of large kettle gongs, horizontally mounted

kenong japan large, low-pitched *kenong*

kenongan phrase marked off by the sounding of a *kenong*

kepatihan Javanese cipher notation system developed at the *Kepatihan* (prime minister's residence) in Surakarta, now in widespread use

keprak small wooden slit gong

kepribadian character, personality

kerep "frequent," "close together"; for *kethuk* playing in large *gendhing*, one *kethuk* stroke on the fourth beat of each group of eight beats; for *kempul* playing in east Javanese *ayak* pieces, one or two *kempul* strokes per beat

kesenian "arts" (Ind.)

ketawang a *gendhing* formal structure, two *kenongan* per *gong* (central Java)

kethoprak a genre of folk theater (associated with Yogya, but popular throughout Java)

kethuk small kettle gong, horizontally mounted; see *arang*, *kerep*

ketipung see *kendhang ketipung*

kèwèran "dangling"; a drum pattern, characterized by triplet playing (Banyumas)

kidung a category of sung poetry

kidungan (= *gandhangan*) singing of rhyming poetry, especially associated with *jula-juli* (east Java)

kijingan style of *saron* resonator, made of several planks, rather than a single block of wood

kinthilan (from *inthil*, "goat droppings") a type of *saron* interlocking

klenèngan performance of gamelan music without dance or drama; gamelan for soft-playing repertory, excludes *bonang* (Solo)

klithik see *wayang krucil*

kluncing triangle used in accompaniment of *gandrung Banyuwangi kodhok ngorèk* "croaking frog"; an archaic gamelan ensemble

kosèk alus an animated, but subtle drumming style (Solo)

kosèkan an animated drumming style, often heard in *wayang* accompaniment (Solo)

krama high Javanese

kraton Javanese palace, court

kreasi baru "new creation" (Ind.); a genre of new *gendhing*, usually with short *gongan* and emphasis on singing

kroncong Indonesian name for a small chordophone of Western origin; an acculturated popular music, using this instrument and other Western instruments

krucil see *wayang krucil*

krucilan a genre of *gendhing* used for east Javanese *wayang* accompaniment

kuda képang hobby-horse trance dance

kulanter small *ketipung*-like drum set vertically (Sunda)

kulon west

kuningan brass

ladrang a *gendhing* formal structure, four eight-beat *kenongan* per *gong*

lagon a type of *sulukan* for calm dramatic situations, accompanied by soft instruments (Yogya)

lagu "song," "melody"; short for *lagu dolanan*; multi-octave implications of *balungan* (= *lagu batin*, "inner melody")

lagu dolanan light composition, featuring singing

lamba "single"; introductory section of a large *gendhing*, with only two *saron* tones per *gatra* (Yogya)

lambang a *gendhing* formal structure, with two sections, each with two sixteen-beat *kenongan* per *gong* (east Java)

lampah (= *laku*, low Jvn.) "do," "walk"; category of *gendhing* for *wayang* accompaniment (Yogya)

lancaran a *gendhing* formal structure, four short *kenongan* (two or four beats) per *gong* (central Java)

langen driyan a genre of dance-drama with all dialogue sung, female dancers, usually presenting stories of Javanese legendary hero Damar Wulan (Solo)

langen mandrawanara a genre of dance-drama with all dialogue sung, male dancers, usually presenting stories from Indic epic *Ramayana* (Yogya)

langgam a category of *kroncong*, usually in Javanese and often performed with gamelan, rather than *kroncong* instrumentation

laras tuning, scale

lawung a martial dance in strong male style

légong a genre of Balinese dance, for pre-pubescent girls

lènggèr singer-dancer (female or impersonator) (Banyumas)

lengkap "complete" (Ind.); gamelan *lengkap*, see gamelan *gedhé*

let "skip"; *let loro* = an interval separated by two keys

lima name of a tone (5); one of three standard *pélog pathet* (central Java)

lincah happy, lively (Ind.)

lirihan (from *lirih*, "soft") *gendhing* performed with soft instrumentation and singing

lomba contest (Ind.)

ludruk/ludrug a genre of comic folk theater, with all-male cast

lugu ordinary, unadorned

luwung a *gendhing* formal structure, with four eight-beat *kenongan* per *gong* (east Java)

macapat a category of *tembang*, each with characteristic melodies, number of syllables per line, and final vowel for each line

maju advanced, progressive (Ind. and low Jvn.)

Mana Suka listener's choice radio program

mandheg "to stop"; to stop for *andhegan*; a type of *ciblon* pattern *manyura* one of three standard *sléndro pathet* (central Java); a *pathet* category within *pélog bem* (= *nyamat*, *nyamat mas*)

mares march; see *gati*

mataraman/mentaraman relating to the central Javanese kingdom of Mataram; term for full seven-tone *pélog* gamelan (east Java)

mbalung to sound the tones of the *balungan*

mbandhèk standard Javanese pronunciation (characterized by "aw" vowel sound), found in most of Java east of Banyumas

mbok-mbokan first major section in large *gendhing* (east Java)

minggah see *inggah*; middle section, followed by *dhawah*, in a few rare large *gendhing* (Yogya); to continue from a large *gendhing* to a small one, usually in *ketawang* or *ladrang* form

minir "minor" (from Dutch *mineur*), see *miring*

mipil "to pick off one by one"; type of *bonang* playing (= *pipilan*); type of dance movement and accompanying drumming pattern

miring a *pélog pathet* category comparable to central Javanese *pathet barang* (east Java); (= *minir*, *barang miring*, *sléndro miring*) vocal scale deviating from fixed-pitch *sléndro* instrumental scale (central and east Java)

mlaku (= *mlampah*, high Jvn.) "to walk," "to move"; a type of *bonang* playing (Yogyanese equivalent of *mipil*); *balungan* with four tones per *gatra* (e.g., 3532); a type of *ciblon* pattern

mondrèng small gamelan ensemble, emphasizing loud-playing instruments, but bossed metal-keyed instruments replacing knobbed gong (Banyumas), cf. *ringgeng*

monggang an archaic gamelan ensemble; (see also *ponggang*)

muyèn singing of *macapat* (Banyumas)

nacah lamba "single chopping"; type of *peking* playing

nacah rangkep "double chopping"; type of *peking* playing

ndhugal joking, mischievous

ndoro-ndoro a piece sung at *tayuban* by the *tandhak*, prior to a dance set (east Java)

nduduk a *bonang* technique, reiterating one tone in groups of three (Solo)

nduduk gembyang performance of *nduduk* with some octave duplication

nduduk tunggal performance of *nduduk* only in low register (Solo)

nem name of a tone (6); one of three standard *sléndro pathet* (central Java); one of three standard *pélog pathet* (central Java)

ngaji recitation of the Koran

ngapak in contrast to *mbandhèk*, pronunciation characterized by "a" or "ak," rather than "aw", found in Banyumas and West Java

ngapak-mbandhèk line, boundary between regions in which *ngapak* pronunciation is prominent and those in which *mbandhèk* pronunciation is prominent

ngaplak "slap"; a drum pattern, characterized by triplet playing (Solo)

ngelik "to become small"; section of a *gendhing*, often characterized by singing and playing in the higher register

ngencot see *cecegan*

nggembyang to play in octaves, especially on *bonang*

nglagu a type of interlocking on *calung* (Banyumas)

ngoko low Javanese

ngracik style of *balungan* with eight tones per *gatra*; in east Java, a technique of *bonang* playing, comparable to Yogyanese *mlaku*

ngrémo popular dance associated with *ludruk* and now performed for opening of many genres of east Javanese performing arts

nibani "to fall on, intentionally"; *balungan* with only two tones per *gatra* (on second and fourth beats; e.g., .3.2); see *pancer nibani*

nintili a technique of *saron peking* playing, anticipating each *balungan* tone in an even, continuous rhythm (east Java)

nyamat (= *nyamat mas*) see *manyura* (*pélog*)

nyamber "swoop"; brisk dance movement executed on tiptoes, often to symbolize flying (Yogya); the triplet drumming pattern that accompanies this movement (Yogya)

nyegat see *gembyangan nyegat*

omprok helmet-like head-dress worn by *gandrung* singer-dancer (Banyuwangi)

padésan "of the village"; *sulukan padésan* = *sulukan* in a style found in the villages (and not the courts)

pakeliran padat short performances of *wayang kulit*, a genre developed at STSI/ASKI

palaran vocal pieces accompanied by the gamelan instruments, but with *bonang* and *balungan* instruments silent (Solo)

pamijèn special, exceptional

pancer recurrent sounding of a single tone on weak beats

pancer nibani a *bonang* technique characterized by sounding a *pancer* between *saron* beats and joining with the *saron* on strong *balungan* beats (east Java)

pancer rangkep the use of double pancer (e.g., 3.32 3.35) in *saron* part (east Java)

panceran the use of *pancer*

panembung low register member of instrument family (*bonang*, *gendèr*); see also *ponggang*

panggul stick beater, used for playing *kendhang* for some pieces in Semarang and east Java traditions

pangkat ndhawah transition to the *dhawah* section (Yogya)

parikan a genre of Javanese poetry in rhyming couplets

pasisir (= *pesisir*) coastal area, north coast of Java

pathet Javanese modal classification

patut "fit," "appropriate"; indication of type of drumming (Yogya)

péci small hat or cap, usually of black velvet, worn by many Indonesian men

pedhotan "broken off," "interrupted"; in the performance of a *gendhing*, a pause during which solo vocalist sings unaccompanied by gamelan (Banyumas)

pejah (= *mati*, low Jvn.) "dead"; a type of *imbal* playing for *saron demung*

peking see *saron panerus*

pélog one of two Javanese tuning systems/scales, with seven uneven intervals per octave, usually only five or six tones used in a single piece

pembangunan development (Ind.)

pèndèt a Balinese welcoming dance, performed by female dancers

pendhapa pavilion, open on three sides

pengarep "the one in front"; *gambang pengarep* = *gambang barung* (Banyumas)

pengasih east Javanese synonym for *bem* scale

penggedhé "the large one"; *gambang penggedhé* = *gambang barung* (Banyumas)

penodhos "the one that drills"; *gambang penodhos* = *gambang barung* (Banyumas)

penthung see *jengglong*

penunggul first scale degree in *pélog* (central Java)

perlombaan contest, competition (Ind.)

pesindhèn female singer

pinggir-rekso line, boundary between central and east Javanese cultural areas

pinjalan alternate term for *imbal* on *bonang* (Yogya)

pipilan see *mipil*

pitutur didactic, moralistic

ponggang (= *monggang*, *panembung*) low-pitched set of kettle gongs (east Java)

prasaja plain, straightforward, simple

prenès light, suggestive, flirtatious

pringgitan (= *pewayangan*) term for gamelan smaller than *gamelan gedhé*, used to accompany *wayang kulit* (Solo)

prunggu bronze (Ind.)

punakawan clown-servants in *wayang*

purwa see *wayang kulit purwa*

putut gelut name of a frequently used *céngkok*

raksasa giant, ogre

rakyat the people, the masses

rambangan vocal pieces accompanied by the gamelan instruments, but with *bonang* and *balungan* instruments silent (Yogya)

ramé busy, noisy (in good sense)

rangkep double; see *irama rangkep, nacah rangkep, pancer rangkep*

rawit intricate

rebab spike fiddle

reyog general category of village processional performance

reyog kendhang a genre of *reyog* in which participants play drums or small gongs (east Java)

reyog Ponorogo a genre of *reyog* characterized by elaborate masks, including a mythical lion, associated with the town of Ponorogo

reyong Balinese single-row gong chime

ricik alternate term for *barung* in reference to *saron*

rinengga "decorated," "embellished"; a traditional *gendhing* with newly added vocal melodies and texts

ringgeng small gamelan ensemble, emphasizing loud-playing instruments, but flat metal-keyed instruments replacing knobbed gong (Banyumas), cf. *mondrèng*

rojèh large, flat cymbal used in archaic gamelan

ronggèng singer-dancer (female or impersonator)

RRI Radio Republik Indonesia, national radio station

sabrangan "from overseas," "foreign"; a type of *kendhang* pattern in *ladrang* form (Yogya)

sampak a genre of *gendhing* used primarily for dramatic accompaniment (central Java)

sanga "nine"; one of three standard *sléndro pathet* (central Java); one of four standard *sléndro pathet* (east Java); third scale degree (east Java); one of three *pathet* categories within *pélog bem* scale (Malang); one of three *pathet* categories within *pélog barang* scale (Malang); see *saron sanga*

santri someone who embraces Islam to the exclusion of other religious belief systems

saron single-octave metallophone, with 6–9 keys resting over a trough resonator

saron barung (= *saron ricik*) middle-register *saron*

saron demung low-register *saron*

saron panerus (= *peking*) high-register *saron*

saron sanga nine-keyed *saron*, associated with *wayang kulit* (Solo)

sedeng middle, average

sedih sad (Ind.)

sekar see *tembang*

sekaran see *kembangan*

sekati Islamic holy week in Java; gamelan *sekati* = large archaic gamelan ensemble sounded throughout this week

sèlèh "settle"; point of repose, usually end of a *gatra*

selomprèt double-reed aerophone (Banyumas, east Java)

senggakan a kind of interpolated vocal phrase, often humorous

sepuluh "ten"; in former times, possibly a *pathet* category in Semarang; one of four standard *sléndro pathet* (east Java); one of three *pathet* categories within *pélog bem* scale (Malang); one of three *pathet* categories within *pélog barang* scale (Malang)

serang one of four standard *sléndro pathet*, associated with last portion of all-night *wayang kulit* (east Java), cf. *galong*; one of three *pathet* categories within *pélog barang* scale (Malang)

seseg fast, squeezed together

sigegan east Javanese equivalent of *sirep*

sindhènan the vocal part sung by the *pesindhèn*

sirep a soft interlude, usually signalled in performance by drummer or puppeteer (central Java) *siter* small zither, with 10–26 strings

siteran small ensemble featuring one or more *siter*

siyem see *gong suwukan*

slawatan songs in Arabic accompanied by tambourines and frame drums, like *jani-janèn*, but with less overt Islamic content (Banyumas); songs in Arabic, Javanese, or combination, accompanied by tambourines and frame drums, associated with Islam (central and East Java)

sléndro one of two Javanese tuning systems/scales, with five nearly equidistant intervals per octave

sléndro miring see *diatonis, miring*

slenthem see *gendèr panembung*

slentho a single-octave metallophone with knobbed keys, tuned an octave lower than *demung*

slomprèt see *selomprèt*

SMKI Sekolah Menengah Karawitan Indonesia: performing arts high school conservatories (Solo, Yogya, Surabaya, Banyumas – also Den Pasar, Bali; Padang Panjang, West Sumatra; Ujung Pandang, South Sulawesi)

soran performed in loud-playing style (Yogya)

sorog pélog bem scale (east Java); first degree of scale (east Java); a *pathet* category (east Java)

srepeg/srempeg a formal structure/genre of *gendhing* for east Javanese *wayang* accompaniment

srepegan a formal structure/genre of *gendhing* for central Javanese *wayang* accompaniment

srimpi female style court dance, usually performed by four dancers (Yogya, Solo)

sronèn (= *srunèn*) ensemble featuring double-reed aerophone (Madura and Madurese East Java)

sroni (= *sruni*) double-reed aerophone (Madura and Madurese East Java)

sruti interval (derived from Indian usage)

STKW Sekolah Tinggi Kesenian Wilwatikta, performing arts college (Surabaya)

STSI Sekolah Tinggi Seni Indonesia, performing arts college (Surakarta and Den Pasar, Bali)

suling end-blown bamboo flute

sulukan mood songs of shadow puppetry and related genre, sung by *dhalang*

sunan title for king of Surakarta

surjan jacket, part of men's formal dress (Yogya)

suwuk ending of performance of a *gendhing*

suwukan see *gong suwukan*

talèdhèk female singer-dancer (Yogya, Solo)

tamban slow

tandhak female singer-dancer (east Java)

tari dance (Ind.)

tayuban ritual celebrations in which men drink liquor and dance with singer-dancers

tembang (= *sekar*, high Jvn.) sung poetry

tengah (see *gulu*)

tenggok (see *gulu*)

terbang frame drums used for *slawatan* and related genres

terompèt double-reed aerophone (Semarang, Sunda, and [?] east Java)

tetegan (= *timbangan*) a technique of *saron peking* playing that interlocks with *bonang panerus* part

tètèt double-reed aerophone (Banyuwangi, East Java)

timbangan (see *tetegan*)

timur east (Ind.)

titilaras musical notation

titipati a *gendhing* formal structure, with two sections, each with four eight-beat *kenongan* per gong (east Java)

topèng mask; masked dance-drama

topèng dhalang masked dance-drama with narrator
tradisional traditional (Ind.)
trisig brisk dance movement executed on tiptoes, often to symbolize flying (Solo)
tugu monument
tumbuk common tone, shared between *sléndro* and *pélog* (often tone 6, but may vary from one
    gamelan set to another)
tuntunan manual, guide
umpak minggah transition to the *inggah* section (Solo)
umyung clangorous, slightly out of tune (intentionally) (Yogya)
uran-uran regionally neutral synonym for *palaran* (Solo), *rambangan* (Yogya)
uyon-uyon gamelan music performed without dance or dance-drama (Yogya)
wangsalan a genre of Javanese poetry, consisting of 12-syllable lines in couplets, in which
    words in the first line suggest, by sound or meaning, words in the second line
waranggana "angel," "nymph"; term for female singer (= *pesindhèn*)
wayang general term for a variety of theatrical genres; abbreviated term for *wayang kulit*
wayang gedhog a form of shadow puppetry presenting stories of Javanese legendary hero Panji
wayang golèk a form of puppetry using three-dimensional wooden dolls, most popular in
    Sunda
wayang jengglong a form of shadow puppetry (Semarang and Pekalongan)
wayang krucil/klithik a form of puppetry using flat, wooden puppets and presenting stories of
    Javanese hero Damar Wulan (central and east Java)
wayang kulit shadow puppetry using leather puppets
wayang kulit purwa shadow puppetry presenting stories based on the Indic epics *Ramayana*
    and *Mahabharata*
wayang orang Ind. for *wayang wong*
wayang topèng masked dance-drama
wayang wong dance-drama with spoken dialogue, gamelan accompaniment, presenting
    stories of *wayang kulit purwa* repertory
wayang wong panggung commercial *wayang wong*, performed on stage (associated with Solo)
wela "rest" in *kempul* part
wesi iron
wétan east
wolu "eight"; one of four standard *sléndro pathet* (east Java); one of three *pathet* categories
    within *pélog bem* scale (Malang area)

Notes

Throughout the present study, in order to distinguish provincial units from cultural and geographic regions, I use upper case for the former and lower case for the latter (e.g., Central Java *vs.* central Java).

1 Introduction: gamelan and cultural diversity in Java

1 Lindsay has written compellingly of some of the issues faced by performing artists, with particular attention to the court and court-derived style of Yogyakarta (1985). As she demonstrates, Western concepts, such as "classical" and "folk," introduced during Dutch colonial times, have become central to Javanese categorization.

2 This may well be in response to the decision by members of the national government, who decreed in 1977 that all public conservatories of traditional music and performing arts would be called "High Schools" (Sekolah Menengah) or "Academies" (Akademi) of "Indonesian Karawitan." Hence the Sekolah Menengah Karawitan Indonesia and Akademi Seni Karawitan Indonesia in Padang Panjang, West Sumatra, and the Sekolah Menengah Karawitan Indonesia in Ujung Pandang, South Sulawesi.

3 Florida's catalogue of manuscripts in the libraries of Surakarta (Florida n.d.) serves as an invaluable guide to the extensive holdings there (and now in microfilm copy at Cornell University, the Arsip Nasional in Jakarta, as well as the libraries where the manuscripts were filmed), complementing Pigeaud's exhaustive study of Javanese literature collections in the Netherlands (Pigeaud 1967–70). Microfilms have recently been made of the manuscripts held at the Yogyakarta library (available at the Sonobudoyo Museum in Yogyakarta, the Arsip Nasional in Jakarta, Australian National University, University of Sydney, and the Center for Research Libraries in Chicago) and of the manuscripts held at the Sonobudoyo Museum (available at the Museum, the Arsip Nasional and Perpustakaan Nasional in Jakarta, Australian National University, and the Center for Research Libraries in Chicago) (Behrend 1989:15–19). See also Lindsay's work (1984) on the holdings of the Yogyakarta palace library, and her dissertation (1985), with *gendhing* lists from several early sources.

4 In the early twentieth century much of this version was published in romanized form, based on a copy held in the Netherlands in Leiden: Soeradipura *et al.*, 1912–15. The complete *Serat Centhini* is currently being published by the Yayasan Centhini Yogyakarta; as of July 1989, seven of the planned twelve volumes were in print.

5 On the known history of this work, see Lindsay 1984. Much of the commentary, less the notation, is accessible as part of the Sonobudoyo Museum Library collection, in a romanization by Pigeaud dated 1934.

6 The latter, comprising an entire issue of *Djawa*, the journal of Het Java-Instituut, is a lengthy study (290 pages) and is currently being translated into English for publication by Linda Burman-Hall.

7 Outside Indonesia, Javanese music is taught at institutions in the United States, Holland, England, Germany, France, Australia, Japan, and the Philippines. We find a burgeoning collection of master's theses, dissertations, and other student work at the universities which offer formal instruction in gamelan performance and graduate programs in ethnomusicology: notably, at the Universities of California (UCLA and Berkeley), Hawaii, Michigan, Wisconsin, and Wesleyan University in the USA; Universities of Amsterdam and Leiden in Holland; Universities of York, Durham, Oxford, Cambridge, and London (SOAS) in Great Britain; Monash in Australia; Tokyo University in Japan; and the University of the Philippines in Manila.

2 Rival traditions in the courtly centers: gamelan music of Surakarta and Yogyakarta

1 For a more comprehensive coverage of the history of this era, see Ricklefs 1974: *passim* and Ricklefs 1981:91ff.

253

2 Historical records provide a partial picture of important developments within these traditions, but it is not my intention here to focus on history. Tracing the course of historic development for any of the arts within either of the two courts is a difficult task. Not that such a line of inquiry would not be valuable, but, as Lindsay suggests in the preface to her insightful and carefully researched dissertation, it would be an "immense subject, and immensely difficult" (1985:v). Lindsay had formerly wished to devote her dissertation to "the emergence of Yogyakarta gamelan as a style distinctive from that of Surakarta," but found the subject too vast (1985:v). Still, Lindsay makes some important and well substantiated observations on musical development prior to the twentieth century.

3 The account of the story given by Peter Carey (1986:19) is based on what G. Resink heard in Yogyakarta during the 1930s and corresponds with versions I encountered in the 1970s. On the understanding of the term "Mataram" to refer either to an older, united central Java, or to Yogyakarta, see Sutton 1984:223–27, and Clara van Groenendael 1985:66–72.

4 These terms are Carey's translation of the commentary written by Willem van Hogendorp in 1827 and published in H. van Hogendorp 1913:141, as cited in Carey 1986:21–22.

5 It would be a lengthy and difficult task to sort out the various interlocking threads of court and village origin. We have clear evidence for the introduction into the Yogyanese court of village (or at least "non-court") pieces (many identified as *gending talèdhèkan*, i.e., pieces for the singer-dancer known as *talèdhèk*) and the related middle-sized drum (*batangan*) and drumming style. It is generally believed that the style of interlocking between the two gong-chime instruments (*bonang*) known as *pinjalan* or *imbal*, which has been practiced in both courts at least since the late nineteenth century, also derived from village practice.

6 The manuscript entitled *Pakem Wirama: Wileting Gendhing Berdangga*, compiled by Kertanegara and usually referred to as the *Pakem Wirama*, contains a section entitled "Pratelan Kawontenanipun Kagungan Dalem Gangsa ing Karaton Ngayogyakarta Hadiningrat" ("List of the King's Gamelan in the Palace of Yogyakarta"). A romanization by Pustakamardawa of one copy of this manuscript lists the instrumentation for fourteen large gamelan of the Yogya court, including the crown prince's residence (*kadipatèn*) and the prime minister's residence (*kepatihan*). The title page of the *Pakem Wirama*, in the several versions I have examined, lists 1889 as the date the writing of the manuscript was initiated. Accretions seem to have been made through the first three or four decades of the twentieth century. The manuscript specifies which instruments were added to existing gamelan under the reign of Hamengku Buwana VIII (1921–39). An inventory of the Solonese kraton gamelan can be found in the manuscript entitled *Sadaya Kagungan Dalem Gongsa* ("All the King's Gamelan"), compiled by R. T. Harungbinang, with an introduction by Sasradipura dated 1900, housed at the Radya Pustaka Library in Surakarta. Hereafter the Yogyanese manuscript is referred to as the *Pakem Wirama* (Kertanegara [1889?]) and the Solonese manuscript as Harungbinang [1900?].

7 The Solonese *kenong* set consisted of tones 5, 6, and high ı̇. The *kempul* set was the same, sometimes excluding the high ı̇. The Yogyanese male *kenong* were tuned to pitch 5 and pitch 6, with the *kenong japan* tuned to pitch 5 in the lower octave and generally considered to be more ancient that the male *kenong*. *Kempul* was tuned to pitch 6. The historical information presented here is based on oral tradition in both cities and is corroborated in Solonese and Yogyanese lists of gamelan instruments: Harungbinang [1900?] and Kertanegara [1889?].

8 *Sléndro* and *pélog* ensembles, even though they may be housed together and played by the same players in a single performance, have separate names and are listed separately in the inventory of gamelan in the possession of the ruler (*sunan*) of the Surakarta *kraton* (Harungbinang [1900?]). Six of the sixteen large gamelan listed include two *demung* and four *saron barung* (*Kyai Kancil Belik*, *Kyahi Guntur Madu*, *Kyahi Udan Arum*, *Kyahi Kutha Windu*, *Kyai Windu Sana*, *Kyahi Semar Ngigel*). In addition, *Kyahi Udan Asih* includes two *demung* and three *saron barung*, and *Kyahi Lokananta* two *demung* and two *saron barung*. The other seven have only one *demung* and two *saron barung*, though it is noted that one *saron barung* was removed from *Kyahi Pengasih* and one *demung* from *Kyahi Rarasati*. The smaller ensembles identified as *klenèngan* (for soft-playing pieces) and *pringgitan* (for *wayang kulut* accompaniment) include only one or two *saron* and no *demung*.

9 Of the sixteen large Solonese court gamelan whose instruments are listed in Harungbinang [1900?], eight have two *saron panerus* and eight have only one. Those with two *saron panerus* are *Kyahi Kancil Belik*, *Kyahi Guntur Madu*, *Kyahi Udan Arum*, *Kyahi Udan Asih*, *Kyahi Kutha Windu*, *Kyahi Windu Sana*, *Kyahi Semar Ngigel*, and *Kyahi Lokananta*. *Kyahi Rarasati* formerly had two, but the manuscript shows one to have been removed. The gamelan *klenèngan* and *pringgitan* listed have no *saron panerus*.

10 The gamelan inventory in the *Pakem Wirama* indicates that five of the fourteen large Yogyanese ensembles include four *demung* and eight *saron barung*. The others have two *demung* and four *saron*, except *Kyahi Puspanadi*, with only two of each. It is noteworthy that no Yogyanese court gamelan has more than one *peking*, and seven of them have no *peking* at all.

11 The individual forms have been discussed in much of the literature and will only be briefly reviewed here. See further Becker 1980:105–47; Sutton 1982:305–12.

12 These pieces may be shaped and edited in response to dramatic requirements in the Solonese dance-drama genre *wayang wong panggung* and the dances excerpted from this genre. See further Susilo 1984.

13 The vast majority of these have been composed by Ki Nartosabdho, who was born in a small town between Yogya and Solo, and lived in Semarang from the late 1940s until his death in 1985. His pieces have incorporated influences from a number of regions (see chapter 8), but his basic musical style is Solonese. His *lagu dolanan* have become widespread, with only a broad regional association (as "central Javanese").

14 Lindsay counts 157 (1985:313–40). If we consider *Pujangga Anom sléndro nem* and *Pujangga Anom sléndro manyura* to be separate pieces, then my count would be 154. However, I am basing my count of 153 on *gendhing* titles. Although Javanese music was not notated until the latter part of the nineteenth century, one can assume that the formal structures associated with the pieces listed are mostly the same today.

15 This manuscript is part of the Yogyakarta court's Krida Mardawa collection of manuscripts. See Lindsay 1985:207 for an explanation of the dating and Lindsay 1985:341–47 for an alphabetical list of these *gendhing*.

16 From 112 to 119 (73 percent to 78 percent). The precise count depends upon how cautious one chooses to be in comparing. For example, *Barang Éndhol-éndhol* appears in HBV and *Éndhol-éndhol* appears in the *Serat Centhini*; *Gliyung* in HBV and *Glayung* in the *Serat Centhini*.

17 The piece *Sarebegan* (= *Srepegan*?) is explicitly listed as a *ketawang*, and thus is clearly not a *gendhing lampah*. It also appears as a *ketawang* in Mloyowidodo 1976(II):182.

18 Of these twenty-five, three (*Ayamsepenang*, *Kodhok Ngorèk*, and *Monggang*) are known to be performed not on gamelan *sekati* but on the archaic gamelan ensembles *Kodhok Ngorèk* (*Ayamsepenang* and *Kodhok Ngorèk*) and *Monggang*.

19 On differences between Yogyanese and Solonese versions of Gendhing *Krawitan*, see Lindsay 1985:255–66.

20 Full score transcriptions of excerpts from *gendhing*, showing all parts in Western staff notation, are given in Hood and Susilo 1967:19 (reproduced in Apel 1969:438–39) and Malm 1977:39–42.

21 Greater length is not always an indication that a piece is Yogyanese. The Solonese *mérong* for Gendhing *Titipati*, *sléndro pathet nem*, consists of four repeatable *gongan*, the Yogyanese *mérong* only two. See Sutton 1982:119, note 9.

22 The *Pakem Wirama* describes this kind of playing not for the *slenthem*, but for the now obsolete instrument known as the *slentho*, a single-octave metallophone like a *demung*, but whose keys are knobbed and tune an octave lower. The *slenthem* was simply to sound two tones per *gatra*, like the *bonang panembung*, for example, .3 .2.

23 To avoid dipping into the lower register for a passage that is middle and high – for example, i 6 5 3 in *pélog* – some Solonese musicians will play the disjunct 16165353. Yogyanese would play 16165353, or some variant thereof.

24 One teacher likened the *suling* to a bird in the distance. If it sings, it will not bother any conversation and may enhance the general mood, but if it is quiet, it will not be missed.

25 The first Solonese notation I have discovered dates from 1925, in *Buku Piwulang Nabuh Gamelan*

(Komisi Pasinaon Nabuh Gamelan 1925). Yogyanese have yet to publish notation for *batangan*, as far as I am aware.

26 For a detailed account of the state of musical life in the Yogyanese *kraton* in the early 1980s, see Vetter 1986.

3 A flourishing tradition in west central Java: gamelan music of Banyumas

1 "Banyumas" is the name given to the entire ex-residency, one of the four *kabupaten* within that ex-residency, and a small town within the *kabupaten*. Unless specified otherwise, I will use the term to refer to the entire ex-residency.

2 On the quilt-like division of central Java between the Solonese Sunan Paku Buwana III and the Yogyanese Sultan Hamengku Buwana, see Pringgodigdo 1950, especially the map in Bijlage V. On more recent administrative divisions in Java, see Gooszen 1985.

3 In Banyumas today, these *wayang* pieces are often interspersed with Solonese versions, at least of *Srepegan*. But while the Solonese versions are recognized by most Banyumas musicians as "Solonese," the others are identified as the "Banyumas" versions. It is interesting that these pieces are some of the few that are widely played throughout the Yogya region and not just within court circles. The many larger pieces that form the Yogyanese court repertory do not seem to have been played in Banyumas.

4 See Sekretariat Nasional 1983:161. I have heard this sequence used several times in the Yogyakarta area. It was standard there until about 1950, according to B. Y. H. Pustakamardawa (formerly Sastrapustaka).

5 In the previous chapter several differences were pointed out between Solonese and Yogyanese ensembles, but the two were shown to be very similar.

6 I heard these at several *calung* performances. An unpublished report by a team from ASKI Surakarta on *calung* and *angklung* music in Banyumas, also reports the playing of these and thirteen other *gendhing* from the court traditions (Supanggah *et al.* [1981]:41).

7 Supanggah *et al.* list twelve *calung* pieces deriving from Indonesian popular songs, including *dangdut* ([1981]:41). Many others have entered the *calung* repertory since 1981. On the *dangdut* genre, see Frederick 1982.

8 Though Rasito does not compose in *pélog pathet lima* or *sléndro pathet nem*, some of S. Bono's pieces are classified as *pélog pathet lima*, for example, *Mangga Mampir*, *Rembang Ngumandang*.

9 *Èbèg* music is undergoing an accommodation to changing musical tastes in the region. See Sutton 1986a: 123–24.

10 Detailed notation of Solonese *ciblon* drumming is available in two published sources: Martopangrawit 1972b:149–62 and Sumarsam 1987:171–203. The standard paradigm for *ladrang* is given also in Sutton 1982:325. Yogyanese practice is said to derive from Solonese and follows it very closely (although some of the terminology differs). Banyumas drumming is notated in the senior papers of students at SMKI Banyumas and in Departemen PDK 1980.

11 The alternation of male and female can be built into many Banyumas pieces, in which the male voices sing a complete *parikan* between phrases by the solo *pesindhèn*.

12 This is one reason why there is a lack of consensus on the application of Solonese *irama* terminology to Banyumas performance style. See Sutton 1986b for an account of the recent adoption of Solonese musical theoretical terms, including the STSI/ASKI *irama* levels (*lancar*, *tanggung*, *dadi*, and *wilet*) in Banyumas.

13 And even in one *èbèg* performance I witnessed in 1984, the musicians played the standard Solonese and Yogyanese Lancaran *Béndrong*, rather than either of the Banyumas pieces with similar names (*Béndrong Kulon* or *Béndrong Jawa*).

4 Partial survival of a tradition in north central Java: gamelan music of Semarang

1 I visited both towns in 1983 and interviewed local representatives of the Department of Education and Culture, met several puppeteers and gamelan directors, and attended several rehearsals.

2 I know of no gamelan makers in the Semarang area, but it is likely that some instruments, at least of brass or iron, are manufactured locally. The musicians I spoke to indicated that bronze ensembles in

Semarang have mostly been brought in from Surakarta. On the manufacture of *gongs* in Semarang, see Jacobson and van Hasselt 1907. An English translation by Andrew Toth can be found in volume 19 of *Indonesia*.

3 It is not clear whether his *pélog* included the heptatonic singing that is now called *diatonis* or, sometimes, *sléndro miring*. Hardjo apparently differentiates these latter two only as contrasting approaches to notation. See Hardjo 1982: 4–5; 12–13; 22–23.

4 This opinion was expressed by the Semarang-born musician A. Salim, by the Solonese-born director of the RRI studio gamelan musicians in Semarang, Ponidi, and by the Yogyanese-born director of the RRI studio gamelan musicians in Yogyakarta, Suhardi. The opinions of Salim and Ponidi are documented in Hardjo (1982:5). Suhardi probably arrived at his opinion independently, having only seen the Hardjo document in 1986, years after he had expressed his opinion to me (1980). However, Ponidi told me in 1986 that he felt that the piece *Dhendhang Semarangan* might be derived from the Western-influenced *kroncong* genre; see the discussion of repertory below.

5 See McNamara 1980 and Mloyowidodo 1976. Gendhing *Okrak-okrak* is generally played as a *gendhing-bonang*, although it is not listed explicitly as such in either source.

6 The young Solonese musician and *wayang* puppeteer Sri Djoko Raharjo felt strongly that this piece derived from east Java. While I did not find this piece performed by east Javanese, I found other pieces in east Java that combined *sléndro* instruments with essentially Western *diatonis* singing (some renditions of *Jamong* and *Srampat*, among others).

7 No *gendhing* has been composed based on the other "*diatonis*" *macapat*, *Dhandhanggula*, but the melody is sometimes heard as a solo interlude in gamelan performance. On the commercial tape *Rujak Sentul* (Lokananta ACD-058), a solo *pesindhèn* sings *Dhandhanggula Semarangan*, accompanied by occasional tones played on the *sléndro gendèr*, leading into the related *Dhendhang Semarangan*. Both as performed and as noted in Hardjo (1982:21–22), the first four tones are *sléndro* (2 5 6 6), followed by *diatonis* or *sléndro miring*. (The listing on the cassette cover of a *Dhandhanggula Banyumasan* preceding the *Dhandhanggula Semarangan* is erroneous.)

8 *Gagah-Sétra* (= *Gagak-sétra*) is known in Solo, Yogya, and is especially popular in the Malang area of East Java. *Génjong* is known in both Solonese and Yogyanese repertories. *Gunungsari* is the title of one of the favorite pieces in the Banyumas repertory, though almost always performed in *sléndro* there. Pieces with the titles *Génjong*, *Clunthang*, *Sumyar* and *Wani-wani* are well-known in Yogya and Solo. I know of no other reference to a *gendhing* entitled *Jemparing*.

9 I found no special Semarang terms for *irama* level. Musicians with whom I spoke used Solonese terminology (*dadi*, *wilet*, and so on) and apparently with the same meanings as in Solonese tradition. It should be remembered, however, that a definition of *irama* level by ratio of *peking* strokes to *balungan* beats, as one finds in some Solonese definitions (Martopangrawit 1969) would not translate to Semarang, where the *peking* maintains a constant ratio of 2:1 with the *balangan* beat regardless of the tempo.

10 In one of those inevitable near-misses of field work, I arrived in Semarang a day after this *wayang* – unaware that it had been scheduled – and learned that no recording had been made, despite the fact that, by all odds, this would be the last performance of *wayang* in Semarang style.

11 Also recorded on commercial cassette by RRI Semarang musicians is the musical comedy-drama *Bancak Doyok*, which begins with a discussion by the actors in which Surakarta is named as their cultural center. The songs make use of standard Solonese texts, such as the *Wédhatama* (attributed to Prince Mangkunegara IV). All this suggests a sense of regional identity as mainstream "central Javanese," without a marked Semarang regional component.

5 A major East Javanese tradition: gamelan music of Surabaya-Mojokerto-Malang

1 Much has been written on music and performing arts in Banyuwangi and on the Osing Javanese. See especially Brandts Buys and Brandts Buys-van Zijp 1926; Scholte 1927; Pigeaud 1932 and 1938; Crawford 1980; Soelarto and Ilmi n.d.; Soepardi 1986; Wolbers 1986, 1987, and 1989.

2 Justisi Laras can be heard on the commercial cassettes issued by Lokananta: ACD-085, ACD-086, ACD-093, ACD-094, ACD-095, ACD-102, ACD-103, and ACD-104. Various groups from Trenggalek, Tulungagung, and Blitar are recorded by Fajar and Ira-Record.

3 Though repertory and performance style generally go hand in hand in Java, borrowed repertory (from Banyuwangi, central Java, etc.) is often reinterpreted in east Java with drumming and other instrumental practices typical of east Javanese style.

4 Small courts have existed in Bangkalan, Pamekasan, and Sumenep. However, the Dutch placed severe limits on the local rulers in Madura and by 1887 had reduced their status to that of the Javanese bupati: "they were merely aristocratic regency heads, under direct Dutch rule." (Ricklefs 1981:126)

5 The best known descriptions are in the *Serat Centhini*. See the romanized publication R. Ng. Soeradipura *et al.*, eds, 1912–15: (vol. 7) 3–30. The same passage is quoted in full in Suharto 1980:82–111.

6 See J. Becker's forthcoming work on Tantrism and Javanese performing arts, in which she argues that they never did.

7 *Topèng* groups currently exist in Jabung and Glagah Dowo (near Tumpang, east of Malang city), and Kedhung Monggo (near Pakisaji, south of Malang city).

8 One does find some central Javanese influence in aspects of both dance choreography and musical accompaniment at the SMKI conservatory in Surabaya, however. See Matsyachir [1977]:23–30.

9 On *ludruk* in historical context, see Pigeaud 1938 and Wongsosewojo 1930. On *ludruk* since Indonesian independence, see the studies by Hatley (1971) and Peacock (1968).

10 This is the list given by Wongsosewojo 1930:204. Writing in Dutch, he lists the aerophone as *trompet* (= trumpet in English). However, the term is sometimes used in Indonesia – primarily in Sunda – to refer to a double-reed aerophone, and it is likely that this is what is intended here. In East Java today, double-reed aerophones are sometimes called *slomprèt, sroni/sruni* or *tètèt* and the ensemble music incorporating this instrument is called *sronèn/srunèn*.

11 As will be seen below, the meaning of *Jula-juli* is somewhat ambiguous, referring not only to a specific piece, but also to a genre, a formal structure, and a style of singing and instrumentation. Pigeaud reports this (*jola-juli*) as the name of one of the pieces played to accompany hobby-horse dancing in Sidoarjo, south of Surabaya (1938:241).

12 In August 1986 I attended a wedding celebration in Trowulan, near Mojokerto, and heard the group of the well-known *dhalang* Ki Piet Asmoro perform concert pieces during most of the afternoon and early evening and continue to perform for a full *wayang kulit* performance until dawn.

13 In central Java, one finds a similar instrument called *slentho* in some older ensembles. And the instrument now known in central Java simply as *slenthem* was often called *slenthem gantung* (literally, "suspended *slenthem*") in the past.

14 Kunst records some variations in terminology in several areas of East Java, as well as other Javanese and Madurese gamelan traditions. For *sléndro* in Mojokerto (and Banyuwangi), he lists *sorog* ("substitute key") as the term for the tone known elsewhere as *barang* ("thing" – tone 1), *tengah* ("middle") or *tenggok* ("upper neck") for *gulu* ("neck" – tone 2) and *sanga* (literally, "nine") for *dhadha* ("chest" – tone 3). For *pélog* in Mojokerto, again he lists *tengah* and *tenggok* as the terms for *gulu* (tone 2), *sanga* for *dhadha* (tone 3), and *sorog* as the term for central Javanese *bem* or *penunggul* (tone 1). In Probolinggo, the term *pengasih* ("lover") was used as well as *sorog* for tone 1. Otherwise the terms correspond with the standard central Javanese set (*barang, gulu, dhadha, lima,* and *nem* in *sléndro; bem* or *penunggul, gulu, dhadha, pélog, lima, nem,* and *barang* in *pélog*). See further Kunst 1973 I:102.

15 In Banyumas, for example, *Dhawet Ayu, Malangan, Kunang-kunang Mabur, Dhobèr, Jaksan,* and *Senggot* all exhibit these characteristics.

16 Nevertheless, in the Surabaya and Mojokerto areas, for these moments of greatest tension and battle, musicians play a special piece known as *Gemblak* or *Krucilan Gemblak*, with dense *kempul* playing and a different *balungan* than the usual *Krucilan*. Soenarto R.P. referred to it simply as *Gemblak* when it was played during a *wayang* performance near Mojokerto we both attended; on the commercial cassette *Toakan* (IR-070) it is listed as *Krucilan Gemblak, sléndro pathet serang*. This is not to be confused with the piece in Ronoatmodjo 1981a entitled *Gemblak*, but with sparser *kempul* and gong punctuation. At Trowulan I notated i 3 i 2 i 3 i 6G.

17 Some recent choreographies by the famous *ngrémo* expert Munali Fatah and others eliminate the

singing, making the *ngrémo* more accessible to dance students who might not feel comfortable singing. In these choreographies the instrumental piece changes *irama* level several times, but in the slower sections the dancers continue to dance, rather than stopping to sing.

18 Neither of these sources gives notation for a second section for Gendhing *Trenggalèk*. If they did, the piece would probably then be classified as *titipati* form or, more appropriately, *gagahan* (see Figure 5.6). I have heard this piece performed several times with only this first section. Yet on the commercial cassette from which I transcribed the drumming pattern in Figure 5.28 a second section, with contrasting *balungan*, is played. On the drumming for this second section, see further, below.

19 The great *ludruk* performer, *ngrémo* dancer, and choreographer Pak Munali Fatah, whom I visited a number of times at his home in Sidoarjo during the mid-1980s, mentioned several famous *suling* players from the era prior to World War II: Pak Minin (famous *ngrémo* dancer), Pak Ngari (famous clown), and even Pak Durasim (probably the most famous *ludruk* performer).

20 See the comment on the identifying marks of east Javanese *karawitan* in Munardi *et al.*, after mentioning the special look and sound of the drum: "Permainan menonjol pada bonang penerus, gender penerus, dan peking" – literally, "the playing stands out on *bonang panerus*, *gendèr panerus*, and *peking*" (1983:2).

21 See Hardjoprawiro 1985:20, 23. The term *kidung* is generally understood to refer to Javanese sung poetry (cf. *tembang*) or a variety thereof. The verb *ngidung* may mean to sing or compose *tembang* (or *kidung*), but in the context of east Javanese gamelan music it refers to the singing of rhyming couplets and quatrains that many would identify as *parikan*.

22 The well-known musician Pak Wongsokadi is said to be the first to introduce female singing into east Javanese *karawitan*, with the group he formed in 1918. According to most older performers I spoke to (Pak Diyat Sariredjo in Surabaya, Pak Piet Asmoro in Trowulan, Mojokerto, Pak Kasdu and Pak Karimun in Malang) there were no female singers for east Javanese *wayang kulit* prior to the 1950s. And in some areas, such as rural Malang, *wayang kulit* was without *pesindhèn* until the 1970s.

23 This according to the owner of Bumi Putra/Jayabaya cassette company in Malang, who produced the tape *Tari Topeng Bapang* with *sindhènan* added to a variety of *wayang topèng* pieces. It is presumed, as with the hobby-horse trance genre (*èbèg*) of Banyumas, that a commercial tape will sell better with *sindhènan*, even if the genre represented has traditionally been instrumental dance accompaniment. Following the release of such tapes in Banyumas, *èbèg* groups have begun to incorporate *pesindhèn* in the groups that accompany live performance. It seems inevitable that the same will occur in the Malang for *wayang topèng*.

24 Photographs dating from 1927 of *gandrung* dancers show them barefooted. (See Scholte 1927 and reproduction in Wolbers 1986 and Soelarti and Ilmi n.d.) But since the 1930s they have normally worn white socks or stockings.

25 For a fascinating account of an *angklung caruk*, see Wolbers 1987. This performance context is mentioned by Crawford (1980:206), but without any indication of the intensity of the competition as described by Wolbers (and as described to me by musicians I spoke to in Banyuwangi in 1986).

26 Though his account claims to describe the "Javanese" rather than just those (east) Javanese in the Gresik area, the prefatory paragraph, written in 1852, warns the reader that most of the account is based on his observations in that area. He distinguishes a "gamelan *surabayan*" from other ensembles, including gamelan *saléndro* (i.e., *sléndro*), gamelan *pélog*, and gamelan *mentaraman*. Certainly his reference to gamelan *mentaram*, which Kunst also indicates was a term prevalent in East Java for *pélog* ensembles, and to gamelan *surabayan* suggests that his sources on gamelan music were local.

6 Gamelan, performing arts, and government policy

1 Particularly since Suharto came to power in the 1960s, the government has stressed the notion of "development" (*pembangungan*) in all aspects of life, including what are now seen across the board as "the arts" (*kesenian*), although "art" as a separate entity is not a concept indigenous to many of

Indonesia's cultures. Policy emanating from the Javanese-dominated central government has often failed to take into account the contours and nuances of particular local cultures. On the problems of the Indonesian government's involvement in a range of activities pertaining to national "development," see Dove 1988.

2 While the only television broadcasts are by the government stations (TVRI), a number of private radio stations and recording companies thrive alongside the national radio stations (RRI) and the national recording company (Lokananta). Little has appeared on the national radio station and its programming policies. Yampolsky, however, offers us a thorough look at the Lokananta recording company and the trends in its output over a period of nearly thirty years (Yampolsky 1987). See further chapter 7.

3 For example, a recent student handbook from ASKI lists one of the main goals of the institutions to be the fostering of "a knowledgeable society that is cultured, follows the morals of the Five Principles, and has an Indonesian identity/personality" ("masyarakat ilmiah yang berbudaya, bermoral Pancasila dan berkepribadian Indonesia") (Anon. 1986:1).

4 Two of the best known artists involved in the initial conception of the Surabaya KOKARI are the gamelan musician and expert drummer Diyat Sariredjo, and the *ludruk* actor and *ngrémo* dancer Munali Fatah, both of whom worked at RRI Surabaya and are now retired.

5 What follows here is a somewhat abridged account of key events and issues that arose at that time. Elsewhere, I have provided a lengthier analysis, including discussion of the contest requirements in Yogya. See Sutton 1984.

6 See Nettl's marvelous discussion of a certain breed of ethnomusicologist who seeks "to keep change at arm's length – to stave off death, as it were – and restore a measure of vitality through the antibiotic-injections of festivals and government-sponsored authenticity and through the intensive-care activities of collecting-projects and national archives" (Nettl 1978:147).

7 It is not clear how far back one might trace a definable Solonese style in gamelan playing, nor when the standardization was crystallized. On the steps toward standardization in Solonese *wayang kulit* tradition, which seem to have occurred some decades prior to the revolution and been inspired in part by Dutch notions of high culture, see Sears's "Power and Performance in Javanese History."

8 Banyumas musician Rasito informed me that groups from Banyumas have won or been placed second in the province-wide contests several times in the last decade, and have done so by nature of their accomplished renditions of Solonese *gendhing*. My records do not indicate in which years the Banyumas groups won.

7 Regional traditions and the media

1 The first radio station in Indonesia, and predecessor to NIROM, was Batavia Radio Veremiging, which began broadcasts in Jakarta in the early 1920s (Moses and Maslog 1978:58).

2 NIROM and VADERA were owned and operated by the Dutch government, whereas MAVRO was independent. Only MAVRO maintained a group of musicians for regular gamelan broadcasts, usually from the Dalem Ngabéan, a noble residence adjoining the *kraton*. For broadcasts of gamelan music on the other stations, the equipment was brought to one of the court gamelans – usually the *kraton* or Pakualaman. From the late 1920s until the Japanese occupation, gamelan music in Surakarta was broadcast on SRV from the Mangkunegaran and SRI from the *kraton*. Though it was mostly the Dutch who could afford to own radios, some Javanese did as well. The broadcast signals were, I am told, strong enough for Yogyanese stations to be picked up at least as far away as Solo and Solonese stations in Yogya. More research is needed on the early days of radio in Java. I am grateful to the elderly musicians, Pak Pustakamardawa, Pak Prajasudirja, and Ki Tjokrowasito (K.R.T. Wasitodiningrat), who have spoken to me about this topic.

3 The actual salaries were very low before 1980, although affiliation with RRI gave these musicians a decided advantage in the market for live performance engagements at wedding receptions and other ritual or ritual-related events. Although the transition to civil servant status has brought somewhat higher salaries and the right to a modest pension at retirement, it has nevertheless been a mixed blessing – both in terms of individual welfare and in terms of performance quality. Salaries are

determined not only by musical ability and seniority, but partially by level of formal education. This has meant that young and relatively inexperienced musicians often make higher salaries than the older experts whose knowledge happens to have come from years of experience and informal learning as performers, rather than as students in degree-bearing programs. And the emphasis on formal education in hiring is now keeping some of the best musicians out of the ranks of the RRI performers altogether. The civil servant status has also been a hardship for healthy performers in their mid-fifties or older, who, once they were made civil servants, were forced to retire, reducing their income to levels lower than they had received beforehand. For the old and ailing musicians who had to drag themselves to the studio for a late night broadcast, however, the chance to retire and draw a pension has been a long-awaited blessing. And the kind of political security, of social invisibility through conformity, provided by the claim to civil servant status has enabled RRI musicians to feel a greater sense of fit with the world of contemporary Indonesia.

4 The year was either 1955 or 1956; Yampolsky documents the disagreement among sources (1987:33, note 3).
5 Here I have only mentioned the companies with the greatest presence in the market-place. A number of other companies produce at least some gamelan music cassettes that are distributed throughout Java and hence not regionally-based.
6 For statistics on availability and sales of different regional gamelan music in eight Javanese cities, see Sutton 1985a:59.
7 Thio Tjem Lien, also known as Antono Wardoyo Martioso, a Chinese businessman who also owned and operated several movie theatres in Purwokerto.
8 I first encountered *èbèg* with *pesindhèn* on cassettes released around 1983; in 1986 René Lysloff witnessed and photographed a live performance of *èbèg* with *pesindhèn*, apparently inspired by the cassette recording.
9 Most companies also restock some of the older titles, though not consistently. The buying public tends to want new releases, according to cassette store owners I spoke to, even if those releases contain *gendhing* that are available on older cassettes.
10 The identification of drum pattern, in Yogyanese fashion, is given on some Borobudur cassettes of *gendhing* performed by Siswa Among Beksa.
11 The use of a different set of terms for *pathet* in east Java has also led to some confusing cases where both central and east Javanese systems are used on the same cassette, as mentioned in chapter 5.

8 Regional pluralism in the music of renowned Javanese

1 For a more detailed account of Nartosabdho's life and views on the arts, see my transcription of an interview Peggy Choy and I conducted with him at his home in April 1979. The interview appears as part of my chapter "Music of Indonesia" in the second edition of the textbook *Worlds of Music* (Titon, forthcoming).
2 The only exception of which I am aware is an early recording of *Godril* on the cassette *Djakarta Indah*, an unnumbered release on the Irama label. The Banyumas gendhing *Godril* is given a new vocal part composed by Nartosabdho and the piece is listed on the cassette cover as "Gending Godril Rinenggo" (i.e., Gendhing *Godril [Banyumasan] Rinengga*).
3 Neither recording dates nor release dates are given on most Javanese cassettes. Yampolsky's work in the Lokananta archives has turned up these dates for most of Lokananta recordings. See Yampolsky 1987.
4 The regional categories that are now standard in tracing the history of jazz in the United States (New Orleans, Chicago, Kansas City, and so on) are less clearly the result of one individual's contribution. But the mobility of jazz musicians has been such that it would be difficult, for example, to attribute anything intrinsically "Chicagoan" to the early jazz made there, mostly by musicians who moved up the Mississippi from New Orleans.
5 This is apparently not a reworking of a Banyuwangi piece, but rather a new composition by Nartosabdho. I was alerted to the possible earlier existence of a Banyuwangi *Éling-éling* by Philip Yampolsky, who found it listed as one of several pieces on a 1934 recording by HMV (His Master's

Voice) under the category "*lagu* Bali" (Balinese songs). The recording is unavailable, but the other songs listed, such as *Kembang Waru* and *Érang-érang* are both known today in the Banyuwangi *gandrung* repertory. The proximity to Bali both geographically and in some aspects of style may have caused confusion on the part of the recording company. Still, there appears to be no piece known as *Éling-éling* in the active repertory of Banyuwangi today.

6 The first is found on *Aja Lamis*, Ira-Record WD-511; the second on *Gendhing Tayub Madiun Vol. 2*, Ira Record WD-761; and the third on *Timur Mas*, Kusuma KGD-023.

7 See Humardani's writing on the "melting" of regional boundaries and the consequent enrichment of the artistic treasury (1982–83:10).

9 Conclusion

1 For example, see Gellner 1983. In ethnomusicology, see Lomax on the "cultural grey-out" (Lomax 1968:4–6).

2 On the development in Java of a Dutch conception of artistic and other cultural categories, see Lindsay 1985: chapter 1. On other European colonial constructions of "tradition," see the essays by Cohn (on India) and Ranger (on Africa) in Hobsbawm and Ranger 1983. Hobsbawm defines "tradition" somewhat differently than I have in this study to mean "a set of practices, normally governed by overtly or tacitly accepted rules and of a ritual or symbolic nature, which seek to inculcate certain values and norms of behaviour by repetition, which automatically implies continuity with the past" (Hobsbawm 1983:1).

3 The *hadiluhung* performances mark the sultan's Javanese "birthdays," which occur every thirty-five days, reckoned by the coincidence of the seven-day week with the Javanese five-day market week. His Highness Sultan Hamengku Buwana IX, who died in 1988, was born on Saturday (*Setu*) in the seven-day week and *Pahing* in the five-day week. Every time these two days fell together (i.e., every thirty-five days – five times seven) the *kraton* musicians presented an evening performance of gamelan music and singing, which, though closed to the public, was broadcast on RRI Yogyakarta. For an extensive account of gamelan activities in the Yogyakarta *kraton* in recent years, prior to the death of Sultan Hamengku Buwana IX, see Vetter 1986.

4 What of certain practices peculiar to other regions not considered, for example? Koentjaraningrat identifies a subcultural region of Bagelèn, in southern Central Java between Banyumas and Yogyakarta (Koentjaraningrat 1984:27, 220–22). I have heard gamelan music accompanying *wayang golèk* puppetry from Kebumèn, in this region, in which pieces I had not encountered elsewhere were played. Perhaps another "tradition"? Perhaps, but not one known to most Javanese. At STSI/ASKI gamelan musicians learn some of these pieces in order to accompany this kind of *wayang golèk*, but it is not, to my knowledge, represented on commercial cassette or in the broadcast media. The few items of Semarang repertory, on the other hand, are much more widely known.

  I should mention here also the town of Sragen, near the border between the provinces of Central and East Java north east of Surakarta, whose name in the 1980s has frequently appeared on the covers of commercial cassette advertising lively music under the rubric of *badhutan Sragen*. The musical repertory presented on these cassettes varies widely – from standard Solonese *gendhing* to an occasional item from Banyuwangi. *Gendhing* associated primarily with the east Javanese heartland are not unusual on these cassettes either, but the playing style is mostly central Javanese. Other than the characteristic use of wide glissandi in some of the female singing on these recordings, Javanese musicians I spoke to denied the existence of a "Sragen" gamelan style, let alone a Sragen tradition. They concurred that the mention of Sragen is commercially appealing because Sragen is an area known for lively *tayuban*, with clown (*badhut*). The *gendhing* may be from anywhere as long as they are mostly lively. Nevertheless, I am unable to report what conceptions local residents of Sragen might have about a local style or tradition there; my inquiries concerning *badhutan* Sragen were limited to musicians in Solo and in Yogya familiar with the recordings.

5 She goes on to state that "Objects are likely to change meanings when they are switched from one community of meaning-attributors to a radically different one" (Errington 1989:49). Of course none

of the regions or "communities" we have discussed are radically different from one another. A Yogyanese playing Solonese Gendhing *Prawan Pupur*, or Banyumas musician playing the east Javanese *Jula-juli*, is not the same as an American such as myself attempting to play either of these pieces, for both pieces can be seen as "Javanese" as well as Solonese or east Javanese. They would not, despite Americans playing them, be considered American.

Bibliography

Adiana, Meilia 1986 *Lengger Kesenian Tradisionil Jawa di Kecamatan Panti Kabupaten Jember* [Lènggèr: A Traditional Javanese Art in Kecamatan Panti, Kabupaten Jember]. Yogyakarta: Proyek Penelitian Dan Pengkajian Kebudayaan Nusantara (Javanologi), Departemen Pendidikan Dan Kebudayaan.

Anderson, Benedict 1972 "The idea of Power in Javanese culture" in Claire Holt (ed.) *Culture and Politics in Indonesia*. Ithaca: Cornell University Press, pp. 1–69.

Anon. 1980 "Cengkok sindhen dadi rembug" [Melodic patterns of female vocalists are discussed]. *Mekar Sari* 23 (24, February 15):4 and 21.

Anon. 1986 *Buku Petunjuk 1986–87, ASKI Surakarta* [1986–87 Handbook, ASKI Surakarta]. Surakarta: ASKI, Kampus Kentingan Jebres.

Apel, Willi, ed. 1969 *Harvard Dictionary of Music*, 2nd ed., rev. and enl. Cambridge, MA: Belknap Press of Harvard University Press.

Asmoro, Piet 1971 *Tuntunan Karawitan Djawa Timuran* [Manual of East Javanese Gamelan Music]. Modjokerto: Kantor Pembinaan Kebudayaan.

Baier, Randal, and Peter Manuel 1986 "Jaipongan: indigenous popular music of West Java." *Asian Music* 18(1):91–110.

Bakhtin, Mikhail 1953 "Discourse in the novel" in Michael Holquist (ed.) *The Dialogic Imagination*. Austin: University of Texas Press, 1981, pp. 259–442.

Barth, Fredrik 1969 "Introduction" in *Ethnic Groups and Boundaries: The Social Organization of Culture Difference*. Boston: Little, Brown and Co., pp. 9–38.

Becker, Judith 1972 "Traditional music in modern Java." Unpublished Ph.D. diss., University of Michigan.

   1980 *Traditional Music in Modern Java: Gamelan in a Changing Society*. Honolulu: University of Hawaii Press.

   n.d. "In the presence of the past: gamelan stories, tantrism, and aesthetics in central Java." Book manuscript, in preparation.

Becker, Judith, and Alan Feinstein, eds. 1984, 1987, and 1988 *Karawitan: Source Readings in Javanese Gamelan and Vocal Music*. 3 vols. Ann Arbor: University of Michigan, Center for South and Southeast Asian Studies.

Behrend, Timothy E. 1989 "Report on the Proyek Mikrofilm Museum Sonobudoyo." *Caraka, "The Messenger": A Newsletter for Javanists* 14 (June):15–26.

Bohlman, Philip V. 1988 "Traditional music and cultural identity: persistent paradigm in the history of ethnomusicology." *Yearbook for Traditional Music* 20:26–42.

Brandts Buys, J.S., and A. Brandts Buys–van Zijp 1925 'Oude klanken" [Old Sounds]. *Djawa* 5(1):16–56.

   1925 and 1926 "Toeters en piepers" [Honkers and pipers]. *Djawa* 5:311–19; and *Djawa* 6:27–31, 76–82, and 318–32.

   1926–27 "Over fluiten" [On flutes]. *Nederlandsch-Indie Oud & Nieuw* 11:57–62 and 115–21.

   1926 "Over muziek in het Banjoewangische" [On music in Banyuwangi]. *Djawa* 6:205–28.

   1928a "Over spleettrom–orkestjes" [On split–drum orchestras]. *De Muziek* 2:389ff. and 437ff.

   1928b "De toonkunst bij de Madoereezen" [The music of the Madurese]. *Djawa* 8:1–290.

Budaya 1953, 1954, 1958 "Berita kebudajaan" [Cultural news]. *Budaya* 2(10 and 11):47; 2(12):53; 3(11 and 12):63; 7(1):51.

Carey, Peter 1986 "Yogyakarta: from sultanate to revolutionary capital of Indonesia, the politics of cultural survival." *Indonesia Circle* 39 (March):19–29.

Chernoff, John Miller 1979 *African Rhythm and African Sensibility: Aesthetics and Social Action in African Musical Idioms*. Chicago: University of Chicago Press.

Clara van Groenendael, Victoria M. 1985 *The Dalang Behind the Wayang*. Verhandelingen van het Koninklijk Instituut voor Taal–, Land– en Volkenkunde 114. Dordrecht, Holland: Foris Publications.

Clifford, James 1988 *The Predicament of Culture: Twentieth–century Ethnography, Literature, and Art*. Cambridge, MA: Harvard University Press.

Clifford, James and George Marcus, eds. 1986 *Writing Culture: The Poetics and Politics of Ethnography*. Berkeley: University of California Press.

Cohn, Bernard S. 1983 "Representing Authority in Victorian India" in Eric Hobsbawm and Terence Ranger (eds.) *The Invention of Tradition*. Cambridge: Cambridge University Press, pp. 165–209.

Crawford, Michael 1980 "Indonesia: East Java." *The New Grove Dictionary of Music and Musicians*. 6th ed., vol 9:201–7.

Departemen Pendidikan dan Kebudayaan (Indonesia) 1973 *Cultural Policy in Indonesia: A Study*. Paris: Unesco.

Departemen Pendidikan dan Kebudayaan, Wilayah Propinsi Jawa Tengah, Kabupaten Banyumas [cited "Departemen PDK"] 1980 *Sumbangan Pikiran Tentang Karawitan Banyumasan* [Contribution to Thoughts about Banyumas Gamelan Music]. Purwokerto, Central Java: Departemen Pendidikan dan Kebudayaan, Wilayah Propinsi Jawa Tengah, Kabupaten Banyumas.

Devereaux, Kent 1986 "Profile: University of Michigan: an interview with Judith Becker and René Lysloff." *Balungan* 2(1–2):19–22.

Djakoeb and Wignjaroemeksa [Jakub and Wignyarumeksa] 1913 *Lajang anjoeroepaké Pratikelé bab Sinaoe Naboeh sarto Panggawéné Gamelan* [Writings on Methods for Studying the Playing and Making of Gamelan]. Volkslectuur, publication no. 94. Batawi [Jakarta]: Pirma Papirus.

1919 *Serat Enoet Gending Sléndro* [Book of *Gendhing* in *Sléndro*]. Volkslectuur, publication no. 169. Batavia: Landsdrukkerij.

Doorn, Jacques van 1980 *Javanese Society in Regional Perspective: Some Historical and Sociological Aspects*. Rotterdam: Comparative Asian Studies Programme, Erasmus University.

Dove, Michael R., ed. 1988 *The Real and Imagined Role of Culture in Development: Case Studies From Indonesia*. Honolulu: University of Hawaii Press.

Dungga, J. A. 1953 "Disekitar perkembangan musik Indonesia" [Concerning the development of Indonesian music]. *Indonesia, Madjalah Kebudajaan* 4(December):702–6.

Errington, Shelly 1989 "Fragile Traditions and Contested Meanings." *Public Culture* 1(2 Spring):49–59.

Esser, B. J. 1927 "Het dialect van Banjoemas: Inzonderheid zooals dit in de Regentschappen Poerbolinggo en Poerwokerto Gesproken Wordt" [The dialect of Banyumas: Especially that which is spoken in the Regencies of Purbalingga and Purwokerto]. *Verhandelingen van het Bataviaasch Genootschap van Kunsten en Wetenschappen* 68(1):1–77.

Florida, Nancy K. n.d. "Javanese language manuscripts of Surakarta, Central Java: a descriptive catalogue" (draft), 9 vols. John M. Echols Collection, Olin Library, Cornell University, Ithaca, NY.

1987 'Reading the unread in traditional Javanese literature." *Indonesia* 44 (October):1–15.

Frederick, William 1982 'Rhoma Irama and the dangdut style: aspects of contemporary Indonesian popular culture." *Indonesia* 34:102–30.

Geertz, Clifford 1960 *The Religion of Java*. New York: The Free Press.

1963 *Agricultural Involution: The Processes of Ecological Change in Indonesia*. Berkeley: University of California Press.

1973 *The Interpretation of Cultures*. New York: Basic Books.

1983 *Local Knowledge: Further Essays in Interpretive Anthropology*. New York: Basic Books.

Gellner, Ernest 1983 *Nations and Nationalism*. Ithaca: Cornell University Press.

Gooszen, A. J. 1985 "Administrative division and redivision on Java and Madura, 1880–1942." *Indonesia Circle* 36:23–53.

Gourlay, K. A. 1978 "Towards a reassessment of the ethnomusicologist's role in research." *Ethnomusicology* 22(1):1–35.

    1982 "Towards a humanizing ethnomusicology." *Ethnomusicology* 26(3):411–20.

Groneman, J. 1890 *De Gamelan te Jogjakarta* [The Gamelan in Yogyakarta]. Foreword "Over onze Kennis der Javaansche Muziek" by J. P. Land. Amsterdam: Johannes Müller.

Groot, A.D. Cornets de 1852 "Bijdrage tot de kennis van de zeden en gewoonten der Javanen" [Contribution to the knowledge of the manners and customs of the Javanese]. *Tijdschrift voor Nederlandsch Indie* 14(2):257–80; 346–67; 393–424.

Hannerz, Ulf n.d. "The world system of culture: the international flow of meaning and its local management." Manuscript (cited in Clifford, 1988).

Hardjo, W. S. 1982 *Macapat Semarangan* [Semarang–style *Macapat* Songs]. Semarang: Departemen Pendidikan dan Kebudayaan, Daerah Tingkat I, Jawa Tengah.

Hardjoprawiro, Kunardi 1985 *Kajian Bentuk Dan Lagu Kidungan Jawa Timuran* [Knowledge on The Form and Melody of East Javanese *Kidungan*]. Yogyakarta: Proyek Penelitian dan Pengkajian Kebudayaan Nusantara (Javanologi), Departemen Pendidikan dan Kebudayaan.

Hardjowigati, D. 1957 "Basa Djawi Banyumas" [Javanese language of Banyumas]. *Medan Bahasa* 2(4, April):18–19.

Harungbinang, R. T. [1900?] "Sadaya kagungan dalem gongsa" [All the king's gamelan], with introduction by Sasradipura. Manuscript, Radya Pustaka Library, Surakarta.

Hatch, Martin F. 1980 "Lagu, laras, layang: rethinking melody in Javanese music." Unpublished Ph.D. diss., Cornell University.

Hatley, Barbara 1971 "Wayang and ludruk: polarities in Java." *The Drama Review* (Special Issue: Theatre in Asia) 15(3):88–101.

Hatley, Ron 1984 "Mapping cultural regions of Java" in *Other Javas Away from the Kraton*, by Ron Hatley, Jim Schiller, Anton Lucas, and Barbara Martin–Schiller. Clayton, Victoria: Monash University Centre of Southeast Asian Studies.

Hefner, Robert W. 1985 *Hindu Javanese: Tengger Tradition and Islam*. Princeton, NJ: Princeton University Press.

    1987 "The politics of popular art: *tayuban* dance and culture change in East Java." *Indonesia* 43(April):75–94.

Hobsbawm, Eric 1983 "Introduction, inventing traditions" in Eric Hobsbawm and Terence Ranger (eds.) *The Invention of Tradition*. Cambridge: Cambridge University Press, pp. 1–14.

Hobsbawm, Eric, and Terence Ranger, eds. 1983 *The Invention of Tradition*. Cambridge: Cambridge University Press.

Hogendorp, H. van 1913 *Willem van Hogendorp in Nederlandsch–Indie 1825–30*. The Hague: Martinus Nijhoff.

Holt, Claire 1967 *Art in Indonesia: Continuities and Change*. Ithaca: Cornell University Press.

Hood, Mantle 1954 *The Nuclear Theme as a Determinant of Patet in Javanese Music*. Groningen: J. B. Wolters. (Reprinted by Da Capo Press, New York, 1977).

Hood, Mantle, and Hardja Susilo 1967 *Music of the Venerable Dark Cloud: Introduction, Commentary, and Analysis*. Los Angeles: University of California Press.

Humardani, S.D. 1982–83 *Kumpulan Kertas tentang Kesenian* [Collected Papers on the Arts]. Surakarta: Akademi Seni Karawitan Indonesia.

Hüskens, Frans 1981 "Regional diversity in Javanese agrarian development: variations in the pattern of involution." Working Paper No. 10. Bielefeld: University of Bielefeld, Sociology of Development Research Centre.

Jacobson, Edward, and J. H. van Hasselt 1907 *De Gong–Fabricatie te Semarang*. Rijks Ethnographisch Museum Serie II, No. 15. Leiden: E. J. Brill. English translation and introduction by Andrew Toth as "The manufacture of gongs in Semarang." *Indonesia* 19(April, 1975):127–72.

Kartamihardja, R. Prajoga 1978 *Kesenian Jawa Timur* [East Javanese Arts]. Surabaya: Team Pelaksana Penelitian dan Pencatatan Kebudayaan Daerah Jawa Timur, Departemen Pendidikan dan Kebudayaan.

Kartomi, Margaret 1973 "Music and trance in Central Java." *Ethnomusicology* 17(2):163–208.

1976 "Performance, music, and meaning of reyog Ponorogo." *Indonesia* 22(October):85–130.

Kayam, Umar 1981 *Seni, Tradisi, Masyarakat* [Art, Tradition, and Populace]. Jakarta: Sinar Harapan.

1985 *The Soul of Indonesia: A Cultural Journey.* Baton Rouge, Louisiana State University Press.

Keil, Charles 1979 *Tiv Song: Art in a Classless Society.* Chicago: University of Chicago Press.

Kertanegara, K. R. T. [1889 ?] "Pakem wirama: wileting gendhing berdangga" [Manual of rhythm: melodic patterns of gamelan compositions]. Three manuscript versions: 1. Javanese script, in possession of dance club and gamelan club Siswa Among Beksa, Yogyakarta; 2. portions romanized by T. Pigeaud, 1934, Sana Budhaya Museum Library, Yogyakarta; 3. sections in Javanese script and romanized, in possession of B. Y. H. Pustakamardawa (in Yogyakarta).

Koentjaraningrat 1984 *Kebudayaan Jawa* [Javanese Culture]. Seri Etnografi Indonesia, No. 2. Jakarta: P.N. Balai Pustaka.

Komisi Pasinaon Nabuh Gamelan 1924 *Buku Piwulangan Nabuh Gamelan* [Lesson Book for Playing Gamelan]. Vol. 1. Surakarta: Pangecapan Swastika.

1925 *Buku Piwulangan Nabuh Gamelan* [Lesson Book for Playing Gamelan]. Vol. 2. Surakarta: Budi Utama.

Kunst, Jaap 1973 *Music in Java: Its History, Its Theory, and Its Technique.* 2 vols. 3rd rev. and enl. ed., E. L. Heins (ed.). The Hague: Martinus Nijhoff. (Earlier English edition 1949; first published in Dutch as *De Toonkunst van Java,* 1934).

Kussudiardjo, Bagong 1955 "Seni tari di Djawa Timur" [The art of dance in East Java]. *Budaya* 4(3): 142–5.

1981 *Tentang Tari* [About Dance]. Yogyakarta: Nur Cahaya.

Larassumbogo, Ki Wedana, R. Murtedjo, and Adisoendjojo 1953 *Titilaras Gending Ageng* [Notation of Large Pieces]. Vol. 1. Jakarta: Noordhoff–Kolff N.V.

Lindsay, Jennifer 1984 "The Krida Mardawa manuscript collection." *Bijdragen tot de Taal–, Land–, en Volkenkunde* 140:248–62.

1985 "Klasik kitsch or contemporary: a study of the Javanese performing arts." Unpublished Ph.D. diss., University of Sydney.

Lomax, Alan 1968 *Folk Song Style and Culture.* AAAS Publication No. 88. Washington, DC: American Association for the Advancement of Science.

Lysloff, René T. A. 1982 "The gong–chime bonang barung in the Central Javanese gamelan: aspects of musical function and idiom in contemporary practice." Unpublished M.A. thesis, University of Hawaii.

1990 "Srikandhi dances lènggèr: a performance of shadow–puppet theater in Banyumas (west central Java)." Unpublished Ph.D. diss., University of Michigan.

Malm, William P. 1977 *Music Cultures of the Pacific, the Near East, and Asia.* 2nd ed. Englewood Cliffs, NJ: Prentice-Hall.

Marcus, George, and Michael Fischer 1986 *Anthropology as Cultural Critique.* Chicago: University of Chicago Press.

Mardjana, M. 1933 *Layang Isi Kawroeh bab Basa Djawa Sawetara* [Writing Containing Various Knowledge about Javanese Language]. Groningen: J. B. Wolters.

Martopangrawit, R. L. 1969 *Pengetahuan Karawitan* [Knowledge of Gamelan Music]. Vol. 1. Surakarta: Akedemi Seni Karawitan Indonesia. Translation into English by Martin Hatch in Becker and Feinstein 1984 (Vol. 1), pp. 1–121.

1972a *Pengetahuan Karawitan* [Knowledge of Gamelan Music]. Vol. 2. Surakarta: Akademi Seni Karawitan Indonesia. Translation into English by Martin Hatch in Becker and Feinstein 1984 (Vol. 1), pp. 123–244.

1972b *Titilaras Kendangan* [Drum Notation]. Surakarta: Akademi Seni Karawitan Indonesia.

1973 and 1976 *Titilaras Cengkok–cengkok Genderan dengan Wiletannya* [Notation of *Gendèr* Patterns and their Variations]. 2 vols. Surakarta: Akademi Seni Karawitan Indonesia.

1975 *Titilaras Gending dan Sindenan Bedaya–Srimpi Kraton Surakarta* [Notation of Gamelan Pieces and Vocal Parts for Female Court Dances of the Surakarta Palace]. Surakarta: Akademi Seni Karawitan Indonesia.

Matsyachir, Djoddy [1977] "Jawa Timur menuju kesatuan gaya seni" [East Java moves towards a single style/tradition of art]. Typescript, SMKI Library, Surabaya.

McNamara, Molly Ann 1980 "Solonese gending bonang: the repertoire and playing style." M.A. thesis, Wesleyan University.

Mloyowidodo, S. 1976 *Gending–gending Jawa, Gaya Surakarta* [Javanese Gamelan Pieces, Surakarta Style]. 3 vols. Surakarta: Akademi Seni Karawitan Indonesia.

Moore, Sally Falk 1989 "The production of cultural pluralism as a process." *Public Culture* 1(2, Spring):26–48.

Moses, Charles, and Crispin Maslog 1978 *Mass Communication in Asia: A Brief History*. Singapore: Asian Mass Communication Research and Information Centre.

Mudianto and A. Tasman [1983] *Notasi Genderan Sena'in* [Notation of Sena'in's *Gendèr* (*Panerus*) Playing]. Surabaya: Sekolah Tinggi Kesenian Wilwatikta.

Mudjanattistomo, R. M.; R. Ant. Sangkono Tjiptowardoyo; R. L. Radyomardowo; and M. Basirun Hadisumarto 1977 *Pedhalangan Ngayogyakarta* [Yogyanese Shadow Puppetry Performance]. Jilid I. Yogyakarta: Yayasan Habirandha.

Munardi, A.M. 1975 *Dramatari Topeng Jabung: Sebuah Pengantar Penelitian* [Masked Dance Drama of Jabung: An Introductory Investigation]. Surabaya: Konservatori Karawitan Indonesia.

Munardi, A.M.; Koesdiono; Djumiran R.A.; Fx. Djoko Waluyo; and Suwarmin 1983 *Pengetahuan Karawitan Jawa Timur* [Knowledge of East Javanese Gamelan Music]. Jakarta: Departemen Pendidikan dan Kebudayaan, Direktorat Pendidikan Menengah Kejuruan.

Murgiyanto, Sal M.; and A.M. Munardi 1979 *Topeng Malang* [Masked Dance of Malang]. Jakarta: Proyek Sasana Budaya, Departemen Pendidikan dan Kebudayaan.

Nettl, Bruno 1978 "Persian classical music in Tehran: the processes of change" in Bruno Nettl (ed.) *Eight Urban Musical Cultures*. Urbana: University of Illinois Press.

Oemarmadi, R. and M. Koesnadi Poerbosenojo 1964 *Babad Banjumas* [Banyumas Legendary History]. Jakarta: Amin Sujitno Djojosudarmo.

Parsana An., I.M. Hardjito, and Sutarno 1972 *Titilaras Genderan Bahan Pelajaran Baku* [*Gendèr* Notation, Materials for Elementary Study]. Surakarta: Akademi Seni Karawitan Indonesia.

Peacock, James 1968 *Rites of Modernization: Symbolic and Social Aspects of Indonesian Proletarian Drama*. Chicago: University of Chicago Press.

Pemerintah Daerah Jawa Timur 1975 *Jawa Timur Membangun: Kini dan Esok* [East Java Develops: Today and Tomorrow]. Surabaya: Pemerintah Daerah Propinsi Tingkat I Jawa Timur.

Pigeaud, T. 1932 "Aantekeningen betreffende den Javaanschen oosthoek" [Notes regarding the eastern end of Java]. *Tijdschrift voor de Indische Taal-, Land- en Volkendunde* 72:215–313.

1938 *Javaanse Volksvertoningen: Bijdrage tot de Beschrijving van Land en Volk* [Javanese Folk Performances: Contribution to the Description of Land and People]. Batavia: Volkslectuur.

1967–70 *The Literature of Java: catalogue* raisonné *of Javanese manuscripts in the Library of the University of Leiden and other public collections in the Netherlands*. 3 vols. The Hague: Martinus Nijhoff.

Powers, Harold S. 1980 "Mode" in *The New Grove Dictionary of Music and Musicians*. 6th ed. Vol. 10:376–450.

Pringgodigdo, R. M. A. K. 1950 *Geschiedenis der Ondernemingen van het Mangkoenagorosche Rijk* [History of the estates/undertakings of the Mangkunegaran Kingdom]. The Hague: Martinus Nijhoff.

Probohardjono, R. Ng. S. 1957 *Gending–gending ingkang kanggé Nabuhi Wajangan Purwa* [Gamelan Pieces for Accompanying Shadow Theatre]. Yogyakarta: P. T. Sinduniti.

Proyek Penelitian dan Pencatatan Kebudayaan Daerah 1976 *Ensiklopedi Seni Musik dan Seni Tari*

Daerah Jawa Timur [Encyclopedia of Music and Dance in the East Java Region]. Surabaya: Proyek Penelitian dan Pencatatan Kebudayaan Daerah, Departemen Pendidikan dan Kebudayaan.

Proyek Rehabilitasi/Pengembangan S.M.K.I. Jawa Timur 1979 *Tari Jejer, Tari Pemaju, dan Tari Padangulan* [*Jejer* Dance, *Pemaju* Dance, and *Padangulan* Dance]. Surabaya: Sekolah Menengah Karawitan Indonesia.

Ranger, Terence 1983 "The invention of tradition in colonial Africa" in Eric Hobsbawm and Terence Ranger (eds.) *The Invention of Tradition*. Cambridge: Cambridge University Press, pp. 211–62.

Rasito 1986 "Kehidupan seni karawitan calung di Banyumas" [The life of the art of bamboo xylophone playing in Banyumas]. Banyumas: [Sekolah Menengah Karawitan Indonesia], published in stencil form.

Repelita 1979 *Rencana Pembangunan Lima Tahun Ketiga 1979/80–1983/84* [Third Five Year Development Plan, for 1979/80–1983/84]. 4 vols. Jakarta: Departemen Penerangan.

1984 *Rencana Pembangunan Lima Tahun Keempat 1984/85–1988/89* [Fourth Five Year Development Plan, for 1984/85–1988/89]. 4 vols. Jakarta: Departemen Penerangan.

Ricklefs, M.C. 1974 *Yogyakarta under Sultan Mangkubumi 1749–1792: A History of the Division of Java*. London: Oxford University Press.

1981 *A History of Modern Indonesia, c. 1300 to the Present*. Bloomington: Indiana University Press.

Ronoatmodjo, A. Tasman; with Soenarto R. P. and Diyat Sariredjo 1981a *Notasi Gending Mojokerto–Suroboyo* [Notation of Mojokerto and Surabaya Gamelan Pieces]. Surabaya: Departemen Pendidikan dan Kebudayaan Propinsi Jawa Timur and Sekolah Tinggi Kesenian Wilwatikta.

Ronoatmodjo, A. Tasman; Diyat Sariredjo; Suwarmin 1981b *Notasi Rebaban Gending–gending Suroboyo* [Rebab Notation for Surabaya Gamelan Pieces]. Surabaya: Departemen Pendidikan dan Kebudayaan Propinsi Jawa Timur and Sekolah Tinggi Kesenian Wilwatikta.

Rosaldo, Renato 1989 *Culture and Truth: The Remaking of Social Analysis*. Boston: Beacon Press.

Saleh, Boejoeng 1956 "Kebudajaan nasional, kebudajaan–kebudajaan daerah dan tatanegara Indonesia" [National Culture, regional cultures, and the Indonesian government]. *Indonesia, Madjalah Kebudajaan* 7(Juni):242–53.

Saputro, Darmono 1984 "Garap kidungan Jula–juli Surabayan di dalam laras slendro" [Singing kidungan for *Jula–juli* of Surabaya, in *sléndro* tuning]. Thesis for Sarjana Muda Kesenian Degree, Sekolah Tinggi Kesenian Wilwatikta, Surabaya.

1987 "Interaksi antara karawitan dengan pakeliran wayang kulit purwa wetanan" [Interaction between music and puppetry in east Javanese shadow puppet theater]. Thesis for Sarjana Lengkap Degree, Sekolah Tinggi Kesenian Wilwatikta.

Scholte, J. 1927 "Gandroeng van Banjoewangi" [Gandrung of Banyuwangi]. *Djawa* 7:144–53.

Sears, Laurie Jo n.d. "Power and performance in Javanese history." Unpublished manuscript.

Sekretariat Nasional Pewayangan Indonesia "Sena Wangi" 1983 *Pathokan Pedhalangan Gagrag Banyumas* [Standard Guidelines for Shadow Puppetry in Banyumas Style]. Jakarta: P.N. Balai Pustaka.

Sena'in, Diyat Sariredjo, and Supadi 1982 *Notasi Genderan* [Notation of *Gendèr (Panerus)* Playing]. Surabaya: Sekolah Tinggi Kesenian Wilwatikta.

Sindusawarno, Ki 1955 *Ilmu Karawitan* [Study of Gamelan Music]. Surakarta: Konservatori Karawitan Indonesia. Translation into English by Martin Hatch in Becker and Feinstein 1987 (Vol. 2), pp. 311–87.

Siswanta, M; Kawindrasutikna; S. Sumanggakarsa, Sabirun 1974 *Gending–gending Beksan* [Gamelan Pieces for Dance]. Yogyakarta: Konservatori Tari Indonesia.

Siswanto 1983 *Pengetahuan Karawitan Daerah Yogyakarta* [Knowledge of Gamelan Music of the Region of Yogyakarta]. Proyek Pengadaan Buku Pendidikan Menengah Kejuruan. Jakarta: Departemen Pendidikan dan Kebudayaan.

Soebiyatno 1979 "Pembuatan gamelan calung" [The making of *calung* gamelan]. Senior Thesis, Akademi Seni Karawitan Indonesia, Surakarta.

Soekanto 1953 "Konservatori Karawitan dan kebudajaan nasional" [The Karawitan Conservatory and national culture]. *Budaya* 2 (Feb):21–25.

Soekarno 1978–79 *Wayang Jengglong: Kabupaten Batang* [*Wayang Jengglong* in the Kabupaten of

Batang]. Penyusun Naskah Kesenian Tradisi. Semarang: Pusat Pengembangan Kebudayaan Jawa Tengah, Departemen Pendidikan dan Kebudayaan.

Soelarto, B. 1979 *Topeng Madura (Topong)* [Masked Dance of Madura]. Jakarta: Proyek Pengembangan Media Kebudayaan, Departemen Pendidikan dan Kebudayaan.

Soelarto, B., and S. Ilmi n.d. *Gandrung Banyuwangi* [The *Gandrung* of Banyuwangi]. Jakarta: Proyek Pengembangan Media Kebudayaan, Departemen Pendidikan dan Kebudayaan.

Soenarto, A.S. 1982 "Reog" [*Reyog*]. in *Penata Tari Muda* [Young Choreographers]. Jakarta: Dewan Kesenian Jakarta. pp. 19–32.

Soenarto, R.P. 1980 *Tuntunan Belajar Dasar–dasar Tabuhan Karawitan Jawa Timuran* [Manual for Studying the Fundamentals of East Javanese Gamelan Playing]. Surabaya: Sekolah Menengah Karawitan Indonesia.

Soenarwi, with A. Tasman n.d. *Notasi Gending–gending Sumenep* [Notation of Sumenep Gamelan Pieces]. Surabaya: Sekolah Tinggi Kesenian Wilwatikta.

Soepardi 1986 *Seni Gandrung, Kesenian Jawa Osing di Banyuwangi* [*Gandrung*, Art of the Osing Javanese in Banyuwangi]. Yogyakarta: Proyek Penelitian dan Pengkajian Kebudayaan Nusantara (Javanologi), Departemen Pendidikan dan Kebudayaan.

Soeradipura, R. Ng., *et al.*, eds. 1912–15 *Serat Tjentini: Babon Asli Saking Kita Leiden ing Negari Nederland* [The Book of Centhini: From an Original Manuscript in Leiden, The Netherlands]. 8 vols. (published as 4). Betawi [Jakarta]: Ruygrok.

Soeroso 1975 *Rebaban Gending* [Rebab Parts for Gamelan Pieces]. Surakarta: Akademi Seni Karawitan Indonesia.

Soleh Adi Pramono, Mochamad 1984 "Gerak permainan Gunungsari Patrajaya: sebuah analisa bentuk dan gaya pada wayang topeng Malang" [Movements in the play of Gunungsari and Patrajaya: an analysis of form and style in the masked dance–drama of Malang]. Thesis for the Seniman Seni Tari Degree, Akademi Seni Tari Indonesia, Yogyakarta.

Sosrowidagdo, Sudarmo 1977 *Gending–gending Pakurmatan* [Ceremonial Gamelan Pieces]. Surakarta: Akademi Seni Karawitan Indonesia.

Sri Suyamti, V.M. 1985 "Garap sindenan gending–gending Surabaya di dalam laras slendro" [Female singing for Surabaya gamelan pieces in *sléndro* tuning]. Thesis for Sarjana Muda Kesenian Degree, Sekolah Tinggi Kesenian Wilwatikta, Surabaya.

Suharto, Ben 1980 *Tayub: Pengamatan Dari Segi Tari Pergaulan serta Kaitannya dengan Unsur Upacara Kesuburan* [Tayub: Survey of a Social Dance and its Relation to Elements of Fertility Ceremony]. Yogyakarta: Proyek Pengembangan Institut Kesenian Indonesia, Departemen Pendidikan dan Kebudayaan.

Sukardi, Kris, and Sogi Sukidjo 1976a *Gending–gending Jawa, Gaya Yogyakarta* [Javanese Gamelan Pieces, Yogyakarta Style]. Surakarta: Akademi Seni Karawitan Indonesia.

1976b *Balungan gending–gending, Gaya Yogyakarta* [Skeletal Melodies of Gamelan Pieces, Yogyakarta Style]. Surakarta: Akademi Seni Karawitan Indonesia.

1976c *Kendangan Gaya Yogyakarta* [Drum Patterns, Yogyakarta Style]. Surakarta: Akademi Seni Karawitan Indonesia.

Sukidjo, Sogi, and Dibyomardowo 1976 *Balungan gending–gending, Gaya Yogyakarta* [Skeletal Melodies of Gamelan Pieces, Yogyakarta Style]. Surakarta: Akademi Seni Karawitan Indonesia.

Sumarsam 1984 "Inner melody in Javanese gamelan" in Judith Becker and Alan Feinstein (eds.) *Karawitan: Source Readings in Javanese Gamelan and Vocal Music*. Vol. 1. Ann Arbor, MI: Center for South and Southeast Asian Studies, University of Michigan, pp. 245–304.

1987 "Introduction to Ciblon Drumming in Javanese Gamelan" in Judith Becker and Alan Feinstein (eds.) *Karawitan: Source Readings in Javanese Gamelan and Vocal Music*. Vol. 2. Ann Arbor, MI: Center for South and Southeast Asian Studies, University of Michigan, pp. 171–203.

Sundoro, Mohamad Hadi 1986 *Seni Macapat Jawa di Kabupaten Jember: laporan penelitian* [The Art of Javanese *Macapat* in the Kabupaten of Jember: a research report]. Yogyakarta: Proyek Penelitian Dan Pengkajian Kebudayaan Nusantara (Javanologi), Departemen Pendidikan Dan Kebudayaan.

Supadmi 1984 *Cengkok–cengkok Srambahan dan Abon–abon* [Basic Melodic Patterns and Filling–in Phrases]. Surakarta: Akademi Seni Karawitan Indonesia.

Supanggah, Rahayu 1984 *Pengetahuan Karawitan* [Knowledge of Gamelan Music]. Kertas Kerja Sarasehan [Symposium Working Paper]. Surakarta: Akademi Seni Karawitan Indonesia.

Supanggah, Rahayu; Roestopo; and Arsenio Nicolas [1981] Untitled manuscript on "Musik bambu di daerah Banyumas" [Bamboo music in the Banyumas area]. Akademi Seni Karawitan Indonesia, Surakarta.

Suparno, T. Slamet 1981 *Bawa Gawan Gending* [Solo Songs Leading into Gamelan Pieces]. Surakarta: Akademi Seni Karawitan Indonesia.

Susanto, Astrid 1978 "The mass communications system in Indonesia" in Karl D. Jackson and Lucian W. Pye (eds.) *Political Power and Communications in Indonesia.* Berkeley: University of California Press, pp. 229–58.

Susilo, Hardja 1967 "Drumming in the context of Javanese gamelan." M.A. thesis, University of California at Los Angeles.

1984 "Wayang wong panggung: its social context, technique and music" in Stephanie Morgan and Laurie Jo Sears (eds.) *Aesthetic Tradition and Cultural Transition in Java and Bali.* Monograph Series, No. 2. Madison: University of Wisconsin, Center for Southeast Asian Studies, pp. 117–61.

Sutojo 1981 *Tari Jawa Timur* [East Javanese Dance]. Surabaya: Sekolah Menengah Karawitan Indonesia.

Sutrisno 1983 *Topeng Dalang Madura* [Madurese Masked Dance with Narrator]. Surabaya: Departemen Pendidikan dan Kebudayaan.

Sutton, R. Anderson 1975 "The Javanese gambang and its music." M.A. thesis, University of Hawaii.

1978 "Toward a grammar of variation in Javanese *gendèr* playing." *Ethnomusicology* 22(2):275–96.

1979 "Concept and treatment in Javanese gamelan music, with reference to the gambang." *Asian Music* 11(1):59–79.

1982 "Variation in Javanese gamelan music: dynamics of a steady state." Unpublished Ph.D. diss., University of Michigan. (Revision to be published as *Variation in Central Javanese Gamelan Music.* DeKalb, IL: Northern Illinois University, Center for Southeast Asian Studies.)

1984 "Change and ambiguity: gamelan style and regional identity in Yogyakarta" in Stephanie Morgan and Laurie Jo Sears (eds.) *Aesthetic Tradition and Cultural Transition in Java and Bali.* Monograph Series, No. 2. Madison: University of Wisconsin, Center for Southeast Asian Studies.

1985a "Musical pluralism in Java: three local traditions." *Ethnomusicology* 29(1):56–85.

1985b "Commercial cassette recordings of traditional music in Java: implications for performers and scholars." *The World of Music* 27(3):23–45.

1986a "The crystallization of a marginal tradition: music in Banyumas, west Central Java." *Yearbook for Traditional Music* 18:115–32.

1986b "New theory for traditional music in Banyumas, west Central Java." *Pacific Review of Ethnomusicology* 3:79–101.

1987 "Identity and individuality in an ensemble tradition: the female vocalist in Java" in Ellen Koskoff (ed.) *Women and Music in Cross-Cultural Perspective.* Contributions in Women's Studies, Number 79. Westport, CT: Greenwood Press, pp. 111–30.

in press *Variation in Central Javanese Gamelan Music.* DeKalb, IL: Northern Illinois University, Center for Southeast Asian Studies.

Sutton, R. Anderson, and Peggy A. Choy 1986 "Harmonious Feeling (Ki Nartosabdho and Condong Raos)" in Colby H. Kullman and William C. Young (eds.) *Theatre Companies of the World.* Westport, CT: Greenwood Press, pp. 55–58.

Team Penulisan Naskah Pengembangan Media Kebudayaan Jawa Timur 1977 *Sejarah Seni Budaya Daerah Jawa Timur* [History of Regional Art and Culture of East Java]. Jakarta: Proyek Pengembangan Media Kebudayaan, Departemen Pendidikan dan Kebudayaan.

Timoer, Soenarto 1978–79 *Reog* [= *Reyog*, processional performances]. Jakarta: Proyek Sasana Budaya, Departemen Pendidikan dan Kebudayaan.

1979–80 *Topeng Dhalang di Jawa Timur* [Masked Dance with Narrator in East Java]. Jakarta: Proyek Sasana Budaya, Departemen Pendidikan dan Kebudayaan.

1988 *Serat Wewaton Pedhalangan Jawi Wetanan* [Standards of East Javanese Shadow Puppetry]. 2 vols. Jakarta: P.N. Balai Pustaka.

Titon, Jeff Todd, ed. forthcoming *Worlds of Music*. 2nd edition. New York: Schirmer Books.

Toth, Andrew F. 1970 "The gamelan sekati of Central Java." Honors thesis, Wesleyan University.

Vetter, Roger R. 1986 "Music for 'the lap of the world': gamelan performance, performers, and repertoire in the kraton Yogyakarta." 2 vols. Unpublished Ph.D. diss., University of Wisconsin–Madison.

Wallis, Roger, and Krister Malm 1984 *Big Sounds from Small Peoples: The Music Industry in Small Countries*. New York: Pendragon.

Warsadiningrat, R. T. 1979 *Wedha Pradangga* [Sacred knowledge about gamelan music]. Surakarta: Sekolah Menengah Karawitan Indonesia. Translation into English by Susan Pratt Walton in Becker and Feinstein 1987 (Vol. 2), pp. 21–170.

Wibisono, Tri Broto 1982 *Ngremo* [The *Ngrémo* Dance]. Surabaya: Proyek Pengembangan Kesenian Jawa Timur.

Wolbers, Paul A. 1986 "Gandrung and angklung from Banyuwangi: remnants of a past shared with Bali." *Asian Music* 18(1):71–90.

    1987 "Account of an angklung caruk, July 28, 1985." *Indonesia* 43 (April):66–74.

    1989 "Transvestism, eroticism, and religion: in search of contextual background for the gandrung and seblang traditions of Banyuwangi, East Java." *Progress Reports in Ethnomusicology*, University of Maryland Baltimore County. Vol. 2, No. 6 (printed as part of a Special Issue, together with Nos. 4, 5, and 7).

Wongsosewojo, R. Ahmad 1930 "Loedroek." *Djawa* 10:204–7.

Yampolsky, Philip 1987 *Lokananta: A Discography of the National Recording Company of Indonesia, 1957–1985*. Bibliography Series, No. 10. Madison: University of Wisconsin, Center for Southeast Asian Studies.

Discography

The discography is divided into two major sections: recordings released on 33 1/3 r.p.m. discs, and recordings released on cassette tape. The list is not comprehensive, nor is it intended to be. Recordings referred to explicitly in the text are included, along with additional selections representative of the genres, performance styles, and repertories discussed in the preceding pages. For readers outside Indonesia, American and European releases (mostly on disc) are more likely to be available than the Indonesian releases. The Indonesian discs, mostly of high performance quality, are no longer produced or sold. And while commercial cassettes are sold widely, they are largely ephemeral; availability is in many cases unpredictable. Those released by Lokananta are the most widely available in Java and, if not found in stores, are all available at the main office in Surakarta (for a complete listing to 1985, see Yampolsky 1987). Arrangements are now being made for limited distribution of Lokananta cassettes in the United States and elsewhere overseas through the American Gamelan Institute (PO Box A36, Hanover, NH 03755, USA). The Mills Music Library of the University of Wisconsin-Madison has an archive of nearly 1,300 cassettes released commercially throughout Indonesia, including 450 cassettes of gamelan music and related dramatic genres from central and east Java. The author's collection includes many of the discs and all of the cassette recordings listed below.

Discs:

Yogyakarta:

Gending Djawa. RRI Jogjakarta, directed by R. Ng. Tjokrowasito. BRD-005 (B), 006, 007, 009, 010 (strong influence from Solonese tradition).

Indonesia I: Java Court Music. Unesco Collection, a Musical Anthology of the Orient. RRI Yogyakarta and Pura Pakulaman musicians, directed by K. R. T. Wasitadipura. Bärenreiter-Musicaphon BM 30 SL 2031 (strong influence from Solonese tradition).

Java: Gamelans from the Sultan's Palace in Jogjakarta. Raden Rja Gondokusumo, director (one example by RRI Yogyakarta, directed by Mujiono). Musical Traditions in Asia. Archiv 2723 017.

Java: L'art du Gamelan. Musiques de l'Asie Traditionelle, Vol. 7. RRI Yogyakarta [directed by Mujiono]. Playa Sound PS 33507 (strong influence from Solonese tradition).

Java: "Langen Mandra Wanara," Opéra de Danuredjo VII. Musiques traditionelles vivantes III. R.M. Projowiwaha, director; gamelan musicians directed by Morjiyo; R.S. Banjaransari, dalang/narrator. 3 discs. Ocora 558 507/9.

Javanese Court Gamelan from the Pura Paku Alaman, Jogyakarta. K.R.T. Wasitodipuro, director. Nonesuch Explorer Series H-72044 (strong influence from Solonese tradition).

273

Javanese Court Gamelan, Vol. III, recorded at the Kraton, Yogyakarta. Nonesuch Explorer Series H-72083.

Surakarta:

Gending Djawa. RRI Surakarta, directed by R. Ng. Hardjosasmojo. Lokananta BRD-002, 003, 004, 005 (A), 011.

Gamelan Garland: Music from the Mangkunegaran at Surakarta, Performed on Gamelan Kjai Kanjut Mesem. M. Ng. Surowirjono and Nji Ng. Yati, directors. Fontana 858 614 FPY.

Gamelan Music from Java, recorded in the Kraton, Surakarta, directed by Raden Tumenggung Warsodiningrat. Philips 831 209 PY.

Gending Beksan: Tari Gambir Anom/Tari Golek. RRI Surakarta, directed by P. Atmosunarto. Lokananta BRD-022.

Java: une nuit de wayang kulit legende de Wahju Tjakraningrat. Musiques et Traditions du Monde. Dalang Sudarmin, Gamelan of Glagah Wangi (Klaten), directed by Kardi Rahardjo Pramono.

Javanese Court Gamelan Vol. II, recorded at the Istana Mangkunegaran, Surakarta. Nonesuch Explorer Series H-72074.

Musique de Java: l'école de Loka Wangi, Centre Java. D.R.S. Pramono, director. Disques Alvarès C462.

Surakarta and Yogyakarta:

Java: Historic Gamelan. Unesco Collection, Musical Sources, Art Music from Southeast Asia Series, IX-2. Philips 6586 004 (archaic ensembles).

Java: Music of the Theatre. A: RRI Jogjakarta, directed by K.R.T. Wasitodipuro; B: Mangkunegaran musicians, directed by Sundoro Mintoeno Widyatmodjo, with vocalists directed by Soejati Mintoraras. EMI Odeon 64 2403201.

East Java:

Gongseng Kentjono. Ludruk RRI Surabaya, directed by Sinandi; Karawitan RRI Surabaya, directed by Tjak Dijat Sariredjo. Serimpi SLP-1011.

Ki Nartosabdho:

Gara-gara. Ki Nartosabdho and RRI Surakarta. Lokananta BRD-014.

Ki Nartosabdho. Ki Nartosabdho and RRI Surakarta. Lokananta BRD-017.

Mixed:

Kembang Glepang. Nji Suratmi B29, with Karawitan Karya Waditra, directed by Sri Widodo. Aneka Record ANL [1001?] (includes *gendhing* from Banyumas and Solonese traditions).

Getuk Goreng. Nji Suratmi B29, with Karawitan Karya Waditra. Aneka Record ANL 1002 (includes *gendhing* from Banyumas, Semarang, and Solonese traditions).

Cassettes:

Yogyakarta:

NB All performances by RRI Yogyakarta have strong influence from Solonese tradition in performance style, though repertory is primarily Yogyanese.

Dhandhanggula Kentar. RRI Yogyakarta, directed by Ki Suhardi. Lokananta ACD-262.

Gendhing Iringan Tari Klasik Yogyakarta: Gatutkaca Pregiwa. Karawitan Mardowo Budhoyo, directed by Romo Sasminto Mardowo. Pusaka cassette [series unnumbered].

Gendhing Iringan Tari Klasik Yogyakarta: Janoko Suprobowati. Karawitan Mardowo Budhoyo, directed by Romo Sasminto Mardowo. Pusaka cassette [series unnumbered].

Gending-gending Mataram: Surengrana. Karawitan P.L.T. Bagong Kussudiardja. Pusaka cassette [series unnumbered].

Golek Lambangsari. Karawitan Mardowo Budhoyo, directed by Romo Sasminto Mardowo. Borobudur Recording [series unnumbered].

Jonggrang Wirang. Ketoprak Mataram Sapta Mandala/Kodam VII/Diponegoro, directed by Bagong Kussidiardja. Fajar 9022.

Madyaratri. RRI Yogyakarta, directed by Ki Suhardi. Lokananta ACD-187.

Megamendhung. RRI Yogyakarta, directed by Ki Suhardi. Lokananta ACD-188.

Pamularsih. RRI Yogyakarta, directed by Ki Suhardi. Lokananta ACD-189.

R.A. Kartini: Gendhing-gendhing Kreasi Palaran Gobyog 9. RRI Yogyakarta, directed by Ki Suhardi. Lokananta ACD-260.

Rena-rena. RRI Yogyakarta, directed by Ki Suhardi. Lokananta ACD-190.

Sarimulya: Uyon-uyon Ngayogyakarta. Karawitan Warga Laras, directed by Ki Suparman. Kencana Record IR-005.

Sinom Jenggleng. RRI Yogyakarta, directed by Ki Suhardi. Lokananta ACD-261.

Soran: Gending Gajah Hendra. Yayasan Siswa Among Beksa, directed by R. M. Dinusatama. Borobudur Recording [series unnumbered].

The Sultan's Pleasure: Javanese Gamelan and Vocal Music from the Palace of Yogyakarta. Music of the World (Brooklyn, NY), cassette T-116.

Uyon-uyon Gobyog. RRI Yogyakarta, directed by Moedjiono. Lokananta ACD-024.

Uyon-uyon Kraton Ngayogyakarta. [Palace musicians, Yogyakarta] Fajar 903.

Wahyu Tejamaya: Wayang Kulit. Ki Suparman, dhalang. 8 cassettes. Fajar 966.

Surakarta:

Bondhan Kinanthi. Klenengan Pura Mangkunegaran, directed by R.M. Tarwo Sumosutargio. Lokananta ACD-164.

Gathutkaca Rebutan Kikis: Wayang Orang. Karawitan Sarwa Irama, directed by Sumarso. 2 cassettes. Lokananta ACD-098, A and B.

Gendhing Beksan. Karawitan Sanggar Budaya Dwi Tunggal. P2SC [series unnumbered].

Kakrasana Rabi. Ki Anom Suroto, dhalang. 8 cassettes. Lokananta ACD-036 (A-H).

Ketawang Puspawarna. Klenengan Pura Mangkunegaran, directed by R.M. Tarwo Sumosutargio. Lokananta ACD-163.

Klenengan Gobjog. RRI Surakarta [directed by P. Atmosunarto, with some items directed by R. Ng. Hardjosasmojo]. Lokananta ACD-001, ACD-002.

Lambangsari. RRI Surakarta [directed by P. Atmosunarto]. Lokananta ACD-106.

Larawudhu. RRI Surakarta, directed by P. Atmosunarto. Lokananta ACD-070.

Mijil Sulastri: Waranggana Kaloka Vol. 1, Warsa Kawuri. RRI Surakarta, directed by R. Ng. Hardjosasmojo. (Cassette release of items recorded in 1950s and 1960s, some released on Lokananta discs, including BRD-002, 004.) Lokananta ACD-235.

Rujak Jeruk: Tayub Royal Gaya Solo. Karawitan Kridha Irama, directed by Wakidjo. Lokananta ACD-275.

Wahyu Purba Kayun. Wayang kulit; Ki Anom Suroto, dhalang. 8 cassettes. Kusuma KWK-026, 1–8.

Ranumenggala: Waranggana Kaloka Vol. 2, Warsa Kawuri. RRI Surakarta, directed by R. Ng. Hardjosasmojo. (Cassette release of items recorded in 1950s and 1960s, some released on Lokananta discs, including BRD-003, 004, 005.) Lokananta ACD-236.

Banyumas:

Abimanyu Kingkin: Gagrag Banyumasan. Ki Soegito Purbocarito, dhalang. 8 cassettes. Gita Record/ Jaya Record [series unnumbered]. (Live performance in Banyumas style for Pekan Pagelaran Wayang Kulit Indonesia, 1983).

Bismo Gugur: Wayang Kulit Banyumasan. Ki Soegito Purbocarito, dhalang. 8 cassettes. Gita Record/ Jaya Record [series unnumbered] (strong influence of Solonese tradition).

Blenderan. Karawitan Purba Kencana, directed by Rasito. Kusuma KGD-033.

Blenderan. Karawitan Purba Kencana, directed by Rasito. Lokananta ACD-231.

Èbèg-èbègan. Calung Asli Banyumasan, Banjar Waru, lengger Kampi; Calung Budi Makarya, directed by Madiyono. Borobudur Recording [series unnumbered].

Gendhing-gendhing Banyumasan Populair/Kreasi Vol. 1: Jalak Pita Banyumasan. Karawitan Purba Kencana, directed by Rasito. Lokananta ACD-227.

Gendhing-gendhing Iringan Tari dan Tayub Banyumasan: Tari Pasihan. Karawitan Purba Kencana, directed by Rasito. Lokananta ACD-228.

Glaha-Glehe. Karawitan Linggamas, directed by S. Bono. Lokananta ACD-159.

Kulu-kulu Banyumasan. Karawitan Purba Kencana, directed by Rasito. Lokananta ACD-230.

Malang Dhei. Karawitan Purba Kencana, directed by Rasito. Lokananta ACD-229.

Mustakaweni: Jemblung Banyumasan. S. Parman, Peang Penjol. 3 cassettes. Hidup Baru Record 7804.

Sintren: Calung Banyumasan. Taruna Budaya, Geduren, directed by Bapak Sikum Suwargo. Royal Sound Stereo [series unnumbered].

Srikandhi mBarang Lengger: Wayang Banyumas. Ki Sugino Siswocarito, dhalang; [Karawitan Purba Kencana, directed by Rasito]. 8 cassettes. Kusuma KWK-097. (Transcribed, translated and annotated in Lysloff 1990).

Prawan Gunung. Karawitan Linggamas, directed by S. Bono. Lokananta ACD-161.

Renggong manis. Karawitan RRI Purwokerto, directed by Hadisutjipto. Lokananta ACD-162.

Senggot. Karawitan Calung Sekar Budhaya, directed by Tawiasa. Lokananta ACD-158.

Waru Dhoyong. Karawitan RRI Purwokerto, directed by Hadisutjipto. Lokananta ACD-160.

Semarang:

Bancak Doyok. RRI Semarang, directed by Ponidi. Lokananta ACD-048.

Gending Bonang Semarangan. RRI Semarang, directed by Ponidi. Lokananta ACD-049.

Gending Bonang. RRI Surakarta, directed by P. Atmosunarto (Side A), RRI Semarang, directed by Ponidi (Side B). Lokananta ACD-050. (Side A = Solonese *gendhing*; Side B = Semarang *gendhing*).

Rujak Sentul. RRI Surakarta, directed by P. Atmosunarto. Lokananta ACD-058. (Contains several items from Semarang tradition.)

Other Central Javanese:

Identified by locale, but with mixture of repertory:

B 3 B: Badhutan Sragen Kreasi Baru. Karawitan Trimo Lowung, directed by Suradi and Sudadi Besur. Lokananta ACD-279.

Goyang Sragen: Badhutan Sragen Kreasi Baru. Karawitan Trimo Lowung, directed by Suradi and Sudadi Besur. Lokananta ACD-278.

Seleksi Tayub Blora: Arum Manis. Karawitan Ngudi Laras, directed by Hadi. Pusaka Cassette [series unnumbered].

East Java:

From west of *Pinggir-rekso* line, predominance of central Javanese tradition:

Bontit. Karawitan Justisi Laras, directed by Soekarno SH. Lokananta ACD-103.

Budheng-budheng. Karawitan Justisi Laras, directed by Soekarno SH. Lokananta ACD-093.

Gambirsawit: Gendhing-gendhing Tayub Trenggalek. Karawitan Ngesthi Wirama, directed by Tambir. Budaya BD-2037.

Gemes: Gendhing Tayub Kediri. Karawitan Ngesthi Laras, directed by Gondo Soedjito. Ira-Record WD-722.

Hasrikaton. Karawitan Justisi Laras, directed by Soekarno SH. Lokananta ACD-104.

Montro. Karawitan Justisi Laras, directed by Soekarno SH. Lokananta ACD-094.

Perkutut Manggung. Karawitan Justisi Laras, directed by Soekarno SH. Lokananta ACD-086.

Prawan Pupur. Karawitan Justisi Laras, directed by Soekarno SH. Lokananta ACD-102.

Renyep. Karawitan Justisi Laras, directed by Soekarno SH. Lokananta ACD-085.

Reyog Ponorogo. Mbah Djojo, director. 4 vols. Borobudur Recording [series unnumbered].

Thengul: Gendhing-gendhing Tayub Gaya Tulungagung. Karawitan Mardi Budaya, directed by Ki Yono Prawita. Kencana Record IR-090.

From Surabaya-Mojokerto-Malang region, east Javanese cultural region:

Aneka Tari Jawa Timur. 3 vols. Bina Tari Jawa Timur, directed by Tribroto Wibisono. Nirwana Records [series unnumbered].

Bagong Gendro: Wayang Kulit Jawa Timuran. Ki H. Suwoto Ghozali, dhalang, karawitan Krido Rawito, directed by Diyat Sariredjo. 6 cassettes. Bumi Putra/Jayabaya [series unnumbered].

Banyu Panguripan. Ludrug RRI Surabaya, directed by Cak Munali Fatah [karawitan RRI Surabaya, directed by Diyat Sariredjo]. Lokananta ACD-151.

Begawan Gelap Bumi: Wayang Kulit Jawa Timuran. Ki Piet Asmoro, dhalang. 6 cassettes. CHGB Recording [series unnumbered].

Bonangan Jawa Timuran: Giro Becek. Karawitan Semanggi Surabaya, directed by Cak Kandar. Ira-Record WD-653.

Cindhe Kembang: Klenengan Jawa Timur. Karawitan Semanggi Surabaya, directed by Cak Kandar. Ira-Record WD-670.

Cokronegoro: Klenengan Jawa Timur. RRI Surabaya, directed by Diyat Sariredjo. Lokananta ACD-078.

Gending-gending Langen Beksan Lumajang. Bapak Soebekti, director. 2 vols. Pinokio Record [series unnumbered].

Gending Tayub Terop Malang. 3 vols. Wedaring Budoyo, directed by Nursi P. Derin. Jayabaya 505–7.

Jula-juli Kananthi: Gendhing Tayub Gaya Blitar. Karawitan Karia Mukti, directed by Andhik Suwandi. Ira-Record WD-666.

Lahire Ontorejo: Wayang Kulit Wetanan, Gaya Jawa Timuran. Ki Suleman. 6 cassettes. Bumi Putra/Jayabaya 045.

Loro Pangkon: Upacara Tradisional Pengantin Surabaya. Karawitan Mulyo Laras, directed by Ki Suleman. Lokananta ACD-202.

Pandawa Pitu. Ki Matadi, dhalang; Karawitan Ngesti Laras, directed by Toni Sudharmadi. 7 cassettes. Fajar 9180.

Pangkur Surabaya: Gending-gending Jawa Timur. Karawitan Bintang Timur, directed (*asuhan*) by Tuty Sukardjo. Kencana Record IR-078.

Srampat: Gendhing-gendhing Tayub Jombangan. Karawitan Tunjung Bang, directed by Sigit Saioen. Kencana Record IR-041.

Tari Topèng Bapang: Topèng Tradisional. Karawitan Kedung Monggo, Malang, directed by Bapak Karimun. Jayabaya 098.

Toakan: Gendhing-gendhing Tayub Jawa Timur. Karawitan Bintang Timur, directed (*asuhan*) by Tuty Sukardjo. Kencana Record IR-070.

From Banyuwangi:

Angklung Caruk: Mangir Lawan Pasinan. Ria Record 102.

Angklung Gending Banyuwangian. 2 vols. Arbas group, directed by Sutrisno. Nirwana Recording [series unnumbered].

Keok-keok. Gandrung Blambangan, Vol. 1. Soegiati-Atun Hanipah, gandrung. Lokananta ACD-216.

Ketemu Maning. Gandrung Blambangan, Kreasi Baru, Vol. 2. Soegiati-Atun Hanipah, gandrung. Lokananta ACD-217.

Klasik Banyuwangian [Gandrung]. Bumi Putra [series unnumbered].

Manasi Ati. Gandrung Blambangan, Vol. 2. Soegiati-Atun Hanipah, gandrung. Lokananta ACD-218.

Padhang Bulan: Ngajak Kawin. Gandrung Blambangan, Kreasi Baru, Vol. 1 Soegiati-Atun Hanipah, gandrung. Lokananta ACD-215.

Ki Nartosabdho:

(recordings of regional repertories, performed by Ki Nartosabdho and his group Condhong Raos)

Semarang Regional Focus:

Gending-gending Semarangan. Fajar 9265.

Gending-gending Semarangan, Vol. 2. Fajar 9313.

Sarwa-sarwi Semarangan. Fajar 980.

Banyumas Regional Focus:

mBang Lepang [= Kembang Glepang]. Fajar 9109.

Gending-gending Banyumasan. Fajar 9201.

Mixed Regional Focus:

Aja Lamis. Ira-Record WD-511. (Includes Ladrang *Gecul Surawangi*, based on styles of East Java).

Aneka Pangkur. Ira-Record WD-508. (Yogyanese and Solonese styles).

Asmaradana Kebar. Ira-Record WD-512. (Yogyanese and Solonese styles).

Cluntang Mataram. Ira-Record WD-535. (Yogyanese and Solonese repertory).

Djakarta Indah. Irama cassette [series unnumbered]. (Includes Macapat *Asmaradana Banyumasan* and *Godril [Banyumasan] Rinengga*).

Gendhing Tayub Madiun. 2 vols. Ira-Record WD-642 and WD-761. (*Gendhing* associated with Central Java and East Java).

Jangkrik Genggong. Lokananta ACD-025. (Includes Ladrang *Gegot Semarangan*).

Jula-juli Suber. Fajar 9124. (Includes *gendhing* associated with Sunda, Banyumas, Surakarta, and east Java).

Jungkeri. Lokananta ACD-052. (Includes *gendhing*, mostly by Ki Nartosabdho, performed in styles identified as Banyumasan, Semarangan, and Surabayan [east Javanese]).

Kinanti Sandung. Ira-Record WD-561. (Solonese and Yogyanese styles).

Pangkur Jenggleng. Ki Nartosabdho and Condhong Raos, with Basiyo and Suparmi. Fajar 917. (Includes Macapat *Pangkur Banyumasan* and *Éling-éling Banyumasan*, *Pangkur palaran* [Solonese], and *Pangkur rambangan* [Yogyanese]).

Sebet: Gending-gending Jawa. Ki Nartosabdho and Condhong Raos. Fajar 954. (*Gendhing* by R.C.

Hardjosoebroto and Ki Wasitodipoero, including several with Balinese and one with Banyuwangi influence).

Timur Mas. Kusuma KGD-023. (Includes *Untul-Luwuk [Banyumasan]*, *Othok-owok [Jawa Timuran]*, and Nartosabdho's combination, Lagu *Timur Mas*).

Udan Palaran. Ki Nartosabdho and Condhong Raos, with Sapta Mandala. Fajar 9057. (*Palaran* [Solonese] and *rambangan* [Yogyanese] versions of several *macapat*).

Other cassettes with mixtures of regional repertories and styles:

Gending-gending Tari Kreasi Baru. Pusat Latihan Tari Bagong Kussudiardja. Fajar 9071. (Arrangements and original compositions for dances choreographed by Bagong Kussidiardja, gamelan music influenced by or adapted from Sunda, Yogyakarta, and East Java [*reyog* and *ngrémo*]).

Gunungsari. Riris Raras Irama [studio musicians of RRI Surakarta], directed by S. Ciptosuwarso. Kusuma KGD-024. (Includes Macapat *Asmaradana Banyumasan*, several Banyumas *gendhing* and *langgam/kroncong* pieces arranged for gamelan).

Palaran Gobyog 8. RRI Surakarta, directed by M. Ng. Dalimin Pw.P. Lokananta ACD-238. (Includes *Srepegan* from Solonese, Yogyanese, and Banyumas traditions).

Index